INSPIRE / PLAN / DISCOVER / EXPERIENCE

NEW ENGLAND

DK EYEWITNESS

NEW ENGLAND

CONTENTS

DISCOVER 6

EXPERIENCE BOSTON 58

EXPERIENCE NEW ENGLAND 158

NEED TO KNOW 332

Left: Assortment of pumpkins in Rhode Island
Previous page: Fall foliage near Killington, Vermont
Front cover: Green Mountain National Forest, Vermont

DISCOVER

A misty valley in rural Vermont

WELCOME TO
NEW
ENGLAND

Sublime beaches and wooded trails. Historic firsts and world-class museums. Fall foliage and fabulous seafood. Whatever your dream trip entails, this DK Eyewitness travel guide is the perfect companion.

1 Mountain lifts, Stowe.

2 Sunset at Marshall Point Lighthouse, Maine.

3 Platter of oysters, clams, shrimp, and lobster.

4 Hikers admiring Connecticut's breathtaking fall scenery.

New England beckons with every season. In spring and summer, beachgoers swoon over Cape Cod's expansive dune-backed bays, while hard-core hikers rise to the challenge of the Green and White Mountains of Vermont and New Hampshire. In fall, drivers tunnel through vibrant canopies as the annual wave of golden hues unfolds from north to south. And with some of the best skiing and snowsports areas in the whole of the US, winter won't disappoint.

History lives on in New England's urban centers, where you can follow the footsteps of America's forefathers on Boston's Freedom Trail, explore the historic vessels of Mystic Seaport, Connecticut, and admire grand Gilded Age mansions in Newport, Rhode Island. But these vibrant cities also look to the future, with world-class museums and cutting-edge theater that will stoke your imagination, while classical ensembles, jazz combos, and live gigs are sure to get you on the dancefloor. Foodie culture dominates the dining scene – innovative chefs and the local fishermen and farmers who supply them guarantee a distinctive regional taste on every plate.

With so many options, it is easy to feel overwhelmed. This guide breaks New England down into easily navigable chapters, with detailed itineraries, expert local knowledge, and comprehensive maps to help plan your perfect trip. Whether you're here for a flying visit or a grand tour, this DK Eyewitness travel guide will ensure you see the very best the region has to offer. Enjoy the book, and enjoy New England.

REASONS TO LOVE
NEW ENGLAND

Mountaintop vistas and craggy coastlines. Vibrant cities and picture-perfect villages. Revolutionary firsts and haunted histories. There are so many reasons to love New England; here are a few of our favorites.

1 HISTORIC BOSTON

Savor past and present on the streets of Boston – from colonial-era Beacon Hill *(p92)* to the vibrant restaurants and nightlife of 21st-century Seaport and the Waterfront.

HIKING THE APPALACHIAN TRAIL 2

New England holds a third of this epic mountain trail. Some sections make good day hikes, but the Hundred Mile Wilderness to Mount Katahdin challenges even the very best.

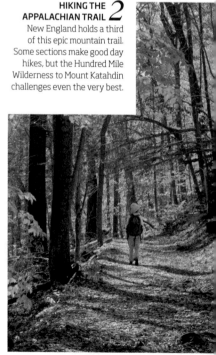

3 MARITIME HISTORY

New England is a region shaped by the ocean that surrounds it. Seafaring heritage comes to life as you tread the decks of America's last whaling ship, or its oldest warship, USS *Constitution (p98).*

CAPE COD NATIONAL SEASHORE 4

Swimmers frolic in the waves, surfers catch big curls, seals bask on the beaches, and whales swim offshore along the 40-mile (64-km) Cape Cod National Seashore (p180).

POSTCARD VILLAGES 5

White churches with heaven-pointed spires flank the serene lawns of New England's village greens, where grazing livestock have given way to town fairs and regular civic gatherings.

WITCH CITY 6

The spooky and the goofy intersect in Salem (p164), where Halloween lasts a whole month. Witches were executed here in the 1690s; now they ride pedicabs in the annual parade.

LIGHTHOUSES ALONG THE ROCKY COAST 7

Dangers lurk all along the 6,000-mile (9,656-km) shoreline. These beacons of light guide ships through rocky straits to snug harbors sheltered from the restless sea.

IVY LEAGUE SCHOOLS 8

New England's top universities have educated presidents, Oscar-winners, and dotcom billionaires. To this day, schools such as Harvard *(p150)* and Yale *(p238)* exude culture and youthful exuberance.

9 REVOLUTIONARY SPIRIT

The feisty rebellion against British rule set New England's tone from the outset. That birthright of innovation, spawned during the American Revolution, lives on in education, music, and art.

10 WHITE AND GREEN MOUNTAIN SLOPES

From giant snowfields above the timberline and steep black diamond runs to novice hills, the slopes of New Hampshire and Vermont are among the best in the US.

KING CRUSTACEANS 11

Crack steamed lobster with a fist-sized rock at a coastal seafood shack – or let a Boston star chef surprise you with an innovative twist on this New England delicacy.

DAZZLING FALL FOLIAGE 12

An electrifying palette of red, yellow, orange, and even purple foliage illuminates the landscape as fall descends on New England's forested hills and valleys.

EXPLORE
NEW ENGLAND

This guide divides New England into seven
color-coded sightseeing areas, as shown
on the map below. Find out more about
each area on the following pages.

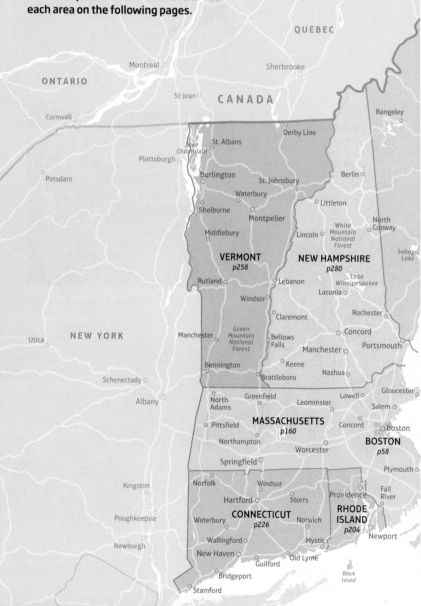

QUEBEC

ONTARIO

Montreal

Sherbrooke

St-Jean

CANADA

Cornwall

Rangeley

Potsdam

Lake
Champlain

St. Albans

Derby Line

Plattsburgh

Burlington

Berlin

St. Johnsbury

Waterbury

Littleton

Shelburne

Montpelier

Lincoln

White
Mountain
National
Forest

North
Conway

Middlebury

VERMONT
p258

NEW HAMPSHIRE
p280

Sebago
Lake

Rutland

Lebanon

Lake
Winnipesaukee

Windsor

Laconia

Claremont

Rochester

NEW YORK

Manchester

Green
Mountain
National
Forest

Bellows
Falls

Concord

Utica

Manchester

Portsmouth

Bennington

Keene

Schenectady

Brattleboro

Nashua

Albany

North
Adams

Greenfield

Leominster

Lowell

Gloucester

Pittsfield

MASSACHUSETTS
p160

Concord

Salem

Northampton

Worcester

Boston

Springfield

BOSTON
p58

Kingston

Norfolk

Windsor

Providence

Plymouth

Hartford

Storrs

RHODE
ISLAND
p204

Fall
River

Poughkeepsie

Waterbury

CONNECTICUT
p226

Norwich

Newburgh

Wallingford

Mystic

Newport

New Haven

Old Lyme

Bridgeport

Guilford

Black
Island

Stamford

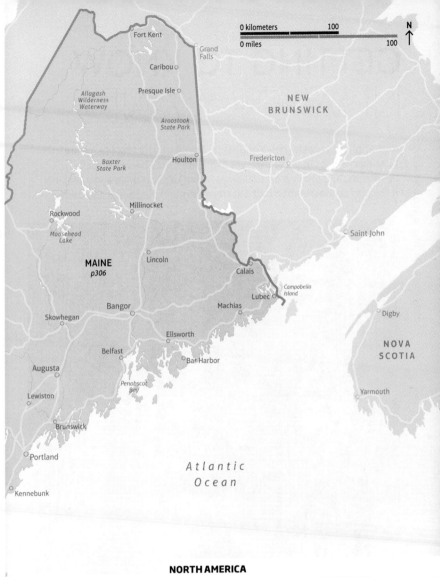

Fort Kent

Grand Falls

Caribou

Presque Isle

NEW BRUNSWICK

Allagash Wilderness Waterway

Aroostook State Park

Baxter State Park

Houlton

Fredericton

Rockwood

Saint John

Millinocket

Moosehead Lake

MAINE
p306

Lincoln

Calais

Campobello Island

Digby

Lubec

Machias

NOVA SCOTIA

Bangor

Skowhegan

Ellsworth

Belfast

Bar Harbor

Yarmouth

Augusta

Penobscot Bay

Lewiston

Brunswick

Portland

Kennebunk

Atlantic Ocean

0 kilometers   100
0 miles   100

N

Provincetown

Cape Cod

Cape Cod Bay

Orleans

Hyannis

Falmouth

Martha's Vineyard

Nantucket Island

NORTH AMERICA

CANADA

Seattle

USA

Chicago

NEW ENGLAND
Boston

San Francisco

New York

Los Angeles

Washington, DC

Atlantic Ocean

Atlanta

Houston

Pacific Ocean

MEXICO

Gulf of Mexico

Miami

GETTING TO KNOW
NEW ENGLAND

New England's coastal cities of Boston, Portland, and Providence are buzzing cosmopolitan centers, yet exquisite sandy beaches, rocky headlands, and pristine natural areas lie only a short drive away, making it the perfect destination for both city-goers and outdoor enthusiasts.

BOSTON

PAGE 58

All New England roads lead to Boston, the region's hub of culture, education and dining, where the city's streets are imbued with Revolutionary history, and the urban wilds of the Emerald Necklace and Boston Harbor Islands are only minutes away. Home of Harvard University and the Boston Symphony Orchestra, Boston is center stage when it comes to live music. Its foodie scene, too, is sure to impress – some of the oldest restaurants in the US serve up delicious Boston scrod and apple cobbler, while cutting-edge chefs celebrate the day's catch and fresh bounty of nearby farms.

Best for
History and fine dining

Home to
Museum of Fine Arts, Trinity Church, Charlestown Navy Yard

Experience
Gliding through the Public Garden lagoon on an elegant Swan Boat

MASSACHUSETTS

PAGE 160

The Bay State stretches from briny Cape Cod in the east to the towering summit of Mount Greylock in the west. Its museums and historic homes tell enthralling tales of pirates, authors, Native Americans, and the first settlers who disembarked the *Mayflower* at Plymouth Rock. Classical music, theater, and modern dance dominate the summer calendar in the villages of the Berkshires near the New York border, while the aroma of fried clams, a signature dish of this seafaring state, wafts through the coastal villages from Cape Ann to Cape Cod.

Best for
Historic firsts, pristine beaches, performing arts

Home to
Salem, Plymouth, the Berkshires

Experience
A swim in Atlantic waters at Cape Cod National Seashore

RHODE ISLAND

PAGE 204

Rhode Island is nicknamed the Ocean State for good reason. Most of America's smallest state – also known as "little Rhody" – lies along its 384-mile (618-km) coastline. Bathing beaches with gentle waves line the shores of South County, while the majestic Gilded-Age mansions of Newport perch high on a cliff between surfing beaches and America's top yachting harbor. In addition to serving as the state's political capital, the vibrant city of Providence, the state capital, is a national leader in design and fine arts, as well as a champion of chef-driven contemporary cuisine.

Best for
Gilded-Age mansions, ocean views

Home to
Providence, Newport

Experience
The interplay of music, flames, and the river as they cast their spell at Providence's WaterFire festival

PAGE 226

CONNECTICUT

The sandy beaches, rocky promontories, and bird-filled marshes of Connecticut have changed little since American Impressionists painted them over a century ago. Today, kayakers, swimmers, and fishermen far outnumber artists with easels. The towns of New London and Mystic recall the state's long engagement with the sea. The rolling landscape of the Litchfield Hills attracts New York's rich and famous. Hartford, the capital city, stages arts and music festivals on the Connecticut River banks, while New Haven is home to Yale University's museums and theater.

Best for
Easy-going adventure, art museums

Home to
Mystic Seaport, Mark Twain House, Yale University

Experience
Spotting eagles and ospreys on a nature cruise on the Connecticut River

PAGE 258

VERMONT

While other New England states look to the sea, Vermont looks to the sky. Lacking an ocean coastline, Vermont stretches across the spectacular Green Mountain range from Lake Champlain eastward to the Connecticut River. Black and white dairy cows graze its hillside pastures while pretty villages with high-steepled white churches nestle in sheltered valleys. The largest city, Burlington, is a foodie hotspot with a lively music scene and active lifestyle – perfectly placed on the shores of Lake Champlain for swimming, boating, and cycling along the shore.

Best for
Mountain hiking, winter sports, fall foliage

Home to
Burlington, the Shelburne Museum, the Green Mountain National Forest

Experience
Hiking the Mount Mansfield ridgeline in Stowe for a taste of the Appalachian Trail

PAGE 280

NEW HAMPSHIRE

The passes, or "notches," through the White Mountains divide New Hampshire in half. North of Franconia and Pinkham Notches are the steep mountain ski runs and rugged granite peaks beloved by hikers. To the south, broad alpine lakes serve as summer playgrounds for campers and waterskiers. The Atlantic coastline is short but features several swimming beaches and Portsmouth, with its locavore dining scene and quirky boutiques.

Best for
Outdoor adventures, tax-free shopping

Home to
Portsmouth, Franconia Notch State Park, Canterbury Shaker Village

Experience
A ride on the cog railway to the summit of Mount Washington, New England's highest point

PAGE 306

MAINE

Maine's northern wilderness is famed for fishing and moose-watching, but most vacationers gravitate to the coast. Historic maritime villages such as Kennebunk and Ogunquit are blessed with sandy beaches. Nestled in the cup of Casco Bay, the sophisticated city of Portland enjoys exciting dining and art scenes. Along Maine's fabled rocky coast, tiny fishing villages bring in crates of fresh lobster, and windjammer sails billow in the sea breeze. Visitors can enjoy island hopping in the summer, while photographers flock to the bucolic landscape of Acadia National Park to snap the highest rocky headlands on the US Atlantic coast.

Best for
Stunning lighthouses, rugged coastline, moose-spotting, lobster

Home to
Portland, Penobscot Bay, Acadia National Park

Experience
A drive up Cadillac Mountain to watch the first sunrise on the US coast

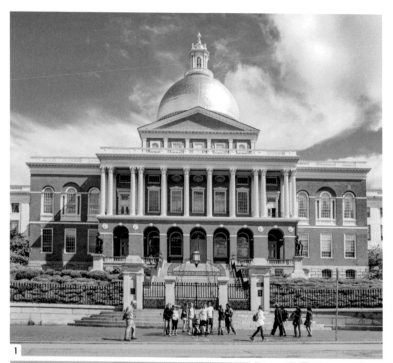

←

① Massachusetts State House, Boston.

② Plimoth Patuxet Museums.

③ Fresh clams at Al Forno.

④ A boat sailing on the Cape Cod Canal at sunset.

From the piney silence of a forest trail to its buzzing art scene, contrasts abound in New England. Whether you're here to enjoy the salty breeze from a schooner's deck or exult in the bustle of city life, let these itineraries inspire your journey.

2 WEEKS
in Southern New England

Day 1

Start your trip on Boston's historic Freedom Trail (p74), then stop in the distinctly Italian North End to refuel at one of the area's many trattorias. Once replenished, take the T to the Isabella Stewart Gardner Museum (p138) to view the collections of one of Boston's most enduring characters. Dine on dumplings in Chinatown (p89) before catching a show in the nearby Theater District (p90).

Day 2

An hour south of Boston is Plymouth (p170), where English Pilgrims first settled in 1620. Hear their story at Pilgrim Hall Museum, and tour *Mayflower II*, a replica of the ship that crossed the ocean. Nearby, Plymouth Rock marks its apocryphal landing site. South of town, explore re-created Pilgrim settlements at Plimoth Patuxet Museums (p172). Weather permitting, swim at White Horse Beach before checking in at the historic John Carver Inn (johncarverinn.com).

Day 3

Continue south, crossing the Cape Cod Canal over the Sagamore Bridge, to the town of Sandwich (p179). Learn about the construction of the waterway at the Cape Cod Canal visitor center, and walk or cycle along the canal path. Catch a glassmaking demonstration at the Sandwich Glass Museum, and spot birds in the marsh from the long boardwalk to Town Beach. The Belfry Inn & Bistro (belfryinn.com) will provide a warm welcome for the evening.

Day 4

Cross the Bourne Bridge back to the mainland to the New Bedford Whaling National Historical Park (p189). Continue west to Providence, Rhode Island (p208) to stroll the Benefit Street Mile of History, and, once you've worked up an appetite, enjoy baked pastas and wood-grilled meats at the celebrated but casual restaurant Al Forno (577 S Water St).

Day 5

Follow Narragansett Bay south to Crescent Park, where even adults can't resist a spin on its restored carousel. Continue through Rhode Island to Bristol (p216) to visit the sprawling Blithewold Mansion and Gardens. If gardens are your passion, stop at Green Animals Topiary Garden (p218) in Portsmouth en route to a fish dinner at the harbor and an overnight stay in elegant Newport (p212).

→

Day 6

Newport bristles with the masts of private yachts and excursion boats. Explore the many boutiques that line the former shipping wharves, and grab a quick lunch before jumping on the hop-on, hop-off trolley to see the rest of town. Take an audio tour of The Breakers (p214) for an insight into the lavish lifestyles of the Gilded Age, then stroll the Cliffwalk for spectacular views of the beach below.

Day 7

From Newport, head west over two bridges to North Kingstown for wide ocean views. Stop for lunch at Mystic Pizza (p245), then on to re-created maritime village, Mystic Seaport (p244). Stay at the waterfront Steamboat Inn (steamboatinnmystic.com).

Day 8

On the coastal route west, stop for lunch in Noank, where Abbott's Lobster in the Rough (117 Pearl St) serves hot lobster rolls, a Connecticut specialty. A half hour west, the village of Old Lyme (p253), was once the center of American Impressionist painting. As you stroll through these unspoiled streets, it's easy to imagine life here over a century ago. Visit the Connecticut River Museum, a short distance west in Essex (p252), then take a boat tour in nearby Haddam. Round off with an evening of musical theater at Goodspeed Opera House in East Haddam.

Day 9

An hour north is Hartford (p230), Connecticut's capital. Wander the halls of the Wadsworth Atheneum, and amble through Bushnell Park, home to another vintage carousel. After lunch, venture west to the Mark Twain House, home to one of America's best-loved novelists. Dine at City Steam Brewery (p232), in a show at the comedy club downstairs.

Day 10

The bucolic high country of the Litchfield Hills (p240) begins west of Hartford. Visit Kent Falls State Park for a picnic lunch before following the trail to the state's

1 Mystic Seaport Harbor.
2 Victorian Carousel, Hartford.
3 Fall colors, Litchfield Hills.
4 Art by Sol LeWitt, Mass MoCA.
5 Hancock Shaker Village.
6 Snow-covered Lowell.

most impressive waterfall. Then on to the ominously named Satan's Kingdom Gorge in New Hartford for an easy-going tubing on the Farmington River. Rifle through Woodbury's many antiques shops before stopping in Litchfield for dinner.

Day 11

The Litchfield Hills segue seamlessly into the Massachusetts Berkshires (p182). An hour's drive will take you to Stockbridge, where the Red Lion Inn (p184) is a perfect base for an arts-oriented day. Visit Chesterwood, the home and studio of sculptor Daniel Chester French, and the Norman Rockwell Museum. In Lenox, pick up picnic fare to enjoy at an evening concert at Tanglewood, summer home of the Boston Symphony Orchestra.

Day 12

Follow the Housatonic River north, pausing at Hancock Shaker Village (p200) before continuing north to Williamstown (p199), home of The Clark. From here, hike the trail up Stone Hill for magnificent

Green Mountain views before returning to town for dinner and lodgings.

Day 13

In nearby funky North Adams, visit the Massachusetts Museum of Contemporary Art (p199) to admire its huge installations. Head east on the Mohawk Trail, one of the region's most scenic drives, stopping at Shelburne Falls to walk across the flower-bedecked railroad bridge and grab a bite in one of the diners along Bridge Street. Continue south to Deerfield (p200) to stay the night at the Deerfield Inn (p200).

Day 14

Begin the day touring Historic Deerfield, once the western frontier of English settlement, then head east to Lowell National Historical Park (p188) to learn about America's first major textile mill in touching detail. Pay your repects to Beat author Jack Kerouac at his grave in Edson Cemetery. In the evening, stroll Merrimack and Middle streets where you'll be spoiled for dining options.

7 DAYS

A Scenic Tour of Northern New England

Day 1

Begin in Downeast Maine at Mount Desert Island, home of Acadia National Park *(p318)*. The 27-mile (44 km) Park Loop Road offers highlights on the park's eastern side. Walk the cliffs around booming Thunder Hole, and challenge yourself to an icy dip at Sand Beach followed by tea and popovers – a Maine specialty – on the lawn of Jordan Pond House. Spend the night in Bar Harbor, with its many shops and restaurants.

Day 2

Start early for the three-hour drive to Portland *(p310)*, Maine, a nationally acclaimed foodie city. Stop for lunch at Duckfat *(43 Middle St)* in the East End. It's a short stroll across Franklin Street into the Old Port with its eclectic assortment of boutiques, galleries, and clothing stores. Maine's rugged beauty has long inspired artists and you can peruse their work at the Portland Museum of Art. Make dinner reservations at Fore Street *(288 Fore St)*, a pioneer of farm-to-fork dining where locally sourced produce is cooked in a wood-fired oven.

Day 3

An hour south, just across the Piscataqua River in New Hampshire, is Portsmouth *(p284)*. While art and architecture buffs can spend an entire day touring its historic house museums, most visitors are content with an hour or two at the Strawbery Banke village museum *(p286)*, leaving time to explore the quirky boutiques that occupy 18th-century warehouses. Take a harbor cruise to see the Portsmouth Naval Shipyard and photograph lighthouses and mansions from the water. Book dinner at the Black Trumpet bistro and wine bar *(29 Ceres St)*.

Day 4

Just a one-hour drive northwest, Wolfeboro is the eastern gateway to sprawling Lake Winnipesaukee *(p304)*, the largest body of water in New Hampshire. The genteel, slow pace of the community stands in marked contrast to Weirs Beach on the lake's western end. With its amusement rides, beach food-vendors, and docks for boat excursions, Weirs Beach is favored by children and the young-at-heart. There's a sandy beach for swimming

5

1 Still waters of Jordan Pond, Acadia National Park.

2 Portland Museum of Art.

3 Strawbery Banke Museum.

4 Boardwalks at Flume Gorge, Franconia Notch.

5 White Mountain descent.

and sunbathing, and multiple options for getting out on lake, from sedate tours on a historic excursion boat to buzzing around on a rented jet ski.

Day 5

One of the few east-west routes in the White Mountains, the Kancamagus Highway (p301) is an exhilarating drive with stops to picnic near the Saco River rapids or hike wooded trails. On the west end, it's a short detour south to Franconia Notch State Park (p290), where a self-guided trail leads through the majestic Flume Gorge. Ride the Cannon Mountain aerial tramway for spectacular summit views over New Hampshire, Maine, Vermont, New York, and Canada. Return north to spend the night in North Woodstock (p300) at the Woodstock Inn Brewery (p300).

Day 6

Fuel up on a pancake breakfast with New Hampshire maple syrup at Polly's Pancake Parlor (pollyspancakeparlor.com) in Sugar Hill. Drive west to Hanover

(p296), enjoy the ride, as the road descends from the steep slopes of the White Mountains to the broad lowlands of the Connecticut River Valley. The town's main attractions are on the Dartmouth campus, which can be easily explored on foot. Stop by the Hood Museum of Art and nearby Baker-Berry Memorial Library, where the reading room is lined with José Clemente Orozco's mural cycle, The Epic of American Civilization. Spend the night at the refined Hanover Inn (2 East Wheelock).

Day 7

Begin the day with a one-hour drive north to Montpelier (p270), Vermont, to see the formidable Vermont State House and pick up coffee at Capitol Grounds (p271) – a pioneer coffee roaster. Stop by Ben & Jerry's Ice Cream Factory (p270) for an amusing tour and tasting, then continue north to Burlington (p262) for lunch at the Farmhouse Tap & Grill (p263). After an afternoon sightseeing cruise on Lake Champlain, shop and dine in Burlington's Church Street Marketplace.

1 Pemaquid Point
Lighthouse at sunset.

2 Yachts in Camden Harbor.

3 Fresh steamed Lobster.

4 Artists view of the waves,
Monhegan Island.

5 DAYS

Lobster and Lighthouses in Midcoast Maine

Day 1

Morning Throw your sense of direction out the window as you yo-yo up and down Maine's midcoast peninsulas from Bath to Searsport. From Bath, head to Five Islands Lobster (*1447 Five Islands Rd, Georgetown*) to sample your first bite.

Afternoon Continue north to Wiscasset. Cross the bridge to Edgecomb for some Maine-themed ceramics, and then on to Boothbay Harbor (*p326*).

Evening At Robinson's Wharf pub (*20 Hendricks Hill Rd, Southport*), dine on steamed clams as local musicians play.

Day 2

Morning Start the day with a lobster boat tour to see how traps are hauled.

Afternoon Drive to Damariscotta to dine on world-famous oysters, then on to Pemaquid Point Light (*p327*). Crack open steamed lobsters at Shaw's Fish & Lobster Wharf (*129 ME-32, New Harbor*).

Evening Stay in Port Clyde at the tip of the St. George peninsula.

Day 3

Morning Catch the ferry to arty Monhegan Island (*p315*) for the day.

Afternoon Hike the trail to see the lighthouse and small museum at the summit of the island's central hill.

Evening Marvel at the wash of stars splashed across the inky sky.

Day 4

Morning Hop on a ferry back to Port Clyde, and drive to Marshall Point, where there is a museum in the keeper's house.

Afternoon McLoon's Lobster Shack (*315 Island Rd, South Thomaston*) is a local favorite. Continue north to see Owl's Head Light. Two miles north in Rockland (*p315*), the Maine Lighthouse Museum is a must.

Evening Catch a show at Rockland's Strand Theatre (*www.rocklandstrand.com*).

Day 5

Morning Start the day with breakfast at the Atlantic Baking Company (*351 Main St*) before driving north to Camden (*p315*), where the harbor is filled with yachts and the main street is lined with boutiques. Continue north to Belfast.

Afternoon Enjoy yet another lobster lunch overlooking the Passagassawaukeag River at Young's Lobster Pound (*2 Fairview St*) in east Belfast. Nearby, in the tiny village of Searsport (*p316*), the Penobscot Marine Museum recaptures the town's maritime heyday.

Evening Return to Belfast to explore its shops and art galleries before dining at Perennial Farm Kitchen (*84 Main St*).

←

1 Fall foliage near Killington.

2 Hiking Mount Mansfield.

3 Vermont Country Store.

4 Children meet the residents of Billings Farm and Museum, Woodstock.

3 DAYS

On the trail of
Vermont's Fall Foliage

Day 1

Morning Start your journey in the bohemian river city of Brattleboro *(p278)* at one of its many bakeries or coffee shops before driving west on Route 9, also known as the Molly Stark Trail. Pause at the high switchback on Hogback Mountain where the scenic overlook lives up to its name as the 100 Mile View.

Afternoon Wilmington *(p279)* marks the start of the VT Route 100. As you drive north, pause to enjoy the country elegance of West Dover, the quirky galleries of arty Jamaica, and the roadside riverbanks lined with trees in their fall finery. The Norway maples are ablaze in scarlet and orange, the sugar maples in cardinal reds, while the birches, beeches, and alders glow luminous yellow. In Weston, the Vermont Country Store *(657 Main St)* will tempt you with more kinds of candy than you knew existed.

Evening Spend the night in a luxurious room complete with a whirlpool tub at the Inn at Weston *(630 Main St)*.

Day 2

Morning After a cooked breakfast at the inn (don't miss bacon smoked with apple wood), head north on Route 100, stopping frequently to take photographs. This section of the famous foliage road follows a glacial valley. The shores of the narrow roadside lakes support brilliant stands of yellow alders punctuated by the purplish and slender red leaves of basswood and the pin cherry. Continue north.

Afternoon Shortly after Route 100 joins Vermont Route 4, watch for the signs to Killington Ski Resort *(p274)*, where the K-1 gondola provides breathtaking views en route to the high summit of Killington Peak. Come back to earth and detour east on Route 4, passing Woodstock, to marvel at the the Quechee Gorge *(p278)*. Backtrack to genteel Woodstock *(p279)* to visit Billings Farm and Museum.

Evening Make dinner reservations at one of Woodstock's many inns; they get booked up quickly during the fall season.

Day 3

Morning Pick up Route 100 in Killington *(p274)* to follow the Mad River Valley *(p271)* alongside the Green Mountains. Follow the lead of Nobel laureate poet Robert Frost and enjoy an ice cream soda at the Rochester Café *(55 N Main St, Rochester)*.

Afternoon Tour the Ben & Jerry's Ice Cream Factory *(p270)*, and continue north to Stowe *(p268)*, a quintessential mountain village. Stretch your legs along the easy ridgeline trail on Mount Mansfield, the highest peak in Vermont.

Evening Book ahead at Stowe's Trapp Family Lodge *(700 Trapp Hill Rd)* to spend the night and dine in the Von Trapp Brewing Bierhall.

Pemaquid Point
Lighthouse on
Maine's rocky coast ↑

NEW ENGLAND FOR
NATURAL BEAUTY

New England was born in fire and ice. For 25,000 years glaciers shaped volcanic stone far below. They melted to reveal the rocky spine of the Green and White Mountains, the sandy glacial deposits of Cape Cod's beaches, and the breathtaking slate and shale ledges of the north coast.

Dramatic Heights

On a clear day, you can almost see forever from the trails and scenic highways that crisscross New England's section of the Appalachian Mountains. This majestic chain of mountains runs from the Litchfield Hills (p240) and Berkshires (p182) through the Green and White mountains and across Maine to Cadillac Mountain in Acadia National Park (p318).

A hiker reaching the snowcapped summit of Mount Washington

A Continent's Shattered Face

Maine's long and spectacular coastline won't disappoint travelers seeking a primal landscape. Icy, aquamarine Atlantic waters churn angrily at the base of rocky cliffs, and even the gentler bays between sentinel headlands are covered with fist-sized pebbles tumbled smooth by the waves. Lighthouses planted on the highest rocks warn mariners that these ledges and ridges also lurk offshore, ready to rip a ship from beneath its captain.

 HIDDEN GEM
Summer Blooms

Rhododendron State Park *(www.nhstate parks.org)* in Fitzwilliam, New Hampshire, is home to a grove of tree-sized rhododendrons. See them bloom bright pink in mid-July.

Green and Fertile Valleys

Stretching 410 miles (660 km) from source to sea, the Connecticut River is New England's arterial waterway. Hillside farms and hardwood forests flank its upper valley, while farm stands line the fertile flood-plain from Mount Sugarloaf southward, bursting with the valley's bounty through summer and fall. Downstream, the river meets the ocean and overhead, ospreys whirl and dive for fish.

→ The slow-moving waters of the Connecticut River

Sandy Shores

Stroll across the soft sands of Connecticut's Long Island Sound, or visit wild Nauset Beach on the Cape Cod National Seashore *(p180)*, where breakers boom as the tide comes rolling in. Their cannon-like explosions echo off the dunes, but hardly stir the seals sunning themselves on nearby sand bars.

Expansive dune-backed bay, Cape Cod National Seashore ↑

Make a Splash

The 20-ft (6-m) drop of Magic Falls on Maine's Kennebec River *(p331)* will certainly get your adrenaline pumping. And that's Maine's "easy" river compared to the Penobscot. Different stretches of the Deerfield River in western Massachusetts offer floats for families and class IV rapids for athletic thrill-seekers.

→

Whitewater rafting on Deerfield River

NEW ENGLAND FOR
OUTDOOR ADVENTURES

New England's mountainous peaks, majestic shorelines, fast-flowing rivers and leafy trails challenge visitors to stretch their muscles, feel their hearts pump, and exult in the many sporting activities for which the region is justly famous.

Hit the Slopes

From the black diamond runs on Mount Mansfield *(p268)* and Killington Peak *(p274)* in Vermont's Green Mountains to the vast snowfields and glade skiing of Sunday River and Sugarloaf *(p329)* in Maine, New England has a ski mountain to match every style and level of skill.

←

Group of skiers on the Narrow Gauge Trail, Mount Sugarloaf

A Hiker's Haven

Hikers can choose from more than 900 miles (1,450 km) of trails in Vermont's Green Mountain National Forest *(p274)* and more than 1,200 miles (1,930 km) of trails in New Hampshire's White Mountain National Forest *(p302)*. Both forests lie along the popular Appalachian Mountain Trail, which continues another 250 miles (400 km) north through Maine to Mount Katahdin.

→

Hikers crossing the Greeley Ponds on the Kancamagus highway

Surf's Up!

With cold ocean temperatures, New England surfing definitely calls for wetsuits, even in mid-summer. Surfers look like seals as they bob offshore, waiting for the next big break. Take it easy on the shores of Rhode Island's South County, catch the sharp break at Newport's Easton's Beach *(p212)*, or ride the really big swells hitting the dunes on Cape Cod National Seashore *(p180)* or Maine's Reid State Park, Georgetown.

←

A surfer heading for the chilly Atlantic waters of Longnook Beach, Cape Cod

TOP 3 HIGH-FLYING ZIP LINE TOURS

Alpine Adventures
🔺 C3 📍 Lincoln, NH
🌐 alpinezipline.com
Soar high above the treetops on up to six lines per tour.

Berkshire East
🔺 A5 📍 Charlemont, MA
🌐 berkshireeast.com
Glide over the Berkshire hills as you zip between two peaks.

Highflyer Zipline
🔺 C7 📍 Mashantucket, CT
🌐 foxwoodshighflyer.com
Zip down the roof of 33-story Fox Tower on the longest zipline in Connecticut.

Pedal Power

Bypass the traffic by pedaling along the Minuteman Bikeway from Cambridge to Bedford, Massachusetts, explore the leafy interior of Cape Cod on the Cape Cod Rail Trail *(p179)*, or cruise past marshes, farms, and gardens on Rhode Island's East Bay Bike Path from East Providence to Bristol.

↑ Cyclists on the East Bay Bike Path, Narragansett Bay, Rhode Island

Pemaquid Point
Lighthouse, Maine ↑

Beacons of Light

Lighthouses, ubiquitous on New England's coast, are an irresistible subject matter. But context is key to getting that truly atmospheric shot. Shoot from below to include the rocky cliffs at Maine's Pemaquid Point, or capture Cape Cod's Race Point Lighthouse as the sun sets over its sandy spit.

NEW ENGLAND FOR
PHOTOGRAPHERS

From the glass towers of Boston's skyline to a solitary lighthouse on a rocky promontory, New England dazzles with the sheer range of its imagery. Every visiting photographer is challenged to make it new, and place their own personal stamp on the region's timeless and quintessential scenes.

Spectacular Cityscapes

Boston has two skylines. The classic harbor view of Rowes Wharf can be photographed aboard a harbor cruise boat. For a great view across the harbor, take the T's Blue Line to East Boston and set up your tripod in Piers Park. Back Bay and Beacon Hill skyline is best snapped from the Cambridge side of the Charles River between Longfellow and Harvard bridges.

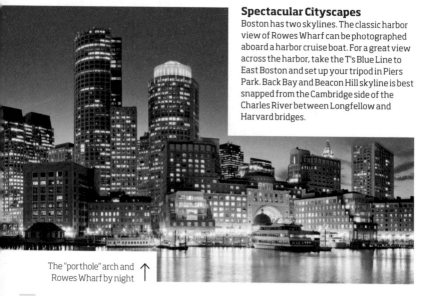

The "porthole" arch and
Rowes Wharf by night ↑

Catching the Wind

The schooners of Maine's iconic windjammer fleet show off their plumage during summer gatherings in Camden, Rockland, Boothbay Harbor, and Brooklin. Photograph them from the harbor piers or breakwaters. Newport, Rhode Island, hosts regattas and races all summer. The best vantage points are Fort Adams and Goat Island.

←

Racing boats off the coast of Newport, Rhode Island

PICTURE PERFECT
Motif #1

This red fishing shack on Bradley Wharf in the tiny town of Rockport, Massachusetts, is the most painted building in America. Photograph it in the early morning or late afternoon from adjacent T Wharf.

The Great Picture Show

Give your colorful fall foliage snaps extra pop by including manmade objects in the frame. Vermont State House (p270) has a hardwood forest backdrop and colorful maple trees out front. Fallen leaves can also be beautiful, and are especially atmospheric in an ancient graveyard like Copp's Hill (p101) in Boston. Or capture a white church spire as it rises above the golden trees in Guilford, Connecticut.

←

Vermont State House set against a backdrop of multi-hued leaves

Bygone Bridges

New England's wooden covered bridges evoke a bygone age of horse-drawn wagons traveling forested trails. Many can be found in Swanzey, New Hampshire, and Brattleboro, Vermont. Either shoot from the riverbank below, or, for a tale of two centuries, wait for a vehicle to poke its hood into the sunlight as it comes out of the bridge.

→

Wooden interior of a covered bridge in Bethel, Maine

Native American and Folk Arts

See the artistic genius of Maine's Penobscot, Passamaquoddy, Mi'kmaq, and Maliseet artists at the Abbe Museum *(p327)* in Bar Harbor and the Hudson Museum at the University of Maine, Orono. You'll marvel over the wit and whimsy of the folk art collections in Vermont's Shelburne Museum *(p266)*. →

Artifacts at the Shelburne Museum

Weatherbeaten (1894), Winslow Homer ↑

Shores of Inspiration

New England's coastline is fascinating to painters. See Maine artist Winslow Homer's seascapes at the Portland Museum of Art *(p310)*. Visual artist Andrew Wyeth spent years painting the people and saltwater farm landscape of the Olson House in Cushing, Maine, now owned by the Farnsworth Art Museum *(p315)*.

NEW ENGLAND FOR
ART LOVERS

Lavish landscapes, monumental sculpture, contemporary Native American art, and cutting-edge installations. From the encyclopedic collections of world-class art museums to the specialized holdings of the top teaching institutes, New England has a museum for every taste and interest.

Dazzling Masterpieces

While New England is filled with small specialized museums, you could easily spend a few days exploring the Museum of Fine Arts, Boston *(p132)* and the Wadsworth Atheneum *(p230)* in Hartford, Connecticut. Both museums cover all the bases from ancient Egypt, Greece and Rome to French Impressionism to American Moderns.

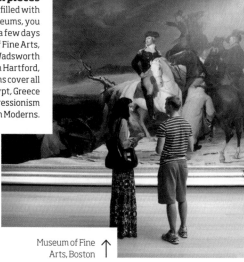

Museum of Fine ↑
Arts, Boston

 INSIDER TIP
Gallery Nights

Provincetown, MA, holds gallery openings on Friday nights in summer. Locals hop from gallery to gallery, treating wine and cheese as dinner.

Cutting-Edge Contemporary

Bewilderment and enchantment are the stock in trade of New England's contemporary art museums. In North Adams, The Massachusetts Museum of Contemporary Art (Mass MoCA) *(p199)* transformed old factories into expansive galleries. Enjoy harborfront views at the Institute of Contemporary Art *(p122)* in Boston – along with the cutting-edge exhibitions inside. The Center for Maine Contemporary Art in Rockland *(p315)* features local artists' work in changing installations.

↑ *Zoran Orlić Campus Building 7 Wall Drawing 340*, by Sol LeWitt

Three Dimensions

The deCordova Sculpture Park and Museum *(p191)* in Lincoln displays over 60 sculptures in its grounds. Chesterwood *(p185)* in Stockbridge mounts summer installations in a woodland setting. Walk the lawns of Aspet, the summer home of Augustus Saint-Gaudens, in Cornish *(p297)*, to see castings of his most famous works.

↑ The deCordova Sculpture Park and Museum in Lincoln

The Struggle for Freedom

While New England traders and merchants profited from the exploitation of enslaved people, some in the region also championed the abolition of the slave trade. Learn more about this complex history on Boston's Black Heritage Trail (p87), which includes sites such as the African Meeting House and other key locations on the Underground Railroad (p55).

←

Costumed guide on a walking tour, Boston

NEW ENGLAND FOR
HISTORY BUFFS

Visitors can follow the adventures of the Age of Sail, or relive the heady danger of plotting revolution against the king. Learn about the fight for equality, and see first-hand how the descendants of New England's original inhabitants continue to honor their forebears.

Spirit of Revolution

Standing in Boston's Faneuil Hall or Old South Meeting House, you can imagine the fiery rhetoric that fanned the flames of rebellion. Words became action with the 1775 Battle of Lexington and Concord, as told at the Minute Man National Historical Park (p168). Ascend the Bennington Battle Monument (p275) in Vermont that marks the 1777 battle where momentum shifted to the American cause.

NARRAGANSETT POWWOW

The Narragansett Indian Tribes August Meeting Powwow has welcomed members and outsiders from far and wide for song, dance, and ceremonies annually since 1676, making it the oldest recorded powwow in the country (www.narragansett indiannation.org).

Historical reenactment at Minute Man National Historical Park, Concord ↑

New England at Sea

New England grew rich on the sea. At Mystic Seaport *(p244)*, you can explore a re-created 19th-century port village and board the last wooden whaling ship afloat. The New Bedford Whaling National Historical Park *(p189)* tells the tale of the dangerous work of hunting whales. The saga of far-flung international trade is the subject of the Salem Maritime National Historic Site *(p166)* in Massachusetts and the Penobscot Marine Museum *(p316)* in Maine.

→

The *Charles W. Morgan*, now moored in Mystic Seaport harbor

Did You Know?

The *Charles W. Morgan* embarked on a total of 37 voyages, with most lasting more than three years.

The First New Englanders

Indigenous people lived in this region long before English puritans established the first colony here in 1620. But upon their arrival, the Europeans brought disease and warfare, decimating the Indigenous population. Find out more about the impact of the settlers on the Indigenous people at the Wampanoag Homesite at the Plimoth Patuxet Museums *(p172)*, Massachusetts, and the Mashantucket Pequot Museum *(p251)*, Connecticut.

←

Strolling through Plimouth Patuxet Museums in character

Leaders of a Nation

Many politicians have called this region home. Two US presidents, John Adams and his son John Quincy Adams, were born at the Adams National Historical Park *(p189)* in Quincy, Massachusetts. The home of the laconic Calvin "Silent Cal" Coolidge *(p278)* in Plymouth Notch, Vermont, reveals the upbringing of the 30th president, while the John F. Kennedy Library and Museum *(p124)* memorializes Boston's most famous son.

→

Statue of Abigail Adams and son John Quincy Adams, Quincy

NEW ENGLAND'S CONTEMPORARY WRITERS

Even today, New England remains fertile literary ground. Stephen King and Richard Russo (Pulitzer Prize) are closely associated with Maine. Andre Dubus III writes from his roots on the Massachusetts North Shore. The elite universities also harbor award-winning writers with global roots. Jamaica Kincaid (American Book Award), Junot Diaz (Pulitzer Prize), and Ha Jin (National Book Award) live and teach in New England.

Murals above the ↑ famous Brattle Book Shop in Boston

NEW ENGLAND FOR
BOOKWORMS

America's first publisher set up in Cambridge, Massachusetts, in 1639, and New Englanders haven't stopped writing since. The region is the undeniable birthplace of American literature, and book-lovers will enjoy the regular festivals and literary events that honour these luminaries.

Literary Festivals

Beat Generation author Jack Kerouac draws fans to his hometown for the Lowell Celebrates Kerouac Festival *(www.lowellcelebrates kerouac.org)*. The Boston Book Festival *(bostonbook fest.org)* features readings by top authors, while four days of readings and talks highlight Vermont's Brattleboro Literary Festival *(brattleboroliteraryfestival. org)*. All three festivals take place in October.

Authors discuss the craft of memoir at the 2018 Boston Book Festival.

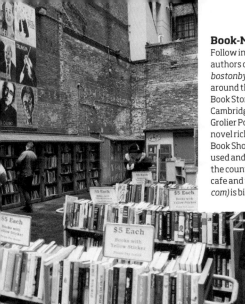

Book-Mad Boston

Follow in the footsteps of Boston's greatest authors on a literary walking tour (*www.bostonbyfoot.org*), or go on a self-guided walk around the city's many bookstores. Harvard Book Store (*p155*) anchors the extensive Cambridge scene, which includes the all-verse Grolier Poetry Book Shop and the graphic novel riches of Million Year Picnic. The Brattle Book Shop (*p88*) is Boston's leading source for used and antiquarian volumes – the largest in the country. Meanwhile, with its excellent cafe and free wifi, Trident (*tridentbookscafe.com*) is bibliophile heaven in Back Bay.

Did You Know?
—
Boston-based Anne Bradstreet became the first published writer from the American colonies in 1650.

Birthplace of American Literature

In the mid-1800s, writers around Ralph Waldo Emerson launched a new American literature. Visit Emerson House (*p169*) to see where they gathered. At neaby Orchard House, Louisa May Alcott wrote *Little Women*. Herman Melville's Arrowhead (*p183*) hasn't changed since he wrote *Moby-Dick*, while the Mark Twain House (*p232*) chronicles the author at his peak.

← Desk where Louisa May Alcott wrote

Frost Country

The quintessential New England poet, Robert Frost etched the rural landscape and hardscrabble life in immortal lines. Glimpse the master at the outset of his career in the Robert Frost Farm (*p293*) in Derry, New Hampshire, and later, as he won his first Pulitzer Prize in the Robert Frost Stone House Museum (*p272*) in Shaftsbury, Vermont.

→

A busy poetry event at Robert Frost Farm

A Burgeoning Foodie Scene

A pioneer city in the foodie revolution, Boston continues to roll out the gastronomic carpet for new ideas and taste sensations. The armada of food trucks along the Rose Kennedy Greenway *(p117)* serves everything from Korean *bulgogi bibimbap* (a rice dice with various toppings) to Mexican *tortas* and grilled cheese sandwiches. Chinatown *(p89)* has enough to satisfy all food cravings and set taste buds alight, with pho and dumplings being lunchtime standbys. You can eat scrod and baked beans at Boston's oldest restaurant, Union Oyster House *(unionoysterhouse.com)*, founded 1832, or savor Boston-bred superchef Barbara Lynch's upscale pastas at the modern and stylish Sportello *(sportello boston.com)* in the Seaport.

$\rightarrow$

Chefs preparing and serving shellfish at the Union Oyster House

NEW ENGLAND FOR
FOODIES

From the sweet lobster hauled from the sea in summer to the tangy crunch of apples picked in the fall, New England has a signature taste in every season. You can find the flavors at the source by connecting with the foragers, farmers, and fishermen whose skills bring them to the table.

King Crustaceans

Lobster shacks all along coastal New England serve steamed whole lobster, usually with melted butter and corn on the cob. The most elemental shacks give you a lobster and a fist-sized rock to crack the shell. If you're less ambitious, go for a lobster roll. Abbott's Lobster in the Rough *(abbots lobster.com)* in Noank, Connecticut, serve theirs hot and grilled in butter.

$\rightarrow$

Lobster served with butter

 INSIDER TIP
Food Tours

Walk and sample your way through Boston's North End on the "Little Italy" North End Market Tour, led by Boston Food Tours *(www.boston foodtours.com)*.

From Farm to Fork

As diners seek authentic local food, New England farmers often cut out the middleman. Rural roads are lined with farmstands that range from a table with cucumbers and tomatoes to small barns filled with bins of produce. Farmers' markets like those in Portland, Maine *(portlandmainefarmers market.org)* and Bennington, Vermont *(www.bennington farmersmarket.org)* are great places to pick up picnic fare. You may even be shopping with chefs from hot local restaurants.

→

Fresh produce at a
Farmer's Market in
Massachusetts

Syrupy Sweetness

When winter's first thaw makes the maple sap rise, New England sugar houses boil the juice into thick syrup. Some sugar houses also cook big farm breakfasts with pancakes. Maple Sugar and Vermont Spice *(vtsugarand spice.com)* in Mendon, Vermont and Heritage Farm Pancake House *(heritagefarm pancakehouse.com)* in Sanbornton, New Hampshire are local favorites.

→

Pancakes drizzled
in maple syrup

The Art of Distillation

Craft distilleries in New England are experimenting with gins laden with complex botanicals and whiskeys aged in local oak, and most have tasting rooms and offer educational distillery tours. Head to New England Distilling (www.newengland distilling.com) in Portland, Maine and Bully Boy Distillers (www.bullyboydistillers.com) in Boston to find out more.

←

Fermentation tank at a craft distillery in Portland

NEW ENGLAND
BY THE GLASS

New England has always favored a sip of beer, cider, mead, wine, and any number of distilled spirits, but the recent growth of craft brewers, vintners, and distillers has vastly expanded the world of drink here. As you explore the riches, be sure to have a designated driver.

The Coastal Wine Trail

Thanks to the moderating effects of the Gulf Stream, coastal Connecticut, Rhode Island, and Massachusetts have a climate well-suited to the wine grapes of Burgundy and Bordeaux. Plan on two to three days to explore the craft wineries of the Coastal Wine Trail (www.coastalwinetrail. com). Pack your own picnics, as most wineries offer picnic tables or grassy lawns where you can enjoy a meal with a bottle of whatever you just discovered in the tasting room.

Serving white wine at a vineyard in Rhode Island ↑

Did You Know?

The *Mayflower* Pilgrims were desperate to come ashore because the ship was running out of beer.

Craft Breweries of Vermont

With 55 craft breweries, Vermont brews more beer per capita than any other US state. Visit the tap rooms of craft beer legends like Idletyme (*www.idletymebrewing.com*) in Stowe and Long Trail near Killington (*www.longtrail. com*). The breweries tend to cluster around ski resorts and mountainous areas, offering thirst-quenching delights after skiing and hiking.

→

Idletyme beer on tap at the legendary Stowe brewery

Merry Mead Halls

The ancient drink fermented from wildflower honey is enjoying a revival in New England. Visit the three tasting rooms of Maine Mead Works (*www.mainemeadworks.com*) - in Portland, Kennebunk, or Rockland - for a tasting or to drink by the glass. Sap House Meadery (*www. saphousemeadery.com*) in Center Ossipee, New Hampshire, makes traditional, barrel-aged, and sparkling mead and offers hive-to-bottle tours.

←

Tempting range at Maine Mead Works

↑ Touring the Merrimack Brewery

This Bud's for You

Budweiser is the massive Clydesdale draft horse to the craft brewers' diminutive ponies. The Merrimack, New Hampshire, facility brews all the Budweiser and Bud Light for New England. Visit to nibble and sip at the Biergarten or take one of the Brewmaster tours (*www.budweisertours.com*) to see how dependable lager is made on an industrial scale.

Did You Know?

A blanket of fallen leaves is nature's way of protecting seeds on the forest floor during winter.

→

Fall foliage on the Kancamagus Highway

Hit the Highway

Place your hands at ten and two on the wheel to motor the impressive array of foliage drives. Vermont's Route 100 meanders along a maple-lined river valley from Arlington north to Smuggler's Notch. Your heart will pump as the Kancamagus Highway (p301) tunnels through the stunning White Mountain National Forest. Ridgeline views from the much-loved Mohawk Trail (www.mohawktrail.com) climax at the Hairpin Turn as it spirals down to the valley below.

NEW ENGLAND FOR
LEAF PEEPERS

Bulk up on memory for your camera or phone if you're visiting New England in the fall. Blazing foliage rolls north to south across the region from mid-September through October. You can see plenty of nature's palette on foot, more if you drive, and still more if you take to the air or water.

Make for the Coast

Don't overlook the more subtle colors of fall. On the coastal trails of the Rachel Carson National Wildlife Refuge in Maine (www.fws. gov), marshes glow in a dozen shades of gold, taupe, and chocolate brown. For even more variety, hike across Sandy Neck in Barnstable on Cape Cod (p177), where wild grasses sway in the breeze above the golden cordgrass, and cattails poke their bulrush bulbs into the air. Framing it all, staghorn sumac shrubs blaze crimson red.

←

Dunes at Sandy Neck Beach in Barnstable, Cape Cod

All Hands on Deck

You'll get an entirely different foliage perspective from an excursion boat. Starting in the north at Burlington, Vermont, *Spirit of Ethan Allen (p262)* cruises Lake Champlain for panoramic views of Vermont's Green Mountains and New York's Adirondacks shrouded in a banket of golden leaves. In central New Hampshire, MS *Mount Washington (cruise nh.com)* motors slowly from scenic port to scenic port on Lake Winnipesaukee. The naturalist aboard *Riverquest (ctriverquest.com)* will point out eagles and ospreys amid dazzling fall displays at the mouth of the Connecticut River.

BOSTON'S FALL COLORS BY BIKE

Fall is the perfect time to use Boston's bike-sharing program *(www.bluebikes.com)* to see the range of New England foliage in a single 7-mile (11 km) trail along the parks of the Emerald Necklace *(p141)*. From stately elms on Boston Common and golden-crowned willows in the Public Garden you'll pedal past the serenely luminous marshes of the Back Back Fens and see the swamp maples reflected in Jamaica Pond. Finally, climb Bussey Hill in the Arnold Arboretum for a view of Boston's city skyline over brilliantly colored treetops.

← MS *Mount Washington*, on Lake Winnipesaukee

A Birds-Eye View

The ski mountains blanketed in snow from November into April pop with color during foliage season, so several ski resorts start running their lifts early. Ride the K1 gondola at Killington *(p274)* in Vermont for incredible views of the electric yellow birch foliage on nearby Pico Peak. The aerial tramway at Cannon Mountain *(p290)* in New Hampshire offers a bird's-eye perspective on the red-and-orange hillsides of Franconia Notch *(p290)*.

↑ Ski lifts surrounded by colorful foliage at Pico Peak, Killington

Isle of Wine

The tiny island of South Hero (*p271*) at the northern tip of Lake Champlain is a rustic wonderland connected to Vermont by a two-lane blacktop highway. Most visitors come to pedal the back roads and visit the crafts shops. Vineyards of riesling and pinot noir wine grapes grow amid the apple orchards, thanks to the lake's warming effects. Visit Snow Farm Vineyard (*www.snowfarm. com*) for a taste.

→

Sun shining over Lake Champlain

4,000

The number of islands in New England; 3,166 of them sit off the coast of Maine.

NEW ENGLAND
OFFSHORE

Every New England island is a unique escape. From tiny rocks only exposed at low tide to large land masses that support several villages, literally thousands of islands dot the shores of New England. Embrace an island state of mind and leave the mainland behind as you reach these outposts.

Whaling Capital

For a century before the discovery of petroleum, Nantucket (*p190*) dominated the whaling industry with whale oil lamps and candles. Now the island trades in memories of these bygone days. Compare the Nantucket Whaling Museum's 46-ft (14 m) sperm whale skeleton to its 28-ft (8 m) whaleboat to see how the odds weren't always on the hunter's side.

←

A giant sperm whale skeleton at the Nantucket Whaling Museum

Cyclists' Delight

Named one of the top dozen natural areas in North America by the Nature Conservancy, Block Island (p224) has about 30 miles (48 km) of natural trails. Since most of the island lies within 200 ft (60 m) of sea level, you'll have easy pedaling to swimming beaches, hiking trails, birding marshes, or the red clay Mohegan Bluffs with their sentinel lighthouse.

→

Taking a break from cycling on a warm day on Block Island

Painterly Monhegan

Whether you're walking through the stunning village or hiking the rocky bluffs, you're bound to encounter an artist at an easel, studiously scrutinizing the island's unspoiled landscape. Fewer than 100 people live year-round on Monhegan Island (p315), located far offshore in the Gulf of Maine. However, its population of commercial fishermen swells in the summer as a host of artists arrive in pursuit of that elusive magical sea light.

←

An artist delicately paints the Monhegan landscape

SCENIC CRUISING IN THE THIMBLE ISLANDS

Of an estimated 365 dots of land in the Thimble Islands (p253) archipelago off the Connecticut coast in Long Island Sound, only 25 are actually inhabited. Many of the homes date from the late 19th century and have all the gingerbread trimmings. Cruises sail past some of the most impressive and recount tales of legendary visitors, including the pirate who possibly buried his treasure here. Visit Thimble Islands Cruise (www.thimbleislands.com) to book an adventure.

Presidential Favorite

You don't have to be commander in chief to enjoy the excellent dining, golf courses, and beaches of Martha's Vineyard (p194), a summertime favorite of former presidents Bill Clinton and Barack Obama. Meanwhile, rocky and remote Campobello Island (p320) was beloved by Franklin Delano Roosevelt.

↑ Barack Obama enjoying a day of golf at Martha's Vineyard

A YEAR IN
NEW ENGLAND

JANUARY

Moby Dick Marathon *(1st weekend)*. Live reading of Herman Melville's whaling epic at the New Bedford Whaling Museum, Massachusetts.

△ **Winter Carnival** *(late Jan)*. An ice-carving competition, snow golf tournament, and other chilly activities celebrate the winter season in Stowe, Vermont.

FEBRUARY

Dartmouth Winter Carnival *(early Feb)*. College students and winter sports teams put together an exuberant weekend of outdoor events in Hanover, New Hampshire.

△ **US National Toboggan Championships** *(early Feb)*. The country's only organized wooden toboggan race takes place in Camden, Maine.

MAY

△ **Cape Cod Maritime Days** *(throughout)*. Boat tours, lighthouse visits, and more celebrate the area's enduring link to the sea.

Abbe Museum Indian Market *(mid-May)*. Native American artists and performers from New England and beyond gather in Bar Harbor, Maine.

JUNE

△ **International Festival of Arts & Ideas** *(early Jun)*. Two-week festival in New Haven, Connecticut, with 200, mostly free, performances and lectures.

Windjammer Days *(last week)*. Viewing windjammers under full sail entering Boothbay Harbor, Maine, is the highlight of this festival.

SEPTEMBER

△ **Norwalk Oyster Festival** *(early Sep)*. The coastal community of Norwalk celebrates Connecticut's oyster industry with tastings, entertainment, and nautical displays .

The Big "E" *(mid-late Sep)*. New England's largest agricultural fair is known for its variety of food and entertainment in West Springfield, Massachusetts.

OCTOBER

△ **Haunted Happenings** *(throughout)*. With its witch-related past, and penchant for all things spooky, Salem, Massachusetts, observes Halloween in dazzling style.

Jack-O-Lantern Spectacular *(throughout)*. More than 5,000 carved pumpkins bring Halloween thrills to Roger Williams Park and Zoo in Providence, Rhode Island.

MARCH

△ **St. Patrick's Day Celebrations** *(mid-Mar)*. Green beer flows throughout New England while Boston and Holyoke, Massachusetts host spirited parades.
Vermont Maple Open House Weekend *(late Mar)*. Visitors are welcome to watch sugar makers boil sap to make maple syrup to celebrate the first crop of the season.

APRIL

Boston Marathon *(3rd Mon)*. America's oldest marathon draws runners and spectators from around the world.
△ **Patriot's Day** *(3rd Mon)*. The battles that sparked the American Revolution are reenacted in Lexington and Concord, Massachusetts.

JULY

△ **Independence Day Celebrations** *(Jul 4)*. Parades, fireworks, and celebratory concerts take place throughout New England.
Newport Folk Festival *(late Jul)*. This legendary folk festival takes over Fort Adams State Park, Rhode Island.

AUGUST

Maine Lobster Festival *(1st weekend)*. Boiled lobster dinners highlight this Rockland, Maine, festival which honors maritime life.
△ **Newport Jazz Festival** *(1st weekend)*. This renowned festival brings jazz stars to Fort Adams State Park, Rhode Island.
Annual Craftsmen's Fair *(early–mid)*. The country's oldest crafts fair features more than 300 craftspeople in Newbury, New Hampshire.

NOVEMBER

Cider Days *(1st weekend)*. Orchards and cider mills celebrate local heritage apples and the New England cider-making tradition in Franklin County, Massachusetts.
△ **Thanksgiving** *(4th week)*. Plymouth, Massachusetts, marks the holiday with dinners at the historic Plimoth Patuxet Museums, with parades and other events in the modern town.

DECEMBER

Christmas at the Newport Mansions *(throughout)*. Three of Rhode Island's Gilded-Age mansions sparkle with holiday decorations in Newport.
△ **New Year's Eve Celebrations** *(Dec 31)*. New England ushers in the new year with fireworks, parades, and spectacular live performances.

A BRIEF
HISTORY

Home to the first enduring English settlement in North America, New England was also the first region of the American colonies to reject British rule. Even following the sea-to-sea expansion of the US, New England continued to influence the nation's political, economic, and intellectual life.

Settlement and European Encounters

Settled *c.* 9000 BC by ancestors of the modern Wabanaki peoples, the first inhabitants of New England had only minor interactions with Europeans until 1600. French and English explorers partially chartered the coast from 1497 to 1603, but it was John Smith who named the region "New England" on his 1616 map. In 1620 religious refugees aboard the *Mayflower* settled in Plymouth. The land rush was on, and the English planted numerous settlements all along the coast. The Puritan-run Massachusetts Bay Colony and its capital of Boston soon dominated the regional political landscape.

80,000
—
The population of New England when European ships first arrived.

Timeline of events

9000 BC
Algonkian villages populate the landscape after deglaciation.

AD 1000
Vikings sail to Newfoundland, Canada, and move along the coast.

1620
Pilgrims land at Plymouth aboard the *Mayflower*.

1692
Salem's infamous witch trials begin, resulting in the execution of 20 innocent people.

1773
Boston Tea Party: colonists protest new taxes by dumping tea in Boston Harbor.

Colonial New England

Colonists from Massachusetts Bay expanded quickly inland and southward along the coast. Meanwhile, buffeted by European disease and encroachment on their lands, New England's Indigenous peoples went into serious decline. The brutal defeat of eastern populations in King Philip's War in 1676 established European dominance, clearing the way for settlement of the interior. In western Massachusetts and Vermont, settlement expanded mainly after the French and Indian War ended in 1763.

Forming a New Nation

Trading restrictions and royal taxes stoked tensions between Britain and the American colonies. New Englanders began talking rebellion, forming militias, and stockpiling arms. When the Boston garrison of British Redcoats marched on Concord and Lexington in April 1775, the ensuing battle sparked the American Revolution. A newly formed Continental Army lay siege to Boston, forcing the evacuation of British forces. The battles soon shifted south, but New Englanders helped write the Declaration of Independence and the US Constitution.

[1] 1716 Homann Map depicting New England as "Nova Anglia."

[2] Landing of the Mayflower at Plymouth Rock in 1620.

[3] King Philip's War, fought between English colonists and Native American tribes led by Metacomet, the Wampanoag chief.

[4] Patriots attack the Redcoats on their return to Boston after the Battle of Concord, 1775.

1793
Slater Mill in Pawtucket, RI, launches the Industrial Revolution with the first water-powered textile mill in America.

1836
Samuel Colt of Connecticut invents the six-shot revolver.

1839
Kingscote sees in era of extravagant summer homes for America's elite in Newport, RI.

1783
Treaty of Paris signals end to Revolutionary War.

1789
George Washington is the first president of the United States.

Fishing and International Trade

Revolution had a high price. New England merchants had grown wealthy on the so-called Triangle Trade of enslaved people, molasses, and rum with Africa and the West Indies. With the ports of the British empire closed to them, the merchant traders of Boston, Salem, and other New England ports opened up lucrative trade routes with China and, eventually, Japan, with stops in the Pacific Northwest to stock up on furs. New England fishermen had been key to the economy from the first settlements of the region, but New England ships also soon dominated the world's whaling industry. Whale oil lit the cities and greased the machinery of the early Industrial Revolution. New England shipyards could barely keep pace with the expanding fleets.

The Wheels of Industry Begin to Spin

The creation of Lowell, Massachusetts, in 1826 as a purpose-built mill town increased the scale of industrial textile manufacturing exponentially. Successful from the outset, Lowell became a template for canal-powered mill developments throughout New England, where many

1 The last whaling ship, *Charles W. Morgan*. ↑

2 Boott Cotton Mills Museum in Lowell, MA.

3 Portrait of American poet Emily Dickinson.

4 Painting of the Battle of Fort Wagner, 1863.

Did You Know?

During the Civil War, the Union counterfeited Confederate currency to cause inflation in the South.

Timeline of events

1820
Nantucket Islanders begin to hunt Atlantic sperm whales off the coast of New England.

1854
Thoreau's *Walden*, a seminal text for the environmental movement, is published.

1865
Railroads begin to span the country as industry expands.

1863
The 54th Massachusetts is the first regiment of Black soldiers to fight in the Civil War.

1880
The Newport Casino opens in Rhode Island and introduces lawn tennis to the US.

1897
The first subway in the country opens in Boston.

immigrants found their first jobs. Manufacturing, fishing, and whaling fortunes converged, as New Englanders built banks and financed America's railroads, while refugees from Ireland and central Europe provided the labor for expansion. A vibrant economy was matched by intellectual ferment. By the mid-19th century, New England authors such as Ralph Waldo Emerson, Nathaniel Hawthorne, Henry David Thoreau, and Emily Dickinson spawned a distinctively American body of literature.

Civil War and Aftermath

As part of the intellectual awakening, New England was a hotbed of the movement to abolish slavery in the US. Even though the region's factories depended on cotton grown by enslaved people in America's southern states, the outbreak of the Civil War proved good for business. New England textile mills switched from cotton to wool to produce the Union's military uniforms, and its Connecticut River arms manufacturers provided weapons. But the war devastated rural New England, as many men gave up farming to go to war. Many never returned, and others relocated their families to more fertile land.

THE UNDERGROUND RAILROAD

Boston was a center for prominent protest against slavery, which was firmly entrenched in the southern states and reviled in much of the northern states. The Underground Railroad was a secret network of escape routes and safehouses for enslaved people fleeing the South and making their way to freedom in the free states of the North and Canada.

Early 1900s
American Impressionist painters establish a base in Old Lyme, CT.

1918
White Mountain National Forest established in New Hampshire and Maine.

1919
Boston police strike for the right to form a trade union.

1917
American entry into WWI, despite Wilson's efforts to remain neutral.

1901
Boston Red Sox founded as a charter franchise of the American League.

1

2

3

The Gilded Age and Immigrant New England

Industrialization and rural flight transformed New England in the last third of the 19th century, as the region became less English and Protestant and more Irish, French, Polish, Italian, and Catholic. These immigrants, who filled the ranks of factory workers and the building trades, also came to dominate the newly resurgent Democratic party and the labor union movement. Wealth in New England became increasingly stratified, and labor strife contributed to the loss of jobs to the non-unionized American South. Meanwhile, between the Civil War and World War I, the New England rich endowed such cultural institutions as the Boston Symphony Orchestra and several major art museums.

New England on the Move

The period between the world wars was rough on New England, as the economy faltered. Poverty and unemployment soared in the mill towns and cities. Yet there were also bright spots. The New Deal of the 1930s brought a vast expansion of roads and airports, and many parts of New England capitalized on the

AMERICA'S FIRST WORKING WOMEN

The Lowell mill girls came to work in textile mills in Lowell, MA, during the Industrial Revolution. One of the first young women recruited was Lucy Larcom. She went on to become a poet and a teacher, and later in life she chronicled her experience as a mill girl in her book, *A New England Childhood.* "I defied the machinery to make me its slave," she wrote.

Timeline of events

1924
Massachusetts Investors Trust brings investment to middle classes.

1929
Stock market crash marks the beginning of the Great Depression.

1930s
Invention of aerial lifts revolutionizes New England's ski industry.

1937
The Appalachian Trail debuts as a footpath from Georgia to Maine.

1947
John F. Kennedy begins his career as US Congressman from Massachusetts.

new infrastructure by creating a tourism industry. By the 1970s, manufacturing was concentrated in high-technology fields such as pharmaceuticals, jet engines, and the nascent computer industry. The region's colleges and universities began to work hand in hand with private capital, spawning hardware and software companies and laying the groundwork for the explosive growth of biotechnology, robotics, and internet companies at the end of the 20th century.

Education and the Knowledge Economy

By the early years of the 21st century, the New England economy had transitioned almost entirely from manufacturing to knowledge and service industries. Higher education remains a mainstay of the region's identity and fiscal strength. Today, many recent college graduates land lucrative positions with innovative Internet-based companies, biomedical corporations, robotics giants, and in finance, largely based in the region's urban centers. Meanwhile, a demand for local food has transformed farming into a boutique industry producing raw materials for a chef-driven dining culture.

[1] Danny Kaye conducting the Boston Symphony Orchestra in 1957.

[2] Lowell mill girls, c. 1913.

[3] Modern interior of Yale University Library.

[4] Stata Center at MIT, Cambridge, MA.

Did You Know?

Email was invented in Cambridge, Massachusetts, by programmer Ray Tomlinson.

1961

President John F. Kennedy signs a bill that authorizes the creation of the Cape Cod National Seashore.

1954

The world's first nuclear submarine is built in Groton, Connecticut.

2013

Terrorist bombs at Boston Marathon kill three and injure hundreds.

2013

Massachusetts is the first US state to legally recognize same-sex marriage.

2019

New England Patriots win sixth Super Bowl since 2002.

EXPERIENCE BOSTON

Boston's Theater District at night

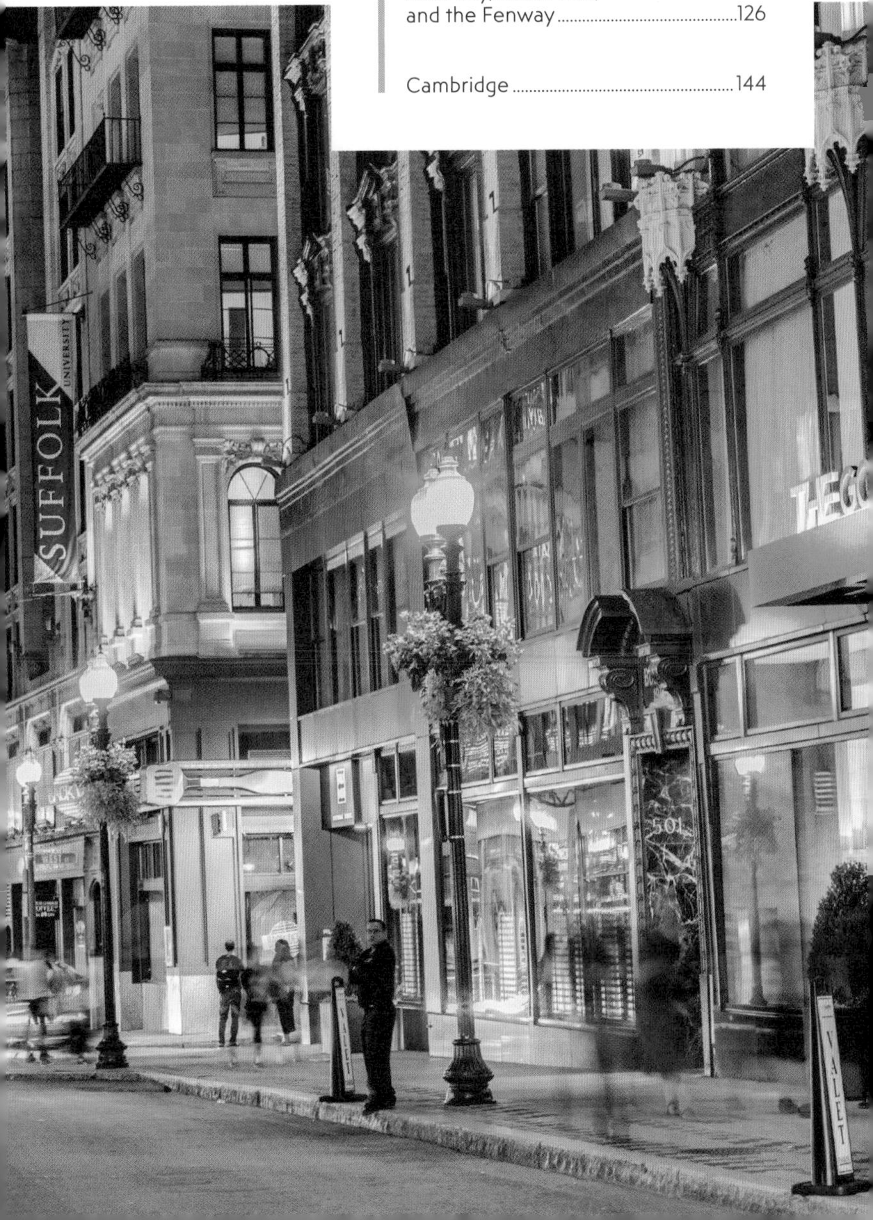
SUFFOLK
UNIVERSITY
501
VALET
VALET

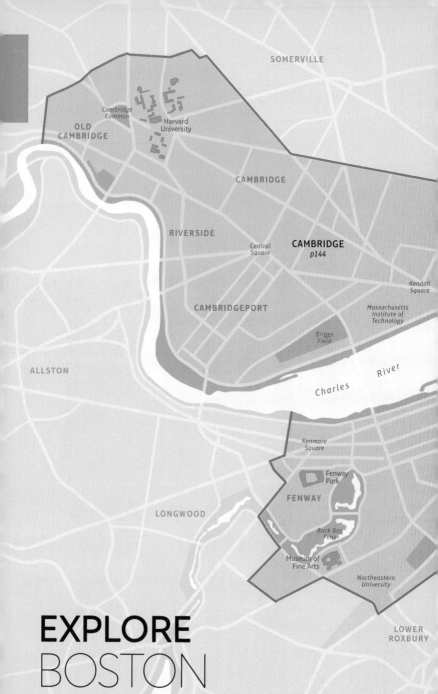

SOMERVILLE

OLD CAMBRIDGE

Cambridge Common

Harvard University

CAMBRIDGE

RIVERSIDE

Central Square

CAMBRIDGE
p144

Kendall Square

CAMBRIDGEPORT

Massachusetts Institute of Technology

Briggs Field

ALLSTON

Charles River

Kenmore Square

Fenway Park

FENWAY

LONGWOOD

Back Bay Fens

Museum of Fine Arts

Northeastern University

LOWER ROXBURY

EXPLORE
BOSTON

This guide divides Boston into five main sightseeing areas, as shown on this map. Find out more about each area on the following pages.

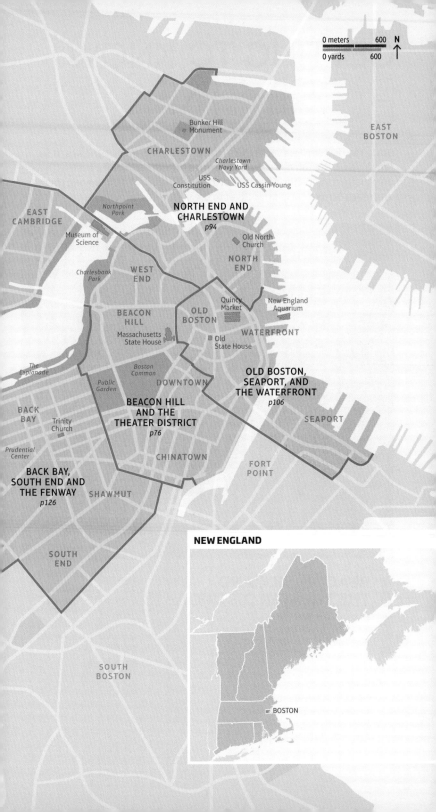

0 meters 600
0 yards 600
N

EAST
BOSTON

Bunker Hill
Monument

CHARLESTOWN

Charlestown
Navy Yard

USS
Constitution

USS Cassin Young

NORTH END AND
CHARLESTOWN
p94

EAST
CAMBRIDGE

Northpoint
Park

Museum of
Science

Old North
Church

NORTH
END

Charlesbank
Park

WEST
END

BEACON
HILL

OLD
BOSTON

Quincy
Market

New England
Aquarium

WATERFRONT

Massachusetts
State House

Old
State House

The
Esplanade

Boston
Common

DOWNTOWN

OLD BOSTON,
SEAPORT, AND
THE WATERFRONT
p106

Public
Garden

BACK
BAY

Trinity
Church

BEACON HILL
AND THE
THEATER DISTRICT
p76

SEAPORT

Prudential
Center

CHINATOWN

FORT
POINT

BACK BAY,
SOUTH END AND
THE FENWAY
p126

SHAWMUT

SOUTH
END

NEW ENGLAND

SOUTH
BOSTON

BOSTON

GETTING TO KNOW
BOSTON

Since the first settlers split between the North End and South Cove (now Chinatown), Boston has spawned a series of neighborhoods, each with its own distinct character. The city's attractions are spread out among them, and reach across the Charles River to the youth-driven culture of Cambridge.

PAGE 76

BEACON HILL AND THE THEATER DISTRICT

Saunter the quaint brick sidewalks of Beacon Hill to get a taste for how the city's first moneyed class – the Boston Brahmins – once lived. Many of their stately mansions and townhouses were the handiwork of Charles Bulfinch, architect of the Massachusetts State House that sits proudly at the summit. For all its air of privilege, Beacon Hill touches on the more democratic open spaces of Boston Common and Public Garden, enjoyed by locals and visitors alike. At the foot of this historic hill is Boston's dynamic Theater District, where grandiose playhouses perform sell-out shows.

Best for
Black history, architecture and theater

Home to
Boston Common and Public Garden, and the Massachusetts State House

Experience
Walking the hidden alleys and warrens of Beacon Hill on the Black Heritage Trail

NORTH END AND CHARLESTOWN

Facing each other across the mouth of the Charles River, North End and Charlestown are packed with essential stops on Boston's famous Freedom Trail, such as Old North Church and Bunker Hill. But they are much more than history lessons. These vibrant residential neighborhoods have been shaped by their immigrant origins. Visitors especially enjoy the traditional Italian character of the North End, with its *caffès*, restaurants, and vibrant street life. Across the Charles River, Charlestown Navy Yard is replete with history and the scenic Paul Revere Park hosts art installations and concerts.

Best for
Revolutionary history and exploring Boston's maritime past

Home to
Old North Church and Charlestown Navy Yard

Experience
Panoramic views of Boston and its harbor from atop the Bunker Hill Monument

→

OLD BOSTON, SEAPORT, AND THE WATERFRONT

Colonial Boston flows seamlessly into the glass and steel glamour of the financial district. As you stroll downhill from the red-brick landmarks of old Boston, you'll cross the soothing linear park of the Rose Kennedy Greenway. At the waterfront, take a harbor cruise, visit the aquarium, or just enjoy the sea air. Follow the shore across Fort Point Channel to the Seaport District, a lively, all-new section of the city.

Best for
Presidential history, harbor cruises, and beaches

Home to
New England Aquarium, Old State House, and Faneuil Hall Marketplace

Experience
A ferry trip to the Boston Harbor Islands

PAGE 126

BACK BAY, SOUTH END, AND THE FENWAY

When you strut down the shopping sidewalks of Newbury Street or stroll the leafy Commonwealth Avenue Mall, the regular grid and sense of order may make you wonder if you're still in Boston. Top boutiques and some of the city's hottest restaurants populate the parallel neighborhoods of Back Bay and the more residential South End. Farther west, the Fenway's meandering parkland complements the city's major art museums.

Best for
World-class art museums, buzzing restaurants, and boutique shopping

Home to
Trinity Church, Museum of Fine Arts, and Isabella Stewart Gardner Museum

Experience
Watching the Boston Red Sox in Fenway Park, America's most iconic baseball park

PAGE 144

CAMBRIDGE

Although part of the greater Boston metropolitan area, Cambridge is a city in its own right. Principally a college town, it is a veritable haven of culture and education, with a vibrant student population. At the heart of it all, Harvard Square is a lively crossroads of street life, independent boutiques, and academia. Funky Central Square looks its best after dark, when the area's plethora of diverse restaurants come alive, and crowds gather for evening entertainment in the area's many bars. The impressive collections of Harvard University's numerous museums attract students, visitors, and *cognoscenti* from far and wide, while students, young coders, and biotech workers let their hair down in the hip spots of Kendall Square near MIT.

Best for
University museums and nightlife

Home to
Harvard University, Museum of Science, and MIT

Experience
Listening to the street musicians busking on the sidewalks of Harvard Square

←

1 Ornate Trinity Church.

2 Boston's Theater District.

3 Visitors admiring exhibits at the Museum of Fine Arts.

4 Fresh oysters at the historic Union Oyster House.

3 DAYS
in Boston

Day 1

Morning Fortified with a cup of Boston's favorite Dunkin' coffee, enjoy a crash course on Boston's history on the Freedom Trail (p74). Start at the Massachusetts State House (p82) and wind your way to Old State House (p112). Continue down to Faneuil Hall (p116) and be sure to catch the Park Service Ranger tour.

Afternoon After lunch at the Union Oyster House (p117), explore the shops of Faneuil Hall Marketplace, then resume your history tour by visiting the Paul Revere House (p102), Old North Church, and Copp's Hill Burying Ground (p100). Time to spare? Cross the bridge to Charlestown to visit "Old Ironsides" in Charlestown Navy Yard (p98) and climb the Bunker Hill Monument (p104).

Evening You've earned this. Backtrack to Hanover Street in the North End, Boston's Italian neighborhood, for all manner of inventive pasta dishes at Bricco (p103).

Day 2

Morning After croissants and coffee in the Newsfeed Cafe of the Boston Public Library (p137), admire the architecture, paintings, and sculpture of the library's original building before crossing Copley Square to visit Trinity Church (p130), one of the top 10 buildings in the US. Stop at the BosTix kiosk (p90) to score same-day tickets to a play in the Theater District.

Afternoon Unless you've been lucky enough to bag tickets to an afternoon Red Sox game at Fenway Park (p140), split your after-lunch hours between the Museum of Fine Arts (p132) and the Isabella Stewart Gardner Museum (p138), both of which face the green parkland of the Back Bay Fens.

Evening Dine early in Chinatown (p89) before your show. Afterward, adjourn to the Aujourd'hui Lounge in the Four Seasons (200 Boylston St).

Day 3

Morning Breathe in the salty air of the Seaport District on a tour of the Boston Tea Party Ships (p123) and learn how high taxation inspired rebellion. And speaking of rebellion, catch one of the revolutionary exhibitions at the nearby Institute of Contemporary Art (p122). Grab lunch at the Barking Crab (88 Sleeper St), a classic seafood shack on the waterfront.

Afternoon At South Station, hop on the T's Red Line subway to Harvard Square (p154) in Cambridge. Take the student-led Harvard University tour for an insight into life on campus (p150). Finish the afternoon browsing the boutiques and bookstores of Harvard Square before heading to Noir Bar (1 Bennett St) for small bites and an artisanal cocktail.

Evening Stick around Harvard Square for dinner and live music at the Beat Brew Hall (www.beatbrewhall.com).

Summer Celebrations

The city's biggest free event is the July 4 Boston Pops Fireworks Spectacular on the Charles River Esplanade. Performed by the Boston Pops Orchestra, it is a veritable feast for the ears, followed by a fireworks extravaganza. For a smaller crowd, the rehearsal the night before includes all the fantastic music but none of the pyrotechnics. The Esplanade stays busy all summer, with weekly concerts by the Boston Landmarks Orchestra, and Friday night screenings of classic movies. Commonwealth Shakespeare mounts a different play each year on Boston Common *(p81)*, while more than 400 free performances in Berklee's Summer in the City program mean you could encounter musicians playing almost anywhere.

→

Boston Landmarks Orchestra performing on the Esplanade

Did You Know?

Founded in 1885, the Boston Pops is the most recorded orchestra in the country.

BOSTON
ON A
SHOESTRING

You don't always have to dig in your pocket to have a good time in Boston. Free guided tours of the city's most iconic buildings combine with stunning gardens and leafy parks to keep visitors entertained all day long. Moreover, some of Boston's biggest outdoor celebrations don't cost a penny.

Go Green

Boston is a city of parks. Public art exhibitions on the Rose Kennedy Greenway *(p120)* sit alongside dynamic fountains and colorful gardens. Plant lovers delight in the encyclopedic array of blooms at the Arnold Arboretum, and can smell more than 1,500 rose bushes at the Kelleher Rose Garden in the Back Bay Fens *(p140)*.

←

The Rose Kennedy Greenway, an oasis in the heart of Boston

TOP 5 | **FREE GUIDED TOURS**

Massachusetts State House
Peek inside the chambers (p82).

Boston Public Library
Discover the library's history (p137).

Freedom Trail
Park rangers bring history to life (p74).

Black Heritage Trail
African-American history of Beacon Hill (p87).

Harvard Yard
Take a student-led tour (p150).

Starry Nights

City lights make it hard to appreciate the night sky without the aid of powerful optics. Fortunately, you can drop in on Friday nights (mid-April to October) at the Museum of Science (p148) for "Astronomy After Hours" at the Gilliland Observatory. On Wednesday evenings, the Judson B. Coit Observatory at Boston University (www.bu.edu) also offers free viewings.

→
Starry skies over Boston Harbor

The Sound of Music

Boston is a top training ground for musicians. Most of the concerts on the New England Conservatory's schedule are free, as are many at Berklee College of Music (p138). You might catch an up-and-coming opera diva or pop performer. Don't overlook less conventional venues either; contemporary, jazz, folk, and classical musicians often play at King's Chapel (p114), and organists perform at Trinity Church (p130).

←
Darynn Dean and the NEC Jazz Orchestra

▷ Cheer on the Boston Marathon

Top distance runners from around the globe flock to Boston every April to compete in the Boston Marathon, the oldest annual marathon in the world. Spectators line the entire 26.2-mile (42.2-km) course from suburban Hopkinton to Back Bay. Favorite viewing spots include Chestnut Hill and the final turn from Commonwealth Avenue down Boylston Street to the finish line at the Boston Public Library.

◁ Batter Up with the Boston Red Sox

Since 1912, the legendary Boston Red Sox have played their home games at Fenway Park *(p140)*, the oldest, best-loved park in Major League Baseball. Cheer on the Red Sox at a game, or take a guided tour *(www.redsox.com)*.

BOSTON FOR
SPORTS FANS

Boston sports fans are truly crazed, and they have every right to be. Boston's professional sports teams are up there with the very best. From sports bar chatter to experiencing the energy at games, visitors can rub shoulders with some of the most knowledgeable and passionate fans in the US.

△ Touchdown Fever

The storied New England Patriots, one of the dominant teams of the NFL, have appeared in more Super Bowls than any other club. Hop aboard the MBTA to Gillette Stadium in Foxborough to see them play, rain or shine.

◁ See the Celtics Score a Slam Dunk

One of the eight founding teams of the National Basketball Association, the Boston Celtics have won 17 NBA championships - and counting. They play on the removable parquet floor of the TD Garden, a venue they share with the Boston Bruins hockey team. You'll spend more time standing and screaming at the top of your lungs than sitting in that seat you paid for. But it's all part of the experience.

◁ Brave the Bruins on Ice

You'll be glad for the glass wall shielding the stands when a Boston Bruin thunders toward you, sending a spray of ice in the air and slamming into the boards. The oldest professional hockey team in the US (since 1924), the Bruins were once known for their extremely physical brand of hockey, where time in the penalty box was seen as a badge of honor. Today the team emphasizes speed, pinpoint shooting, and dominant goaltending.

INSIDER TIP
Score Game Day Tickets

Tickets for Boston's biggest sporting events are available from Ace Ticket *(www.aceticket. com)* or StubHub *(www. stubhub.com)*. If you can't score a ticket on game day, fear not, you can always join the rest of the fans in rooting for the home team at a nearby sports bar, where the energy is equally infectious.

△ Head of the Charles Regatta

Every October up to 11,000 athletes row their shells in graceful synchronicity over the winding course of the Head of the Charles Regatta. The grassy embankments on either side of the river make great picnic spots to watch the two day competition. To get even closer, stake out a spot on the Weeks Footbridge.

Rock, Rhythm, and Blues

The House of Blues *(www.house ofblues.com)* national chain of music and supper clubs launched in Cambridge, Massachusetts, and its nightly music program still anchors the renowned Lansdowne Street entertain-ment district. Meanwhile, the historic and outrageously opulent Orpheum Theatre *(www.orpheumtheatre maboston.com)* at Downtown Crossing presents an eclectic stream of touring performers. Mingle with the Allston student crowd at the Paradise Rock Club *(www.paradiserock.club)*, where bands strive to play with a definite edge.

→

George Clinton and Parliament Funkadelic perform at House of Blues

BOSTON FOR
MUSIC LOVERS

When the sun goes down in Boston, the clubs light up. From Irish fiddle music and laid-back jazz to punk wailers and thunderous rock, there's a venue for almost every style. If you're a visiting musician, you might want to sit in on a *seisiun* or even take the spotlight at one of many open mic nights.

 HIDDEN GEM
The Verb Hotel

Pop into The Verb *(www.theverbhotel. com)*, a music-inspired boutique hotel in Kenmore Square to see its vast collection of more than a half-century of memorabilia and collectables recounting Boston's rock 'n' roll legacy. The hotel also owns an extensive vinyl library for guests' exclusive use.

Legendary Jazz

Boston has been a jazz mecca since the early 20th century. Major recording artists headline the shows at the Regattabar *(regattabarjazz.com)* in Harvard Square and Scullers Jazz Club *(www.scullersjazz.com)* in Allston. In South End, The Beehive *(www.beehiveboston.com)* features nightly music, mostly with a jazz or Latin jazz edge.

→

Lenny White's band performing at Regattabar, Charles Hotel

Boston is home to a large and vibrant Latin American community, and while Latin bands play some of the city's bars, especially in South End, the most consistent spot to get up and dance to salsa and *bachata* is the Havana Club in Central Square (*www.havana clubsalsa.com*). It's essentially a house party minus the alcohol. Start with a dance lesson, then hit the floor to recorded music until after midnight.

Toe-Tappin' Folk

Originally called Club 47, Club Passim in Harvard Square (*p154*) was instrumental in the American folk music revival of the late 1950s and 1960s. Folkies still play their hearts out on the small downstairs stage. Several Irish pubs schedule *seisiuns* of traditional music. The Burren (*www.burren.com*) and The Druid (*www. druidpub.com*) host them regularly.

←

A seisiun at The Druid pub in Cambridge

The Indie Scene

Alt rockers adore the Middle East (*www. mideastoffers.com*) in Central Square – this Cambridge club gave many budding musicians their start. Youngsters from the hustings figure this is where they'll get their break. A slightly more mature indie group converges at Lizard Lounge (*www. lizardloungeclub.com*) just up Massachusetts Avenue from Harvard Square.

↑ Musician Sango performs at the Middle East

A LONG WALK
THE FREEDOM TRAIL

Distance 2.5 miles (4 km) **Walking time** 1 hour **Terrain** Generally flat and paved; the route is clearly marked by a painted red line on sidewalks **Stopping point** Quincy Market

Boston has more sites directly related to the American Revolution than any other city. The most important of these, as well as some that relate to other freedoms gained by Bostonians, form "The Freedom Trail", starting at the information center on Boston Common and ending at Bunker Hill in Charlestown. The first section weaves its way through the central city and Old Boston. Distances begin to stretch out on the second half as the trail meanders through the narrow streets of the North End to Charlestown, where Boston's settlers first landed. For more details on this historic route, visit www.thefreedomtrail.org.

↑ The gold dome of the Massachusetts State House illuminated at dusk

Before reaching the **Massachusetts State House**, the trail passes the Robert Gould Shaw and the 54th Massachusetts Infantry Regiment memorial, which honors the first African-American volunteer unit in the American Civil War.

The Freedom Trail starts at the Visitor Information Center on **Boston Common** (p80), where angry colonials once rallied against their British masters. Political speakers still expound from soapboxes here, and the Common remains a center of civic activity.

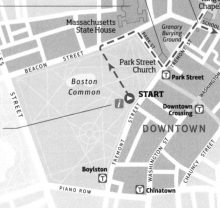

The towering granite obelisk above the Charlestown waterfront is **Bunker Hill Monument** (p104), which commemorates those lost in the battle of June 17, 1775 that ended with a costly victory for British forces.

An iron bridge over the Charles River links the North End with Charlestown.

Continuing along Tremont Street you will come to **King's Chapel and Burying Ground** (p114).

On School Street, a hopscotch-like mosaic embedded in the sidewalk commemorates the site of the first public school, established in 1635. At the bottom of the street is the **Old Corner Bookstore** (p114).

A bulwark of the anti-slavery movement, **Park Street Church** (p87) took the place of an old grain storage facility, which gave its name to the adjacent **Granary Burying Ground**.

FINISH

Bunker Hill Monument

MONUMENT SQUARE

SOLEY AVE

Winthrop Square

WARREN STREET

PARK ST

CHELSEA STREET

CONSTITUTION

Revere Landing Park

Charlestown Bridge

NEW SUDBURY STREET

CAMBRIDGE ST

CITY HALL PLAZA

Government Center

King's Chapel

SCHOOL ST

BOWDOIN STREET

Granary Burying Ground

PARK ST

TREMONT ST

Massachusetts State House

CHARLES STREET

BEACON STREET

Boston Common

STREET

Park Street Church

Park Street

WASHINGTON ST

START

Downtown Crossing

DOWNTOWN

TREMONT STREET

WASHINGTON ST

CHAUNCY STREET

Boylston

PIANO ROW

Chinatown

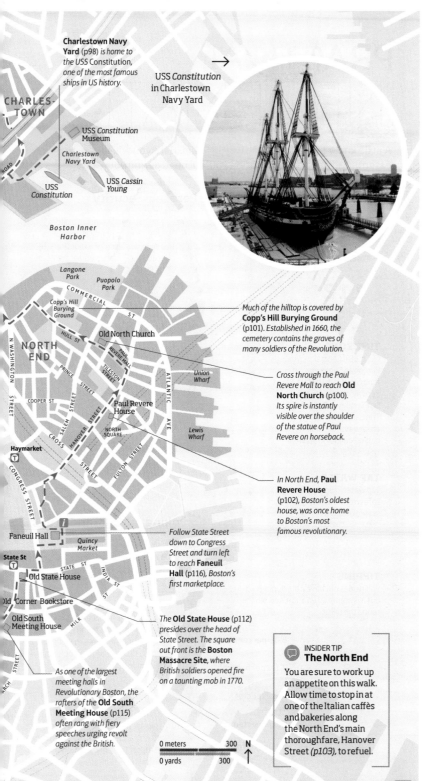

Charlestown Navy Yard (p98) *is home to the USS* Constitution, *one of the most famous ships in US history.*

USS *Constitution* in Charlestown Navy Yard

CHARLES-TOWN

USS *Constitution* Museum

Charlestown Navy Yard

USS *Cassin Young*

USS *Constitution*

Boston Inner Harbor

Langone Park

Puopolo Park

COMMERCIAL ST

Copp's Hill Burying Ground

HULL ST

Old North Church

NORTH END

PAUL REVERE MALL

N WASHINGTON STREET

PRINCE STREET

TILESTON STREET

ATLANTIC AVE

Union Wharf

COOPER ST

SALEM STREET

HANOVER STREET

Paul Revere House

NORTH SQUARE

Lewis Wharf

CROSS STREET

Haymarket

FULTON STREET

CONGRESS STREET

Faneuil Hall

Quincy Market

State St

STATE ST

INDIA ST

Old State House

Old Corner Bookstore

Old South Meeting House

MILK ST

ARCH STREET

Much of the hilltop is covered by **Copp's Hill Burying Ground** (p101). *Established in 1660, the cemetery contains the graves of many soldiers of the Revolution.*

Cross through the Paul Revere Mall to reach **Old North Church** (p100). *Its spire is instantly visible over the shoulder of the statue of Paul Revere on horseback.*

In North End, **Paul Revere House** (p102), *Boston's oldest house, was once home to Boston's most famous revolutionary.*

Follow State Street down to Congress Street and turn left to reach **Faneuil Hall** (p116), *Boston's first marketplace.*

The **Old State House** (p112) *presides over the head of State Street. The square out front is the* **Boston Massacre Site**, *where British soldiers opened fire on a taunting mob in 1770.*

As one of the largest meeting halls in Revolutionary Boston, the rafters of the **Old South Meeting House** (p115) *often rang with fiery speeches urging revolt against the British.*

> 💬 INSIDER TIP
> **The North End**
>
> You are sure to work up an appetite on this walk. Allow time to stop in at one of the Italian caffès and bakeries along the North End's main thoroughfare, Hanover Street *(p103)*, to refuel.

0 meters 300
0 yards 300

N ↑

BEACON HILL AND THE THEATER DISTRICT

Literally and figuratively the loftiest perch in downtown Boston, Beacon Hill was the city's first exclusive address. The rows of brick townhouses embody Boston's finest Federal architecture, and many larger manses were the work of Charles Bulfinch, designer of the 1798 State House on the hill's summit. The majestic south slope faces leafy Boston Common, and the foot of the hill flows down to the Public Garden. While Boston's gentry occupied the south slope, the north slope of Beacon Hill has always been more democratic. It was home to the city's leading 19th-century community of free African Americans, and later welcomed waves of Eastern European Jewish immigrants.

Near the Common on Boylston and Washington streets, Boston's Theater District bloomed with glamorous playhouses in the late 19th and early 20th centuries. Many of the theaters have been restored to their original grandeur, and the nightlife scene extends into adjacent Chinatown, where Asian restaurants thrive on the pre- and post-theater trade.

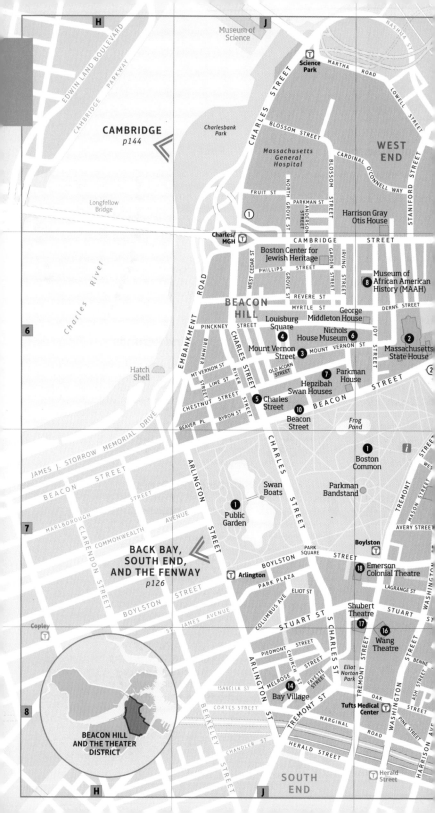

BEACON HILL AND THE THEATER DISTRICT

Must Sees
1. Boston Common and Public Garden
2. Massachusetts State House

Experience More
3. Mount Vernon Street
4. Louisburg Square
5. Charles Street
6. Nichols House Museum
7. Hepzibah Swan Houses
8. Museum of African American History (MAAH)
9. Boston Athenaeum
10. Beacon Street
11. Granary Burying Ground
12. Park Street Church
13. Downtown Crossing
14. Bay Village
15. Chinatown
16. Wang Theatre
17. Shubert Theatre
18. Emerson Colonial Theatre
19. Citizens Bank Opera House

Eat & Drink
1. Alibi Bar & Lounge
2. No. 9 Park

Shop
3. Brattle Book Shop

BOSTON COMMON AND PUBLIC GARDEN

🅠 K7　🅣 Park Street, Boylston, Arlington　ℹ️ 139 Tremont St; www.boston.gov/parks/boston-common

These two adjacent urban oases form part of Boston's Emerald Necklace. Swan boats drift beneath weeping willows, children splash in fountains, and a bronzed George Washington oversees the proceedings from his his lofty steed.

Acquired by Boston in 1634 from first settler William Blackstone, Boston Common served at various times as common pasture, military drill ground, and gallows site. British troops camped here during the 1775–6 military occupation. In the 19th century, it was a hub for Civil War recruitment and anti-slavery rallies, playing host to many anti-war demonstrations and civil rights protests. Meanwhile, the adjacent Public Garden exudes old world charm. Opened in 1839, it was the first botanical garden in the US, and is emblematic of Boston at its most enchanting. The **Swan Boats**, a fleet of pontoon pleasure boats, operate on the Public Garden lagoon.

Swan Boats
🅐 Boston Public Garden　🅞 Mid-Apr–mid-Sep: 10am– 5pm daily (subject to change)　🅦 swanboats.com

Did You Know?
———
During World War II, the Common donated most of its iron fencing as scrap metal for the war effort.

↑ *Make Way For Ducklings,* a sculpture by Nancy Schön in Boston Public Garden

↑ A summer boat ride on the lagoon in Boston Public Garden

Seasonal Guide

Spring

Boston Common and Public Garden awake from their winter slumber in April. More than 23,000 tulips burst into bloom around the Garden and the Swan Boats - and resident swans - return to the Public Garden Lagoon to enjoy the warmer weather. Not to be outdone, the Common's mid-20th century carousel begins spinning next to the Frog Pond.

Summer

▷ Shaded areas of the Common offer respite during the hot summer months. Sunbathers bask on its hillside, while park league baseball games take over the field, and the park transforms into an outdoor venue for numerous festivals and events. By the Parkman Bandstand, theater lovers can enjoy free performances of Shakespeare on the Common *(www.commshakes.org),* with an ice cream in hand. Work on your Vinyasa flow at free yoga sessions held every Thursday by the Frog Pond, while excitable toddlers cool off in the nearby Spray Pool.

Autumn

◁ The delicate Japanese maples of the Public Garden turn bright crimson and deep burgundy to inaugurate the fall foliage spectacle in both parks. Just as the Carousel ends its season, the Frog Pond holds an annual lighted pumpkin float.

Winter

▷ Walkways, kiosks, and bridges stand out in stark relief, as white winter snow blankets the parks. December sees the Common's bare branches draped with lights, and the city decorates a giant Christmas tree. Don't miss skating on the Frog Pond!

←

Verdant Boston Common is a tranquil haven among the towering buildings of downtown Boston

MASSACHUSETTS STATE HOUSE

QK6 **↑**24 Beacon St **T**Park Street **◷**10am-3:30pm Mon-Fri (reservations recommended) **W**malegislature.gov

The Puritan founders of Boston envisioned a "shining city upon a hill." Two centuries later, the state of Massachusetts built its palace of government as a domed Neoclassical temple at the city's highest point.

The cornerstone of the Massachusetts State House was laid on July 4, 1795, by Samuel Adams and Paul Revere. Completed on January 11, 1798, this Charles Bulfinch-designed center of state government served as a model for the US Capitol Building in Washington, DC, and as an inspiration for many of the state capitols around the country. Later additions were made, but the original building remains the archetype of American government buildings. Its dome, sheathed in copper and gold, serves as the zero-mile marker for Massachusetts, making it, as physician and poet, Oliver Wendell Holmes Sr remarked, "the hub of the universe."

The Great Hall, used for state funtions, is the latest addition to the State House.

Beautiful stained-glass windows decorate the main staircase.

The House of Representatives is home to the Sacred Cod, which hangs over the gallery.

The Wings, added in 1917, sit rather incongruously with the rest of the structure.

1 The Massachusetts State House has a striking facade.

2 The Great Seal of the Commonwealth features in the stained-glass windows by the main staircase.

3 Seals of the original 13 colonies are displayed in the Hall of Flags skylight above Massachusetts battle flags.

EXPERIENCE   Beacon Hill and the Theater District

THE CHANGING COLORS OF THE STATE HOUSE DOME

Paul Revere's company covered the leaky wooden dome of Massachusetts State House in copper in 1802 to protect it from leakage. It was later painted pale yellow to resemble gold leaf, before it was covered with the real thing in the 1870s. During World War II, matte black paint camouflaged the dome to keep it hidden from enemy eyes. In 1997, the original gilt was replaced with 23-carat gold leaf.

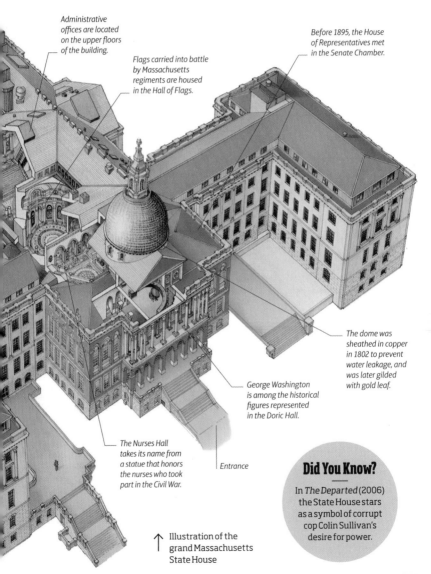

Administrative offices are located on the upper floors of the building.

Flags carried into battle by Massachusetts regiments are housed in the Hall of Flags.

Before 1895, the House of Representatives met in the Senate Chamber.

The dome was sheathed in copper in 1802 to prevent water leakage, and was later gilded with gold leaf.

George Washington is among the historical figures represented in the Doric Hall.

The Nurses Hall takes its name from a statue that honors the nurses who took part in the Civil War.

Entrance

↑ Illustration of the grand Massachusetts State House

Did You Know?

In *The Departed* (2006) the State House stars as a symbol of corrupt cop Colin Sullivan's desire for power.

EXPERIENCE MORE

3

Mount Vernon Street

 J6 Charles/MGH, Park Street

In the 1890s the novelist Henry James called Mount Vernon Street "the most civilized street in America," and it still retains that air of urbane culture. Most of the developers of Beacon Hill chose to build their private homes along this street. Architect Charles Bulfinch envisioned Beacon Hill as a district of freestanding mansions on spacious grounds, but building costs ultimately dictated much denser development. The sole remaining example of Bulfinch's vision is the second Harrison Gray Otis House, built in 1800 at No. 85 Mount Vernon Street. The Greek Revival row houses next door (Nos. 59–83) were built to replace the single mansion belonging to Jonathan Mason, Otis's chief development

partner, and torn down after his death in 1836. The Bulfinch-designed houses at Nos. 55, 57, and 59 were built by Mason for his daughters. No. 55 was passed on to the Nichols family in 1885.

4

Louisburg Square

J6 Charles/MGH, Park Street

Home to best-selling authors, millionaire politicians, and corporate moguls, Louisburg Square is perhaps Boston's most prestigious address. Developed in the 1830s as a shared private preserve on Beacon Hill, the square's tiny patch of greenery surrounded by a high iron fence sends a clear signal of the square's continued exclusivity. The last private square in the city, its Greek Revival bow-fronted townhouses sell for a premium; even the on-street parking spaces are deeded. The traditions of Christmas Eve carol singing and candlelit windows are said to have begun on Louisburg Square. A statue of Christopher Columbus stands at its center.

Did You Know?

Between 1659–81, Christmas celebrations were banned in Boston, as Puritans declared it a corrupt holiday.

5

Charles Street

J6 Charles/MGH

This street originally ran along the bank of the Charles River, although subsequent landfill projects have removed it from the riverbank by a considerable distance. The

TOP 3 ANTIQUES STORES

Upstairs Downstairs
J6 93 Charles St
Find vintage furniture and jewelry spanning three centuries here.

Eugene Galleries
J6 76 Charles St
Books, maps, and prints from Boston and beyond.

Good
J6 98 Charles St
Fine pieces by local artists mingle with a range of antiques.

→ The red-brick facades of townhouses facing onto Louisburg Square

↑ A bustling junction on Charles Street, one of Boston's main dining and shopping districts

main shopping and dining area of the neighborhood, the curving line of Charles Street hugs the base of Beacon Hill, giving it a quaint, village-like air. Many of the buildings' upper stories are residential, while street level and cellar levels were converted to commercial uses long ago. Though most of the street dates from the 19th century, widening in the 1920s meant that some houses on the west side acquired new facades. The Charles Street Meeting House, designed in 1807, was built for a Baptist congregation that practiced immersion in the adjacent river. Charles Street was one of the birthplaces of the US antiques trade and now has a high concentration of antiques dealers.

Nichols House Museum

◉ J6 **⌂** 55 Mount Vernon St **Ⓣ** Park Street **◷** Apr–Oct: 11am–4pm Tue–Sat; Nov–Mar: 11am–4pm Thu–Sat **ⓦ** nicholshouse museum.org

The Nichols House Museum was designed by Charles

Bulfinch in 1804. Modernized in 1830 by the addition of a Greek Revival portico, the house is nevertheless a superb example of Bulfinch's domestic architecture. It also offers an insight into the life of a true Beacon Hill character. Rose Standish Nichols moved into the house in 1885, aged 13. She left it as a museum in her 1960 will. A woman ahead of her time, the strong-willed and famously hospitable Nichols was, among other things, a self-styled landscape designer, who traveled extensively to write about gardens.

Hepzibah Swan Houses

◉ J6 **⌂** 13, 15, & 17 Chestnut St **Ⓣ** Park Street **⊘** To the public

The only female member of the Mount Vernon Proprietors, Mrs. Swan had these houses built by Bulfinch as wedding presents for her daughters in 1806, 1807, and 1814. They are backed by Bulfinch-designed stables that face onto Mount Vernon Street. The height of the stables was restricted to avoid impeding the view over

the street. In 1863–5, No. 13 was home to Dr. Samuel Gridley Howe, who founded the first school for the blind in the US in 1833.

EAT & DRINK

Alibi Bar & Lounge
Set in the former "drunk tank" of the Charles Street Jail, this hotel bar is a top spot for cocktails and evening snacks.

◉ J5 **⌂** 215 Charles St **◷** 5pm–2am daily **ⓦ** alibiboston.com

$ $ $

No. 9 Park
This place is just downhill from the Massachusetts State House, so its fine dining is popular with local lawmakers.

◉ K6 **⌂** 9 Park St **ⓦ** no9park.com

$ $ $

Museum of African American History (MAAH)

📍K6 🏠46 Joy St
🚇Park Street ⏰10am-4pm Mon-Sat 🚫Public hols 🌐maah.org

Built from plans designed by Asher Benjamin, the African Meeting House (centerpiece of the museum) was dedicated in 1806. The oldest Black church building in the US, it was the political and religious center of Boston's African-American society. The plain interior rang with the oratory of some of the 19th century's most fiery abolitionists: from Sojourner Truth and Frederick Douglass to William Lloyd Garrison, who founded the New England Anti-Slavery Society in 1832. The meeting house basement was Boston's first school for African-American children until the adjacent Abiel Smith School was built in 1831. When segregated education was barred in 1855, however, the school closed. The meeting house became a Hasidic synagogue in the 1890s, as most of Boston's African-American

community moved to Roxbury and Dorchester. The synagogue closed in the 1960s, and in 1987 the African Meeting House reopened as the linchpin site on the Black Heritage Trail.

Boston Athenaeum

📍K6 🏠101/2 Beacon St
🚇Park Street ⏰Noon-8pm Tue, 10am-4pm Wed-Sat 🌐bostonathenaeum.org

Organized in 1807, the collection of the Boston Athenaeum quickly became one of the country's leading private libraries. Sheep farmer Edward Clarke Cabot won the 1846 design competition to house the library, with plans for a gray sandstone building based on Palladio's Palazzo da Porto Festa in Vicenza, a building Cabot knew from a book in the Athenaeum's collection. Included in over half a million

> Organized in 1807, the collection of the Boston Athenaeum quickly became one of the country's leading private libraries.

volumes are rare manuscripts, maps, and newspapers. Among the Athenaeum's major holdings are the personal library of George Washington and the theological library supplied by King William III of England to the King's Chapel (p114). In its early years the Athenaeum was Boston's chief art museum, but transferred much of its collection to the Museum of Fine Arts when it opened.

Beacon Street

📍J6 🚇Park Street

Beacon Street is lined with urban mansions facing Boston Common. The 1808 William Hickling Prescott House at No. 55, designed by Asher Benjamin, offers regular tours of its rooms from April to October. The American Meteorological Society in No. 45 occupies Harrison Gray Otis's last and finest house. It had

The book-lined shelves of the brimming Boston Athenaeum

11 bedrooms and an elliptical room behind the front parlor, where the walls and even the doors are curved.

The elite Somerset Club stands at Nos. 42–43 Beacon Street. Between the 1920s and the 1940s, Irish Catholic mayor James Michael Curley would lead election night victory marches to the State House, pausing at the Somerset Club to taunt the Boston Brahmins inside.

The Parkman House at No. 33 Beacon Street is now a city-owned meeting center. It was the home of Dr. George Parkman, who was murdered by Harvard professor and fellow socialite Dr. John Webster in 1849. Boston society was torn apart when the presiding judge, a relative of Parkman, sentenced Webster to be hanged.

⑪ Granary Burying Ground

🅠 K6 🅐 Tremont St 🅣 Park Street 🅞 9am–5pm daily

Named after the early grain storage facility that once stood on the adjacent site of Park Street Church, the Granary Burying Ground dates from 1660. Buried here were three important signatories to the Declaration of Independence – Samuel Adams, Robert Treat Paine, and John Hancock – as well as Paul Revere, Benjamin Franklin's parents, and victims of the Boston Massacre.

The orderly array of gravestones is the result of modern groundskeeping. Few stones, if any, mark the actual burial site of the person memorialized. In fact, John Hancock may not be here at all; some believe that his body was removed in the 19th-century.

⑫ Park Street Church

🅠 K6 🅐 1 Park St 🅣 Park Street 🅞 Mid-Jun-Aug: 9:30am–3pm Tue-Sat; Sep-Jun: by appointment 🅦 parkstreet.org

Park Street Church's 217-ft (65-m) steeple has punctuated the intersection of Park and Tremont streets since its dedication in 1810. Designed by English architect Peter Banner, who adapted a design by Christopher Wren, it was commissioned by parishioners wanting to establish a Congregational church in the heart of Boston. The church remains one of the city's most influential pulpits.

Contrary to popular belief, the church's sermons did not earn the intersection the nickname of "Brimstone Corner." Rather, the name dates from the War of 1812 when the US militia stored its gunpowder in the church basement for safekeeping against bombardment from the British Navy. In 1829, William Lloyd Garrison, gave his first abolition speech from the Park Street pulpit. In 1849 a speech entitled "The War System of Nations" was addressed to the American Peace Society by Senator Charles Sumner. In 1893, the anthem *America the Beautiful* by Katharine Lee Bates debuted here. Today the church is involved in religious, political, cultural, and humanitarian activities.

BOSTON'S BLACK HERITAGE TRAIL

This Boston city trail links several key sites, ranging from the African Meeting House to a number of private homes, which are not open to visitors. The walking tour also leads through streets such as Holmes Alley, once used by fugitives to flee professional slave catchers. Free tours of the trail are led by National Park Service rangers from June through August (check *www.nps.gov/boaf* for times). Self-guided tour maps are available at the MAAH.

↑ The towering steeple and red-brick exterior of Park Street Church

13

Downtown Crossing

📍K7 🏠Washington, Winter & Summer sts 🚇Downtown Crossing

As an antidote to heavy traffic congestion, this shopping-district crossroads – located at the intersection of Washington, Winter, and Summer streets – was laid

SHOP

Brattle Book Shop

This jam-packed store is an essential stop for keen readers and serious collectors of antiquarian books. The sale bins offer an excellent selection of beach reads.

📍K7 🏠9 West St 🚫Sun 🌐brattlebookshop.com

out as a pedestrian zone between 1975 and 1978. Downtown's single remaining department store is Macy's, although the area also offers a range of other outlets, including bookstores, camera stores, and a jewelry district. Street vendors and summer lunchtime concerts create a lively scene.

The bustling Macy's department store is one of a chain found throughout the US, with the best-known store located in New York. Across Summer Street, the building that housed Filene's Department Store remains a local landmark. A decade-long redevelopment maintained the original 1912 Beaux-Arts facade and added a sleek condominium tower. The complex also features shops and restaurants. Nearby is a branch of Roche Brothers supermarket chain, with abundant fresh fruit and take-out lunch options.

The historic multistory building at 333 Washington Street is known locally as the "jewelry building"

because it houses more than 70 small jewelry shops as well as jewelry repair shops across its five floors. Swing by to window-shop the sparkling wares.

14

Bay Village

📍J8 🏠Bounded by Tremont, Arlington, & Charles St South 🚇Tufts Medical Center, Boylston

Originally an expanse of mud flats, the Bay Village area was drained in the early 1800s and initially became habitable with the construction of a dam in 1825. Many carpenters, cabinetmakers, artisans, and house painters involved in the construction of Beacon Hill's pricier townhouses built their own modest but well-crafted residences here. There are consequently many marked similarities between the two neighborhoods. Fayette Street was laid out in 1824 to coincide with the visit of

→

Artist Stefanie Rocknak's statue of Edgar Allan Poe on Boylston Street, Bay Village

the Marquis de Lafayette, the French general who allied himself with George Washington during the American Revolution (p53). Bay Street, located just off Fayette Street, features a single dwelling and is generally regarded as the city's shortest street. In 1809, author Edgar Allan Poe was born in a boarding house on Carver Street, where his parents were staying while touring with a traveling theatrical company. Poe was never fond of Boston (he referred to residents as "Frogpondians"), but the city honored him with a statue. Erected in October 2014 on the corner of Boylston Street and Charles Street South, it depicts Poe in mid-stride, holding a suitcase overflowing with manuscripts and a raven at his side. During Prohibition in the 1920s, clandestine speakeasies gave Bay Village its bohemian ambience. More recently, the neighborhood has become a center for Boston's LGBT+ community.

15

Chinatown

Q K7 **A** Bounded by Kingston, Kneeland, Washington, & Essex sts **T** Chinatown

This area is the third-largest Chinatown in the US after those in San Francisco and New York. Pagoda-topped telephone booths, as well as a three-story gateway guarded by four marble lions, set the neighborhood's Asian tone.

The first 200 Chinese to settle in New England came by ship from San Francisco in 1870, recruited to break a labor strike at a shoe factory. Another wave of immigration from California in the

←

The dramatic three-story decorative gateway to Boston's Chinatown

 INSIDER TIP
Delicious Dumplings

Many restaurants in Chinatown serve tasty dumplings, but for a quick lunch and lots of choice, head to Dumpling Café (695 Washington St) or Gourmet Dumpling House (52 Beach St).

1880s was prompted by an economic boom that led to job openings in construction. Boston's Chinese colony was fully established by the turn of the 19th century.

Political refugees from China, who emigrated here after World War II, as well as more recent immigrants from Vietnam, Korea, Thailand, Laos, and Cambodia, have swelled Chinatown's population. Along with the area's garment and textile industries, restaurants, food markets, and dispensers of Chinese medicine are especially numerous along the main thoroughfare of Beach Street, as well as on Tyler, Oxford, and Harrison streets.

Grand Lobby and seven-story auditorium are designed in Renaissance Revival style, with gold chandeliers, stained glass, ceiling murals, and jasper pillars.

Today the theater hosts Broadway road shows, visiting dance and opera companies, concerts, motion-picture revivals, and local productions. The Wang and Shubert theaters are the primary venues of the non-profit Boch Center.

INSIDER TIP
BosTix Booths

For discounts of up to 80 percent on theater, dance, and music performances, check the offerings at the BosTix booths at Faneuil Hall and Copley Square, or search calendar.arts boston.org.

1.3 million

The average number of passengers who travel on Boston's subway every day.

 16

Wang Theatre

📍 K8   🏠 270 Tremont St   🚇 Boylston, Tufts Medical Center   🕐 Times vary, check website   🌐 bochcenter.org

Opened in 1925 as the Metropolitan Theatre and later named the Music Hall, New England's most ornate variety theater was inspired by the Paris Opera House, and was originally intended to be a movie theater. Designed by Clarence Blackall, the theater's auditorium was once one of the largest in the world. It was restored and renamed as the Wang Center for the Performing Arts in 1983, but is now known simply as the Wang Theatre. The five-story

 17

Shubert Theatre

📍 K7   🏠 265 Tremont St   🚇 Boylston, Tufts Medical Center   🕐 Times vary, check website   🌐 bochcenter.org

The 1,500-seat Shubert Theatre rivals the Emerson Colonial Theatre for its long history of staging major pre-Broadway productions. Designed by the architects Charles Bond and Thomas

James, the theater features a white Neoclassical facade with a pair of Ionic columns flanking a monumental, Palladian-style window over the entrance. The theater first opened its doors in 1910, with a production of *The Taming of the Shrew*. During its heyday many stars walked the boards, including Sarah Bernhardt, W. C. Fields, Cary Grant, Mae West, Humphrey Bogart, Ingrid Bergman, Henry Ford, and Rex Harrison. Today, dance, theater, musicals, and opera are showcased here.

 Emerson Colonial Theatre

📍K7 🏠106 Boylston St 🇹Boylston ⏰Times vary, check website 🌐emersoncolonialtheatre.com

Clarence H. Blackall designed 14 Boston theaters during his architectural career, among them the Colonial, which is the city's oldest theater in continuous operation under the same name. Although the exterior is plain, the interior is impressively opulent. Designed by H. B. Pennell, the Rococo lobby has chandeliers, gilded trim, and lofty arched ceilings. The auditorium is decorated with figures, frescoes, and friezes.

The theater opened on December 20, 1900 with an extravagant performance of the melodrama *Ben Hur*, and became well known for putting on lavish musical productions. Impresario Florenz Ziegfeld launched his *Follies* here in 1927 and the theater was used extensively

← The richly decorated interior of the Wang Theatre's Grand Lobby

↑ The busy entrance, and *(inset)* ornate ceiling of the Emerson Colonial Theatre

by lyricist-dramatist Oscar Hammerstein and composer Richard Rodgers to hone their musicals before they went on to Broadway. Nowadays, it mainly hosts touring shows.

 Citizens Bank Opera House

📍K7 🏠539 Washington St 🇹Boylston ⏰Times vary, check website 🌐bostonoperahouse.com

The grande dame of Boston vaudeville houses, built in 1927–8 to honor the memory of impresario B. F. Keith, shines anew as a venue for large-scale Broadway productions and an active Boston Ballet program. Its flamboyant Spanish baroque facade only hints at the grandeur inside. The most recent restoration not only installed replicas of the original carpet that had to be woven on custom-made looms, it applied another 4 lbs (2 kg) of gold leaf on the decorative woodwork and plaster cornices.

THE HISTORY OF BOSTON'S THEATER DISTRICT

Boston's first theater opened in 1793 on Federal Street. Fifty years later, the city had become a major tryout town and boasted many lavish theaters. The US premiere of Handel's *Messiah* opened in 1839, and the premiere of Tchaikovsky's First Piano Concerto in 1875. In the late 19th century theaters came under fire from the censorious Watch and Ward Society. Later, dramas such as Tennessee Williams' *A Streetcar Named Desire* debuted here, alongside musicals that included works by Rodgers and Hammerstein.

A SHORT WALK
BEACON HILL

Distance 1 mile (1.5 km) **Time** 45 minutes
Nearest subway Park Street

From the 1790s to the 1870s, the south slope of Beacon Hill was Boston's most sought-after neighborhood – its wealthy elite decamped only when the more exclusive Back Bay (p126) was built. Many of the district's houses were designed by Charles Bulfinch and his disciples, and the south slope evolved as a textbook example of Federal architecture. Elevation and view were everything, resulting in the finest homes being located either on Boston Common or perched near the top of the hill. Early developers set houses back from the street, but the economic depression of 1807–12 resulted in row houses being built right out to the street. As you walk around Beacon Hill look out for these elegant houses.

Did You Know?

The area is named for a wooden beacon that once stood on the hill to warn residents of attack or fire.

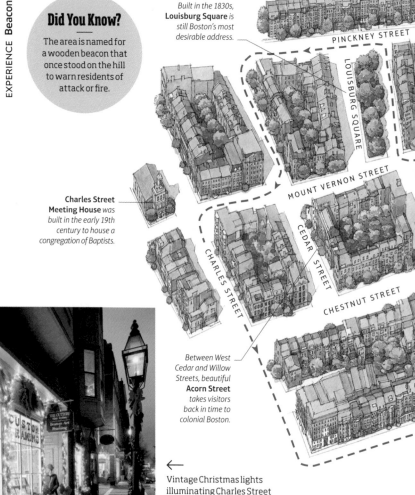

Built in the 1830s, **Louisburg Square** *is still Boston's most desirable address.*

PINCKNEY STREET

LOUISBURG SQUARE

MOUNT VERNON STREET

CEDAR STREET

CHESTNUT STREET

CHARLES STREET

Charles Street Meeting House *was built in the early 19th century to house a congregation of Baptists.*

Between West Cedar and Willow Streets, beautiful **Acorn Street** *takes visitors back in time to colonial Boston.*

←
Vintage Christmas lights illuminating Charles Street during the holidays

↑ Low light on Acorn Street, the most photographed street in Boston

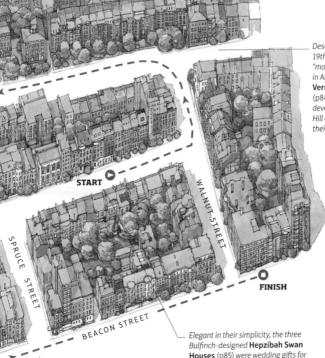

Nichols House Museum (p85) *offers an insight into the life of Beacon Hill resident Rose Nichols, who lived here from 1885 to 1960.*

Described in the 19th century as the "most civilized street in America," **Mount Vernon Street** (p84) *is where the developers of Beacon Hill chose to build their own homes.*

START

WALNUT STREET

SPRUCE STREET

FINISH

BEACON STREET

Elegant in their simplicity, the three Bulfinch-designed **Hepzibah Swan Houses** (p85) *were wedding gifts for the daughters of a wealthy Beacon Hill proprietress.*

The finest houses on Beacon Hill were invariably built on **Beacon Street** (p86). *Grand, Federal-style mansions, some with ornate reliefs, overlook the city's most popular green space, Boston Common.*

0 meters	50	N
0 yards	50	↑

NORTH END AND CHARLESTOWN

Boston's oldest neighborhoods – settled 1631 and 1629, respectively – wear their history with pride. The steeple of Old North Church in the North End literally lit the way for the American Revolution. A century later, the language echoing through the neighborhood's warren of narrow streets was Italian. The North End retains its Italian identity, although most immigrants have now moved on. On summer weekends, festivals of patron saints bring a joyous vitality to its streets.

Charlestown's initial settlement on the Charles River tidal flats was leveled during the American Revolution but rebuilt soon after. Its strategic location at the focal point of Boston Harbor made Charlestown perfect for the creation of one of the new nation's first naval shipyards, and the 1797 famous frigate USS *Constitution* is still moored there. Bunker Hill Monument was finished in 1843, just as an influx of immigrants from Ireland began to repopulate the neighborhood. Although now vanishing with gentrification, the Irish-American "Townie" remains a stock character in Hollywood gangster films.

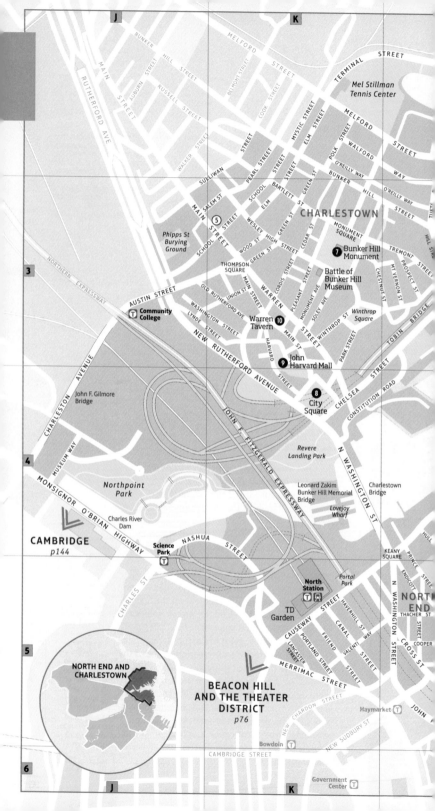

NORTH END AND CHARLESTOWN

Must Sees
❶ Charlestown Navy Yard
❷ Old North Church

Experience More
❸ Copp's Hill Burying Ground
❹ Paul Revere Mall
❺ Paul Revere House
❻ Hanover and Salem Streets
❼ Bunker Hill Monument
❽ City Square
❾ John Harvard Mall
❿ Warren Tavern

Eat & Drink
① Caffè Vittoria
② Bricco Ristorante & Enoteca
③ Ristorante Lucia
④ Brewer's Fork
⑤ Monument Restaurant & Tavern
⑥ Pier 6

Little Mystic Channel

Barry Playground

WALFORD WAY

DECATUR STREET

CHELSEA STREET

TOBIN BRIDGE

FIFTH AVE

16TH STREET

THIRD AVE

FOURTH AVE

11TH STREET

9TH ST

FIRST STREET

9TH STREET

8TH STREET

THIRD AVENUE

5TH ST

FIRST

6TH AVENUE

Shipyard Park

USS Constitution Museum

❶ Charlestown Navy Yard

USS Cassin Young

USS Constitution

Boston Inner Harbor

EAST BOSTON

MAVERICK STREET

SUMNER STREET

Langone Park

Puopolo Park

Fiskes Wharf

COMMERCIAL STREET

CHARTER ST

Battery Wharf

Sumner Tunnel

Callahan Tunnel

❸ Copp's Hill Burying Ground

HULL ST

SHEAFE ST

❷ Old North Church

Paul Revere ❹ Mall

PRINCE STREET

SALEM STREET

N BENNET ST

HANOVER AVE

CLARK ST

St Stephen's Church

Union Wharf

FLEET ST

ATLANTIC AVENUE

❻ Salem Street ①

❺ Paul Revere House

Hanover ❻ Street

NORTH SQUARE

NORTH STREET

RICHMOND STREET

COMMERCIAL STREET

Lewis Wharf

②

CROSS STREET

NORTH ST

FULTON STREET

FITZGERALD SURFACE ROAD

ATLANTIC AVENUE

OLD BOSTON, SEAPORT, AND THE WATERFRONT
p106

| 0 meters | 400 |
| 0 yards | 400 |

N ↑

1 Ⓜ3

CHARLESTOWN NAVY YARD

📍L3 🚇Community College 🚌93 ⛴From Long Wharf 🕐10am–4pm Wed–Sun (late Nov–early Apr: 10am–4pm Fri–Sun); photo ID required for those aged 18 and older 🚫Jan 1, Thanksgiving, Dec 25 ℹ️Building 5; www.nps.gov/bost

Some of the most storied battleships in American naval history began life at Charlestown Navy Yard. Established in 1800, Charlestown remained vital to US security until its decommissioning in 1974. From the wooden-hulled USS *Constitution* built in 1797 to World War II steel destroyer USS *Cassin Young*, the yard gives visitors a unique all-hands-on-deck historical experience unparalleled anywhere else in the United State.

For 174 years, as the US Navy moved from wooden sailing ships to steel giants, Charlestown Navy Yard played a key role in supporting the US Atlantic fleet. On decommissioning, the facility was transferred to the National Park Service to interpret the art and history of naval shipbuilding.

The oldest commissioned warship afloat, USS *Constitution* was built in the North End and christened in 1797. She won 42 battles, lost none, captured 20 vessels, and was never boarded by an enemy. In July 2017, she returned to the water, able to carry her own canvas into the wind once again after a full restoration. The **USS Constitution Museum** documents her history.

USS Constitution Museum

Ⓜ Ⓖ 📍Charlestown Navy Yard 🕐9am–6pm daily (Nov–Mar: 10am–5pm daily) 🌐ussconstitutionmuseum.org

OLD IRONSIDES

Given her 25-inch (63-cm) thick hull at the waterline, it's easy to imagine why USS *Constitution* earned her nickname "Old Ironsides." Pitted against HMS *Guerrière* during the War of 1812, the ship engaged in a shoot-out that left *Guerrière* all but destroyed. Seeing British cannonballs "bouncing" off USS *Constitution's* hull, a sailor allegedly exclaimed, "Huzzah! Her sides are made of iron!" The rest is history.

1 USS *Cassin Young*, named for Pearl Harbor hero Captain Cassin Young (1894–1942).

2 A rigger's scale model of USS *Constitution* at the USS Constitution Museum.

3 Cannons on the deck of USS *Constitution*.

Did You Know?

First tested in action in 1798, USS *Constitution* is the world's oldest warship still afloat.

↑ The wooden top deck, known as the spar deck, of USS *Constitution*

OLD NORTH CHURCH

📍L5 🏠193 Salem St 🚇Haymarket, North Station
🕐Mar–May, Nov, & Dec: 9am–5pm daily; Jan & Feb:
10am–4pm; Jun–Oct: 9am–6pm daily 🌐oldnorth.com

An icon of the American Revolution, the spire of Old North Church still rises high as a visible landmark. The austere serenity of the interior belies its pivotal role in the United States' history

Christ Episcopal Church is the official name of Boston's oldest surviving religious edifice, which dates from 1723. It was built of brick in the Georgian style similar to that of St. Andrew's-by-the-Wardrobe in Blackfriars, London, designed by Sir Christopher Wren. The church was made famous on April 18, 1775, when Christ Church sexton Robert Newman, aiding Paul Revere (p102), hung a pair of signal lanterns in the belfry. These were to alert the patriots that British troops were beginning to move on Concord and Lexington by crossing the Charles River.

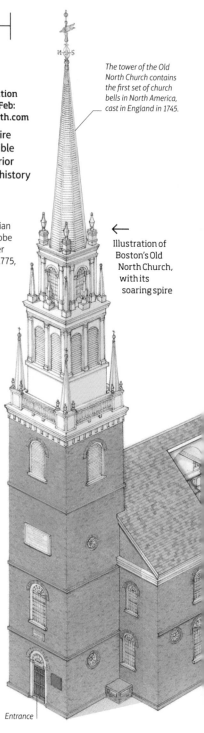

The tower of the Old North Church contains the first set of church bells in North America, cast in England in 1745.

← Illustration of Boston's Old North Church, with its soaring spire

Entrance

↑ Distinctive gold chandeliers hang from the church ceiling

↑ Simple decoration of the Old North Church Altar

↑ Brick exterior and white spire of Old North Church rising above North End

The church's distinctive chandeliers were brought to Boston from England in 1724 and were first lit for the Christmas season.

High-sided box pews contained foot-warmers for wintry weather.

This marble bust of George Washington was presented to the church in 1815.

EXPERIENCE MORE

3

Copp's Hill Burying Ground

📍 L4 🚏 Charter & Hull sts Ⓣ Government Center, North Station 🕘 9am–5pm daily

This is Boston's second-oldest cemetery after the one by King's Chapel (p114). Nicknamed "Corpse Hill," it's real name derives from a local man by the name of William Copp. He owned a farm on its southeastern slope from 1643, and much of the cemetery's land was purchased from him. Other more famous people interred here include Robert Newman, the sexton who hung Paul Revere's signal lanterns in the belfry of Old North Church, and Edmund Hartt, builder of USS Constitution (p98). Increase, Cotton, and Samuel Mather, three generations of a family of influential Puritan ministers, are also buried here, along with hundreds of Boston's Colonial-era enslaved people and freedmen, including Prince Hall, founder of the African Freemasonry Order in Massachusetts.

During the British occupation of Boston, the site was used by British commanders, who had an artillery position here. They would later exploit the prominent hilltop location during the Revolution, when they directed cannon fire from here across Boston harbor toward American positions in Charlestown. King George III's troops were said to have used the slate headstones for target practice, and pockmarks from their musket balls are still visible on some of the graves.

Copp's Hill Terrace, directly across Charter Street, is a prime observation point for views over to Charlestown and Bunker Hill. It was also the site of one of history's strangest tragedies. In January 1919, a 2.3-million-gallon molasses tank exploded, creating a huge, syrupy tidal wave that cascaded through the streets, killing 21 people, and leaving the waters of Boston Harbor stained brown until the summer.

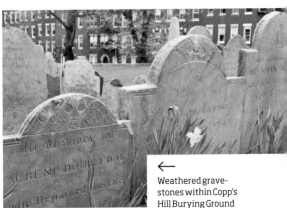

← Weathered gravestones within Copp's Hill Burying Ground

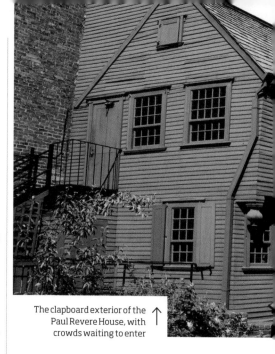

The clapboard exterior of the Paul Revere House, with crowds waiting to enter

4

Paul Revere Mall

📍 L5 🏠 Hanover St
🚇 Haymarket

This brick-paved plaza gives the crowded neighborhood of the North End a precious stretch of open space between Hanover and Unity streets. A well-utilized municipal resource, the Mall is always full of local people: children, teenagers, young mothers, and older residents chatting in Italian and playing cards or checkers. Laid out in 1933, and originally called the Prado, its focal point is Cyrus Dallin's equestrian statue of local hero Paul Revere, which was originally modeled in 1885, but not sculpted and placed here until 1940. Bronze bas-relief plaques on the mall's side walls commemorate a number of North End residents who have played an important role in the history of Boston. Benches, a fountain, and twin rows of linden trees complete the space, which has a distinctly European feel.

At the north end of the Mall is Old North Church (p100), one of the city's most important historical sites. To the south is Hanover Street, which is lined with numerous Italian caffès and restaurants.

5

Paul Revere House

📍 L5 🏠 19 North Sq
🚇 Haymarket 🕐 Mid-Apr–Oct: 9:30am–5:15pm daily; Nov–mid-Apr: 9:30am–4:15pm daily
🚫 Jan–Mar: Mon 🌐 paulreverehouse.org

The city's oldest surviving clapboard-frame house is historically significant, for it was from here on the night of April 18, 1775 that Paul Revere began his legendary horseback ride to warn his compatriots in Lexington of the impending arrival of British troops. This historic event was later immortalized in a boldly patriotic, epic poem by Henry Wadsworth Longfellow (p155). It begins "Listen, my children, and you shall hear of the midnight ride of Paul Revere."

Revere, a Huguenot descendant, was by trade a versatile gold- and silversmith, copper engraver, and maker of church bells and cannons. He and his second wife, Rachel, mother of eight of his 16 children, owned the house from 1770 to 1800. Small, leaded casement windows, an overhanging upper story, and a nail-studded front door all contribute to make it a fine example of 18th-century Early American architecture. By the mid-19th century the house

PAUL REVERE

An American silversmith, engraver, and colonial resistance leader, Paul Revere is best known for his midnight ride to alert colonial militia of approaching British soldiers – although many popular details, such as his supposed cry that "The British are coming!", have been proved fanciful. After the Revolution, Revere expanded to iron casting and bronze bell and cannon casting. Many of the hundreds of bells he cast remain in use more than 200 years later.

EXPERIENCE North End and Charlestown

Caffè Vittoria

Reputedly Boston's first Italian cafe, Caffè Vittoria has been serving up delicious pastries and unbeatable coffee since 1929.

L5 **290-6 Hanover St**
caffevittoria.com

$ $ $

Bricco Ristorante & Enoteca

Boston's North End is a one-stop-shop for Italian-influenced treats. At Bricco, a local heavyweight, authenticity is key, from the house-made pasta to the team of Italian chefs.

L5 **241 Hanover St**
bricco.com

$ $ $

Ristorante Lucia

This family-run restaurant offers a skilful mix of both traditional and innovative Italian-inspired dishes.

L5 **415 Hanover St**
luciaboston.com

$ $ $

had become a decrepit tenement. It was saved from demolition by preservationists' efforts led by one of Revere's great-grandsons, and opened as a museum in 1908. Inside, period artifacts provide a good picture of domestic life in Colonial times.

In the courtyard is a large bronze bell, cast by Paul Revere for a church in 1804. He made nearly 200 church bells, many of which are still in use today.

Other buildings on the campus include the early 18th-century Pierce–Hichborn House, one of the earliest brick townhouses remaining in Boston, and a visitor center with historic exhibitions and a gift shop.

Did You Know?

In 1950, $2.7 million was stolen from a North End bank, the largest robbery in US history at that time.

Hanover and Salem Streets

L5

Cutting from Cross Street to the wharves of Commercial Street, Hanover and Salem streets are the throbbing Italian heart of the North End. Even as the Italian-American families who flocked here in the early 20th century have since moved out to the suburbs, they have kept their restaurants, caffès, bakeries, bars, and even their private cigar-smoking club on these mercantile streets.

So narrow that only a masochist would attempt to drive here, Hanover and Salem streets are best experienced on foot – preferably at a leisurely pace, with plenty of pauses to soak in the atmosphere. During the daytime the streets feel like any busy American neighborhood (aside from the Italian spoken by old men on street corners); but at night, Hanover Street swarms with locals and visitors alike in search of a good meal.

St. Leonard's church, on the corner of Hanover and Prince streets, is the spiritual center of the North End. It was built by Italian immigrants, and the ornate interior is a testament to the fine craftsmanship of the Italian artists who were among the first parishioners. During the weekends of late July and August, the North End streets are filled with food festivals and parades of old-country religious societies.

↑ Bunker Hill Monument illuminated on a foggy Boston night

area as Evacuation Day. The citizens of Charlestown began raising funds for the construction of Bunker Hill Monument in 1823, laid the cornerstone in 1825, and dedicated the 221-ft (67-m) vertical granite obelisk in 1843. There is no elevator, but the 294-step climb to the top is rewarded with spectacular views of the Charles River and Boston skyline. The ground-level museum, which is wheelchair accessible, focuses on the strategies and significance of the Battle of Bunker Hill. The monument is beautifully lit at night to reveal the pyramid that caps the obelisk – a design echoed in the tops of the pylons of the nearby Leonard Zakim Bunker Hill Memorial Bridge. Be aware that, during the winter months, Bunker Hill Monument may be closed due to ice and snow on the stairs.

EAT & DRINK

Brewer's Fork

Local beers, wood-fired pizzas, charcuterie, and inventive brunch plates.

📍L3 🏠7 Moulton St
🌐brewersfork.com

$ $ $

Monument Restaurant & Tavern

Exquisite gastropub fare in a wood and brick room with high ceilings.

📍K3 🏠251 Main St
🌐monument charlestown.com

$ $ $

Pier 6

Casual seafood with waterfront views.

📍M3 🏠18th St
🌐pier6boston.com

$ $ $

7

Bunker Hill Monument

📍K3 🏠Monument Sq
🕐Apr–Jun: 10am–4pm Wed–Sun; late Nov–early Apr: 10am–4pm Fri–Sun
🚫Jan 1, Thanksgiving, Dec 25 🌐nps.gov/bost

In the Revolution's first pitched battle between British and colonial troops, which took place on June 17, 1775, the British won a Pyrrhic victory on the battlefield but failed to create an escape route from the Boston peninsula to the mainland.

Following the battle, American irregulars were joined by other militia to keep British forces penned up until the Continental Army, under the command of General George Washington, forced their evacuation by sea the following March 17, still celebrated in the Boston

---

8

City Square

📍K4

When John Winthrop arrived with three shiploads of Puritan refugees in 1630, they settled first in the marshes at the base of Town Hill, now City Square. A small public park marks the site of Winthrop's Town House the very first seat of Boston government.

The monument is beautifully lit at night to reveal the pyramid that caps the obelisk – a design echoed in the tops of the pylons of the nearby Zakim Bridge.

9

John Harvard Mall

K3

Ten families founded Charlestown in 1629, a year before the rest of Boston was settled. They built their homes and a palisaded fort on Town Hill, a spot now marked by John Harvard Mall. Several bronze plaques within the park commemorate events in the early history of the Massachusetts Bay Colony (p52). A small monument pays homage to John Harvard, the young cleric who ministered to the Charlestown settlers and who left his name, half his estate, and all his books to the fledgling college at Newtowne, when he died in 1638 (p150).

MOB? WHAT MOB?

Charlestown is a safe neighborhood on the verge of gentrification, but you wouldn't know it from its depiction by Hollywood. In the 1950s and 1960s, the Charlestown Mob warred with their counterparts in Somerville, the Winter Hill Gang. When the Charlestown thugs lost, no one wept. But movie-makers found the narrow streets of Charlestown to be a colorful backdrop for such fictional crime movies as *Monument Avenue* (1998), some scenes in *The Departed* (2006) *(below)*, and *The Town* (2010).

10

Warren Tavern

K3 **2 Pleasant St** **Lunch, dinner daily, brunch Sat-Sun** **Jan 1, Thanksgiving, Dec 25** **warrentavern.com**

Dating from 1780, the historic Warren Tavern was one of the first buildings to be erected after the British burned down Charlestown. The tavern was named after Joseph Warren, the president of the Provincial Congress in 1774 and a general in the Massachusetts Army. He enlisted as a private with the Continental Army for the Battle of Bunker Hill, where he was killed in 1775. The tavern, once derelict, has been renovated to reflect its 18th-century style. By contrast, the food is modern fare.

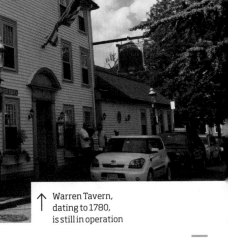

↑ Warren Tavern, dating to 1780, is still in operation

OLD BOSTON, SEAPORT, AND THE WATERFRONT

This is an area in which old and new sit one on top of the other. From the British tax collectors at the Old State House to the fiery revolutionary rhetoric that rang out in Faneuil Hall, the remnants of colonial Boston – some of which predate the American Revolution – have quite a story to tell. Since early Boston fortunes were made at sea, it's unsurprising that State Street connects the original seat of government to Long Wharf, the oldest quay on the waterfront.

Long walled off from the rest of the city by an elevated highway, Boston's waterfront began to revive when the New England Aquarium opened in 1969 and Faneuil Hall Marketplace followed in 1976. When the Big Dig (1991–2007) buried the highway and created the Rose Fitzgerald Kennedy Greenway, the waterfront began to bustle with activity. The extension into South Boston across the Fort Point Channel has created the Seaport District, a dynamic new neighborhood of hotels, restaurants, and the Institute of Contemporary Art.

OLD BOSTON, SEAPORT, AND THE WATERFRONT

Must Sees
1 New England Aquarium
2 Old State House

Experience More
3 King's Chapel and Burying Ground
4 Old Corner Bookstore
5 Omni Parker House
6 Old City Hall
7 Old South Meeting House
8 Custom House
9 Faneuil Hall
10 Post Office Square Park
11 Quincy Market
12 Waterfront Wharves
13 Rose Fitzgerald Kennedy Greenway
14 Government Center
15 Boston Children's Museum
16 Fish Pier
17 Institute of Contemporary Art
18 Boston Tea Pary Ships & Museum
19 John F. Kennedy Library and Museum
20 Edward M. Kennedy Institute for the US Senate
21 Castle Island and South Boston Beaches

Eat
① Union Oyster House
② Salty Dog Seafood Grille & Bar
③ Barking Crab
④ Legal Harborside

Drink
⑤ The Black Rose
⑥ Mr. Dooley's Tavern
⑦ Hennessy's

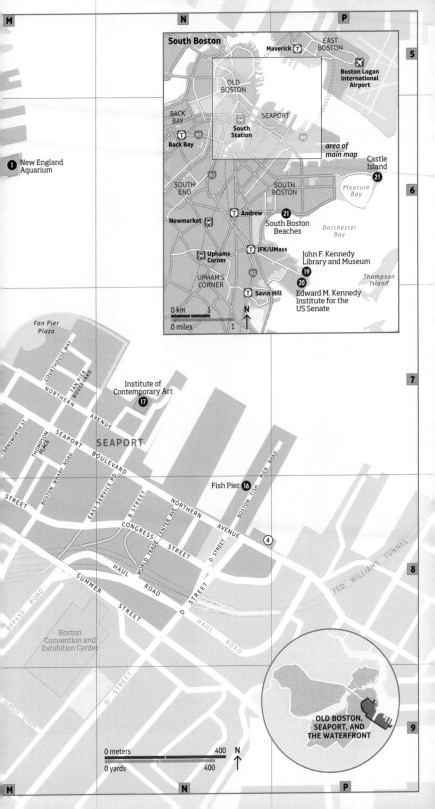

South Boston

EAST BOSTON

Maverick Ⓣ

Boston Logan International Airport

OLD BOSTON

SEAPORT

BACK BAY

90

Back Bay Ⓣ

South Station

area of main map

New England Aquarium ❶

SOUTH END

93

SOUTH BOSTON

Castle Island ㉑

Pleasure Bay

Newmarket Ⓣ

Andrew Ⓣ

South Boston Beaches ㉑

Dorchester Bay

Uphams Corner Ⓣ

JFK/UMass Ⓣ

John F. Kennedy Library and Museum ⓳

Thompson Island

UPHAM'S CORNER

93

Savin Hill Ⓣ

Edward M. Kennedy Institute for the US Senate ⓴

0 km ———— 1

0 miles ———— 1

N ↑

Fan Pier Plaza

COURTHOUSE WAY

FAN PIER BOULEVARD

NORTHERN AVENUE

Institute of Contemporary Art ⓱

FARNSWORTH ST

THOMPSON PLACE

SEAPORT BOULEVARD

SEAPORT

BOSTON WHARF ROAD

STREET

EAST SERVICE RD

B STREET

WORLD TRADE CENTER AVE

CONGRESS STREET

NORTHERN AVENUE

D STREET

BOSTON FISH PIER ROAD

Fish Pier ⓰

④

HAUL ROAD

SUMMER STREET

D STREET

TED WILLIAMS TUNNEL

Boston Convention and Exhibition Center

HAUL ROAD

D STREET

CRANN STREET

BYPASS ROAD

0 meters ———— 400

0 yards ———— 400

N ↑

OLD BOSTON, SEAPORT, AND THE WATERFRONT

① ⟨symbols⟩

NEW ENGLAND AQUARIUM

◉M6 **◫1 Central Wharf** **ⓣAquarium** **◷Jul & Aug: 9am–6pm daily (to 7pm Fri & Sat); Sep–Jun: 9am–5pm daily (to 6pm Sat & Sun** **ⓦneaq.org**

The sea pervades every aspect of Boston life, so it's only natural that the New England Aquarium is one of the city's most popular attractions. What sets it apart is its commitment not only to creating an exciting environment to learn about marine life, but also to conserving the natural habitats of thousands of gilled, feathered, and whiskered inhabitants.

The Waterfront's prime attraction dominates Central Wharf. Designed by a consortium of architects in 1969, the aquarium has a core enclosed by a vast four-story ocean tank, which contains an innumerable array of marine animals, from hundreds of brightly colored tropical fish to sharks, sea turtles, and moray eels. A curving walkway runs around the outside of the tank from top to bottom and provides viewpoints of the interior of the tank from different levels. Also resident at the aquarium are harbor seals, northern fur seals, California sea lions, penguins, rays, sea turtles, and mesmerizing seadragons. The facility also includes a superb IMAX® theater.

200,000

Gallons of salt water fill the New England Aquarium's Giant Ocean Tank.

←

Exterior of the New England Aquarium on Boston's Central Wharf

THE AQUARIUM'S MISSION

The aquarium's aim, first and foremost, is to instigate and support marine conservation. Its Conservation Action fund has fought on behalf of numerous endangered marine animals worldwide, helping to protect humpback whales in the South Pacific, sea turtles in New England, and dolphins in Peru. Closer to home, it also lobbies to protect critically endangered Atlantic whales.

↑ Beautiful sea life in the aquarium's large tank

↑ Penguins perched on rocks at the aquarium's Penguin Exhibit

❷ 🏃 Ⓜ 🏛

OLD STATE HOUSE

📍L6 🏠206 Washington St 🚇State, Govt Centre, Downtown Crossing 🕐9am–5pm daily (Jul & Aug: extended hours) 🚫1st week Feb 🌐revolutionaryspaces.org

Past and present merge seamlessly in the city of Boston, where commuters hop a subway line in the cellars of the British colonial house of governance. The restrained dignity of the 18th-century Old State House recalls a time when the king's word was law.

Dwarfed by the towers of the Financial District, the Old State House was the seat of British colonial government between 1713 and 1776. The royal lion and unicorn still decorate each corner of the East Facade. Following independence, the Massachusetts legislature took possession of the building, and it has had many uses since, including a produce market, merchants' exchange, Masonic lodge, and Boston City Hall. Its wine cellars now function as a downtown subway station. The building houses two floors of exhibits and interactive displays about the city's history and the Boston Massacre.

A Latin inscription, relating to the first Massachusetts Bay colony, runs around the outside of a crest on the West Facade.

A gold sculpture of an eagle, symbol of America, can be seen on the west facade.

Keayne Hall is named after Robert Keayne, who, in 1658, gave £300 so that the Town House could be built.

→

The splendid exterior and elegant interiors of the Old State House

① The traditional exterior of the Old State House contrasts with surrounding skyscrapers.

② A replica unicorn statue is mounted on the roof.

③ The central staircase has two beautiful handrails.

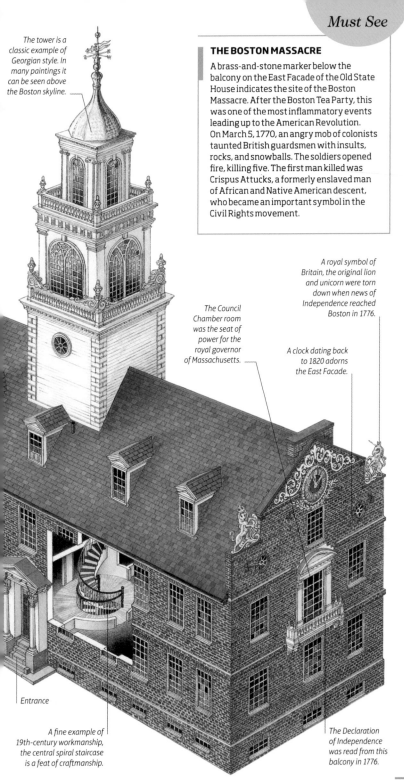

The tower is a classic example of Georgian style. In many paintings it can be seen above the Boston skyline.

THE BOSTON MASSACRE

A brass-and-stone marker below the balcony on the East Facade of the Old State House indicates the site of the Boston Massacre. After the Boston Tea Party, this was one of the most inflammatory events leading up to the American Revolution. On March 5, 1770, an angry mob of colonists taunted British guardsmen with insults, rocks, and snowballs. The soldiers opened fire, killing five. The first man killed was Crispus Attucks, a formerly enslaved man of African and Native American descent, who became an important symbol in the Civil Rights movement.

A royal symbol of Britain, the original lion and unicorn were torn down when news of Independence reached Boston in 1776.

The Council Chamber room was the seat of power for the royal governor of Massachusetts.

A clock dating back to 1820 adorns the East Facade.

Entrance

A fine example of 19th-century workmanship, the central spiral staircase is a feat of craftmanship.

The Declaration of Independence was read from this balcony in 1776.

EXPERIENCE Old Boston, Seaport, and the Waterfront

3

King's Chapel and Burying Ground

📍 K6 🏛 58 Tremont St 🚇 Park Street, State, Government Center 🕐 Times vary, check website 🌐 kings-chapel.org

An Anglican chapel, built in 1688, originally stood on this site. When New England's governor decided a larger church was needed, the present edifice – begun in 1749 – was constructed around the original chapel. After the Revolution, the congregation's religious allegiance switched from Anglican to Unitarian. The sanctuary's raised pulpit dates from 1717 and is one of the oldest in the US. The bell inside the King's Chapel is the largest ever cast by Paul Revere (p102).

Among those interred in the adjacent cemetery are John Winthrop and Elizabeth Pain, who was the inspiration for adultress Hester Prynne in Nathaniel Hawthorne's moralistic novel *The Scarlet Letter.*

4

Old Corner Bookstore

📍 L6 🏛 1 School St 🚇 Park Street, State, Government Center 🚫 To the public

A dormered gambrel roof crowns this brick landmark, which opened as Thomas Crease's apothecary shop in 1718 and was reestablished as the Old Corner Bookstore in 1829. Moving in 16 years later, the Ticknor & Fields publishing company became a gathering place for a notable roster of authors: Emerson, Hawthorne, Longfellow, Thoreau, early feminist writer Margaret Fuller, and *Uncle Tom's Cabin* novelist Harriet Beecher Stowe. The firm is often credited with carving out the first distinctively American literature. The earliest editions of the erudite *Atlantic Monthly* periodical were also printed here. Julia Ward Howe's rousing tribute to American Civil War bravado, "The Battle Hymn of the Republic," first appeared in the February 1862 issue.

5

Omni Parker House

📍 K6 🏛 60 School St 🚇 Park Street, State, Government Center 🌐 omnihotels.com

Harvey D. Parker was so successful a Boston restauranteur that he was able to expand the property into a first-class, grand hotel. His Parker House opened in 1855, standing five stories high and featuring the first passenger elevator ever seen in Boston. The building saw many transformations, and its latest 14-story incarnation has stood across from King's Chapel since 1927.

The hotel quickly attained a reputation for luxurious accommodations and lavish,

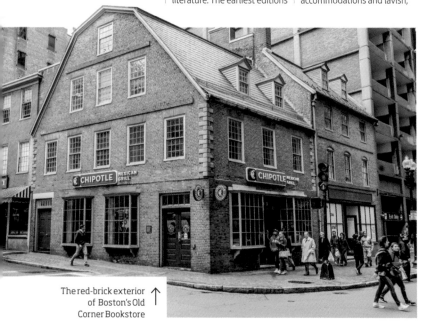

The red-brick exterior of Boston's Old Corner Bookstore ↑

dining. Among Parker House's many claims to fame are its Boston Cream Pie, which was first created here, and the word "scrod," a uniquely Bostonian term loosely translated as the freshest white fish of the day.

Boston politicians have long favored the Parker House public areas. John F. Kennedy announced his candidacy for Congress here, and rascal mayor James Michael Curley was such a constant presence that the whiskey bar is named "The Last Hurrah" after the roman-à-clef based on his life.

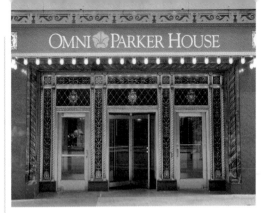

↑ The ornate facade of Omni Parker House, which opened in the late 19th century

6
Old City Hall

K6 🏠 45 School St
Ⓣ Park Street, State, Government Center

This building is a wonderful example of French Second Empire architectural gaudiness and served as Boston's City Hall for over a century from 1865 to 1969. It was eventually superseded by the rakishly imposing new City Hall structure at nearby Government Center, and the renovated 19th-century building now features a steak house.

Previous occupants of the Old City Hall have included such flamboyant mayors as John "Honey Fitz" Fitzgerald and James Michael Curley. There are also statues here that memorialize Josiah Quincy, the second mayor of Boston, after whom Quincy Market is named, as well as Benjamin Franklin, who was born on nearby Milk Street in 1706.

→ A statue outside the Old City Hall, depicting second mayor Josiah Quincy

7
Old South Meeting House

Ⓖ L6 🏠 310 Washington St
Ⓣ Park Street, Government Center, State ⏰ Apr–Oct: 9:30am–5pm daily; Nov–Mar: 10am–4pm daily
ⓦ revolutionaryspaces.org

Built in 1729, this edifice had colonial Boston's biggest capacity for town meetings – a fact capitalized upon by a group of rebellious rabble-rousers calling themselves the Sons of Liberty, who drew large crowds to hear their raging against British taxation and other royal annoyances.

During a candlelit protest rally on December 16, 1773, fiery speechmaker Samuel Adams flashed the signal that led to the Boston Tea Party (p123) several hours later. The British retaliated by turning Old South Meeting House into an officers' tavern and stable. It was saved from destruction and became a museum in 1877. A series of lectures are offered, covering a range of New England topics, and chamber music concerts and other musical performances are also held here. The shop has a wide

DRINK

The Black Rose
Boston's drinking culture harks back to the city's Irish heritage. Head to the Black Rose for Guinness stew, lobster rolls, and live Irish music.

Ⓖ L6 🏠 160 State St
ⓦ blackroseboston.com

Mr. Dooley's Tavern
This is a firm favorite with local musicians for its impromptu sessions.

Ⓖ L6 🏠 77 Broad St
ⓦ mrdooleys.com

Hennessy's
Choose from an excellent list of whiskeys at this great conversation bar.

Ⓖ L6 🏠 25 Union St
ⓦ hennessysboston.com

selection of merchandise, including the ubiquitous tins of "Boston Tea Party" tea.

Directly across Washington Street, sculptor Robert Shure's memorial to the victims of the 1845–9 Irish Potato Famine was added to the plaza in 1998.

Did You Know?

Endangered peregrine falcons have nested on the Custom House tower for more than 20 years.

⑧ Custom House

📍L6 🏠3 McKinley Sq 📞(617) 310-6300 🚇Aquarium
🕐Tower: 2pm & 6pm Sat-Thu

Before landfill altered the downtown topography, early Boston's Custom House was perched at the water's edge. A temple-like Greek Revival structure, the granite building had a skylit dome upon completion in 1847. Since 1915, however, it has supported a 495-ft (150-m) tower with a four-sided clock. For the best part of the 20th century, the Custom House was Boston's only bona fide skyscraper.

The building features an observation tower, which is open to the public and offers stunning views of the harbor and the Financial District skyscrapers that tower over it. It is a great place to enjoy a drink as the sun sets.

⑨ Faneuil Hall

📍L6 🏠Dock Sq
🚇Government Center, Haymarket, State
🕐9am–5pm daily (closed for events)
🌐nps.gov/bost

A gift to Boston from the wealthy merchant Peter Faneuil in 1742, this Georgian brick landmark has always functioned simultaneously as a public market and town meeting place. Today, it

also houses the visitor center of the Boston National Historical Park, and serves as the site where new citizens take the oath of allegiance.

The building is grand. Look out for the grasshopper weathervane which master tinsmith Shem Drowne modeled after the one on top of the Royal Exchange in the City of London, England. Near the end of the 18th century, architect Charles Bulfinch was commissioned to expand the building in order to accommodate larger crowds. The work was completed in 1806, and Faneuil Hall then remained unchanged until 1898, when it was further expanded according to Bulfinch stipulations.

Nicknamed "The Cradle of Liberty," the building started hosting revolutionary figures soon after its construction. In 1763, Samuel Adams rallied against British oppression here. During the 19th century, Faneuil Hall became a central forum for historic antislavery and women's suffrage speeches. With the hall's libertarian history, it may be surprising to learn that Peter

> **During the 19th century, Faneuil Hall became a central forum for historic antislavery and women's suffrage speeches.**

Faneuil engaged in the trade of enslaved persons, and 21st-century sentiments lean toward renaming the structure.

⑩ Post Office Square Park

📍L6 🏠Franklin, Pearl, High, & Congress sts 🚇State, Aquarium 🌐normanbleventhalpark.org

Officially named Norman B. Leventhal Park (after a Bostonian businessman best known for his civic improvements to the city), and occupying land reclaimed when a parking garage was demolished, this beautifully landscaped park is a small island of green amid the soaring skyscrapers of the Financial District. Vines climb a long trellis along one side of the park, and a fountain made of green glass cascades on the square's Pearl Street side. A focal point for the entire area throughout the year, the Post Office Square Park comes into its own in the summer months, when it hosts many special events. A small kiosk sells luncheon fare, jazz concerts are often held at midday, and office workers fill the benches and lounge on the well-kept lawns. The green space is blanketed with free Wi-Fi.

The square is surrounded by several notable buildings,

← Custom House's soaring, four-sided clock tower, which dates from 1915

↑ Visitors at the food stalls, in *(inset)* Old Boston's famous Quincy Market

EAT

Union Oyster House
Established in the 1820s just a stone's throw from Quincy Market, this seafood joint serves up Boston classics in a historic setting.

 L6 41 Union St unionoyster house.com

$$

Salty Dog Seafood Grille & Bar
Established in 1972, this culinary landmark is one of the original vendors of Faneuil Hall Marketplace.

 L6 206 Faneuil Hall Marketplace salty dogboston.biz

$$

not least the former main post office on Congress Street, after which the park is named. The 1929–31 Art Deco masterpiece of geometric and botanical ornamentation that used to be occupied by the post office is now home to the John W. McCormack courthouse. The Langham Boston hotel is housed in a classic Renaissance Revival showpiece. Completed in 1922, it was once the premises of the Federal Reserve Bank. Among the original features that have been carefully preserved are the painted dome and murals by N. C. Wyeth. The most notable edifice on the square is the 1947 late Art Deco building on the south side of Franklin Street. Originally constructed as the head-quarters for the New England Telephone Company, this landmark building also recalls the neighborhood's connection to telephone history. The laboratory of telephone pioneer Alexander Graham Bell was located on nearby Court Street.

Quincy Market

 L6 Between Chatham & Clinton sts State, Government Center 10am–9pm Mon-Sat, 11am-7pm Sun faneuil hallmarketplace.com

This immensely popular shopping and dining complex attracts nearly 18 million people every year. It was developed from the buildings of the old Quincy Market, which was the city's meat, fish, and produce market. These buildings had fallen into dis-repair before they underwent a widely acclaimed restoration in the 1970s. The 535-ft- (163-m-) long colonnaded market hall with a spectacular central rotunda is flanked by the North and South Market buildings. These individual warehouses have also been refurbished to accommodate numerous boutiques, stores, restaurants, and pubs, as well as upstairs business offices. In 2015 the city opened a

new fresh market opposite the Haymarket subway station on the Rose Kennedy Greenway. The year-round Boston Public Market features only locally sourced produce and specialty foods.

Impressive interior of Boston's Quincy Market

12

Waterfront Wharves

📍M6 🏠Atlantic Ave
🚇Aquarium

Boston's waterfront is fringed by many wharves, reminders of the city's past as a key trading port. One of the largest of these is Long Wharf, established in 1710 to accommodate the boom in early maritime commerce. Once extending 2,000 ft (610 m) into Boston Harbor and lined with shops and warehouses, the historic Long Wharf, which was built during 1710–56, provided mooring for the largest ships of the time. Today, many sightseeing excursion boats depart from here, including to Boston Harbor Islands.

For those who would prefer to remain on dry land, this area is also an excellent strolling spot, with miles of pedestrian- and bike-friendly access to the waterfront. Harbor Walk connects Long Wharf with other adjacent 19th-century wharves, including Rowes Wharf, where you'll find the Boston Harbor Hotel, restaurants, and a marina. Long Wharf is also a good access point to the nearby Rose Fitzgerald Kennedy Greenway.

↑ People admiring the Boston skyline from the Rose Fitzgerald Kennedy Greenway

13

Rose Fitzgerald Kennedy Greenway

📍M6 🏠Atlantic Ave
🚇Haymarket, South Station, Aquarium
🕐7am–11pm daily 🌐rosekennedygreenway.org

A contemporary parkland constructed as a roof garden above the superhighway tunnel, the Rose Fitzgerald Kennedy Greenway cuts an organic green swathe for 1.5 miles (2.5 km) through the heart of Boston. This linear park was created in 2008 on land reclaimed from the removal of an elevated highway. Visitors and locals can laze on the lawns, recline on benches, cool off in one of seven fountains, enjoy lunch from one of the many food trucks that dot the site, and post on social media using the free Wi-Fi. There is also a charming modern carousel featuring hand-carved figures of local wildlife – including a skunk, a lobster, a rabbit, and more. Near Rowes Wharf, the permanent Harbor Fog water sculpture evokes the sea with fog, light, and sound. Many public art installations change each year, with recent

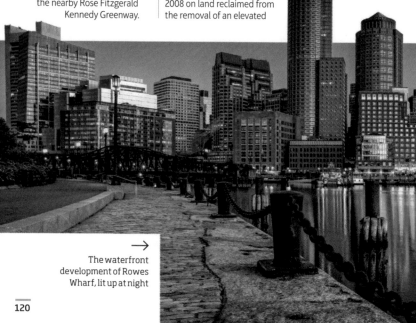

→ The waterfront development of Rowes Wharf, lit up at night

examples including a gigantic mural by Boston-based painter and sculptor Mia Cross; this stretched for 140 ft (43 m) along the greenway. Colorful flower gardens also punctuate the park's walkways.

The site's broad green spaces host a number of special events throughout the year; during warmer months the park is a hotspot for festivals, while its adjacent food market lures picnickers. The Berklee Greenway Concert Series is also held here during the summer, and offers visitors an excellent opportunity to enjoy free performances by some of Berklee College of Music's finest musicians.

An interactive Google map, which helps visitors make the most of their visit to the greenway, can be found on the park's website.

Government Center

◎ L6 **🚇 Cambridge, Court, New Sudbury, & Congress sts** **🚇 Government Center**

This city-center development was built on the site of what was once Scollay Square,

BOSTON HARBOR ISLANDS

Bostonians don't have to go far to escape urban life. The popular landscapes of the Boston Harbor Islands National and State Park offer everything from hiking trails and swimming beaches to snack bars and even campgrounds. You can reach eight of the islands by ferry from Long Wharf between May and October. With its Civil War-era fort, Georges is the hub of the island ferry system. Find ferry schedules and further details at the information booth at Long Wharf, or visit www.bostonharborislands.org.

demolished as part of the trend for local urban renewal that began in the early 1960s. This trend had already resulted in the building of the strikingly Modernist concrete-and-brick City Hall, which stands on the eastern side of the square and houses government offices. The upper stories of this main complex, where city business is conducted, jut out above the lower levels, which house a variety

Did You Know?

A Confederate widow, known as "The Lady in Black," is said to haunt Fort Warren on Georges Island.

of shops and businesses. Some Bostonians viewed the new development as controversial; others did not lament the loss of what was essentially a disreputable cluster of saloons, burlesque theaters, tattoo parlors, and scruffy hotels. The overall master plan for Government Center was inspired by the outdoor vitality and spaciousness often found in Italian piazzas. Architects I. M. Pei & Partners tried to re-create some of this feeling by surrounding Boston's new City Hall with a vast terraced plaza paved in brick. As intended, its spaciousness makes it an ideal place for events such as skateboard contests, political and sports rallies, food fairs, and patriotic military marches. Free concerts usually hosted during the summer, are a particularly big draw.

↑ Visitors exploring colorful exhibits in the lobby at Boston Children's Museum

 15

Boston Children's Museum

 M7 308 Congress St South Station 10am–5pm daily (to 9pm Fri) bostonchildrens museum.org

Overlooking Fort Point Channel, a pair of rejuvenated 19th-century red-brick wool warehouses contain one of the country's best children's museums. The expansive museum offers a host of interesting exhibits on science, culture, environmental awareness, health, and the arts. Youngsters can play games, join learning activities, and hoist themselves up the incredible 30-ft (9-m) New Balance climbing structure in the lobby. Visits to a silk

---

⛰ GREAT VIEW
On the Water

Boston's Institute of Contemporary Art takes full advantage of its waterfront location. Museum admission includes a scenic ferry ride to its satellite Watershed gallery, open late May to Labor Day.

---

merchant's house, which was transplanted from Kyoto (Boston's sister city), inject a multicultural dimension, while careers can be sampled as children work on a mini construction site. A towering milk bottle in front of the museum serves as a summer food stand, and mazes, giant boulders, and performance spaces grace an outdoor park.

 16

Fish Pier

N8 South Station

As the South Boston waterfront continues to develop and gentrify, Boston Fish Pier is a solid reminder of the city's roots in the fishing trade. Built 1912–14, the pier was the largest and most modern facility of its kind at that time. During the 1920s, it processed 250 million lbs (113 million kg) of fish each year and served as home to one of the largest fishing fleets in the US.

Today the pier continues to play a key role in providing New England seafood to the city and the nation. Nearly two dozen fish processors and dealers are based on the pier. The Fish Pier also hosts the annual Boston Seafood

---

EAT

Barking Crab

This urban seafood shack, on Fort Point Channel, serves simple fare. Sit at one of the picnic tables and enjoy the harbor views while munching on delicious crab cakes.

 M7 88 Sleeper St barkingcrab.com

$ $ $

Legal Harborside

Choose from casual fish shack dishes on the first floor; fine dining on the second; and sushi and cocktails on the third floor at this vast seafood hotspot.

 N8 270 Northern Ave legalseafoods.com

$ $ $

Festival in August, which features top chefs, seafood purveyors, and entertainers.

 17

Institute of Contemporary Art

N7 25 Harbor Shore Dr South Station 10am–5pm Tue–Sun (to 9pm Thu & Fri) icaboston.org

Since 1936, when it introduced Americans to the then-radical work of German Expressionism, the Institute of Contemporary

→

The Boston Tea Party Ships & Museum, an interactive site that can be boarded by visitors

↑ The dramatic waterfront bulding that houses the Institute of Contemporary Art

Art (ICA) has made a point of championing cutting-edge innovation and avant-garde expression. Over the years, the ICA has challenged the very definition of art, showing creations often outside the usual art-world boundaries, such as an entire exhibition devoted to blowtorches. The ICA was also in the vanguard of showing and interpreting video art when the technology was still in its infancy.

For its first 70 years, the ICA was an exhibiting but not a collecting institution, in part due to the theory that the definition of "contemporary"

changes from minute to minute. That policy changed in 2006, when the ICA moved from its quaint Back Bay building to a dramatic new wood, steel, and glass structure cantilevered above the Harbor Walk on Fan Pier on the South Boston waterfront. The museum is the creation of the design firm Diller Scofidio + Renfro, and sprawls over 65,000 sq ft (6,040 sq m), including a 325-seat performing arts theater with clear walls that allow the harbor to serve as a stage backdrop, as well as a media center and art lab for educational programs. The

ICA commissions a new installation each summer at its adjunct Watershed space in East Boston.

Boston Tea Party Ships & Museum

📍 M7 🏛 306 Congress St
🚇 South Station ⏰ 10am-5pm daily (to 4pm in winter)
🌐 bostonteapartyship.com

Griffin's Wharf, where the Boston Tea Party, the city's most famous act of rebellion, took place on December 16, 1773, was buried beneath landfill many years ago. Replicas of two British East India Company ships involved in the Tea Party now anchor on the Fort Point Channel, a short distance south of the original wharf site. After exploring the ships – which contain period furnishings and are able to be boarded – and even tossing some boxes of tea overboard, visitors can enter an interactive museum where exhibits put that poignant historic act of protest into its broader context, explaining how political tensions between Boston and the British Crown at that time eventually led to the American Revolution.

John F. Kennedy Library and Museum

◉ P6 🏠 Columbia Point, Dorchester 🚇 JFK/U Mass ⏰ 9am–5pm daily ⛔ Public hols 🌐 jfklibrary.org

The soaring white concrete-and-glass building of the John F. Kennedy Library stands sentinel on Columbia Point, near the mouth of Boston Harbor. This is the city's official memorial to its most famous son, and the extensive museum does not disappoint. Exhibitions chronicle the 1,000 days of the Kennedy presidency with poignant intimacy, and include a re-creation of the Oval Office. Kennedy was among the first politicians to grasp the power of media, and the museum takes full advantage of film and video footage to use the president's own words and image to tell his story, including his campaign for the Democratic Party nomination and landmark television debates with Republican opponent Richard M. Nixon. Gripping film clips capture the anxiety of nuclear brinkmanship during the Cuban missile crisis, as well as the inspirational spirit of the space program and founding of the Peace Corps. The combination of artifacts, displays, and television footage evoke both the euphoria of "Camelot" and the numb horror of Kennedy's assassination in 1963.

Other members of the president's family are also recognized here for their contributions to American history.

INSIDER TIP
Sullivan's Snack Bar

The quintessential order at Sullivan's snack bar *(2080 William J. Day Blvd)* on Castle Island is a hot dog with a raspberry lime rickey to drink. Bostonians consider the late-February seasonal opening of this long-running snack shack to be the first sign of spring.

Within the Kennedy Library, the re-created office of Attorney General Robert F. Kennedy touches on both his deft handling of race relations and the key advisory role he played to his elder brother. Wide ranging exhibits examine the role of First Lady Jacqueline Kennedy as a cultural style-setter and a passionate advocate for the arts and historic preservation.

The impressive exterior and *(inset)* exhibits of the John F. Kennedy Library and Museum ↑

20

Edward M. Kennedy Institute for the US Senate

📍 P6 🏛 Columbia Point, Dorchester 🚇 JFK/U Mass 🕐 10am–5pm Tue–Sun 🚫 Public hols 🌐 emk institute.org

For almost half a century, Ted Kennedy honed his skills as one of the most talented negotiators in the US Senate, known for his ability to connect across the aisle and forge bipartisan legislation. Standing adjacent to the John F. Kennedy Library and Museum, this institute was opened in 2015 to celebrate the youngest Kennedy brother's contribution to American politics. A recreation of his office provides a personal look at the "Lion of the Senate," while interactive exhibits and a full-scale reproduction of the Senate Chamber offer insights on the legislative process. Historical debates are highlighted through film and live action. Visitors can even participate in floor debates on legislation under real-time consideration in Washington, DC.

21

Castle Island and South Boston Beaches

📍 P6 🏛 2010 Day Blvd

Now attached to the South Boston mainland, Castle Island has guarded the entrance to Boston Harbor since 1634. Fort Independence,

↑ Fort Independence, a 17th-Century fort that stands on Castle Island

which was built in 1851, crowns the island, and visitors can explore its bunkers and tunnels during the summer. Edgar Allan Poe was briefly stationed here, and his story, "A Cask of Amontillado," was based on a fort legend. The fort was staffed through the Civil War and reactivated during the Spanish-American War and both World Wars.

Anglers cast for striped bass and bluefish from the Steel Pier, where the island's infill meets the mainland. Another causeway encircles Pleasure Bay, and many local residents jog or strut the circumference as a daily constitutional. The roaring wind makes eavesdropping practically impossible, hence why notorious crime boss James "Whitey" Bulger used to meet here with his lieutenants.

Adjacent L Street, M Street, and Carson Beaches – the South Boston's very own "Riviera" – stretch for three miles along the South Boston shoreline of Dorchester Bay, connecting to Columbia Point

via the Harborwalk. The South Boston beaches are equipped with public restrooms and are serviced by qualified lifeguards from Memorial Day to Labor Day.

HARBORWALK

More than three decades in the making, the Boston Harborwalk (www.bostonharbor now.org) links the city and the sea. The nearly continuous pedestrian walkway stretches for miles from East Boston to Dorchester, passing through Charlestown, the North End, downtown, and South Boston. It's easy to follow short sections for a peaceful stroll or exhilarating jog. Along the way, you'll find beaches, museums, shops, restaurants, and benches to sit on and watch the boats come and go in Boston Harbor.

BACK BAY, SOUTH END, AND THE FENWAY

Until the 19th century, Boston was situated on a narrow peninsula surrounded by tidal marshes. Projects to reclaim Back Bay began in the 1850s, using new inventions such as the steam shovel. Development began immediately, and the marshes were dry land by 1880. Planned along French lines, with elegant boulevards, Back Bay is now one of Boston's most exclusive neighborhoods. The more bohemian South End, laid out on an English model of townhouses clustered around pretty squares, is home to many artists and a focus for much of Boston's LGBT+ community.

The Fenway was also laid out on reclaimed wetlands at the end of the 19th century and quickly became home to such cultural landmarks as Symphony Hall, the Museum of Fine Arts, and the Isabella Stewart Gardner Museum. In the 20th century, Fenway Park became the base of the Boston Red Sox, and Boston University enlivened adjacent Kenmore Square.

BACK BAY, SOUTH END, AND THE FENWAY

Must Sees
① Trinity Church
② Museum of Fine Arts

Experience More
③ The Esplanade
④ Gibson House Museum
⑤ First Baptist Church
⑥ Commonwealth Avenue
⑦ Newbury Street
⑧ Mary Baker Eddy Library & Mapparium
⑨ Boston Center for the Arts
⑩ Boston Public Library
⑪ 200 Clarendon Tower
⑫ Copley Square
⑬ Isabella Stewart Gardner Museum
⑭ Berklee Performance Center
⑮ Boylston Street
⑯ Huntington Theatre
⑰ Symphony Hall
⑱ Jordan Hall
⑲ Back Bay Fens
⑳ Fenway Park
㉑ Kenmore Square
㉒ Massachusetts College of Art and Design

Eat
① Bar Lyon
② Eataly

Drink
③ Bill's Bar
④ Landsdowne Pub
⑤ House of Blues

Stay
⑥ The Newbury Boston
⑦ Fairmont Copley Plaza

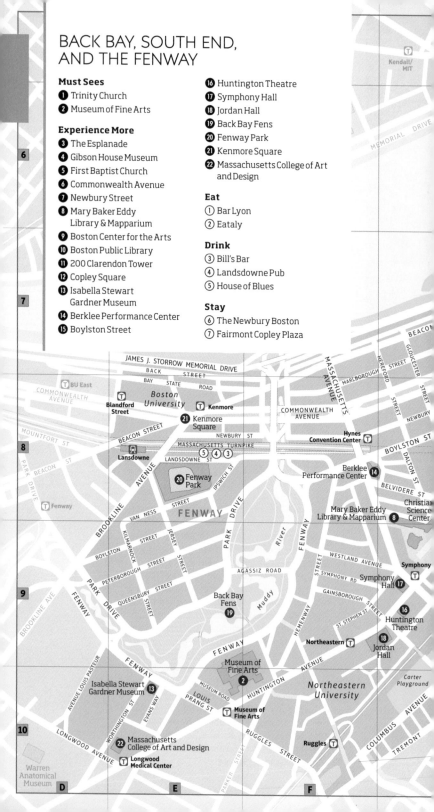

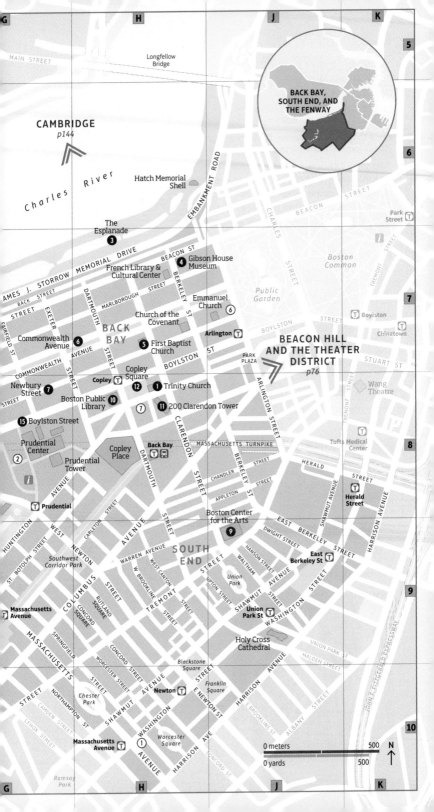

G

H

J

K

5

MAIN STREET

Longfellow
Bridge

BACK BAY,
SOUTH END, AND
THE FENWAY

6

CAMBRIDGE
p144

Charles River

Hatch Memorial
Shell

EMBANKMENT ROAD

CHARLES STREET

BEACON STREET

Park
Street

Boston
Common

TREMONT STREET

7

The Esplanade **3**

MEMORIAL DRIVE

AMES J. STORROW

BACK STREET

French Library &
Cultural Center

Gibson House
Museum **4**

BERKELEY STREET

Public
Garden

DARTMOUTH STREET

MARLBOROUGH STREET

BACK
BAY

Church of the
Covenant

Emmanuel
Church **6**

BOYLSTON STREET

Boylston

i

Chinatown

EXETER STREET

FAIRFIELD ST

Commonwealth
Avenue **6**

COMMONWEALTH AVENUE

First Baptist
Church **5**

Arlington **T**

PARK
PLAZA

BEACON HILL
AND THE THEATER
DISTRICT
p76

STUART ST

Wang
Theatre

Newbury
Street **7**

Copley **T**

Copley
Square

12

Trinity Church **1**

ARLINGTON STREET

Boston Public
Library **10**

7

200 Clarendon Tower **11**

TREMONT STREET

Tufts Medical
Center

8

15 Boylston Street

CLARENDON STREET

Back Bay **T**

MASSACHUSETTS TURNPIKE

BERKELEY STREET

HERALD STREET

Herald
Street **T**

Prudential
Center

2

Copley
Place

DARTMOUTH STREET

CHANDLER STREET

SHAWMUT AVENUE

HARRISON AVENUE

Prudential
Tower

i

APPLETON STREET

T Prudential

AVENUE

CARLETON STREET

Boston Center
for the Arts **9**

EAST BERKELEY STREET

HUNTINGTON AVENUE

WEST NEWTON STREET

WARREN AVENUE

W CANTON STREET

W BROOKLINE STREET

SOUTH
END

WALTHAM STREET

HANSON STREET

DWIGHT STREET

East
Berkeley St **T**

9

ST. BOTOLPH STREET

Southwest
Corridor Park

RUTLAND SQUARE

CONCORD SQUARE

TREMONT STREET

UPTON STREET

Union
Park

SHAWMUT AVENUE

Union
Park St **T**

WASHINGTON STREET

T Massachusetts
Avenue

COLUMBUS AVENUE

SPRINGFIELD STREET

WORCESTER STREET

CONCORD STREET

Blackstone
Square

Holy Cross
Cathedral

UNION PARK ST

MALDEN STREET

JOHN F. FITZGERALD EXPRESSWAY

MASSACHUSETTS AVENUE

NORTHAMPTON STREET

Chester
Park

SHAWMUT ST

Franklin
Square

E NEWTON ST

Newton **T**

HARRISON AVENUE

E BROOKLINE ST

ALBANY STREET

STREET

CAMDEN STREET

LENOX STREET

Massachusetts
Avenue **T**

WASHINGTON AVENUE

i

Worcester
Square

HARRISON AVENUE

CONCORD ST

0 meters   500

0 yards   500

N

10

Ramsay
Park

G

H

J

K

❶ 🛈 Ⓜ

TRINITY CHURCH

📍H8 🅰Copley Sq ⓉCopley 🕐10am–4:30pm Tue-Sat (to 4:30pm Sun) 🌐trinitychurchboston.org

Boston has a knack for creating curious visual juxtapositions, and one of the most remarkable is in Copley Square, where the 19th-century Trinity Church reflects in the sleek, blue-tinted glass of the decidedly modern and imposing 200 Clarendon Tower.

Routinely voted one of America's finest buildings, this masterpiece by Henry Hobson Richardson dates from 1877. It was named a National Historic Landmark in 1971, and has earned the distinction of being listed one of the American Institute of Architects' ten greatest buildings in the country.

This wasn't always home to Trinity Church – it was founded in 1733 near Downtown Crossing, but the congregation moved to this site in 1872. The granite and sandstone Romanesque structure stands on wooden piles driven through mud into bedrock, surmounted with granite pyramids. John LaFarge designed the interior, while some of the windows are designed by Edward Burne-Jones and executed by William Morris.

PHILLIPS BROOKS

Born in Boston in 1835 and educated at Harvard, Brooks was a towering charismatic figure. Rector of Trinity Church from 1869, he gained a reputation for powerful sermons. From 1872 Brooks worked closely with Henry Hobson Richardson on the design of the new Trinity Church – at least five sculpted likenesses of him can be seen in and around the building.

On the wall of the chancel are a series of gold bas-reliefs.

The North Transept Windows were designed by Edward Burne-Jones and executed by William Morris.

The present-day chancel was designed by Charles Maginnis.

The Pulpit features carved scenes from the life of Christ and portraits of great preachers through the ages.

→ The breathtaking Trinity Church, with its bell tower and interior

Bell tower

← Striking interior and stained-glass windows of Trinity Church

→ People relaxing by Copley Square Fountain on a summer's day

The West Portico was modeled on that of St. Trophime in Arles, France.

John LaFarge's lancet windows show Christ in the act of blessing.

Main entrance

2 🎨 🏛 🍴 ☕ 🎁

MUSEUM OF FINE ARTS

📍 F10 🏛 Avenue of the Arts, 465 Huntington Ave ⏰ 10am–5pm daily (to 10pm Wed–Fri) 🚫 Public hols 🌐 mfa.org

Since its establishment in 1870, the Museum of Fine Arts (MFA) has collected some 500,000 pieces from an array of cultures and civilisations, ranging from ancient Egyptian tomb treasures to the latest in cutting-edge contemporary artworks.

This is the largest art museum in New England and one of the great encyclopedic art museums in the United States. Its collection includes around 500,000 objects, ranging from ancient Egyptian artifacts and Greek sculpture to specially commissioned murals by John Singer Sargent.

The MFA's original 1909 Beaux-Arts-style building was augmented in 2010 by the 53 galleries of the Art of the Americas Wing, designed by Foster + Partners. In 2011, the museum transformed its west-facing wing, designed in 1981 by I. M. Pei, into the Linde Family Wing for Contemporary Art.

> 💬 INSIDER TIP
> **Family Fun**
>
> The MFA offers a range of family programs, including MFA play-dates, art-making sessions, and other fun and educational activities to inspire little ones as they explore the museum.

1

1 The MFA is home to the largest Monet collection outside of France; his works can be seen in Gallery 252.

2 *The Blue Boat* (1892) is one of many works by Winslow Homer in the museum's collection.

3 Josiah McElheny's *Endlessly Repeating Twentieth Century Modernism*, 2007 is displayed in Gallery 247.

2

3

GALLERY GUIDE

The Linde Family Wing (west side) displays contemporary art and houses an excellent restaurant and the museum store. European, Classical, Far Eastern, and Egyptian art and artifacts occupy the original MFA building. Arts from North, Central, and South America are displayed over four levels in the Art of the Americas Wing. All works on display are subject to change, since many items are involved in the museum's highly successful Traveling Exhibitions program.

←

Colonnaded entrance and 1909 Beaux-Arts-style exterior of the Museum of Fine Arts

EXPERIENCE MORE

 3

The Esplanade

📍H7 🚇Charles/MGH
🕐24 hrs daily

Running along the Boston side of the Charles River, between Longfellow Bridge and Dartmouth Street, are the lagoons, parkland, and islands known collectively as the Esplanade. The park is used extensively for in-line skating, cycling, and strolling. Most safely enjoyed during daylight hours, it is also the access point for boating on the river and the site of the city's leading outdoor concert space.

In 1929, Arthur Fiedler, then the young conductor of the Boston Pops Orchestra, chose the Esplanade for a summer concert series that became an annual tradition. Fourth of July concerts by the Boston Pops – which are one of the country's oldest Independence Day public celebrations – are followed by fireworks and can attract upward of 500,000 spectators. The Esplanade's iconic Hatch Memorial Shell was constructed in 1939, and its stage is widely used by musical ensembles and other groups throughout the summer.

4

Gibson House Museum

📍H7 🏠137 Beacon St
🚇Arlington 🕐For tours at 1pm, 2pm, & 3pm Wed–Sun
🌐thegibsonhouse.org

Among the first houses built in the Back Bay, the Gibson House reflects the Gilded Age, with its original Victorian decor and furnishings. The 1860 brownstone and red-brick structure was designed in the Italian Renaissance Revival style for the widow Catherine Hammond Gibson, who was one of the few women to own property in this part of the city. Her grandson Charles Hammond Gibson, Jr., a noted eccentric, poet, travel writer, and horticulturalist, arranged for the house to become a museum after his death in 1954. As a prelude to this, Gibson began to rope off the furniture in the 1930s, thus inviting his guests to sit on the stairs to drink martinis.

One of the most modern houses of its day, the Gibson House boasted gas lighting, indoor plumbing in the base-ment, and coal-fired central heating. It is Gibson's preser-vation of the 1860s' decor (with some modifications

in 1888) that makes the museum a true time capsule of Victorian life in Boston.

5

First Baptist Church

📍H7 🏠110 Common-wealth Ave 📞(617) 267-3148 🚇Arlington, Copley
🕐For Sunday worship

This Romanesque-style First Baptist Church was Henry Hobson Richardson's first major architectural commission and became an instant land-mark when it was finished in 1872. Viewed from Commonwealth Avenue, it is one of the most distinctive buildings of the city skyline.

Richardson considered the nearly freestanding bell tower to be the church's most inno-vative structure. It is topped with a decorative frieze and arches protected by an over-hanging roof. The frieze was modeled in Paris by Bartholdi, the sculptor who created the Statue of Liberty. The faces

$\longrightarrow$

Phillis Wheatley, one of the many historical figures on Commonwealth Avenue

Canoeists paddling through one of the Esplanade's scenic lagoons

in the frieze, which depict the sacraments, are likenesses of prominent Bostonians of that time. The trumpeting angels adorning the tower gave the building its nickname, "Church of the Holy Bean Blowers."

Shortly after the church was completed, the Unitarian congregation dissolved because it was unable to bear the expense of the building. The church stood vacant until 1881, when the First Baptist congregation from the South End took it over.

Commonwealth Avenue

H7 Arlington, Copley, Hynes Convention Center

Back Bay was Boston's first fully planned neighborhood, and architect Arthur Gilman made Commonwealth Avenue, modeled on the elegant boulevards of Paris, the centerpiece of the design. The wide avenue became an arena for America's leading architects in the second half of the 19th century. A walk from the Public Garden to Massachusetts Avenue is like flicking through a catalog of architectural styles. Few of the grand buildings on either side of the avenue are open to the public, but strollers along the central mall encounter a number of historic figures in the form of bronze statues. The end of the mall features a heroic bronze of Leif Erikson, erected as a historically unsupported flight of fancy that the

Norse explorer landed at Boston. The statue of abolitionist William Lloyd Garrison is said to capture the man's air of moral superiority. A modern bronze memorializes Phillis Wheatley, the first formerly enslaved woman in the US to publish a book of poetry.

Newbury Street

G8 Arlington, Copley, Hynes Convention Center

Newbury Street is a Boston synonym for "stylish." The Newbury Boston at Arlington Street sets an elegant tone that continues with a mix of prestigious and often well-hidden art galleries, stylish shops, and some of the city's best sidewalk dining.

Churches provide vestiges of a more decorous era. The **Church of the Covenant** at No. 67 Newbury is the largest intact Tiffany church interior, with more than 20 stained-glass windows and an elaborate Tiffany lantern. A chorus and orchestra perform sacred music each Sunday (Sep–May) at Emmanuel Church on the corner of Berkeley Street.

Most of Newbury Street was constructed as town-house residences, but the desirability of these spaces for retail operations has pushed residents to the upper floors, while ground and sub-surface levels are devoted to chic boutiques and eateries.

Church of the Covenant
67 Newbury St
cotcbos.org

↑ Springtime blossoms brightening the sidewalk of Newbury Street

↑ Visitors marveling at the large, illuminated, stained-glass Mapparium

Mary Baker Eddy Library & Mapparium

📍G8 🏠200 Massachusetts Ave 🚇Symphony 🕐10am–5pm daily 🌐marybakereddylibrary.org

Named for the founder of the Christian Science Church, this library is a major scholarly resource. In addition to the archives and community programs, exhibits highlight the life and teachings of Mary Baker Eddy (1821–1910), and the history of the Christian Science movement. The most unusual attraction is the Mapparium, which can only be seen on a guided tour. It is a three-story stained-glass globe which you view from the inside from a glass walkway. Illuminated by LED lighting, the countries represented on the globe's surface are those that existed when it was built in 1935.

EAT & DRINK

Bar Lyon
In the style of its namesake city, Bar Lyon pairs French wine and cider with casual cuisine.

📍G8 🏠1750 Washington St 🌐barlyon.com

Eataly
Try antipasti at the wine bar at this Italian food market, or opt for fine dining at Terra.

📍H10 🏠800 Boylston St 🌐eataly.com

Boston Center for the Arts

📍J9 🏠539 Tremont St 🚇Back Bay/South End 🕐Cyclorama: 9am–5pm Mon–Fri; Mills Gallery: noon–5pm Wed & Sun, noon–9pm Thu–Sat 🔒Public hols 🌐bcaonline.org

The centerpiece of a resurgent South End, the BCA complex includes four stages, an art gallery, and artists' studios as well as the Boston Ballet Building, home to the company's educational programs, rehearsal space, and administrative offices. The Tremont Estates Building, an organ factory in the years after the Civil War, now houses artists' studios, rehearsal space, and an art gallery. The largest of the BCA buildings is the circular, domed Cyclorama, which serves as a performance and exhibition space. It opened in 1884 to exhibit the 50-ft (15-m) by 400-ft (121-m) painting *The Battle of Gettysburg* by French artist Paul Philippoteaux. The painting was removed in 1889 and is now displayed at Gettysburg National Military Park.

The Stanford Calderwood Pavilion, with a 360-seat and a 200-seat theater, opened in 2004 as Boston's first new theater in 75 years. The Mills Gallery houses exhibitions focusing on emerging contemporary artists, with a strong emphasis on

multimedia installations and shows with confrontational, and often provocative, themes.

Boston Public Library

H8 Copley Sq Copley 9am–9pm Mon–Thu, 9am–5pm Fri–Sat, 1–5pm Sun Jun–Sep: Sun; public hols bpl.org

Founded in 1848, the Boston Public Library was America's first free city library for the public. It quickly outgrew its original building, hence the construction of the Italian *palazzo*-style Copley Square building in 1887–95. Designed by Charles McKim, the building is a marvel of fine wood and marble detail, as highlighted in the daily tours. Bates Hall, the main reading room, is noted for its barrel-vaulted ceiling. Sculptor Daniel Chester French fashioned the library's huge bronze doors, Edward Abbey's murals of the Quest for the Holy Grail line the book request room, and John Singer Sargent's religious murals depicting scenes from Jewish and Christian belief cover a third-floor gallery. The library's collection is housed in the 1971 Boylston Street addition, a Modernist structure by architect Philip Johnson.

200 Clarendon Tower

H8 200 Clarendon St Copley To the public

The tallest building in New England, this 790-ft (240-m) rhomboid cuts into Copley Square, with its mirrored facade reflecting the surroundings, including the original Hancock building with its red and blue lights that forecast the local weather. The 60-story office building shares the square with its 19th-century neighbors, the Romanesque Trinity Church and the Italian Renaissance Revival Copley Plaza Hotel, without dwarfing them. Although the building was renamed in 2015, many locals still refer to it as the John Hancock Tower.

Copley Square

H8 Copley

Named after John Singleton Copley, the great Boston painter born nearby in 1737, Copley Square is a hive of civic activity surrounded by some of Boston's most striking architecture. Summer activities include farmers' markets, concerts, and folk-dancing.

The inviting green plaza took years to develop; when Copley was born, it was just a marshy riverbank, which remained unfilled until 1870. Construction of the 200 Clarendon Tower in 1975 anchored the southeastern side of the square, and the Copley Place development on the southwestern corner completed it in 1984. Today's Copley Square, an open space of trees, grass, and fountains, took shape in the heart of the city in the 1990s, after various plans to utilize this hitherto wasted space were tendered.

A plaque honoring the Boston Marathon, which ends at the Boston Public Library, was set in the sidewalk in 1996 to coincide with the 100th race. As well as pushcart vendors, the plaza has a booth for discounted show tickets.

The orderly interior and *(inset)* wide stone facade of Boston Public Library

→

Visitors exploring the galleries of the Isabella Stewart Gardner Museum

Isabella Stewart Gardner Museum

📍E10 🏠25 Evans Way
🚇MFA 🕐11am–5pm Wed–Mon (to 9pm Thu) 🚫Jan 1, Thanksgiving, Dec 25
🌐gardnermuseum.org

The only thing more surprising than a Venetian *palazzo* on The Fenway is the collection of more than 2,500 works of art inside. Advised by scholar Bernard Berenson, the strong-willed Isabella Stewart Gardner turned her wealth to collecting art in the late 19th century, acquiring a notable collection of Old Masters and Italian Renaissance pieces. Titian's *Rape of Europa*, for example, is considered his best painting in a US museum. The eccentric "Mrs. Jack" had an eye for her contemporaries as well; she purchased the first Matisse to enter an American collection. The works are displayed on three levels around a stunning skylit courtyard. Mrs. Gardner's will stipulated that the collection should remain assembled as

she originally intended. Her intentions were thwarted in 1990, when thieves stole 13 priceless works, including a rare Rembrandt seascape. On a more positive note, a wing designed by the Italian architect Renzo Piano opened in 2012 with gallery space and a performance hall for Gardner's concert series.

Berklee Performance Center

📍F8 🏠136 Massachusetts Ave 🚇Hynes Convention Center 🕐For concerts, check website for details
🌐berklee.edu/bpc

The largest independent music college in the world, Berklee College of Music has produced a number of jazz, rock, and pop stars, including producer and arranger Quincy Jones, Dixie Chicks singer Natalie Maines, and jazz-pop pianist/vocalist Diana Krall.

Berklee students and faculty frequently use the Berklee Performance Center

as a showcase. Many concerts are free or low-priced. The warm acoustics and intimate relationship between the performers and the audience produce what is known among audiophiles as "the Berklee sound."

Boylston Street

📍G8 🚇Boylston, Arlington, Copley, Hynes Convention Center

The corners of Boylston and Berkeley streets represent Boston architecture at its finest and most diverse. The stately French Academic-style structure on the west side was erected for the Museum of Natural History, a forerunner of the Museum of Science *(p148)*. It has gone on to house upscale shops and restaurants. The east side spouts a Robert A. M. Stern tower and a Philip Johnson office building that resembles a table radio. Boston jeweler Shreve, Crump & Low occupied the Art Deco building at the corner of

Berklee students and faculty frequently use the Berklee Performance Center as a showcase, and often as a venue for making live recordings.

→

The Neo-Classical facade of Symphony Hall, home of the Boston Symphony

Arlington Street until they decided to relocate to nearby Newbury Street in 2012.

The soaring central tower of the Prudential Tower and Shopping Center greatly dominates the skyline on upper Boylston Street. Adjoining the Prudential is the Hynes Convention Center. It was significantly enlarged in 1988 to accommodate the city's burgeoning business in hosting conventions.

Boylston Street is also home to memorials marking the location of the horrific 2013 Boston Marathon bombings, which killed three and injured hundreds.

The Italian-Gothic-style **New Old South Church**, which is located at the corner of Dartmouth, was built in 1874–5 by the congregation that had met previously at the Old South Meeting House (p115).

New Old South Church
📍 645 Boylston St 🕐 8am-7pm Mon-Fri, 10am-4pm Sat, 8:30am-7pm Sun 🌐 oldsouth.org

---

Huntington Theatre

📍 G9 📍 264 Huntington Ave 🚇 Symphony 🌐 huntingtontheatre.org

An anchor on Boston's "Avenue of the Arts," the company here presents a mix of updated classic plays and new work by established and emerging playwrights. A number of productions have moved to Broadway or Off Broadway. In addition to the approximately 900-seat Huntington Avenue Theatre, the company also performs at two smaller stages in the Calderwood Pavilion at the Boston Center for the Arts. These intimate spaces are well suited to developing new work.

Symphony Hall

📍 G9 📍 301 Massachusetts Ave 🚇 Symphony 🌐 bso.org

Not quite two decades after the founding of the Boston Symphony Orchestra, Symphony Hall opened in 1900. Architects McKim, Mead & White designed a stately Neoclassical home for the orchestra, complete with replicas of Greek and Roman statues in a series of niches. But the architects' greatest achievement was to engage Harvard physics professor Wallace Clement Sabine to apply scientific principles of acoustics to the design of the auditorium, making it one of the world's top concert halls.

Did You Know?

The Gardner Museum still offers $10 million for information leading to the recovery of its stolen artworks.

In addition to the acclaimed orchestra, the Boston Pops also performs light classical and popular music.

Jordan Hall

📍 G9 📍 30 Gainsborough St 🚇 Symphony 🌐 necmusic.edu/jordan-hall

Opened in 1903 and noted for its fine and resonant acoustics, Jordan Hall is the primary performance venue for the students and faculty of the New England Conservatory. It also presents concerts by visiting soloists and ensembles. The conservatory was founded in 1867 and is the oldest independent music school in the United States, with an emphasis on training in classical music, jazz, and contemporary improvisation. The conservatory presents almost 600 concerts per year, often featuring students and faculty, and many of which are free.

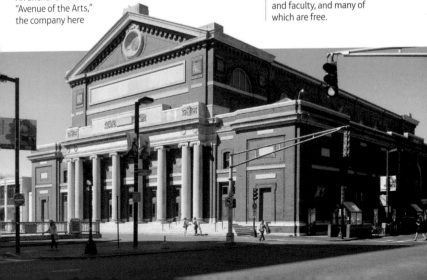

DRINK

Stoked by the crowds of Fenway Park baseball fans and the presence of college students at nearby Boston University, Lansdowne Street is renowned for its buzzy strip of bars and clubs. Check out these local hangouts for a guaranteed great night in the city.

Bill's Bar

Q E8 **A** 5 Lansdowne St **O** 5pm-2am daily **W** billsbarboston.com

Lansdowne Pub

Q E8 **A** 9 Lansdowne St **O** 4pm-2am Mon-Fri, 11am-2am Sat & Sun **W** lansdownepub boston.com

House of Blues

Q E8 **A** 15 Lansdowne St **O** 4-10pm daily **W** houseofblues. com/boston

---

Back Bay Fens

Q G9 **T** Kenmore

Located west of Kenmore Square, the Fens is a sprawling parkland that forms an integral connector to the chain of parks known as the Emerald Necklace, as laid out by Frederick Law Olmsted at the end of the 19th century. Part urban wilderness and part freshwater lagoon, the Back Bay Fens link Kenmore Square and the Fenway neighborhood to such institutions as the Isabella Stewart Gardner Museum (p138) and the Boston Museum of Fine Arts (p132). Several handsome bridges of uncut stone and arching masonry, designed by the architect of Trinity Church, dot the length of the park, and its pathways are popular with joggers and cyclists. The Fenway Victory Gardens are the only remaining continuously operating World War II victory gardens in the US, while the charming Kelleher Rose Garden sits opposite the Museum of Fine Arts. Because the Fens are remote and poorly lit, the area is best frequented by daylight.

Fenway Park

Q E8 **A** 4 Jersey St **T** Kenmore **O** Through the year, check website for event details **W** redsox.com

Whatever their loyalties, sports fans from all over the world flock to this civic icon, the home of the wildly popular Boston Red Sox. Opened in 1912, this is the oldest Major League baseball park still standing and a shrine to the national pastime.

Tickets to games during the baseball season (April to October) can be hard to come by, but one-hour tours are offered daily throughout the

---

 INSIDER TIP
Fenway Tours

Behind-the-scenes tours of Fenway Park Stadium, America's best-loved ballpark, run on the hour from 9am–5pm every day (www. mlb.com/redsox/ ballpark/tours). On game days the last tour departs three hours before the game begins.

year. Knowledgeable tour guides provide visitors with a behind-the-scenes look at the park's many intricacies, including a stop atop the fabled Green Monster, a towering wall that stands 37 ft (11 m) above left-field, originally built to prevent non-ticket-holders from getting a glimpse of the action. The venue has also become a popular summertime concert space, hosting big-name acts such as Bruce Springsteen and The Rolling Stones.

↑ The Citgo sign illuminating Kenmore Square as the sun begins to set

Kenmore Square

◎E8 ⓣKenmore

Known as a launching pad for psychedelic music in the 1960s and punk in the 1970s, Kenmore Square is not quite the Wild West of Boston nightlife that it once was. The last vestige of the seminal music scene survives at the nearby Paradise Rock Club, set farther west on Commonwealth Avenue (p135).

In its more grown-up phase, Kenmore still serves as the nexus of the B, C, and D branches of the MBTA's

Green Line, and forms a busy intersection for several main avenues.

Before and after Boston Red Sox home games, the square is so crowded that walking can be difficult, as Kenmore is the closest stop to the ever-popular Fenway Park. Kenmore Square is also home to Boston University and its 33,000 students. Their presence helps support a plethora of casual restaurants and pizza joints. Pedestrians can find Kenmore at night from miles away, as its highest point is a gigantic, animated Citgo sign, a somewhat surprising city landmark since 1965. Its original neon tubes have been replaced with energy-efficient LEDs.

22
Massachusetts College of Art and Design

◎E10 ⓐ621 Huntington Ave ⓣLongwood ◑noon-6pm Wed-Fri (to 8pm Thu), 10am-6pm Sat & Sun ⓦmassart.edu

The only free-standing publicly funded art school in the US, the Massachusetts

College of Art and Design has played an important role in Boston art and commerce since its founding in 1873. Its free MassArt Art Museum features brilliant exhibitions of contemporary art by well-known artists as well as by emerging figures. A fixture on Boston's excellent contemporary art scene since the late 20th century, the 8,000-sq-ft (743-sq-m), three-floor gallery space underwent a $12.6 million renovation in 2020.

BOSTON'S EMERALD NECKLACE

Best known as designer of New York's Central Park, Frederick Law Olmsted based himself in Boston, where he created parks to solve environmental problems and provide a green refuge for inhabitants of the 19th-century industrial city. The Emerald Necklace includes the green spaces of Boston Common and the Public Garden and Commonwealth Avenue. To create a 5-mile (8-km) ring of parks, Olmsted added the Back Bay Fens, Jamaica Pond, the rustic Riverway, Arnold Arboretum, and Franklin Park.

←

Baseball fans packing the stands on a sunny day in Fenway Park

A SHORT WALK
BACK BAY

Distance 1.5 miles (2.5 km) **Time** 20 minutes
Nearest subway Copley

Traverse this fashionable district as it unfolds westward from the Public Garden (p80) in a grid that departs from the twisting streets found elsewhere in Boston. Commonwealth Avenue, with its grand 19th-century mansions and parkland, and Newbury and Boylston Streets are its main arteries. Newbury Street is a magnet for all of Boston wanting to indulge in some upscale shopping, whereas the more somber Boylston Street bustles with office workers. Copley Square anchors the entire area and is the site of Henry Hobson Richardson's magnificent Trinity Church (p130) and the 60-story 200 Clarendon Tower (p137), which is the tallest building in New England.

↑ Studying in the grand McKim Building at Boston Public Library

Did You Know?

The architect of 200 Clarendon sited the glass tower to reflect and defer to Trinity Church.

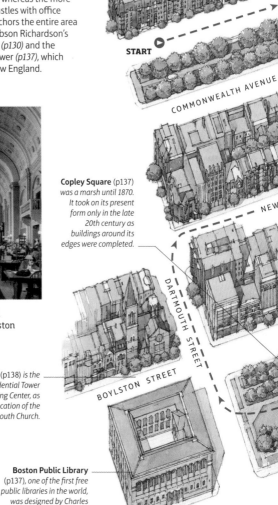

START

COMMONWEALTH AVENUE

NEWE

Copley Square (p137) *was a marsh until 1870. It took on its present form only in the late 20th century as buildings around its edges were completed.*

DARTMOUTH STREET

Boylston Street (p138) *is the site of the Prudential Tower and Shopping Center, as well as the location of the New Old South Church.*

BOYLSTON STREET

Boston Public Library (p137), *one of the first free public libraries in the world, was designed by Charles McKim. Inside are murals by John Singer Sargent.*

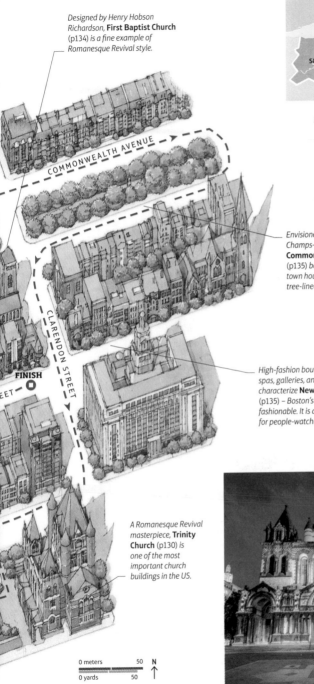

Designed by Henry Hobson Richardson, **First Baptist Church** (p134) *is a fine example of Romanesque Revival style.*

Envisioned as Boston's Champs-Elysées, **Commonwealth Avenue** (p135) *boasts beautiful town houses and a tree-lined central mall.*

High-fashion boutiques, day spas, galleries, and restaurants characterize **Newbury Street** (p135) – *Boston's most fashionable. It is a great place for people-watching.*

FINISH

A Romanesque Revival masterpiece, **Trinity Church** (p130) *is one of the most important church buildings in the US.*

0 meters 50
0 yards 50
N ↑

↑ The monumental façade of Trinity Church lit up at night

CAMBRIDGE

West of central Boston, across the Charles River, lies Cambridge, a city in its own right and home to Harvard University and the Massachusetts Institute of Technology. The leftist bent of its residents earns it the nickname of the "People's Republic of Cambridge," and Cantabrigians often joke that their city is Boston's younger, smarter sister. Founded in 1631, it began to assume its modern character only five years later, when Harvard College was founded in what was then called Newtowne. When the Massachusetts Institute of Technology (MIT) moved to the Cambridge banks of the Charles River in 1916, it cemented the city's position as a college town *par excellence*. Between them, the two universities continue to drive the intellectual, social, and economic life of Cambridge. Harvard Square has the city's historic attractions – Christ Church, Cambridge Common, and the Longfellow House. It is also the city's primary entertainment and shopping district. The explosive 21st-century growth of biotech, information-technology, and robotics companies near MIT, however, has made Kendall Square its hipper, younger rival. Central Square retains the city's working-class roots with a feisty live music scene.

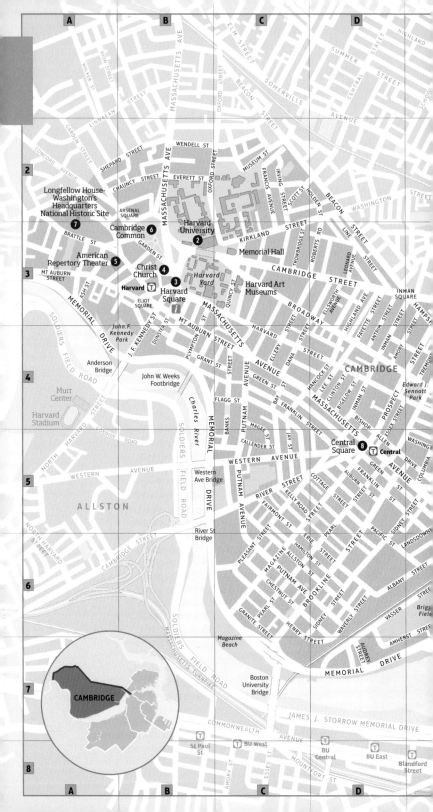

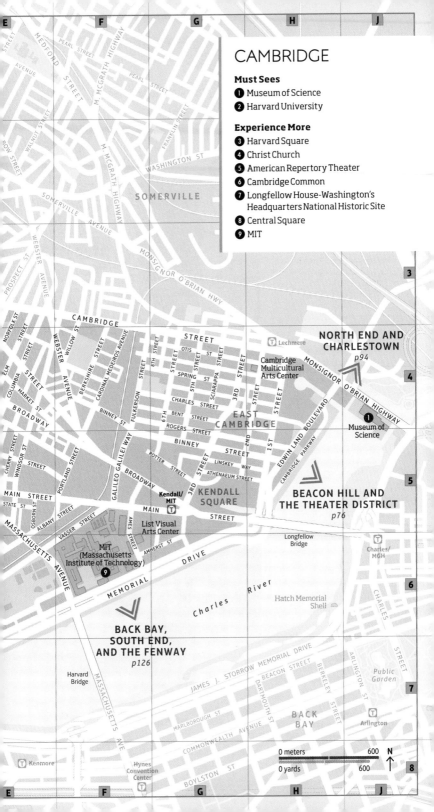

CAMBRIDGE

Must Sees
1 Museum of Science
2 Harvard University

Experience More
3 Harvard Square
4 Christ Church
5 American Repertory Theater
6 Cambridge Common
7 Longfellow House-Washington's Headquarters National Historic Site
8 Central Square
9 MIT

UNMISSABLE EXHIBITS

Hall of Human Life

At the newest and most popular exhibit in the Science Park, visitors are given a barcode wristband that records responses to various challenges and activities. Cutting-edge subjects are explored, such as DNA sequencing, GMO research, and all sorts of medical and nutritional science.

Mugar Omni Theater

This five-story IMAX® theater takes the concept of the "big-screen" to a whole new level. Sit below a 180-degree dome that fills your entire range of vision with spect-acular moving images.

Charles Hayden Planetarium

This notable high-tech planetarium brings the dazzling night sky to life, and presents daily shows about stars, planets, and other celestial phenomena.

To the Moon

Climb into the pilots' seats of replica Apollo Command Module and Lunar Module cockpits to relive the first moon landing. Nearby models show the growth of space stations from Skylab and Mir to the International Space Station.

Theater of Electricity

This live theater show explores the science of electricity. Its star is the world's largest air-insulated Van de Graaff generator, which safely zaps out sizzling lightning bolts of up to 1 million volts.

Did You Know?

The MOS opened in 1864, making it one of the oldest science museums in the US.

Archimedean Excogitation, an audio-kinetic sculpture by George Rhoads ↑

❶ 🔧 💻 🛍️

MUSEUM OF SCIENCE

📍J4 🚇Science Park 🚉Science Park 🕐9am–5pm Mon–Thu & Sat–Sun (Jul–early Sep: to 7pm), 9am–9pm Fri
🚫Thanksgiving, Dec 25 🌐mos.org

With over 700 interactive displays designed to thrill and amaze, it's little wonder that this is Boston's most-visited museum. Popular attractions include a jaw-dropping IMAX® screen, the Hall of Human Life, lightning demonstrations, and live science shows.

The Museum of Science straddles the Charles River atop the inactive flood control dam that sits at the mouth of the Charles River. The museum itself was built in 1951, but the Science Park has taken shape around it since, virtually obscuring the dam structure with theater and planetarium buildings.

With colorful, interactive exhibits covering natural history, medicine, astronomy, computing, and the wonders of the physical sciences, the Museum of Science is largely oriented to families. The Mugar Omni Theater contains a five-story domed screen with a multi-dimensional wrap-around sound system, and shows mostly films with a natural-science theme. The Charles Hayden Planetarium offers laser displays and shows about stars, planets, and other celestial phenomena, ranging from exhibitions on NASA's latest space missions, to a kid-themed exploration of the stars with Sesame Street's Big Bird and Elmo.

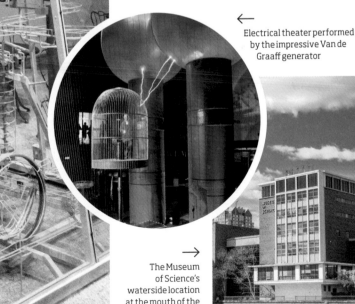

← Electrical theater performed by the impressive Van de Graaff generator

→ The Museum of Science's waterside location at the mouth of the Charles River

2

HARVARD UNIVERSITY

 D5 Harvard 1350 Massachusetts Ave; (617) 495-1573; www.harvard.edu

The country's oldest and arguably greatest institution of higher learning, Harvard has touched every corner of American cultural, political, professional, and business life. Eight American presidents – most recently Barack Obama and George W. Bush – and the heads of state of another 18 nations, as well as 48 Nobel laureates, and 44 winners of the Pulitzer Prize number among its faculty and alumni.

the surrounding community Cambridge after the English city in which they had been educated. Harvard University is now one of the world's most prestigious centers of learning, and it has expanded to encompass more than 400 buildings that sprawl throughout Cambridge and the Boston Metropolitan area. Historic Harvard Yard, however, remains at its heart.

INSIDER TIP
Free Tours
Free walking tours through the university campus depart from the Smith Campus Center on Massachusetts Ave. Tours last around an hour, providing a detailed history of the university and the local area, as well as a unique insight into student life.

1

Harvard Yard

 Massachusetts Ave
 24 hours

In 1636 Boston's Puritan leaders founded a college in Newtowne. Two years later cleric John Harvard died and bequeathed half his estate and all his books to the fledgling college. The colony's leaders bestowed his name on the school and re-christened

↑ Harvard Yard's red-brick buildings, surrounded by beautiful fall foliage

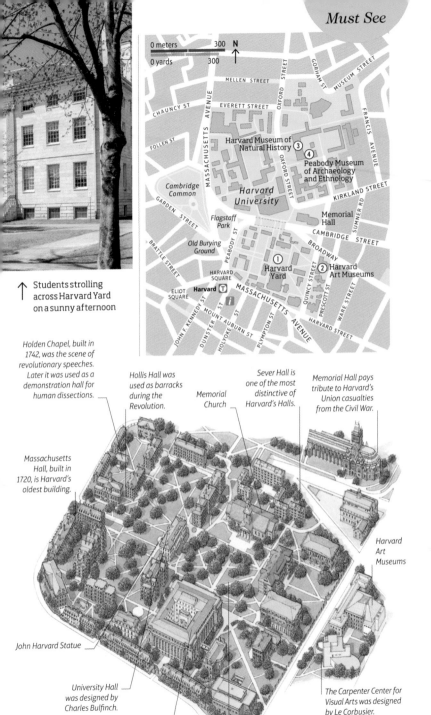

Students strolling across Harvard Yard on a sunny afternoon

0 meters 300
0 yards 300
N

MELLEN STREET
CHAUNCY ST
EVERETT STREET
FOLLEN ST
OXFORD STREET
GORHAM ST
MUSEUM STREET
MASSACHUSETTS AVENUE

Harvard Museum of Natural History ③
④ Peabody Museum of Archaeology and Ethnology

Harvard University

FRANCIS AVENUE

KIRKLAND STREET

Cambridge Common

GARDEN STREET

Flagstaff Park

Old Burying Ground

BRATTLE STREET

PEABODY ST

Memorial Hall

SUMNER RD

CAMBRIDGE STREET

BROADWAY

HARVARD SQUARE

① Harvard Yard

② Harvard Art Museums

QUINCY STREET

PRESCOTT ST

WARE STREET

ELIOT SQUARE

Harvard ⓣ

ℹ

MASSACHUSETTS AVENUE

HARVARD STREET

JOHN F. KENNEDY ST

DUNSTER ST

MOUNT AUBURN ST

HOLYOKE ST

PLYMPTON ST

Holden Chapel, built in 1742, was the scene of revolutionary speeches. Later it was used as a demonstration hall for human dissections.

Hollis Hall was used as barracks during the Revolution.

Memorial Church

Sever Hall is one of the most distinctive of Harvard's Halls.

Memorial Hall pays tribute to Harvard's Union casualties from the Civil War.

Massachusetts Hall, built in 1720, is Harvard's oldest building.

Harvard Art Museums

John Harvard Statue

University Hall was designed by Charles Bulfinch.

The Widener Library, named for Harry Elkins Widener, who died on the Titanic in 1912, is the world's largest university library.

Tercentenary Theater

The Carpenter Center for Visual Arts was designed by Le Corbusier.

Historic Harvard Yard, Harvard University's oldest campus

②   Harvard Art Museums

🏠 32 Quincy St ⏰ 10am–5pm daily 🚫 Public hols 🌐 harvardartmuseums.org

With works of art ranging from the ancient world to the present day, the Fogg Art, Busch-Reisinger, and Arthur M. Sackler museums occupy a state-of-the-art, eco-friendly complex designed by the Italian architect Renzo Piano. Collections from all three institutions are included in a single admission.

A good place to start is the Lightbox Gallery on the top level of the complex, where visitors can explore the collections digitally. This glass-walled space overlooks the courtyard below and allows visitors to glimpse into the labs of the Straus Center for Conservation and Technical Studies, a training ground for fine arts conservation and research.

Beneath the Lightbox on Level 4, the Art Study Center offers students and members of the public the chance to examine original works of art from the

collections. This service is available by appointment only. Lectures, workshops, films, and special events are held throughout the year. On the third floor, three fantastic gallery spaces are dedicated to rotating installations. Adjacent, the special exhibitions gallery space tends to be the busiest in the museum.

The Fogg Art Museum was created in 1895, when Harvard began to build its own art collection. Today it includes extensive holdings of European and American paintings, sculpture, decorative arts, and works on paper from the Post-Classical period to the present day, including works by Bernini, Renoir, Degas, and several masterpieces by John Singleton Copley.

Founded in 1903 as Harvard's Germanic Museum, the superb Busch-Reisinger collections focus on German and Nordic art as well as design from after 1880, with an emphasis on German Expressionism.

Named for a famous philanthropist, physician, and art collector, the Arthur M. Sackler Museum is home to Harvard's collection of ancient, Asian, Islamic, and late Indian art. Located on the first, second, and third floors, the Sackler Museum holds a world-renowned collection of archaic Chinese jades, ritual vessels, and weapons, Chinese and Korean Buddhist sculpture and ceramics, vases, bronzes, and coins from Greece, Rome, Egypt, and the Near East, as well as objects from ancient Mediterranean and Byzantine civilizations. Galleries on the second

← Clay Bodhisattva on display in the Sackler Museum, found in the Mogao complex at Dunhuang

ACKNOWLEDGING THE PAST

In 2017, Harvard Law marked its bicentennial by dedicating a plaque to honor the enslaved whose labor created the wealth on which the school was founded. "May we pursue the highest ideals of law and justice in their memory," it reads. Harvard is one of many universities – including Columbia, Georgetown, and Brown – struggling with historical ties to the trade of enslaved people.

floor hold the Sackler's collections from Islamic lands and India. They include a range of paintings, drawings, calligraphy, and manuscript illustrations from the 8th to the 19th centuries.

③   Harvard Museum of Natural History

🏠 26 Oxford St ⏰ 9am–5pm daily 🚫 Public hols 🌐 hmnh.harvard.edu

The imposing Harvard Museum of Natural History is actually three brilliant museums rolled into one: the Mineralogical and Geological Museum, the Museum of Comparative Zoology, and the Herbaria.

The mineralogical galleries include some of Harvard University's oldest specimen collections, dating from 1783. The zoological galleries date from 1859, the same year Darwin published *On the Origin of Species*. They include the personal arachnid collection of the founder, along with dinosaur skeletons and taxidermied bird, reptile, and mammal specimens. Children are fascinated by the giant kronosaurus (a type of prehistoric sea serpent) and

↑ Blaschka glass flowers at the Harvard Museum of Natural History

Did You Know?

The John Harvard statue is actually modeled on a Harvard student from the class of 1882.

the skeleton of the first triceratops ever described in scientific literature.

The collections in the botanical galleries include the Ware Collection of Blaschka Glass Models of Plants, popularly known as the "glass flowers." Between 1886 and

↑ Totem pole at Peabody Museum's Hall of the North American Indian

1936, father and son artisans Leopold and Rudolph Blaschka created these 4,300 exacting models of 780 plant species, prized for their beauty as well as their scientific utility.

Peabody Museum of Archaeology and Ethnology

🏛 11 Divinity Ave ⏰ 9am–5pm daily 🌐 peabody.harvard.edu

Founded in 1866, the Peabody Museum of Archaeology and Ethnology houses several million artifacts and more than 500,000 photographic images, from all around the world. The Peabody remains, to this day, a world-leading research facility.

The Hall of the North American Indian on the ground level displays totem carvings by Pacific Northwest nations and a wide range of Navajo weavings. The third floor is devoted to Central American anthropology, with casts of some of the ruins uncovered at Copán in Honduras and Chichen Itza in Mexico. The fourth floor exhibit, "All the World is Here," recounts the early history of

the museum collections and the birth of American anthropology through more than 600 artifacts from Asia, Oceania, and the Americas.

TOP 5 HARVARD DROPOUTS

Matt Damon
Academy Award-winning actor, screenwriter, and producer.

Bill Gates
Microsoft co-founder, philanthropist, and one of the richest people in the world.

Frank Gehry
Pioneering architect, and Pritzker Architecture Prize recipient.

Bonnie Raitt
Blues revivalist singer, guitarist, songwriter, and recipient of 10 Grammy Awards.

Mark Zuckerberg
Tech genius who launched Facebook from his dorm to become one of the world's youngest billionaires.

EXPERIENCE MORE

3

Harvard Square

📍B3 🚇Harvard
🌐harvardsquare.com

Even Bostonians think of Harvard Square as the heart of Cambridge; the square was the original site of Cambridge from around 1630, and many of the streets laid out during the 17th century are still in use today. Dominating the square is the Harvard Cooperative Society ("the Coop"), a local institution that sells inexpensive clothes, posters, and books. The square has long been linked to the printed word, and is still home to a high concentration of book stores.

Harvard's large student population is also very much in evidence here, adding color to the character of the square. Many trendy boutiques, inexpensive restaurants, and friendly cafés cater to their needs. Street performers abound, especially on the weekends, and the square has long been a place where pop trends begin. Club Passim, for example, has incubated many successful singer-songwriters since Joan Baez first debuted here in 1959.

4

Christ Church

📍B3 🏠Garden St
🚇Harvard 🕐8am–5pm
Mon–Fri & Sun, 8am–3pm
Sat 🌐cccambridge.org

With its square bell tower and plain, gray, shingled edifice, Christ Church is a restrained example of an Anglican church. Designed in 1759 by Peter Harrison, the architect of Boston's King's Chapel (p114), Christ Church came in for rough treatment as a barracks for Continental Army troops in 1775 – British loyalists had almost all fled Cambridge by this time. The army even melted down the organ pipes to cast musket balls. The church was restored for services on New Year's Eve in 1775, when George Washington and his wife, Martha, were among the worshipers. Anti-Anglican sentiment remained strong in Cambridge, and Christ Church did not have its own rector again until the 19th century. Famously, Theodore Roosevelt taught a Sunday School here.

↑ The stark, gray facade of the 18th-century Christ Church

5

American Repertory Theater

📍A3 🏠Loeb Drama Center: 64 Brattle St; Oberon: 2 Arrow St 🚇Harvard
🕐Times vary, check website
🌐americanrepertory theater.org

The American Repertory Theater (ART) in Cambridge presents the most groundbreaking theatrical work in

↑ Harvard Square, lit by the low glow of evening streetlamps

↑ Cambridge Common, the city's popular park, ablaze with spectacular fall foliage

Greater Boston, and audience members delight in debating the merits of each production. Founded in 1980, the ART is located on the grounds of Harvard University and works closely with the university in nurturing new talent in acting, directing, and other theater disciplines. ART also collaborates with innovative artists from around the world to create new work. Under artistic director Diane Paulus, the company has received several Tony Awards, a Pulitzer Prize and other awards for both new plays and musical revivals. In addition to the main stage in the Loeb Drama Center, the ART develops new artists and performance projects in the club-like atmosphere of its second stage, Oberon, where there is a full on-site bar. Here you might see tap-dancers, poets, or burlesque artists, who constantly strive to stretch theatrical boundaries.

 6

Cambridge Common

📍 B3 🚇 Harvard

Set aside as common pasture and military drill ground in 1631, Cambridge Common has served as a center for religious, social, and political activity ever since. George Washington took command of the Continental Army here on July 3, 1775, beneath the Washington Elm, now marked by a stone. The common served as the army's encampment from 1775 to 1776. Dawes Island, a memorial at the south end of the site, commemorates William Dawes, the less famous colleague of Paul Revere who rode through Cambridge to warn of the British advance.

In 1997 the first monument in the US to commemorate the victims of the Irish Famine was unveiled on the common.

The common is also a major city park as well as a historic landmark. At its north end stands an excellent children's playground. Within it there is a Viking ship structure, complete with sand-and-water play, and a climbing web to be scaled.

 7

Longfellow House-Washington's Headquarters National Historic Site

📍 A3 🏠 105 Brattle St 🚇 Harvard 🕐 Jun-Oct: 9:30am-5pm 🌐 nps.gov/long

This house on Brattle Street, like many around it, was built by Colonial-era merchants loyal to the British Crown during the Revolution. It was seized by American revolutionaries and served as George Washington's headquarters during the Siege of Boston. The poet Henry Wadsworth Longfellow boarded here in 1837, was given the house as a wedding present in 1843, and lived here until his death in 1882. He wrote his most famous poems here, including "Tales of a Wayside Inn" and "The Song of Hiawatha." Longfellow's status as literary dean of Boston meant that Nathaniel Hawthorne and Charles Sumner, among others, were regular visitors.

TOP 4 BOOKSTORES OF HARVARD SQUARE

Grolier Poetry Book Shop
This institution has been a fixture in Cambridge literary life since 1927.

Raven Used Books
Head here for scholarly and literary titles.

The Million Year Picnic
Graphic novels and comic books line the shelves at this local favorite.

Harvard Book Store
Look no further than this eponymous store for an extensive selection of new releases, used books, and remainders.

Did You Know?

Harvard Bridge is measured in "Smoots," a unit equal to the height of 1950s MIT student Oliver R. Smoot.

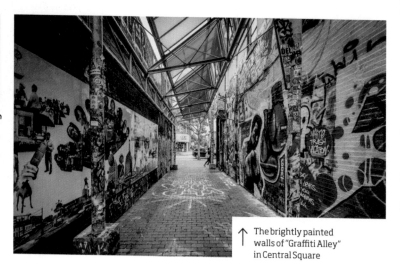

↑ The brightly painted walls of "Graffiti Alley" in Central Square

Central Square

📍D5 🚇Central

Located on Massachusetts Avenue midway between Harvard and MIT, Central Square embraces the diverse cultures and interests of Cambridge with a variety of ethnic restaurants and stores, a large Asian grocery with an adjoining French pastry shop, a couple of art supply stores, and a seasonal farmers' market. The most colorful feature in the square is the so-called "Graffiti Alley," an 80-foot (24-m) wall where artists are encouraged to express themselves across an ever-changing display of bold graffiti. The whole square, in fact, has a strong artistic vibe. The funky performance

spaces at the Middle East Restaurant and Nightclub are legendary venues for indie rock, with a reputation as incubators for local talent and top stops for touring bands. The nearby Dance Complex offers classes for recreational and professional dancers, studio space for dance companies and choreographers, and has a robust calendar of performances.

MIT

📍F6 🏛77 Massachusetts Ave 🚇Kendall, Central 🌐mit.edu

The wellspring of some of the last half-century's most mind-boggling advances in computer hardware and software, gaming technology, robotics, biotech, and internet platforms, the Massachusetts Institute of Technology (MIT) was chartered in 1861 to teach "exactly and thoroughly the fundamental principles of positive science with

application to the industrial arts." The institute has since evolved into one of the world's leading universities in engineering and the sciences, and is a pioneer in commercializing scientific advances.

Several architectural masterpieces dot MIT's 135-acre (55-ha) campus, which sits on the banks of the Charles River. These include architect Eero Saarinen's Kresge Auditorium and the MIT Chapel, built in 1955.

 INSIDER TIP
Float Tour

The city of Boston takes on a new aspect when viewed from the Charles River aboard a rental canoe, kayak, or paddleboard. Guided evening paddles *(www. paddleboston.com)* are also available.

→ Students strolling across the grass-edged paths of MIT's main campus

The Stata Center, designed by the Toronto-born architect Frank Gehry, features radical geometry with its walls-akimbo random curves and angles. The ground floor houses a semi-permanent exhibition of past "hacks" (practical jokes) played by MIT students, including a fire hose drinking fountain and a full size replica of the police car once placed atop the dome of the Rogers Building.

The Wiesner Building is a major collaboration between architect I. M. Pei and several artists, including the American abstract painter Kenneth Noland, whose relief mural "Here-There" dominates the atrium. The building houses the **List Visual Arts Center**, which is the university's contemporary art museum. Originally named the Hayden Gallery, it was established in 1950 and is a champion of avant-garde art from around the world – especially art with a technological twist. Alongside its permanent collection, the gallery presents a number of special exhibitions annually.

MIT PUBLIC ART COLLECTION

Almost 25 outdoor sculptures by major contemporary artists dot the campus of the Massachusetts Institute of Technology. The school welcomes visitors to wander the grounds and reflect on the issues of science and society that the works explore. There is an interactive public art map available on www.listart.mit.edu, or www.listart. oncell.com offers a self-guided campus tour introduced by late Boston native and Star Trek star Leonard Nimoy.

The **Hart Nautical Gallery** in the Pratt School focuses on marine engineering, with exhibits ranging from models of ships to exhibits of the latest advances in underwater research. It is a division of the extremely popular **MIT Museum**, which blends art and science with exhibits such as Harold Edgerton's ground-breaking stroboscopic flash photographs and the latest holographic art.

List Visual Arts Center
🏠 20 Ames St ⏰ Noon-6pm Tue-Sun (to 8pm Thu) 🌐 listart.mit.edu

Hart Nautical Gallery
♿ 🏠 Building 5, 55 Massachusetts Ave 📞 (617) 253-5942 ⏰ 10am-5pm daily

MIT Museum
🏠 314 Main St ⏰ Until summer 2022; check website 🌐 mitmuseum.mit.edu

> **Several architectural masterpieces dot MIT's 135-acre (55-ha) campus, which sits on the banks of the Charles River.**

EXPERIENCE
NEW ENGLAND

Squam Lake, New Hampshire

MASSACHUSETTS

The area now known as Massachusetts has been inhabited since the retreat of the glacial ice sheet around 11,000 years ago. About a dozen distinct nations of people dominated the area, with the Massachusett and Wampanoag being the most prominent along the coast, and the Mahican from the Connecticut River westward. These coastal villages were decimated in what the Wampanoag called the "Great Dying," the 1616–19 epidemic that began with French contact in Maine and spread along trade routes. Indigenous populations abandoned entire villages, especially along the coast, setting the scene for European settlement.

In 1620, Pilgrims sailing to the Virginia Colony were blown off course and forced to land farther north at Plymouth, where they established the first permanent English settlement in North America. Further settlement by a group of Puritan entrepreneurs quickly followed. For all their Englishness, this second group named the bay between Cape Cod and the mainland after the coastal Massachusett Nation, and took the bay's name for their colony. The towns of Salem, Boston, and Plymouth became the beachhead from which the rest of New England was colonized.

Many of American's pivotal events have played out against the backdrop of Massachusetts. In the 18th century, it was here that the seeds of the American Revolution took root, forever altering the course of world history. The machinery of the American Industrial Revolution chugged to life in the early 19th century in Lowell and other mill towns. Later high-tech labs in Cambridge would help lead the nation into the digital age.

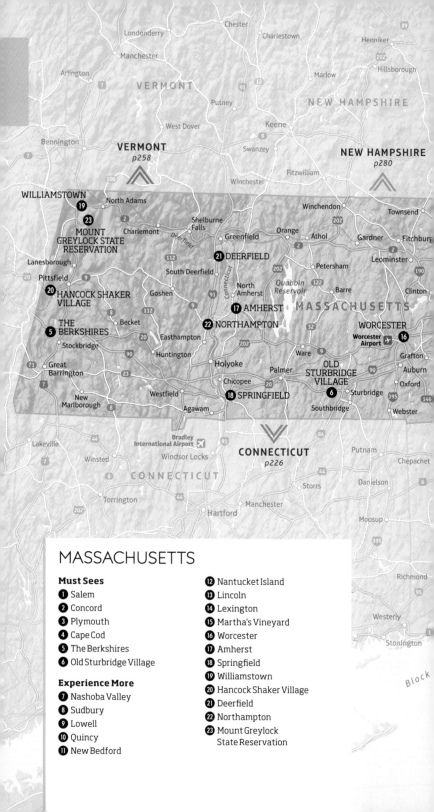

MASSACHUSETTS

Must Sees
1 Salem
2 Concord
3 Plymouth
4 Cape Cod
5 The Berkshires
6 Old Sturbridge Village

Experience More
7 Nashoba Valley
8 Sudbury
9 Lowell
10 Quincy
11 New Bedford
12 Nantucket Island
13 Lincoln
14 Lexington
15 Martha's Vineyard
16 Worcester
17 Amherst
18 Springfield
19 Williamstown
20 Hancock Shaker Village
21 Deerfield
22 Northampton
23 Mount Greylock State Reservation

Dover

York Beach

Concord

Suncook

Durham

Kittery

Goffstown

Manchester

Exeter

Portsmouth

Manchester-Boston
Regional Airport

Hampton

Derry

Amesbury

Nashua

Haverhill

Newburyport

Lawrence

Plum Island

Chelmsford

Andover

Ipswich

9 LOWELL

Topsfield

Essex

Rockport

Gloucester

Wilmington

Reading

Beverly

Manchester-by-the-Sea

NASHOBA
VALLEY

Woburn

SALEM **1**

7

CONCORD **2**

14 LEXINGTON

Marblehead

LINCOLN **13**

Malden

SUDBURY **8**

Boston

Massachusetts
Bay

Framingham

Brookline

Wellesley

10 QUINCY

Dedham

Weymouth

Medfield

Scituate

Randolph

Race
Point

Milford

Stoughton

Marshfield

Franklin

Brockton

Provincetown

Truro

Foxborough

Bridgewater

Kingston

Cape
Cod
National
Seashore

North Attleboro

3 PLYMOUTH

Wellfleet

Attleboro

Taunton

Middleboro

Eastham

RHODE
ISLAND
p204

Tremont

Buzzards
Bay

Cape Cod
Bay

Orleans

Providence

Wareham

Sandwich

CAPE COD

T.F. Green
Airport

Somerset

Bourne

Barnstable

4

Chatham

Warwick

Fall River

Barnstable
Municipal Airport

RHODE
ISLAND

NEW
BEDFORD **11**

Buzzards
Bay

Marshpee

Hyannis

South
Yarmouth

Harwich

Portsmouth

Westport

East Falmouth

Monomoy
Island

Newport

Woods
Hole

Falmouth

Nantucket
Sound

Wakefield

Sakonnet

Vineyard Haven

Oak Bluffs

Great
Point

Narragansett

Edgartown

NANTUCKET
ISLAND

Galilee

15

MARTHA'S
VINEYARD

12

Island Sound

Nantucket

Block
Island

Nantucket
Memorial Airport

Atlantic

Ocean

0 kilometers   20

N

0 miles   20

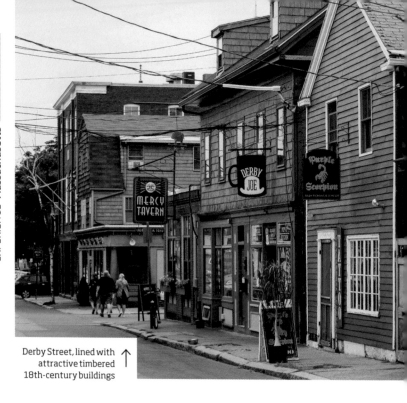

↑ Derby Street, lined with attractive timbered 18th-century buildings

①

SALEM

D5 ✈14 miles (22 km) S in Boston 🚆N in Boston 🚢Long Wharf, Boston ⓘ2 New Liberty St; www.salem.org

Known for its infamous witch trials, Salem has many other, less sensational claims to fame. Founded in 1626, it grew to become one of New England's busiest ports. Present-day Salem is a bustling, good-natured town that celebrates its rich artistic and architectural heritage, all the while playing up its popular image as the witchcraft capital of America.

①

Peabody Essex Museum

🏛East India Sq 🕐10am–5pm Tue–Sun 🌐pem.org

The dramatic soaring glass and brick building designed by Moshe Safdie allows the Peabody Essex galleries to display its collection of more than one million objects, including some of the world's largest holdings of Asian art and artifacts. Among the exhibits are treasures brought back from the Orient, the Pacific, and Africa by Salem's sea captains. Highlights include jewelry, porcelain figures, ritual costumes, scrimshaw, and figureheads. The museum also displays the only complete Qing Dynasty house outside China.

SALEM WITCH TRIALS

In 1692 Salem was swept by a wave of hysteria in which 200 citizens were accused of practicing witchcraft. In all, 150 people were jailed and 19 were executed as witches, while another man was crushed to death with stones. Not surprisingly, when the governor's wife became a suspect, the trials came to an abrupt end.

---

②

Salem Witch Trials Memorial

🏛Charter St 🕐Dawn–dusk

Located next to the old cemetery, this memorial, made up of granite stones, provides a place for quiet contemplation and public

③ 🗺️ 🏛️

Salem Witch Museum

📍 19 ½ Washington Sq N
🕐 10am–4:30pm daily (Jul, Aug, & Oct: extended hours) 🚫 Thanksgiving, Dec 24 & 25 🌐 salemwitch museum.com

Salem's most-visited sight commemorates the town's darkest hour. During the mass hysteria of 1692–93, neighbor turned on neighbor with accusations of practising witchcraft. No one was safe: two dogs were executed on the gallows for being witches. According to some, the author Nathaniel Hawthorne – who was profoundly disturbed by reports of the events – added a "w" to his last name in order to distance himself from other descendants of Judge Hathorne, the man who presided over the witch trials. Exhibits in the Gothic-style building trace the history of witches and witchcraft and evolving perceptions of witches up to the present day. The town capitalizes on its association with witches each year in October with one of the nation's largest and most colorful celebrations of Halloween.

💬 INSIDER TIP
Exploring Salem

Main attractions are situated in clusters in the harbor and downtown areas. The historic waterfront can easily be explored on foot, as can the busy area along Essex and Liberty streets.

↑ Salem Witch Museum, the town's most popular sight

acknowledgment of this tragic event in the area's local history. The memorial was dedicated by Nobel laureate Elie Wiesel in 1992 on the 300th anniversary of the Salem witch trials.

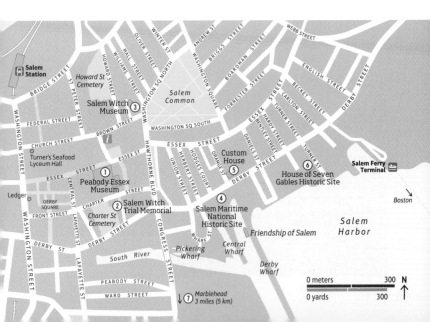

EXPERIENCE Massachusetts

④ 🤿 Ⓜ

Salem Maritime National Historic Site

📍160 Derby St
🕐10am–5pm daily (Nov–mid-May: to 4pm Wed–Sun) 🚫Jan 1, Thanksgiving, Dec 25 🌐nps.gov/sama

Salem's heyday as an important maritime center has been preserved here. At its peak, the town's harbor was serviced by around 50 wharves. Today this busy waterfront complex maintains three working wharves, including the Derby Wharf. The longest of the three, it, was begun in 1762 by wealthy merchant Richard Derby. *The Friendship of Salem*, a reconstruction of an East Indiaman sailing ship built in 1797, is moored here when it is not on tour during the summer.

The interior of the House of the Seven Gables, and *(inset)* the timber-framed exterior

⑤

Custom House

📍176 Derby St 🕐Same times as the Salem National Historic Site 🌐nps.gov/sama

The Federal-style Custom House (1819) was established to collect taxes on imports and now forms part of the Salem Maritime National Historic Site. In the 1840s author Nathaniel Hawthorne (1804–64) worked as a surveyor here. The impressive red-brick structure, with its high ceilings and elaborate furnishings, is described in Hawthorne's novel *The Scarlet Letter* (1850) and contains his office and desk at which he wrote. The building also houses exhibits on the work of the customs service and inspectors.

⑥ 🤿 Ⓜ 🏛

House of Seven Gables Historic Site

📍115 Derby St 🕐10am–5pm daily (Nov–mid-May: 10am–4pm Wed–Sun) 🚫1st two weeks in Jan, Thanksgiving, Dec 25 🌐7gables.org

Fans of author Nathaniel Hawthorne should make a pilgrimage to this 1668 house. The Salem-born writer was so taken with the Colonial-style

↑ Saugus Iron Works at Salem Maritime National Historic Site

home that he used it as the setting in his novel *The House of Seven Gables* (1851). As well as its famous seven steeply pitched gables, the house has a secret staircase. In addition, the site contains other early homes, including Hawthorne's birthplace, a gambrel-roofed 18th-century residence, which was moved from Union Street in 1958.

 7

Marblehead

🏠 3 miles (5 km) S of Salem

Just outside of town lies the area's most picturesque spot: Marblehead. When President George Washington visited the area, he said it had "the look of antiquity." This holds

Did You Know?

Witch trials weren't exclusive to Salem; they also took place in nearby Ipswich and Andover.

true to this day. Settled in 1629 and perched on a rocky peninsula, this village displays its heritage as a fisherman's enclave and a thriving port. Crisscrossed by hilly, twisting lanes, the historic district is graced with a wonderful mix of merchants' homes, shipbuilders' mansions, and fishermen's cottages. With more than 200 houses built before the Revolutionary War, and nearly 800 built during the 1800s, the district constitutes a fine catalog of American architecture. Included among the historic buildings is the spired **Abbot Hall**, the seat of local government, built in 1876, and where *The Spirit of '76* painting (1875) by Archibald Willard (1836–1918) hangs. Built in 1768 for a wealthy businessman, the **1768 Jeremiah Lee Mansion** has a sweeping entrance hall, mahogany woodwork, and superb wallpaper. A drive along the shoreline reveals the lighthouse at Point O'Neck (1835).

Abbot Hall

🏠 Washington Sq ☎ (781) 631-0528 ⏰ Call for hours

1768 Jeremiah Lee Mansion

♿♿ 🏠 161 Washington St ⏰ Jun–Oct: 10am–4pm Thu–Sat 🌐 marbleheadmuseum.org

EAT

Ledger
This place does creative twists on classic New England food and mixes inventive cocktails.

🏠 125 Washington St 🌐 ledgersalem.com

$$$

Turner's Seafood at Lyceum Hall
Seafood favorites served in a historic building with brick walls and high tin ceiling.

🏠 43 Church St 🌐 turners-seafood.com

$$$

 ❷

CONCORD

 C5 ✈ 20 miles (32 km) W in Boston ℹ 58 Main St; (978) 369-3120 🖥 concordchamberofcommerce.org

This small town was central to two important chapters in US history. The first was the Battle of Lexington and Concord on April 19, 1775, which signaled the beginning of the Revolutionary War. The second spanned several generations, as 19th-century Concord blossomed into the literary heart and soul of the US when many of the nation's leading authors and thinkers of the time lived here.

❶ Ⓜ

Minute Man National Historical Park

🖥 nps.gov/mima

This historic park preserves and tells the story of the American victory over at Concord. A militia of ordinary citizens known as Minute Men attacked British soldiers at North Bridge and sent them retreating back to their Boston. This so-called "shot heard round the world" set off the war. Learn more about the fight at the **North Bridge Visitor Center**, while the

Minute Man Visitor Center features a battle mural and a 22-minute multimedia show.

North Bridge Visitor Center

🏠 174 Liberty St 🕐 Apr–Oct 9:30am–5pm daily; Nov–Dec: 11am–3pm Tue–Sat

Minute Man Visitor Center

🏠 Rte 2A, Lincoln 🕐 Apr–Oct: 9am–5pm daily

→

The famous Minute Man statue by Daniel Chester French (1850–1931)

❷

Concord Museum

🏠 Jct of Lexington Rd & Cambridge Tpk 🕐 Jan–Mar: 11am–4pm Mon–Sat, 1–4pm Sun; Apr–Dec: 9am–5pm Mon–Sat, noon–5pm Sun
🖥 concordmuseum.org

The museum's eclectic holdings include decorative arts from the 17th, 18th, and 19th centuries, and the lantern that Paul Revere

↑ North Bridge, site of the opening battle in the Revolutionary War

ordered hung in the steeple of Old North Church to warn of the British advance (p100).

The Old Manse

☐ 269 Monument St ◷ Late Apr-Oct: noon-5pm Tue-Sun; Nov-late Apr: noon-5pm Sat & Sun ◻ thetrustees.org

The parsonage by the North Bridge was built in 1770 by the grandfather of writer Ralph Waldo Emerson (1803–82), who lived here briefly. The building's literary connections were cemented when author Nathaniel Hawthorne and his wife rented the house between 1842 and 1845.

Emerson House

☐ 28 Cambridge Tpk ☎ (978) 369-2236 ◷ Mid-Apr-late Oct: 10am-4:30pm Thu-Sat, 1-4:30pm Sun

Ralph Waldo Emerson lived in this house from 1835 until his death in 1882, writing essays, organizing lecture tours, and entertaining friends and admirers. Much of Emerson's furniture, writing, and family memorabilia is on display.

Walden Pond State Reservation

☐ 915 Walden St ◷ 8am-6:30pm daily ◻ mass.gov

Essayist Henry David Thoreau (1817–62) lived in relative isolation at Walden Pond from July 1845 to September 1847. During his stay, he compiled the material for his seminal work *Walden* (1854), in which he called for a return to simplicity in everyday life and respect for nature. Because of Thoreau's deep influence on future generations of environmentalists, Walden Pond is often considered to be the birthplace of the conservationist movement.

The pond is surrounded by 0.6 sq miles (1.5 sq km) of woodlands and is a popular spot for walking and fishing.

STAY

Concord's Colonial Inn

The 54 rooms in this town center hotel are divided between new and historic buildings.

☐ 48 Monument Sq ◻ concords colonialinn.com

$$⑤⑤⑤$

North Bridge Inn

This traditionally decorated bed and breakfast has six suites, and is just a short walk from the of North Bridge historic battle site.

☐ 21 Monument St ◻ northbridge inn.com

$$⑤⑤⑤$

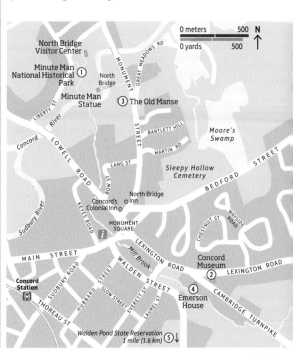

PLYMOUTH

 D6 40 miles (64 km) NW in Boston ⛴ To Provincetown (seasonal) 🛈 130 Water St; www.seeplymouth.com

In 1620, 102 English Pilgrims boarded the Mayflower and sailed into Plymouth harbor to establish what is considered to be the first permanent English settlement in the Americas. Today the town bustles with tourists exploring the sites of America's earliest days, including the fascinating Plimoth Patuxet Museums, an outdoor living-history museum 2.5 miles (4 km) from the center of town.

① The Mayflower

🅰 State Pier 📞 (508) 746-1622

The *Mayflower II*, a replica of the 17th-century sailing ship that carried the Pilgrims over from England, is moored by Plymouth Rock. At just 106 ft (32 m) in length, the vessel seems far too small to have made a transatlantic voyage.

Walking along the cramped deck, visitors will marvel at the Pilgrims' courage. Even after surviving the brutal crossing, many Pilgrims succumbed to illness and malnutrition during their first winter in Plymouth. Their remains are buried across the street on Coles Hill, which is fronted by a statue of Massasoit, the Wampanoag chief who allied himself with the newcomers and aided the survivors by teaching them the growing and use of native corn. It was with Massasoit and his people that the Pilgrims celebrated their first Thanksgiving.

Burial Hill at the head of the Town Square was the site of an early fort and the final resting place of many members of the original colony. The two churches descended from the Pilgrims stand side by side beneath the hill, heirs to a split over theology in the 19th century. Perched on a hilltop overlooking town, the 81-ft (25-m) National

 INSIDER TIP
By Foot or Trolley

Most of the sights can be accessed on foot by the Pilgrim Path. A seasonal sightseeing trolley connects sights and features a 40-minute history of the town.

The *Mayflower II*, a replica of the original ship that set sail for America in 1620

Monument to the Forefathers is dedicated to the Pilgrims who made the first voyage.

Plimoth Grist Mill

◫6 Spring Lane ☎(508) 747-4544 ◷Mid-Mar-Nov: 9am-5pm daily

To appreciate how quickly the Pilgrims progressed from near castaways to hardy settlers, take in the Plimoth Grist Mill, featuring a 1970 reconstruction of the 1636 original grist mill that was destroyed in a fire in 1847. The mill grinds cornmeal with power from a huge water wheel.

③

Spooner House

◫27 North St ☎(508) 746-0012 ◷Jun-Aug: 2-6pm Thu & Sun

Plymouth has several historic homes such as the Spooner House, constructed in 1749 and continuously occupied by one family until 1954, when James Spooner left his home to the Plymouth Antiquarian Society. Its accumulation of artifacts provides a history of Plymouth life.

④

Mayflower Society House

◫4 Winslow St ☎(508) 746-3188 ◷Call for hours

The original section of the Mayflower Society House was built in 1754 and extensively renovated in 1898. What was the old kitchen is now the office for the General Society of Mayflower Descendants.

Its research library has one of the finest genealogical collections in the United States.

⑤

Richard Sparrow House

◫42 Summer St ◷Apr-late Dec: 10am-5pm daily ⋓sparrowhouse.com

A crafts shop, museum and art gallery are housed in the town's oldest home (*c.* 1640).

⑥

Pilgrim Hall Museum

◫75 Court St ☎(508) 746-1620 ◷9:30am-4:30pm daily

Opened in 1824, this is one of America's oldest public

→

Richard Sparrow House, the oldest house in town, dating from around 1640

museums, housing the largest existing collection of Pilgrim-era artifacts, including the only known portrait of a *Mayflower* passenger, as well as personal items such as mugs, bibles and even a cradle.

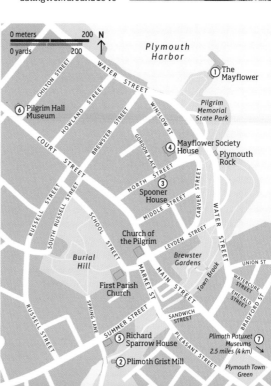

Plymouth
Harbor

① The Mayflower

Pilgrim Memorial State Park

⑥ Pilgrim Hall Museum

④ Mayflower Society House

Plymouth Rock

③ Spooner House

Church of the Pilgrim

Burial Hill

Brewster Gardens

First Parish Church

⑤ Richard Sparrow House

Plimoth Patuxet ⑦ Museums 2.5 miles (4 km)

② Plimoth Grist Mill

Plymouth Town Green

EXPERIENCE Massachusetts

PLIMOTH PATUXET MUSEUMS

🏠 137 Warren Ave ⏰ Mid-Mar-Nov: 9am-5pm daily; check website for winter hours 🌐 plimoth.org

The living history museum of Plimoth Plantation depicts the settlement around 1627, while adjoining Patuxet village shows Wampanoag life in the same era.

Plymouth calls itself "America's home town", as it was the first English settlement in New England and home of the Separatists, who became known as Pilgrims. Plimoth Plantation is a painstakingly accurate re-creation of the Pilgrims' village, right down to 17th-century breeds of livestock. Costumed interpreters portray actual original colonists going about their daily tasks of salting fish, gardening, and musket drills. In the parallel Wampanoag Homesite, descendants of the people who have lived here for 12,000 years speak in modern language about the experiences of the Wampanoag and explore the story of one 17th-century man, Hobbamock, and his family.

Did You Know?

The Pilgrims made their first North American landfall on Cape Cod, not Plymouth.

Hopkins House is named for colonist Stephen Hopkins, whose wife Elizabeth gave birth on the Mayflower.

Outer Palisade

Allerton House was the home of Issac Allerton, the agent who dealt with the colony's financiers.

↑ Culture and history demonstrations at the Patuxet village

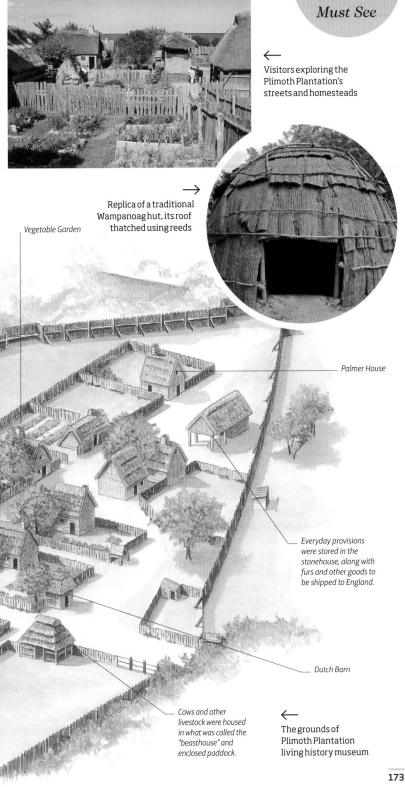

←
Visitors exploring the Plimoth Plantation's streets and homesteads

→
Replica of a traditional Wampanoag hut, its roof thatched using reeds

Vegetable Garden

Palmer House

Everyday provisions were stored in the stonehouse, along with furs and other goods to be shipped to England.

Dutch Barn

Cows and other livestock were housed in what was called the "beasthouse" and enclosed paddock.

←
The grounds of Plimoth Plantation living history museum

4

CAPE COD

🅰 E6 ✈ Barnstable Municipal Airport 🚌 Elm Ave, Hyannis 🚌 Ocean St,
Hyannis; Railroad Ave, Woods Hole ℹ Jct Rtes 132 & 6, Hyannis; www.
capecodchamber.org

Millions of visitors arrive each summer to enjoy the boundless beaches,
natural beauty, and quaint colonial villages of Cape Cod. Extending
some 70 miles (113 km) into the sea, the Cape is shaped like an upraised
arm, bent at the elbow ending with the fist at Provincetown. Crowds
are heaviest along Route 28, where beaches edge the warmer waters
of Nantucket Sound and Buzzard's Bay, while antiques stores and inns
abound in the towns and villages that line Route 6A, the King's Highway.

First-time visitors to Cape Cod are almost always confused when
they are given directions by locals. This is because residents
have divided the Cape into three districts with names that do
not make much sense to newcomers. The Mid- and Upper Cape
is actually the southernmost portion closest to the mainland,
while the Lower Cape is the northernmost section. The Lower,
or Outer, Cape takes in the long elbow of the peninsula that
curls northward and forms Cape Cod Bay. The towns of
Chatham, Brewster, Orleans, Eastham, Wellfleet, Truro, and
Provincetown are all located in this section. Stretching from
Bourne and Sandwich in the west to Yarmouth and Harwich in
the east, Cape Cod's Mid- and Upper sections offer travelers a
broad range of vacation experiences. Be it sunbathing on the
tranquil beaches of Nantucket Sound by day, or partaking in the
fashionable nightlife of Hyannis once the sun has set over Cape
Cod Bay, this section of the Cape has something for every taste.

INSIDER TIP
**The King's
Highway**

Sometimes it pays to
take the slow road. Rte
6A traces the historic
villages along Cape Cod
Bay's shoreline. Known
as The King's Highway,
it shows off Cape Cod
at its most quaint and
picturesque. Tranquil
beaches and verdant
forests line the route.

A coastal sunrise casting golden light over a deserted beach near Provincetown

 Provincetown

This picturesque town has a colorful history. The Pilgrims first landed here in 1620 before pushing on to Plymouth – an event commemorated by the **Pilgrim Monument and Provincetown Museum**. "P-Town," as it is known, later grew into a major 18th-century fishing center. By the 20th century, it had become a busy artists' colony. Today it is one of New England's most vibrant destinations. The region's cultural history is celebrated at the **Provincetown Art Association and Museum**, where works by local artists are displayed. The **Provincetown Public Library** also showcases a striking collection of art, including a half-scale model of the fishing schooner *Rose Dorothea*. MacMillan Wharf is the jumping-off point for whale-watching cruises.

Pilgrim Monument and Provincetown Museum

⊕ 🏛 High Pole Hill Rd ⏰ Apr-Dec: 9am-5pm daily (Jun-mid-Sep: to 7pm) 🌐 pilgrim-monument.org

Provincetown Art Association and Museum

⊕ 🏛 460 Commercial St ⏰ Check website for details 🌐 paam.org

Provincetown Public Library

🏛 356 Commercial St ⏰ 10am-5pm Mon & Fri, 10am-8pm Tue-Thu, 1-5pm Sat & Sun 🌐 provincetownlibrary.org

---

PROVINCETOWN ARTIST COLONY

Artists, writers, and poets have long been inspired by Provincetown's natural beauty. The town's first art school opened its doors in 1901, and Hans Hofmann, Jackson Pollock, Mark Rothko, and Edward Hopper are among the many prominent artists who have spent time here. The roster of resident writers includes John Dos Passos, Tennessee Williams, Sinclair Lewis, and Eugene O'Neill, whose earliest plays were staged at the Provincetown Playhouse on the wharf.

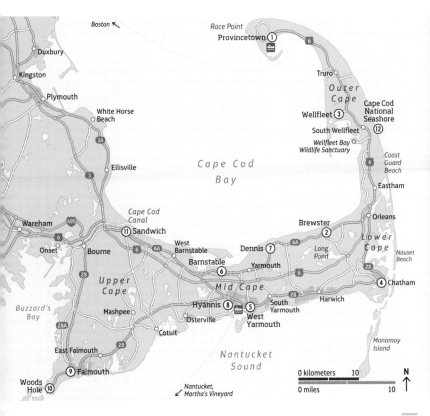

② Brewster

Named for Elder William Brewster (1566–1644), who was a passenger on the *Mayflower*, Brewster is another town graced with handsome 19th-century houses of wealthy sea captains. It is also the site of a particularly lovely church, the 1834 First Parish Brewster Unitarian Universalist Church. Some pews are marked with names of prominent captains.

Children will love the interactive exhibits on display at the **Cape Cod Museum of Natural History**. An observation area looking out on the salt marsh habitat of birds gives visitors close-up views of the natural world, and the museum offers interesting guided walks. Along Cape Cod Bay, Brewster's eight beaches taper gradually toward the ocean, and about 1 mile (1.6 km) of tidal flats is revealed at low tide.

Cape Cod Museum of Natural History

 ☐ 869 Rte 6A ☐ Jun–Sep: 9:30am–4pm daily; check website for winter opening hours ☐ ccmnh.org

③ Wellfleet

Just 17 miles (27 km) south of Provincetown lies Wellfleet, a classic Cape Cod village with a quaint town center and white-washed houses, and surrounded by unspoiled natural landscapes. Renowned

HIDDEN GEM
Wellfleet Drive-In Theatre

It wouldn't be summer without catching a double-feature on the giant screen at this classic 1957 drive-in theater, the only one left on Cape Cod *(www. wellfleetcinemas.com).*

worldwide for its oysters, Wellfleet also is home to numerous other interesting attractions: once an early whaling center it is now home to one of the Cape's largest concentrations of art galleries.

Farther down the Cape is Eastham, home to the **1869 Schoolhouse Museum**, a one-room school built in 1869. Neighboring Orleans is a commercial center with access to the very beautiful Nauset Beach and its much-photographed lighthouse.

1869 Schoolhouse Museum

 ☐ Nauset Rd, Eastham ☐ Times vary, check website ☐ eastham historicalsociety.org/1869-schoolhouse-museum

④ Chatham

This attractive, upscale community sits on the Cape's "elbow," where Nantucket Sound meets the Atlantic Ocean. Chatham offers fine inns, a Main Street filled with attractive shops, and a popular summer playhouse. Housed in an 1887 Victorian train station, the **Chatham Railroad Museum** contains models, memorabilia, and vintage trains that can be boarded. Fishing boats unload their catch at the pier every afternoon, and

↑ A seaside path skirting the coastline near the town of Chatham

the surrounding waters offer good opportunities for amateur anglers.

Chatham is also the best place to plan a trip to the **Monomoy National Wildlife Refuge**. This reserve, on a sandy peninsula, attracts endangered migrating birds such as the piping plover and the roseate tern. Deer are also spotted here, and gray and harbor seals bask on the rocks.

Chatham Railroad Museum

☐ Depot Rd ☐ mid-Jun–mid-Sep: 10am–4pm Tue–Sat ☐ chathamrailroad museum.com

Did You Know?

Cape Cod has more lighthouses that any other part of the United States.

Monomoy National Wildlife Refuge

 Wikis Way, Morris Island
Times vary, check website
fws.gov/refuge/Monomoy

---

⑤

West Yarmouth

The southwest-most of the three villages of Yarmouth, sparsely populated West Yarmouth consists largely of summer cottages near the Nantucket Sound beaches on the south side of slow-going Route 28. Visitors have long appreciated the strip for its ice cream, fast food, and mini-golf, and the recent addition of a pirate museum has only increased its appeal. Named for a ship that sank in a storm after

being captured by pirates, the **Whydah Pirate Museum** exhibits gold doubloons, weapons, clothing, and West African gold jewelry.

Whydah Pirate Museum

 674 Rte 28 Feb-Dec 10am-5pm Tue-Sun
discoverpirates.com

---

⑥

Barnstable

This attractive harbor town is the shire town of Barnstable County, a widespread region extending to both sides of the Cape. The **Coast Guard Heritage Museum**, located in an 1856 customs house, displays artifacts from the Lighthouse, Livesaving, and Revenue Cutter services. The harbor is a great base from which to embark on whale-watching cruises, and conservation properties offer fine hiking opportunities.

Coast Guard Heritage Museum

 Rte 6A, 3353 Main St
May-Oct: 10am-3pm Tue-Sat coastguard heritagemuseum.org

EAT

Mac's on the Pier
Order oyster po' boys at the window and dine at beachside picnic tables.

265 Commercial St, Wellfleet Late May-mid-Oct macsseafood.com

⑤⑤⑤

Chatham Pier Fish Market
Enjoy fresher-than-fresh seafood chowder from this windswept shack by Chatham Pier.

45 Barcliff Ave, Chatham May-mid-Oct

⑤⑤⑤

Mews
Serving gourmet cuisine with an ocean view, Mews is a treat in fine dining. Opt for a more casual experience at the upstairs bistro.

429 Commercial St, Provincetown mews.com

⑤⑤⑤

↑ Boats moored in peaceful Millway Marina, Barnstable

 Kite surfer hitting the waves off West Dennis Beach

 ⑦

Dennis

This gracious village has developed into a vibrant artistic center and is home to the 1927 **Cape Playhouse**, America's oldest professional summer theater, as well as some of the Cape's finest public golf courses. The list of stage luminaries who started their career here is impressive. Playhouse grads include Academy Award-winners Humphrey Bogart, Bette Davis, and Henry Fonda. The Playhouse complex

also includes the **Cape Cod Museum of Art**, displaying the works of many Cape Cod artists. A short drive to the east, the Scargo Hill Tower offers brilliant views of the surrounding landscape.

Cape Playhouse

 🏛820 Rte 6A 🌐capeplayhouse.com

Cape Cod Museum of Art

♿ 🕑 🏛Cape Playhouse grounds 🕐Times vary, check website 🌐ccmoa.org

---

⑧

Hyannis

The Cape's largest village is also a busy shopping center and the transportation hub for regional train, bus, and air services, as well as ferries to Martha's Vineyard (p194) and Nantucket (p190). The harbor is full of yachts and sightseeing boats, but Hyannis' most popular form of transportation does not float. The **Cape Cod Central Railroad** takes travelers for a scenic two-hour round-trip to the Cape Cod canal. Hyannis was one of the Cape's earliest

summer resorts, attracting vacationers as far back as the mid-1800s. The Kennedy compound is best seen from the water aboard a sightseeing cruise. The fascinating **John F. Kennedy Hyannis Museum**, on the ground floor of the Old Town Hall, covers the years he spent here, beginning in the 1930s, and includes photos, oral histories, and family videos.

Cape Cod Central Railroad

♿ 👶 🕐May-late Oct: Tue–Sun; check website for trip times and departure points 🌐capetrain.com

John F. Kennedy Hyannis Museum

♿ 🏛397 Main St 🕐Times vary, check website 🌐jfkhyannismuseum.org

---

⑨

Falmouth

Settled by Quakers in 1661, Falmouth grew into a resort town in the late 19th century. The picturesque village green and historic Main Street reflect a Victorian

↑ Elegant facade of the John F. Kennedy Hyannis Museum in Hyannis

↑ Pretty shops and boutiques lining the streets of Falmouth

heritage. Its coastline is ideal for boating, windsurfing, and sea kayaking. The town is also graced with miles of beaches. Old Silver is the most popular, but Falmouth Heights has the most dramatic views of Vineyard Sound. Visitors will find walking and hiking trails, salt marshes, and ample opportunities for beach-combing and bird-watching. The Shining Sea Bike Path offers breathtaking vistas on the way to Woods Hole.

Woods Hole

This is home to the world's largest independent marine science research center, the Woods Hole Oceanographic Institution (WHOI). Visitors to the **WHOI Exhibit Center** can explore two floors of displays and videos explaining coastal ecology and highlighting some of the organization's findings. Exhibits include a replica of the interior of the *Alvin*, one of the pioneer vessels developed for deep-sea exploration.

WHOI Exhibit Center
⊗ 🏠 15 School St ⏰ Apr–Dec: times vary, check website 🅦 whoi.edu

Sandwich

The oldest town on the Cape is straight off a postcard: the First Church of Christ over-looks a picturesque pond fed by the brook that powers the water wheel of the colonial-era **Dexter Grist Mill**. Built in 1654, it has since been restored, and is now grinding again. Its cornmeal is available at the gift shop.

Another industry is celebrated at the **Sandwich Glass Museum**. Between 1825 and 1888, local entrepreneurs invented a way to press glass. Today, nearly 5,000 pieces of beautiful Sandwich glass are displayed here.

Sandwich's most unusual attraction is **Heritage Museums and Gardens**, a garden and museum built around the collection of pharmaceutical magnate and inveterate collector Josiah Kirby Lilly, Jr (1893–1966). Here, a collection of 39 antique cars is displayed in a reproduction of Shaker barn. The American Art Gallery contains everything from folk art, paintings, and scrimshaw to a working 1912 carousel. Temporary exhibitions are also held in the Special Exhibitions Gallery. In the

grounds, the Hidden Hollow's Splash area is a favorite with youngsters.

Dexter Grist Mill
⊗ 🏠 Maine & Water sts 📞 (508) 888-4361 ⏰ Times vary, call ahead

Sandwich Glass Museum
⊗⊗ 🏠 129 Main St ⏰ Times vary, check website 🅦 sandwichglassmuseum.org

Heritage Museums and Gardens
⊗ 🏠 67 Grove St ⏰ Apr–mid-Oct: 10am–5pm daily 🅦 heritagemuseumsandgardens.org

---

CAPE COD RAIL TRAIL

Beat Cape Cod traffic by hopping on a bicycle for the 25.5-mile (41 km) pedal along a former railroad from Dennis to Wellfleet. The relatively flat route reveals the natural beauty of the Cape as it passes through forests and fields, and skirts marshes and cranberry bogs *(www.mass.gov/locations/cape-cod-rail-trail)*.

→

Wood End Light, and *(inset)* a surfer observing the waves on Nauset Beach

⑫ 🎨

CAPE COD NATIONAL SEASHORE

🅰 Rte 6, Cape Cod 🚹 Salt Pond Visitor Center, Rte 6, Eastham; www.nps.gov/caco

With its stunning dunescapes and seemingly endless expanses of white sand that stretch more than 40 miles (64 km) from Chatham in the south to Provincetown at the northern tip, Cape Cod National Seashore is one of the Eastern Seaboard's true gems.

Conservationists have long treasured the outer Cape. Its dunes and sand cliffs, salt marshes teeming with shorebirds and mollusks, and cedar and pine woodlands are unique in New England. The 1961 creation of the National Seashore put the area under strict environmental protection by removing most existing homes and letting old roads drift over with sand.

However, the seashore encourages non-destructive uses of the park. The Province Lands barrens are laced with exhilarating bicycle trails, while the Atlantic beaches draw the main crowds. Their waters range from gentle surf to large rollers that stir surfers' hearts. Lighthouses above the beaches are scenic and functional, and even the fragile parabolic dunes in Truro can be crossed on a special footpath. Ranger-led programs include beach campfires with storytelling, guided nature walks, canoe trips, birdwatching, and nature programs for children.

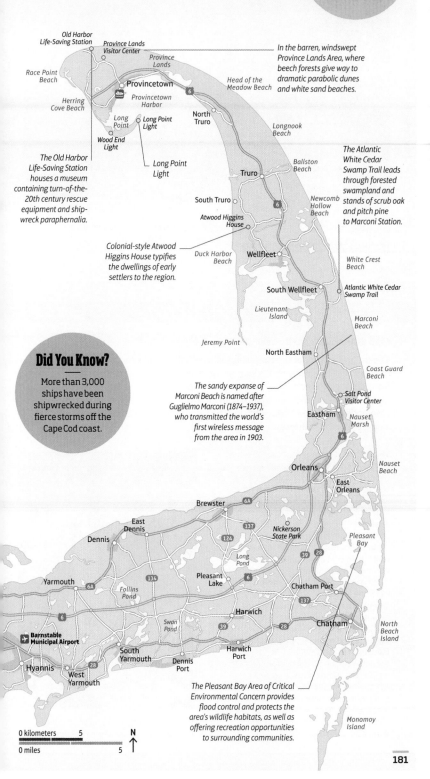

In the barren, windswept Province Lands Area, where beech forests give way to dramatic parabolic dunes and white sand beaches.

The Old Harbor Life-Saving Station houses a museum containing turn-of-the-20th century rescue equipment and ship-wreck paraphernalia.

The Atlantic White Cedar Swamp Trail leads through forested swampland and stands of scrub oak and pitch pine to Marconi Station.

Colonial-style Atwood Higgins House typifies the dwellings of early settlers to the region.

Did You Know?

More than 3,000 ships have been shipwrecked during fierce storms off the Cape Cod coast.

The sandy expanse of Marconi Beach is named after Guglielmo Marconi (1874–1937), who transmitted the world's first wireless message from the area in 1903.

The Pleasant Bay Area of Critical Environmental Concern provides flood control and protects the area's wildlife habitats, as well as offering recreation opportunities to surrounding communities.

Old Harbor Life-Saving Station
Race Point Beach
Province Lands Visitor Center
Province Lands
Provincetown
Herring Cove Beach
Provincetown Harbor
Long Point
Long Point Light
Wood End Light
Long Point Light
North Truro
Head of the Meadow Beach
Longnook Beach
Ballston Beach
Truro
South Truro
Atwood Higgins House
Newcomb Hollow Beach
Duck Harbor Beach
Wellfleet
White Crest Beach
South Wellfleet
Atlantic White Cedar Swamp Trail
Lieutenant Island
Marconi Beach
Jeremy Point
North Eastham
Coast Guard Beach
Salt Pond Visitor Center
Eastham
Nauset Marsh
Nauset Beach
Orleans
East Orleans
Brewster
Nickerson State Park
Pleasant Bay
East Dennis
Dennis
Long Pond
Pleasant Lake
Yarmouth
Follins Pond
Chatham Port
North Beach Island
Harwich
Swan Pond
Chatham
Barnstable Municipal Airport
Harwich Port
Hyannis
West Yarmouth
South Yarmouth
Dennis Port
Monomoy Island

0 kilometers   5
0 miles   5

N

↑ The glorious colors of fall foliage in the verdant Berkshire Hills

5

THE BERKSHIRES

🔺A5 ✈️Albany, NY 🚉Pittsfield 🌐berkshires.org

The natural beauty of the Massachusetts Berkshires beckons visitors in every season – whether it's summertime picnics on the Tanglewood lawns, enjoying electrifying outdoor contemporary dance shows at Jacob's Pillow international dance festival, strolling through the resplendent foliage of fall, or hitting the slopes for exhilarating winter skiing and snowboarding.

Visitors have long been attracted to the peaceful wooded hills, green valleys, rippling rivers, and waterfalls of this western slice of Massachusetts. Equidistant from Boston and New York, the Berkshire Hills and Housatonic Valley became a getaway where wealthy 19th-century urbanites could escape the heat of summer in the city. In the 20th century, the region blossomed as a summer center for music, dance, and theatrical performances. Now the region is a year-round playground, popular for its culture as well as for the ample opportunities it provides for outdoor recreation, such as hiking, mountain-biking, and horse-riding.

The southern Berkshires are speckled with small towns and country villages. Great Barrington to the south and Pittsfield to the north are the commercial centers of the region, while Lenox, associated with the Tanglewood Festival, and Stockbridge, home to the Normal Rockwell Museum, are rich in cultural life. Discover the attractions of northern Berkshires *(pp 199–201)*, which are just as enticing.

↑ Bish Bash Falls in Mount Washington, the highest waterfall in the state

① Pittsfield

This town has a growing cultural scene, including the award-winning **Barrington Stage Company**. Its literary shrine is **Arrowhead**, an 18th-century home in the shadow of Mount Greylock, where Herman Melville lived from 1850 to 1863 and where he wrote his masterpiece *Moby-Dick*.

The **Berkshire Museum** has a large collection of items covering the disciplines of history, natural science, and fine art. The galleries are notable for their works by such 19th-century American masters as Edward Moran (1829-1901) and Thomas Hill (1829-1908).

Barrington Stage Company

🚗30 Union St 🌐barrington stageco.org

Arrowhead

🏛️🎫♿ 🚗780 Holmes Rd 🕐Late May-mid-Oct: 9:30am-5pm daily; rest of year by appt 🌐mobydick.org

Berkshire Museum

♿🏛️ 🚗39 South St 🕐10am-5pm Mon-Sat, noon-5pm Sun 🔒Public hols 🌐berkshiremuseum.org.

② Scenic Hikes

🚗 Rte 41 S 📞(413) 528-0330 🕐Dawn-dusk

The southern Berkshires are replete with outdoor attractions and the hills are crisscrossed by hiking trails. **Bartholomew's Cobble** in Sheffield is known for its spring wildflower bloom, while in the **Bash Bish Falls**

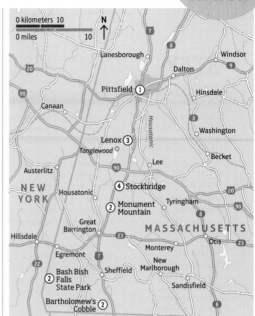

State Park, the cataract of Bash Bish Falls – the highest waterfall in the state – plunges into a serene pool at its base, surrounded by woodlands. On the main road between Stockbridge and Great Barrington, **Monument Mountain** can be climbed via a pair of trails. Herman Melville and Nathaniel Hawthorne met on a joint climb, forming a bond that led to Melville dedicating his novel *Moby-Dick* to his fellow author.

Bartholomew's Cobble

🚗105 Wearohue Rd, Sheffield 🌐thetrustees.org

Bash Bish Falls State Park

🚗Falls Rd, Mt Washington 🌐mass.gov

Monument Mountain

🚗Rte 7, Great Barrington 🌐thetrustees.org

> Herman Melville and Nathaniel Hawthorne met on a joint climb, forming a bond that led to Melville dedicating his novel *Moby-Dick* to his fellow author.

STAY

The Red Lion Inn

Since 1773, the sprawling white-painted Red Lion Inn has been synonymous with hospitality in the Berkshires. Guests can survey it all from front-porch rockers.

 Main St, Stockbridge redlioninn.com

$$ \$\$\$ $$

Tourists

This design-centric riverside motor-lodge retreat balances contemporary style with a woodsy location. The hip restaurant occupies the property's 1813 farmhouse.

915 State Rd, N Adams tourists welcome.com

$$ \$\$\$ $$

③
Lenox

In the late 19th century the gracious village of Lenox became known as the "inland Newport" for the extravagant summer "cottages" built by prominent and wealthy families such as the Carnegies and the Vanderbilts. Before the 1929 Great Depression, there were more than 70 grand estates gracing the area. While some of the millionaires have since moved away, many of their lavish homes remain in service as schools, cultural institutions, resorts, and posh inns. One of the more prominent mansions is **The Mount**, built in 1902 by Pulitzer Prize-winning author Edith Wharton (1862–1937).

Lenox gained new status as a center of culture in 1937, when the 0.8-sq-mile (2-sq-km) Tanglewood estate became the summer home of the Boston Symphony Orchestra. Music lovers flock for concerts to the 1,200-seat Seiji Ozawa Hall or the open Music Shed, where they enjoy picnicking and listening to the music on the surrounding lawn. Jazz and popular concerts are interspersed with the classical program. Tanglewood's name is credited to Nathaniel Hawthorne, who lived in a house on the estate at one time and wrote some of his short stories here.

The Mount

 2 Plunkett St Mid-May–Oct: 10am–5pm daily edithwharton.org

---

④
Stockbridge

Stockbridge was founded in 1734 by missionaries seeking to educate and convert the local Mohegan people. The simple **Mission House** (c. 1739) was built by Reverend John Sergeant for his bride. Today the house contains period pieces and Native American artifacts. The town's quaint

Did You Know?

The Crane Paper Company in Dalton makes the specific paper used for all US currency.

↑ The Mount, Edith Wharton's house, inspired by French, Italian, and English design

main street, dominated by the 1897 Red Lion Inn, has been immortalized in the popular paintings of Norman Rockwell (1894–1978), one of America's most beloved illustrators. The artist lived in Stockbridge for 25 years, and the country's

The Norman Rockwell Museum and *(inset)* Rockwell's *Freedom From Want* painting ↑

largest collection of Rockwell originals can be seen at the **Norman Rockwell Museum**.

The town of Stockbridge has been home to its share of prominent residents, including sculptor Daniel Chester French (1850–1931), who summered at his **Chesterwood** estate. It was here that French created the working models for his famous *Seated Lincoln* (1922) for the Lincoln Memorial in Washington, DC. The models remain in the studio along with other plaster casts. During the summer months the grounds are used to exhibit sculpture.

Naumkeag Museum and Gardens is a graceful 1885 mansion built for Joseph H. Choate, US Ambassador to the UK and one of the era's leading attorneys. The 26-room house is appointed with its original furnishings and an art collection that spans three centuries. The formal gardens are also a work of art.

TOP 5 PERFORMING ARTS VENUES

Tanglewood Music Festival
⌂ Lenox ⓦ bso.org
BSO's summer line-up is not to be missed.

Shakespeare & Co.
⌂ Lenox ⓦ shakespeare.org
Performances year-round.

Jacob's Pillow Dance Festival
⌂ Becket ⓦ jacobspillow.org
Modern dance festival.

Barrington Stage Co.
⌂ Pittsfield
ⓦ barringtonstageco.org
Award winning theater.

Williamstown Theatre Festival
ⓦ wtfestival.org
Lively summer festival.

Mission House
⊗ ⊗ ⌂ 19 Main St ☎ (413) 298-3239 ⊙ Memorial Day–Columbus Day; call for tour hours

Norman Rockwell Museum
⊗ ⊗ ⊙ ⌂ Rte 183 ⊙ May–Oct: 10am–5pm daily; Nov–Apr: 10am–4pm Mon–Fri, 10am–5pm Sat & Sun ⊗ Jan 1, Thanksgiving, Dec 25 ⓦ nrm.org

Chesterwood
⊗ ⊗ ⌂ 4 Williamsville Rd ⊙ Late May–mid-Oct: 10am–5pm daily ⓦ chesterwood.org

Naumkeag Museum and Gardens
⊗ ⌂ Prospect Hill ⊙ Memorial Day–Labor Day: 10am–5pm daily; call for winter hours ⓦ thetrustees.org

6 🚲 🏍 🍴 🖥 🛍

OLD STURBRIDGE VILLAGE

🅰B6 🅰Rte 20, Sturbridge 🕐May–Oct: 9:30am–5pm daily; check website for winter hours 🚫Dec 25 🌐osv.org

Old Sturbridge Village poignantly captures the everyday lives of rural New Englanders, as they worked to build a new country. Visitors can interact with villagers as they work and play.

↑ A horsedrawn stage-coach transports visitors around the village

At the heart of this living-history museum are about 40 vintage buildings that have been restored and relocated from all over New England. Laid out like an early 19th-century village, Old Sturbridge is peopled by costumed interpreters who go about their daily activities. A blacksmith works the forge, farmers tend their crops, and millers work the gristmill. Inside buildings are re-created period settings, antiques, and craft demonstrations. A gallery, education center, and workshops illuminate 19th-century life.

> **A blacksmith works the forge, farmers tend their crops, and millers work the gristmill.**

The Towne House once had a ballroom, and now contains period furniture and porcelains.

Bank

The Center Meetinghouse stands at the foot of the village common.

The Parsonage

Rural stores were link[ed] to the outside world.

STAY

The Old Sturbridge Inn & Reeder Family Lodges

Old or new? The two lodging options at Old Sturbridge Village are the ten-room 1789 Oliver Wight House, which perfectly combines historic ambiance with modern convenience, or one of the modern Reeder Family Lodge units, each with its own private entrance and curbside parking. Visitors should note, the Oliver Wight House is limited to ages 12 and up.

🅰C6 🏠371 Main St, Sturbridge 🌐osv.org

$ $ $

Visitors can enjoy home-cooked seasonal fare in the authentic Bullard Tavern.

EXPERIENCE MORE

7
Nashoba Valley

🅰C5 🛈100 Sherman Ave, Devens; (978) 772-6976

Fed by the Nashoba River, Nashoba Valley is an appealing world of meadows, orchards, and colonial towns built around village greens. The region is particularly popular in May, when the apple trees are in bloom, and again in fall, when the apples are ripe for picking.

The **Fruitlands Museums**, the valley's major attraction, comprises four museums, two outdoor sites, and a beautiful hilltop café. Founder Clara Endicott Sears (1863–1960) built her home here in 1910 and began gathering properties of historical significance. Her first acquisition was Fruitlands, a commune based partly on vegetarianism and self-sufficiency initiated by Bronson Alcott and fellow authors. Alcott was the father of author Louisa May Alcott (1832–88) and was the model for the character of Mr. March in her book *Little Women* (1868). The restored farmhouse now serves as a

82
distinct varieties of apple tree are grown in the orchards of the Nashoba Valley Winery.

museum and includes memorabilia of Alcott, Ralph Waldo Emerson, and other authors and philosophers. Five years later, Sears acquired a 1790 building in nearby Shaker Village, which now houses a collection of traditional Shaker furniture and artifacts.

Also in the area is the **Nashoba Valley Winery**, a petite orchard that produces wine from grapes, and from table fruits such as apples, berries, and pears. The winery has expanded into a microbrewery that produces fine beers and spirits.

Fruitlands Museums
🏠102 Prospect Hill Rd, Harvard ⏰Times vary, check website 🌐thetrustees.org

Nashoba Valley Winery
🏠100 Wattaquadock Hill Rd, Bolton ⏰11am–5pm daily 🌐nashobawinery.com

EXPERIENCE Massachusetts

8 Sudbury

C5 🚆 Boston
w sudbury.ma.us

The picturesque town of Sudbury is home to a number of historic sites, including the 1797 First Parish Church –the earliest religious services of which date back to 1640 – and the 1723 Loring Parsonage. Longfellow's Wayside Inn, which lays claim to being the oldest operating inn in the United States, was built in 1707 and officially began its trade in 1716. The inn was immortalized in Henry Wadsworth Longfellow's poetry collection entitled *Tales of a Wayside Inn* (1863). In the early 1920s the building was purchased by billionaire industrialist Henry Ford (1863–1947), who aimed to turn it into a living history museum. Ford restored the inn, filled it with antiques, and surrounded it with other relocated structures, such as a rustic gristmill, a schoolhouse, and a general store. Today, the inn serves both as a mini-museum of Colonial America as well as offering simple overnight rooms and hearty American fare in its quaint, pub-like restaurant.

> Painter James McNeill Whistler (1834-1903), most famous for his portrait of his mother, was born in Lowell. His birthplace is now the Whistler House Museum of Art.

9 Lowell

 C5 🚆 Boston 🚌 i 61 Market St, Unit 1C; www. merrimackvalley.org

Lowell was America's first industrial city, paving the way for the American Industrial Revolution. In the early 19th century, Boston merchant Francis Cabot Lowell opened a cloth mill in nearby Waltham and equipped it with his new power loom. The increase in production was so great that the mill quickly outgrew its quarters, and the business expanded into the town of East Chelmsford (later known as Lowell). Powered by the Merrimack River, it grew to include 10 giant mill complexes and employed more than 10,000 workers. While the mills prospered as a result, it was at the expense of its workers, many of whom were unskilled immigrants exploited by the mill owners. Eventually laborers banded together, and there were many strikes.

The most successful was the 1912 Bread and Roses Strike, which helped improve working conditions, but relief was temporary. In the 1920s companies began to move south in search of cheaper labor. Although many mills restarted during World War II, the last textile mill closed in the 1960s and adversely impacted the economic growth of the city.

In 1978 the **Lowell National Historical Park** was established to rehabilitate more than 100 downtown buildings and preserve the city's unique history. On Market Street, the Market Mills Visitor Center offers screenings, walking tours maps, guided walks with rangers, and tickets for summer canal boat tours of the waterways. In summer and fall, antique trolleys take visitors to the **Boott Cotton Mills Museum**, where the operation of 88 vintage power looms produce a deafening clatter. Interactive exhibits trace the Industrial Revolution and the growth

↑ The picturesque grounds surrounding Longfellow's Wayside Inn in Sudbury

↑ Vintage power looms churning at the Boott Cotton Mills Museum in Lowell

of the labor movement. While Lowell is best known for its industrial history, the city has many other attractions. The **New England Quilt Museum** displays antique and contemporary quilts, and sponsors talks on trends in current fiber arts. Painter James McNeill Whistler (1834–1903), most famous for his portrait of his mother, was born in Lowell. His birthplace is now the **Whistler House Museum of Art**. A number of the old mill structures have been transformed by artists into hives of creativity, and several galleries have also opened here as a result. **Western Avenue Studios**, which is the largest artists' community on America's eastern seaboard, is open for visitors once a month. Novelist Jack Kerouac, is another famous native of Lowell. He was born here in 1922, though left for New York City shortly after graduating from high school.

Lowell National Historical Park

⊛ ⊛ 🏠 246 Market St
🕐 Times vary, check website
🖥 nps.gov/lowe

Boott Cotton Mills Museum

⊛ 🏠 115 John St 📞 (978) 970-5000 🕐 Late Mar–Nov: 9:30am–5pm daily (call for opening hours off-season)

New England Quilt Museum

⊛ 🏠 18 Shattuck St
🕐 10am–4pm Wed–Sat
🖥 neqm.org

Whistler House Museum of Art

⊛ 🏠 243 Worthen St
🕐 11am–4pm Wed–Sat
🖥 whistlerhouse.org

Western Avenue Studios

🏠 122 Western Ave
🕐 Noon–5pm 1st Sat of month 🖥 westernavenuestudios.com

Quincy

🅰 D5 🚇 180 Old Colony Ave; www.discoverquincy.com

Quincy was once home to four generations of the Adams family, among them the second and sixth presidents of the US. The 544,500-sq-ft (50,600-sq-m) **Adams National Historical Park** includes the John Adams Birthplace, the John Quincy Adams Birthplace, the Old House, where the Quincy family lived, and a church, where John Adams, John Quincy Adams, and both their wives are buried. A trolley provides transportation between sights.

Adams National Historical Park

⊛ ⊛ 🏠 1250 Hancock St
🕐 Mid-Apr–mid-Nov: 9am–5pm daily 🖥 nps.gov/adam

New Bedford

🅰 D6 🚇 133 William St; www.newbedford-ma.gov

In the mid-1800s, profits from whaling made New Bedford the richest port of its size in the world. Hear tales of epic ocean voyages at the Whaling National Historical Park and at the New Bedford Whaling Museum. Nearby, the Seamen's Bethel underscores the great risk involved, with marble cenotaphs memorializing sailors tragically lost at sea.

JACK KEROUAC

Lowell native Jack Kerouac (1922–69) was the leading chronicler of the "Beat Generation," a term that he coined to describe members of the 1950s' disaffected Bohemian movement. Though he lived elsewhere for most of his life, his remains are buried in Lowell's Edson Cemetery. Excerpts from his most famous novel, *On the Road* (1957), and his other writings are inscribed on pillars in the Kerouac Commemorative Park on Bridge Street.

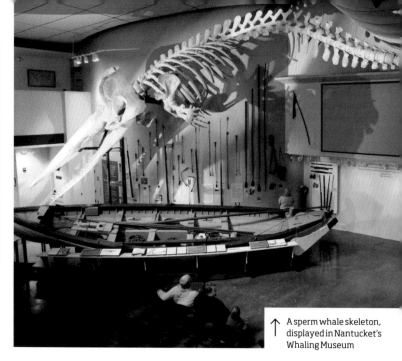

↑ A sperm whale skeleton, displayed in Nantucket's Whaling Museum

12

Nantucket Island

🗺 E7 ✈ West Tisbury
⛴ Hyannis; Harwich port;
New Bedford & Oak Bluffs
ℹ Zero Main St; www.
nantucket.net

Lying off the southern tip of Cape Cod (p174), Nantucket Island is a 14-mile- (22-km-) long enclave of tranquility. With only one town to speak of, the island remains an untamed world of kettle ponds, cranberry bogs, and lush stands of wild grapes and blueberries, punctuated by the occasional lighthouse.

In the early 19th century the town of Nantucket was the envy of the whaling industry, with a fearsome fleet of about 100 vessels. The town's architecture reflects those bygone days, with the magnificent mansions of sea captains and merchants – made rich from their whaling exploits – lining Main Street. Today the town has the nation's largest concentration of pre-1850s houses.

Did You Know?

Nantucket Island was allegedly first purchased for the sum of "thirty pounds and two beaver hats."

The **Nantucket Historical Association (NHA)** operates 11 historical buildings in town. One of the most important sites is the Whaling Museum on Broad Street. The museum features a restored 1847 spermaceti candle factory and a rare complete skeleton of a sperm whale recovered from a Nantucket beach. Historic exhibits include ship models, ships' logs, maps and charts, and more than 45,000 photographs and examples of scrimshaw that highlight the era when Nantucket was the world's leading whaling port, a trade that resulted in the Nantucket whale population being hunted to the brink of extermination by the 1760s.

Nowadays, these magnificent mammals are still a major focal point of life on this island, but in a much more humane way. Nantucket plays an important role in the protection and conservation of North Atlantic whales through organizations such as the Marine Mammal Alliance Nantucket.

Additional buildings of interest include the Hawden House, which was built in 1845 and focuses on the lifestyle of whaling merchants, and the Quaker Meeting House. From an initial meeting in 1701, Quakerism grew to be the religion of Nantucket's elite. The meeting house is still a tiny but active congregation. Also open for tours are the 1686 Jethro Coffin House, the island's oldest house, and the 18th-century Old Mill, a wind-powered grain mill restored to operating condition.

Nantucket Historical Association (NHA)

♿ ♻ 🕐 🏛 15 Broad St
🕐 Times vary, check website
🌐 nha.org

Lincoln

A C3 **i** 16 Lincoln Rd; www.lincolntown.org

Located at the midway point between Lexington and Concord, Lincoln was once called "Niptown" because it was comprised of parcels of land that were "nipped" from neighboring towns. Today this wealthy rural community is noted for its interesting array of sightseeing attractions.

The **DeCordova Sculpture Park** displays some 60 contemporary large-scale American sculptures as part of its changing outdoor exhibition. The estate was bequeathed to the town by wealthy entrepreneur and patron of the arts Julian DeCordova (1850–1945).

Walter Gropius (1883–1969), the director of the original Bauhaus school of design in Germany – and one of the 20th century's most influential architects – fled Adolf Hitler's regime and became a professor at Harvard. In 1937 he designed his modest but unique home, **Gropius House**, by combining traditional New England elements with splendid modern flourishes of chrome banisters and acoustical plaster.

Art and architecture are also celebrated at the **Codman Estate**, built in the 1700s by merchant John Codman. Home to five generations of the Codman family, the three-story house contains wonderful Neoclassical furnishings.

At **Drumlin Farm Wildlife Sanctuary** visitors can see a working farm in action, with hands-on learning activities for children. There are also many nature trails.

DeCordova Sculpture Park and Museum

⊛ ⊛ ⊜ ⊚ **A** 51 Sandy Pond Rd **O** Summer: 10am–5pm daily; winter: Times vary, check website **W** thetrustees.org

Gropius House

⊛ ⊛ ⊚ **A** 68 Baker Bridge Rd **O** May–Oct: 11am–4pm Wed–Sun; Nov–Apr: 11am–4pm Sat & Sun **W** historicnewengland.org

Codman Estate

⊛ ⊛ **A** 34 Codman Rd **O** Jun–mid-Oct: 10am–2pm 2nd & 4th Sat of month **W** historicnewengland.org

Drumlin Farm Wildlife Sanctuary

⊛ ⊚ **A** 208 South Great Rd **O** Mar–Oct: 9am–5pm Tue–Sun (Nov–Feb: to 4pm) **W** massaudubon.org

---

Lexington

A D5 **i** 1875 Massachusetts Ave; www.tourlexington.us

Lexington and neighboring Concord are forever linked in history as the settings for two bloody skirmishes that acted as catalysts for the Revolutionary War. On April 19, 1775, armed colonists called Minute Men clashed here with British troops on their way to Concord in search of rebel weaponry. A statue memorializing this struggle stands on Lexington Battle Green. The battle is reenacted each year in

mid-April. The local **Historical Society** maintains three buildings linked to the battle that now display artifacts from that era. Buckman Tavern served as both a meeting place for the Minute Men and as a makeshift hospital for their wounded. Paul Revere is said to have stopped here following his historic ride (*p102*), as well as at the Hancock-Clarke House to warn Samuel Adams (1722–1803) and John Hancock (1737–93), two of the eventual signatories to the Declaration of Independence. Munroe Tavern served as headquarters for British forces.

Historical Society

⊛ **A** Hancock-Clarke House: 36 Hancock St; Buckman Tavern: 1 Bedford St; Munroe Tavern: 1332 Massachusetts Ave **W** lexingtonhistory.org

← *The Minute Man*, a statue commemorating the fierce battle of Lexington

A catboat atop still waters, off the coast of Nantucket Island

15

Martha's Vineyard

⚐D7 ⊡ West Tisbury
⛴ Woods Hole, Hyannis,
New Bedford ℹ Beach Rd,
Vineyard Haven; www.
mvy.com

"The Vineyard," as the locals call it, is the largest of all New England's vacation islands at 108 sq miles (280 sq km). Just a 45-minute boat ride from shore, it is blessed with a mesmerizing mix of scenic beauty and the understated charm of a beach resort. Bicycle trails abound here, and opportunities for hiking, surf fishing, and some of the best sailing in the region add to the Vineyard's lure. Although they all share sleepy coastal charm, each town has its

The windswept headland of Aquinnah at the western edge of the island is famous for its steep, multi-hued clay cliffs - a favorite subject of photographers.

own distinct mood and style, making them all interesting to explore.

Most visitors arrive on Martha's Vineyard aboard ferries that sail into the aptly named waterfront town of Vineyard Haven, which was built in Victorian style after a fire in the 1800s. Vineyard Haven is sheltered between two points of land known as East and West Chop, each with its own landmark lighthouse.

Another notable building in this town is **Martha's Vineyard Museum**, which has been painstakingly relocated from its original site in Edgartown, and was relaunched early 2019. The museum is now housed in the historic Vineyard Haven Marine Hospital.

As the center of the island's prosperous whaling industry

in the early 1800s, Edgartown was once home to wealthy sea captains and merchants. The streets are lined with their homes.

At the eastern end of the waterfront, visitors can catch the ferry to Chappaquiddick Island, a rural outpost that is popular for its beaches and opportunities for surf fishing, bird-watching, canoeing, and hiking. This quiet enclave was made famous by a fatal accident in 1969, when a car driven by Senator Edward Kennedy (1932–2009) went off the bridge, killing a young woman passenger.

Tourism began on Martha's Vineyard in 1835, when local Methodists began using an undeveloped area, now known as Oak Bluffs, to pitch their tents during their summer revival meetings. The setting proved popular as people came in search of sunshine and salvation. Gradually the tent village gave way to a town of colorful gingerbread cottages, boarding houses, and stores, and was named Cottage City. In 1907 it was renamed Oak Bluffs. The town is home to the **Flying Horses**

Did You Know?

British explorer Bartholomew Gosnold named Martha's Vineyard for his daughter in 1602.

↑ The stately homes of sea captains overlooking Edgartown's busy harbor

LONG POINT WILDLIFE REFUGE

Birders, swimmers, kayakers, paddle-boarders, and hikers all love Long Point, a 600-acre (243-ha) stretch of the south coast of Martha's Vineyard, which is under the stewardship of the Trustees of Reservations (www.thetrustees.org). When striped bass and bluefish appear in the summer, surfcasters stake out stretches of the large sandy ocean beach, especially at the change of tides. Some of the best swimming is in the freshwater Long Pond, where there is no danger of rip tides. In July and August, a concession stand rents paddleboards and kayaks, while hikers can enjoy miles of trails that wind through a sandplain heath and an oak forest.

Carousel, the oldest platform carousel in the country. Today's children delight in riding on it as much as those of the 1870s.

Unlike the Vineyard's busier eastern section, the western shoreline is much more tranquil and rural. The area, which includes the splendid towns of North and West Tisbury, Menemsha, and Aquinnah (formerly Gay Head, but it reverted to the area's original Native American name in 1998), is graced by a number of private homes and pristine beaches, many of which are strictly private.

Tiny West Tisbury remains a rural village of picket fences, rolling landscapes, a white-spired church, and a general store. In Menemsha, a working fishing fleet fills the harbor, and the weathered fishermen's shacks, fish nets, and lobster traps look much as they did a century ago. The windswept headland of Aquinnah at the western edge of the island is famous for its steep, multi-hued clay cliffs – a favorite subject of photographers. The area also lays claim to some of the more picturesque sandy beaches on Martha's Vineyard.

Martha's Vineyard Museum

♿ 🅿 ⓘ 🏛 151 Logan Pond Rd, Vineyard Haven
🕐 10am–5pm Tue–Sun (to 8pm Tue; mid-Oct–late May: to 4pm) 🚫 Public hols
🅦 mvmuseum.org

Flying Horses Carousel

♿ 🅿 🏛 Oak Bluffs Ave, Oak Bluffs 📞 (508) 693-9481
🕐 Apr–mid-Oct: call for hours

← The sun rising over the Edgartown Harbor Light, one of five Vineyard lighthouses

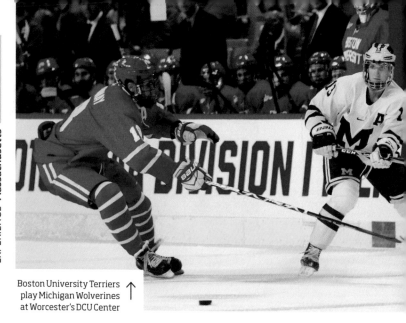

Boston University Terriers play Michigan Wolverines at Worcester's DCU Center

Worcester

🅰️C5 ✈️ Worcester Airport
🚇 🚌 ℹ️ 46 Main St; (508) 753-1550

Worcester has always been on the cutting edge. During the American Industrial Revolution, local designers developed the nation's first mechanized carpet weavers and envelope folders. This spirit of invention reached its pinnacle in 1926, when Worcester native Dr. Robert Goddard (1882–1945) launched the world's first liquid-fuel rocket.

However, not all of Worcester's forward thinking has been reserved for the development of new machines. Over time this city, which is built on seven hills, became home to 10 colleges and universities, as well as a center for biological research that developed the first birth-control pill in the 1950s.

Central Massachusetts' premier event space, the **DCU Center**, contains an indoor arena and convention center. The complex hosts big-name concerts and sporting events, family shows, and conventions.

Since 2021, the "WooSox" AAA affiliate of the Boston Red Sox have played in **Polar Park** in the Canal District.

Set in a late-19th-century stone building, the **Worcester Art Museum** has distinguished itself as an important repository. Its collection contains some 35,000 objects spanning 5,000 years, including a 12th- century chapter house that was rebuilt stone by stone on the premises. The museum houses one of the world's leading collections of medieval armor and weaponry from Europe and Asia. Holdings of East and West Asian art and Japanese wood-block prints are wonderfully balanced by a good number of works by Western masters such as Claude Monet (1840–1926), Thomas Gainsborough (1728–88), and Pablo Picasso (1881–1973).

Just 2 miles (3 km) from downtown Worcester, the **Ecotarium** promotes a better understanding of the region's environment and its wildlife. Interactive exhibits invite hands-on learning experiences. Its surrounding grounds contain a wildlife center for injured and endangered animals and a Wild Cat Station that explores mountain lions in New England. There is also a planetarium within the vast 2,613,600-sq-ft (242,800-sq-m) grounds.

North Grafton, 10 miles (16 km) southeast of Worcester, has a long history of clock-making. In the early 19th century brothers Benjamin, Simon, Ephraim, and Aaron Willard were regarded as some of New England's best craftsmen, designing new styles for timepieces. Their stylish pieces were given such varied names as Eddystone Lighthouse, Skeleton, and Act of Parliament. Today more than 70 Willard timepieces and elegant tall clocks are on display at the **Willard House and Clock Museum**, which is located in the family's original 18th-century homestead and opened as a museum in 1971.

DCU Center
🏛️ 50 Foster St ⏰ For events, check website for details 🌐 dcucenter.com

Polar Park
♿ 🏛️ 122 Madison St
🌐 woosox.com

Willard House and Clock Museum

⊘ ⊘ 🏠 11 Willard St, North Grafton ⏰ 10am–4pm Wed-Sat, 1–4pm Sun (Jan–Mar: Fri–Sun only) 🆆 willardhouse.org

---

17

Amherst

🅰 B5 ✈ 41 miles (66 km) S in Windsor Locks, CT 🚌 🚊 🛈 35 S Pleasant St; (413) 253-0700

This idyllic college town is home to three different institutes of higher learning. The most popular with visitors is Amherst College, with its traditional ivy-covered brick buildings. Founded in 1821 for underprivileged youths hoping to enter the ministry, the school has grown into one of the most selective small colleges in the US. The college is home to both the excellent **Mead Art Museum** – which includes the Rotherwas Room, an ornately paneled hall dating to c. 1600 – and the Beneski Museum of Natural History.

Poet Emily Dickinson was one of Amherst's most famous citizens. In her early 20s, Dickinson withdrew from society and spent the rest of her life in the family home, where she died in 1886. The second-floor bedroom of the **Emily Dickinson Museum** has been restored to the way it was during the years 1855–86, when the reclusive poet wrote her most important verse. Her work remained unpublished until after her death. Over time critics proclaimed it to be the work of a poetic genius. The **Jones Library** has displays on Dickinson's life and works, as well as collections on poet Robert Frost, who taught at Amherst College in the 1940s.

Mead Art Museum

⊘ 🏠 Amherst College 🕿 (413) 542-2335 ⏰ 9am–5pm Tue–Thu (to 8pm Fri) 🚫 Mid-Dec–late Jan

Emily Dickinson Museum

⊘ ⊘ 🏠 280 Main St ⏰ Mar–Dec: times vary; check website for details 🆆 emilydickinsonmuseum.org

Jones Library

🏠 43 Amity St 🕿 (413) 259-3090 ⏰ 9am–5:30pm Mon, Wed, Fri, & Sat; 9am–8:30pm Tue & Thu; 1–5pm Sun 🚫 Jun–Aug: Sun

Worcester Art Museum

⊘ 🈺 🈲 🏠 55 Salisbury St ⏰ 10am–5pm Wed–Sun 🆆 worcesterart.org

Ecotarium

⊘ 🏠 222 Harrington Way ⏰ 10am–5pm Tue–Sat, noon–5pm Sun 🆆 ecotarium.org

---

←

A Colonial Revival building at Amherst College

A statue in the Dr. Seuss National Memorial Sculpture Garden, Springfield ↑

18

Springfield

🅰B4 ✈15 miles (24 km) SW in Windsor Locks, CT 🚌🚉 🚹1441 Main St; (413) 787-1548 or (800) 723-1548

Now a center for banking and insurance, Springfield owes much of its early success to guns. The **Springfield Armory National Historic Site** – the first armory in the US – was commissioned by George Washington (1732–99) to manufacture arms for the colonial forces fighting in the Revolutionary War. Today the historic armory is part of the National Park Service and maintains one of the most extensive and unique firearms collections in the world.

In 1891, Dr. James Naismith (1861–1939), an instructor at the International YMCA Training Center, now Springfield College, invented the game of basketball. The **Basketball Hall of Fame** traces the game's development from its humble beginnings, when peach baskets were used as nets, to its evolution as one of the world's most popular team sports. The state-of-the-art museum features interactive displays and basketball memorabilia.

Court Square on Main Street is the revitalized center of the city. Nearby is **The Quadrangle**, a group of five museums of art, science, and history. The G. W. V. Smith Art Museum displays a noted collection of Oriental decorative arts and Japanese armor. Galleries at the Museum of Fine Arts contain European and American paintings, sculpture, and the decorative arts. Children love the Springfield Science Museum, with its live animal center and Dinosaur Hall, with a life-size model of *Tyrannosaurus rex*. The Wood Museum of Springfield History displays locally made vehicles.

The Dr. Seuss National Memorial Sculpture Garden features the beloved characters of popular children's author and Springfield native Theodor Geisel (1904–91), better known as Dr. Seuss. In 2017, the Quadrangle opened The Amazing World of Dr. Seuss Museum, which provides opportunites for the children to build reading skills through a series of wordplay games and other activities. As one would expect, the museum

→
The three-tiered "reflecting pool" at The Clark, Williamstown

also displays Geisel's impressive collection of zany hats and bow ties.

Some 11 miles (18 km) north, the hamlet of South Hadley is home to Mount Holyoke College (1837), the nation's oldest women's college. Poet Emily Dickinson (1830–86) was one of Mount Holyoke's most famous students. The 1.2-sq-mile (3.2-sq-km) campus encompasses two lakes and a series of nature trails. College sites worth a visit include the art museum and the Victorian-style Talcott Greenhouse.

Springfield Armory National Historic Site

⊛ ♿ One Armory Sq ☎(413) 734-8551 🕐9am–5pm daily; (Nov–late May: Wed–Sun) 🚫Jan 1, Thanksgiving, Dec 25 🌐nps.gov/spar

Basketball Hall of Fame

⊛ ♿ 1000 W Columbus Ave 🕐10am–4pm daily 🚫Dec–Apr: Mon & Tue; Thanksgiving, Dec 25 🌐hoophall.com

The Quadrangle

⊛ ♿ State & Chestnut sts 🕐Times vary, check website 🌐springfieldmuseums.org

> The hilltop grounds of The Clark also include trails through forest and meadow that are open to hikers and, in winter, snowshoers.

19

Williamstown

🅰A5 ✈Albany, NY 🚌 ℹJct Rtes 2 & 7; (413) 458-9077 or (800) 214-3799

Art lovers make pilgrimages to this northwesterly town to visit the stunning facility of **The Clark**. Its private art collection is housed in a postmodern building and is especially strong on French Impressionists, including more than 30 Renoirs. The grounds of this hilltop museum also include trails through forest and meadow that are open to hikers and, in winter, snowshoers. The **Williams College Museum of Art** is also notable for a collection that ranges from ancient Assyrian stone reliefs to Andy Warhol's (1928–87) final self-portrait.

The Williamstown Theater Festival, founded in 1954 and held every summer, is known for its high-quality productions. These often feature big-name Broadway and Hollywood stars, with past performers including Bradley Cooper, Gwyneth Paltrow, and Christopher Walken. More art can be found 7 miles (11 km) east of Williamstown

in North Adams at the **Massachusetts Museum of Contemporary Art** (MASS MoCA). Several interconnected 19th-century factory buildings, with enormous indoor spaces, elevated walkways, and outdoor courtyards, display cutting-edge art that is often too large to fit inside conventional museums. American Conceptual/Minimalist artist Sol Lewitt's wall drawings are a particular highlight. The Gallery space was doubled in 2017 in order to better showcase the rapidly expanding collection.

The Clark

⊛ ⊛ ♿ 225 South St 🕐10am–5pm Tue–Sun (Jul & Aug: daily) 🌐clarkart.edu

Williams College Museum of Art

♿ Main St 🕐10am–5pm Thu–Tue (Jun–Aug: 10am–5pm daily) 🌐wcma.williams.edu

Massachusetts Museum of Contemporary Art

⊛ 🏠 1040 MASS MoCA Way 🕐11am–5pm Wed–Mon (Jul–Sep: 10am–6pm daily) 🌐massmoca.org

20

Hancock Shaker Village

🅰 C4 🅗 Rte 20, outside Pittsfield 🕐 Mid-Apr–Jun: 10am–4pm daily; Jul–mid-Oct: 10am–5pm daily 🌐 hancockshakervillage.org

Founded in 1783, this was the third in a series of 19 Shaker settlements established in the Northeast and Midwest as utopian communities. The Shakers, so-called because they often trembled and shook during moments of worship, believed in celibacy and equality of the sexes, with men and women living separately but sharing authority and responsibilities. At its peak in the 1830s, there were 300 residents living in the village. Now the community has no resident Shakers.

Twenty of the 100 original buildings have been restored, including the tri-level round stone barn, cleverly designed so that as many as 52 heads of cattle could be fed by a single farmhand from a central core. The Brick Dwelling can house up to 100 people, and has a communal dining room, where traditional Shaker fare is served on select evenings.

Presentations on the Shaker way of life include demonstrations of chair-, broom-, and oval box-making. In the Discovery Room visitors may try on reproduction Shaker clothing and also attempt crafts such as weaving.

21

Deerfield

🅰 B5 🛧 Windsor Locks, CT 🛈 18 Miner St, Greenfield; (413) 773-9393

A one-time frontier outpost that saw heavy raids in the late 17th century, Deerfield is home to a mile- (1.6-km-)

A brick building in Hancock Shaker Village, *(inset)* where traditional crafts are made ↓

long center avenue, lined with clapboard homes, known simply as "The Street." Around 60 of these remain within **Historic Deerfield** and are carefully preserved. Some of the houses now serve as museums, exhibiting a broad range of period furniture and decorative arts. The Flynt Center of Early New England Life schedules changing exhibitions on early life in western Massachusetts. Visitors seeking a photo

↑ A visitor exploring the Smith College Museum of Art in Northampton

opportunity can drive to the summit of **Mount Sugarloaf State Reservation** in South Deerfield for views of the Connecticut River Valley.

Historic Deerfield

⊛ ⌂ The Street, Old Deerfield ⊙ Jan-Mar: times vary, check website; Apr-Dec: 9:30am-4:30pm daily ⊗ Thanksgiving, Dec 24 & 25 ⓦ historic-deerfield.org

Mount Sugarloaf State Reservation

⊛ ⌂ 300 Sugarloaf St, South Deerfield ☎ (413) 665-2928 ⊙ May-Dec: 8am-dusk daily

---

 Northampton

Ⓐ B5 ✈ Windsor Locks, CT 🚌 ℹ 99 Pleasant St; (413) 584-1900

A lively center for the arts and known for its bar scene, Northampton has a well-preserved Victorian-style Main Street lined with craft galleries and shops. The town is also home to the 1871 Smith College, the largest privately endowed women's college in the nation. The handsome campus is home

to the notable Smith College Museum of Art and the **Lyman Plant House and Conservatory**, known for its flower shows and the gardens and arboretum. Nearby is the Norwottuck Rail Trail, a popular walking and biking path that runs along an old railroad bed connecting Northampton to neighboring Amherst. In Holyoke, south of Northampton, visitors can explore the trails in the 3-sq-mile (7-sq-km) **Mount Tom State Reservation**.

Lyman Plant House and Conservatory

⌂ College Lane, Northampton ☎ (413) 585-2740 ⊙ 10am-4pm daily ⊗ Thanksgiving, Dec 25-Jan 1

Mount Tom State Reservation

⊛ ⌂ 125 Reservation Rd, Holyoke ☎ (413) 534-1186 ⊙ 8am-dusk daily; Visitor Center: Memorial Day-mid-Oct: Wed-Sun (call for hours)

 Mount Greylock State Reservation

Ⓐ A5 ⌂ Off Rte 7, Lanesborough ☎ (413) 499-4262 ⊙ Times vary, call for hours

The Appalachian Trail *(p10)*, the popular 2,000-mile (3,200-km) hiking path running from Georgia to Maine, crosses Mount Greylock's summit between Pittsfield *(p183)* and North Adams *(p199)*. At 3,491 ft (1,064 m), Greylock is the highest point in Massachusetts, and offers panoramic views of five states. On clear days, visibility can reach up to 90 miles (145 km). The auto road to the summit is open from late May through to October. Hiking trails in the 2-sq-mile (5-sq-km) park remain open and are very popular during fall foliage season. At the mountain's summit, visitors can visit the seasonal lodge.

→ A group of hikers taking in the rolling views from Mount Greylock

A DRIVING TOUR
THE NORTH SHORE

Length 31 miles (50 km) with a detour to Wingaersheek Beach **Stopping-off points** Seafood abounds in Rocky Neck, Gloucester, Rockport, Essex, and Newburyport.

The scenic tip of the North Shore is a favorite escape for harried Bostonians and vacationers who come for the quaint towns, sandy beaches, and whale-watching excursions that are found here in abundance. Ipswich is known for its sandy beaches, dunes and seafood, especially clams. The rocky shores of Cape Ann hold diverse pleasures, including artists' colonies, mansions, and opportunities for swimming and boating.

Locator Map
For more detail see p162

*A wealth of 17th- and 18th-century architecture, such as The Great House at Castle Hill, makes **Ipswich** a fine town to explore.*

*A scenic harbor, luxurious mansions, and a wide beach are town highlights in **Manchester-by-the-Sea**.*

FINISH Ipswich

START Manchester-by-the-Sea

↑ The Great House at Castle Hill in Ipswich, surrounded by lush foliage

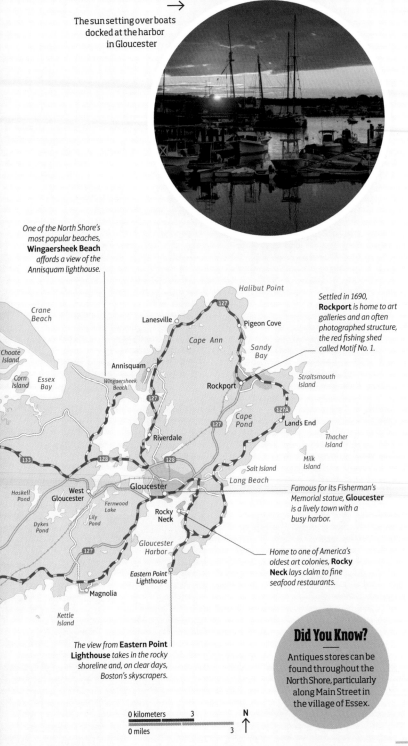

The sun setting over boats docked at the harbor in Gloucester

One of the North Shore's most popular beaches, **Wingaersheek Beach** affords a view of the Annisquam lighthouse.

Settled in 1690, **Rockport** is home to art galleries and an often photographed structure, the red fishing shed called Motif No. 1.

Famous for its Fisherman's Memorial statue, **Gloucester** is a lively town with a busy harbor.

Home to one of America's oldest art colonies, **Rocky Neck** lays claim to fine seafood restaurants.

The view from **Eastern Point Lighthouse** takes in the rocky shoreline and, on clear days, Boston's skyscrapers.

Did You Know?

Antiques stores can be found throughout the North Shore, particularly along Main Street in the village of Essex.

0 kilometers 3
0 miles 3

N ↑

RHODE ISLAND

Like Massachusetts, Rhode Island (or RI) was inhabited long before it was colonized. At the time of European contact, the principal Algonkian-speaking Indigenous peoples were the Narragansett, the Pequot, and the Wampanoag. Reduced in numbers during the 1616–19 plague that swept coastal New England, they welcomed initial European settlement. But friction over land rights led to bloody raids on both English and indigenous towns, culminating in King Philip's War (1675–78). Tribal allies under Metacomet put up a valiant fight, but were ultimately forced to flee or make peace.

Yet, this small state was founded on big ideals. Driven from the Massachusetts Bay colony in 1636 for his outspoken beliefs on religious freedom, clergyman Roger Williams (1604–83) purchased land from the Narragansetts and established a small settlement on the banks of Narragansett Bay. He founded Providence upon the tenets of freedom of speech and religious tolerance – principles that would be formally introduced in the First Amendment to the US Constitution in 1781. This forward-thinking spirit made Rhode Island the site of America's first synagogue and Baptist church, and some of the nation's earliest libraries, public schools, and colleges. In May 1776 Rhode Island formally declared independence from British rule.

Sturbridge
Southbridge
Webster
Douglas
Uxbridge
Bellingham
Franklin

Woodstock
Thompson
Putnam
Burrillville
North Smithfield
5 WOONSOCKET
Cumberland

Pascoag
Smithfield
Lincoln
Central Falls

Glocester
Chepachet
Greenville
PAWTUCKET 4

Foster
PROVIDENCE 1
East Providence

CONNECTICUT
Hampton
Danielson
Brooklyn
Johnston
Cranston
Barrington

Canterbury
RHODE ISLAND
West Warwick
T.F. Green Airport
Warwick

CONNECTICUT
p226
Coventry
Apponaug
East Greenwich

Jewett City
West Greenwich
12 WICKFORD

Pachaug Pond
Austin
Exeter
North Kingstown

Norwich
Liberty
SAUNDERSTOWN
13

Wyoming
Richmond
West Kingston
Kingston
JAMESTOWN 11

Canonchet
SOUTH KINGSTOWN 10
Beavertail State Park

Hopkinton
Wakefield
14

Westerly
CHARLESTOWN
Matunuck
NARRAGANSETT

Mystic
Westerly State Airport
Weekapaug
Galilee
Point Judith

Groton
Stonington
Napatree Point
WATCH HILL 16
Misquamicut Beach
Charlestown Breachway

Fishers Island
Block Island Sound

Block Island
New Shoreham

Scituate
Scituate Reservoir
West Warwick
Worden Pond
Burlingame State Park
15

0 kilometers 10
0 miles 10
N

RHODE ISLAND

Must Sees
1 Providence
2 Newport

Experience More
3 Bristol
4 Pawtucket
5 Woonsocket
6 Tiverton
7 Little Compton
8 Portsmouth
9 Middletown
10 South Kingstown
11 Jamestown
12 Wickford
13 Saunderstown
14 Narragansett
15 Charlestown
16 Watch Hill

↑ Waterplace Park and Riverwalk, warm weather gathering spots

❶

PROVIDENCE

D6 ✈Warwick ☐Providence Station 🚌🚐Point St (to Newport) ℹ1 Sabin St; www.goprovidence.com

Sandwiched between Boston and New York, Providence started life as a small farming community. It became a flourishing seaport in the 17th century, and evolved into an industrial hub in the 19th century, with immigrants from Europe pouring in to work in the burgeoning textile mills. Downtown Providence, to the west of the Providence River, has undergone several renewal phases, and the reclaimed waterfront and developing arts and entertainment district have helped inject new vitality into the city's core. Visitors are best served by exploring on foot.

① Benefit Street's Mile of History

☐Benefit St 🔲mileofhistory.org

The buildings along Benefit Street's Mile of History each tell a story. The **RISD Museum of Art** houses a collection of artworks from Ancient Egyptian to contemporary American. The elegant 1838 Greek Revival **Providence Athenaeum** is where Edgar Allan Poe found inspiration for his poem *Annabel Lee* (1849).

Other architectural gems include the **First Unitarian Church** with a bell cast by Paul Revere (p102).

RISD Museum of Art

 ☐224 Benefit St 🕐10am–5pm Tue–Sun, 10am–9pm 3rd Thu of month 🚫Public hols 🔲risdmuseum.org

Providence Athenaeum

☐251 Benefit St 🕐10am–7pm Mon–Thu, 10am–6pm Fri & Sat, 1–5pm Sun 🚫Summer: Sat pm, Sun 🔲providenceathenaeum.org

First Unitarian Church

☐310 Benefit St 📞(401) 421-7970 🕐Daily

② ♿ Ⓜ

First Baptist Church in America

☐75 N Main St 📞(401) 454-3418 🕐11am–2pm Mon–Fri

Founded in 1638 by Roger Williams and built in 1774–5, the First Baptist Church in America is noted for its Ionic columns, intricately carved wood interior, and large Waterford crystal chandelier. It is also listed as a National Historic Landmark.

↑ Books lining the walls from floor to ceiling at Providence Athenaeum

Governor Stephen Hopkins House

🏠 15 Hopkins St 🕐 11am-2pm Wed (Apr-Nov: also 10am-4pm Sat) 🌐 stephenhopkins.org

The 1707 Governor Stephen Hopkins House belonged to one of the signatories to the Declaration of Independence.

Brown University

🏠 75 Waterman St 🌐 brown.edu

Founded in 1764, Brown is the seventh-oldest college in the US and one of the

Did You Know?

Providence has more doughnut shops per capita than any other region in the United States.

prestigious Ivy League schools. The campus, a rich blend of Gothic and Beaux-Arts styles, is a National Historic Landmark. The Center for Slavery and Justice addresses the source of the family wealth that helped to found the school. Other buildings of note include University Hall, where French and colonial troops were quartered during the American Revolution; Manning Hall, which houses the University Chapel; the John Carter Brown Library, with its fascinating collection of Americana; and the List Art Building, a striking structure that contains classical and contemporary art.

John Brown House

🏠 52 Power St 🕐 Times vary, check website 🚫 Public hols 🌐 rihs.org

This Georgian mansion was built in 1786 for John Brown (1736–1803). A successful merchant and shipowner, he played a lead role in the

INSIDER TIP
WaterFire

See Providence in a new light as over 80 bonfires cast a magical glow on downtown rivers. Lightings take place at sunset on selected evenings from May through October (www.waterfire.org).

burning of the British customs ship *Gaspee* in a pre-Revolutionary War raid in 1772. The John Brown House was the most lavish of its era, introducing Providence to many new architectural elements, including the projecting entrance, Doric portico, and the Palladian window above it. Sparing no expense, Brown ordered wallpapers from France and furniture from famed cabinet-makers Townsend and Goddard. The 12-room house has been impeccably restored and is a repository for some of the finest furniture and antiques of that period.

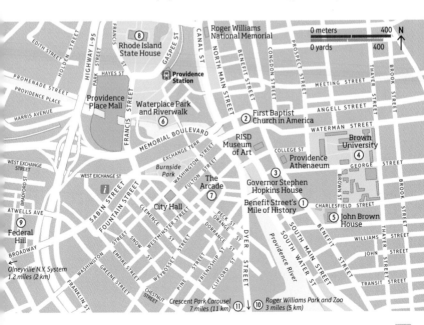

⑥

Waterplace Park and Riverwalk

⌂ Memorial Blvd **⏰** Dawn-dusk daily

One of the brightest additions to downtown Providence is this walkway at the junction of the Moshassuck, Providence, and Woonasquatucket rivers. Visitors can stroll the park's cobblestone paths, float under footbridges in rented kayaks or canoes, take a romantic gondola ride, or enjoy the free concerts and the WaterFire extravaganza during the summer months.

⑦

The Arcade

⌂ 65 Weybosset St
🌐 arcadeprovidence.com

Known as the "Temple of Trade," this 1828 Greek Revival building has the distinction of being the first indoor shopping mall in the US. The massive, three-story stone complex has been acclaimed as "one of the three finest commercial buildings in 19th-century America" by New York's Metropolitan Museum of Art. Inside a skylight extends the entire length of the building, which contains high-end boutiques and restaurants at ground level and micro-lofts above.

⑧

Rhode Island State House

⌂ 82 Smith St **☎** (401) 222-3983 **⏰** 8:30am–4:30pm Mon-Fri **🚫** Public hols

Dominating the city landscape, this imposing building was constructed in 1904 by the prominent New York firm McKim, Mead, & White. The white Georgian marble dome is one of the largest self-supported domes in the world. A bronze statue called *Independent Man*, a longtime symbol of Rhode Island's free spirit, stands atop the magnificent building. Among the displays in the statehouse are a full-length portrait of President George Washington by Gilbert Stuart (1755–1828), a portrait of Providence resident and Civil War General Ambrose Burnside painted by Emanuel Leutze (1816–68), and the original colonial charter of 1663. Tours depart at 9am, 10am, 11am, 1pm, and 2pm.

> Federal Hill is known for its abundance of authentic Italian delicatessens, trattorias, restaurants, bakeries, import stores, and its pleasant old-world piazza.

⑨

Federal Hill

Visitors will know they are in Little Italy once they pass through Federal Hill's impressive arched gateway, decorated with a traditional bronze pine cone. A stripe down the center of the street – in the colors of the Italian flag – confirms that this lively neighborhood in the

↓ Rhode Island State House and *(inset)* its highly decorative inner dome

EAT

Olneyville
N.Y. System

Wieners served on a bun with mustard, onions, celery salt, and secret recipe meat sauce are a signature Rhode Island delicacy. Best enjoyed after a heavy night on the town.

□ 18 Plainfield St
□ till late ⊚ olneyville newyorksystem.com

⑤⑤⑤

↑ Waterside gazebo at Roger Williams Park and Zoo

Federal Hill district is truly Italian in spirit. Bordered by Federal and Broadway streets and Atwells Avenue, Federal Hill is known for its abundance of authentic Italian delicatessens, trattorias, restaurants, bakeries, import stores, and its pleasant old-world piazza.

Roger Williams Park and Zoo

□ 1000 Elmwood Ave
🚌 ⊚ Times vary, check website □ Dec 25
⊚ rwpconservancy.org

In 1871 Betsey Williams, a direct descendant of Roger Williams, donated 0.2 sq miles (0.5 sq km) of prime real estate to the city for use as parkland. Since that time, another 0.5 sq mile (1.3 sq km) of property has been added to the site. Once farmland, the park is now a major recreational resource with ponds, a lake with paddleboats and row-boats for rent, well-trodden jogging and cycling paths, baseball diamonds, and a tennis center. Children especially love the carousel. The park has a number of

exciting attractions such as the Museum of Natural History and Planetarium, which describes itself as "the people's university." Here, exhibits range from curiosities collected in Victorian times to a look at space exploration.

The verdant Roger Williams Park Botanical Center accommodates up to 12,000 sq ft (3,657 sq m) of indoor gardens as well as a lush outdoor garden displaying more than 150 different species of cultivars.

One of the most popular features of the park is the exciting Roger Williams Park Zoo. Go on the Marco Polo Adventure Trek which features animals such as camels, snow leopards, Asian black bears, and endangered red pandas.

⑪

Crescent Park Carousel

□ 700 Bullocks Blvd, Riverside ⊚ Times vary, check website □ Dec 25
⊚ crescentparkcarousel.org

The carvings of the Crescent Park Carousel, built between 1905 and 1910 by carousel innovator Charles I.D. Looff, were models from which other amusement parks could order their own carousels. Considered the apogee of the carousel carving arts, the fully restored ride twirls to the tunes of its historic mechanical band organ.

ROGER WILLIAMS

Williams (1603-83) was a friend of the indigenous inhabitants of Rhode Island. He defied the strict restraints of the Massachusetts Bay Colony, believing that all people should be free to worship as they liked. Banished for his outspoken views, he established his own colony of Rhode Island and Providence Plantations, obtaining the land from the Narragansett people, so that "no man should be molested for his conscience sake." It became the country's first experiment in religious liberty.

↑ Newport's scenic Cliff Walk, lined with stunning mansions

②

NEWPORT

🅰 B1 ℹ️ 23 America's Cup Ave; www.discovernewport.org

A center of trade, culture, wealth, and military activity for more than 300 years, Newport is a true sightseeing mecca. Historical firsts abound in this small city. America's first naval college and synagogue are here, as are the oldest library in the country and one of the oldest continuously operating taverns. Any visit to the city should include a tour of the mansions from the Gilded Age of the late 19th century, when the wealthy flocked here each summer to beat New York's heat.

①

Brick Market Museum and Shop

🏠 127 Thames St 📞 (401) 841-8770 🕙 10am–5pm daily

One of Newport's architectural treasures, the Brick Market, a commercial hub during the 18th century, has been carefully renovated and is now a fascinating museum that provides an excellent introduction to the city's architecture and economic, social, and sporting past. Exhibits include a video of historic Bellevue Avenue. Guided walking tours are also offered.

②

Touro Synagogue

🏠 85 Touro St 📞 (401) 847-4794 🕙 Times vary, call for hours

America's oldest synagogue, Touro was erected in 1763 by Sephardic Jews who had fled Spain and Portugal in search of religious tolerance. Designed by architect Peter Harrison (1716–75), it is considered one of the country's finest examples of 18th-century architecture. Services still follow the Sephardic rituals of its founders. Visitors can learn about prominent Jews in America's early history.

③

Newport Mansions

🏠 424 Bellevue Ave
🌐 newportmansions.org

Built between 1748 and 1902, nine of these summer "cottages," modeled on European palaces, are open for guided tours. The Breakers (p214) is one of the finest examples.

↑ Exhibits at the Touro Synagogue, America's oldest synagogue

④ International Yacht Restoration School

🏠 449 Thames St ⏰ Times vary, check website 🚫 Public hols 🌐 iyrs.edu

This school provides a fascinating insight into yacht restoration. Visitors can observe students from the mezzanine, and tour the waterfront campus. The top-floor library displays artifacts such as miniature model boats and yachting trophies.

---

⑤ Fort Adams State Park

🏠 Harrison Ave 📞 (401) 847-2400 ⏰ Park: sunrise-sunset daily; Fort: summer: 10am-3pm daily

Originally constructed in 1799 to protect the US naval fleet, then based in Newport, Fort Adams was expanded to its mammoth size in 1857, at a cost of $3 million, to house 2,400 soldiers. The surrounding park is popular for boating, picnicking, and soccer and rugby matches. Anglers often fish from the pair of specially designated piers, while boaters use ramps to launch their craft. Views from the Bay Walk trail include stunning sunsets over Conanicut Island. Each summer the grounds host the nationally renowned Newport Jazz and Newport Folk festivals.

> **GREAT VIEW**
> **Cliff Walk**
>
> The 3.5-mile (5.5-km) walk along Newport's rugged cliffs offers some of the best views of the city's grand mansions. The Forty Steps, each step named for someone lost at sea, lead to the ocean.

⑥ International Tennis Hall of Fame

🏠 194 Bellevue Ave 📞 (401) 849-3990 ⏰ 10am-5pm daily 🚫 Jan-Mar: Tue; Thanksgiving, Dec 25 🌐 tennisfame.com

The hall is housed in the Newport Casino, which dates from 1880. The first US National Lawn Tennis Championship, later known as the US Open, was held here in 1881. The museum displays everything from antique rackets to the "comeback" outfit worn by Monica Seles (b.1973). The grass courts are open to the public.

---

⑦ Redwood Library and Athenaeum

🏠 50 Bellevue Ave ⏰ 9:30am-5:30pm Mon-Sat (to 8pm Wed), 1-5pm Sun 🌐 redwoodlibrary.org

Completed in 1750, the Redwood is one of the oldest continuously operating libraries in America and an early example of a temple-form building. As well as rare books and manuscripts, the library's museum contains colonial portraits, sculpture, and furniture.

> **PINEAPPLE SYMBOLISM**
>
> While on trade missions to Africa and the West Indies, Newport's sailors ate fresh fruit to ward off scurvy. What they did not eat, they brought home to their families. It became a tradition to place a pineapple on the gate-post when the seagoing man of the house had returned. The fruit became a local symbol of hospitality and was often incorporated into the front door. Pineapples appear on many old Newport homes.

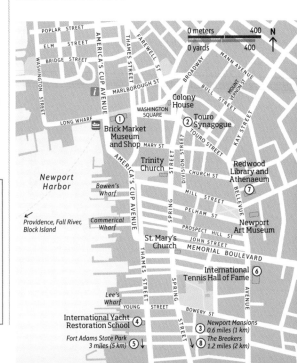

⑧

THE BREAKERS

📍 Ochre Point Ave 🕐 Mid-May-Aug: 9am-6pm daily; Sep-Oct 9am-5pm daily; check website for winter hours 🚫 Thanksgiving, Dec 25 🌐 newportmansions.org

The most elaborate of the Newport Mansions, the gilt and marble encrusted interior of The Breakers is a breathtaking insight into the preeminance of the Vanderbilt family.

The architecture and ostentation of the Gilded Age *(p56)* of the late 1800s reached its pinnacle with The Breakers, the summer home of railroad magnate Cornelius Vanderbilt II (1843–99). Completed in 1895, the four-story, 70-room limestone structure surpassed all other Newport mansions in extravagance. US architect Richard Morris Hunt modeled the building after the 16th-century palaces in Turin and Genoa. Its interior is adorned with marble, alabaster, stained glass, gilt, and crystal. The Breakers also hosts a number of special events, including lectures, film screenings, and flower shows.

> ## A MAGNATE'S LIFE
>
> Cornelius Vanderbilt II inherited the mantle as head of the Vanderbilt empire in 1885. He directed the family businesses, mainly railroads, with his brother for 11 years, before suffering a paralyzing stroke. He died in 1899 at the age of 56. At which time, the local gossip held that he had more money than the US Mint.

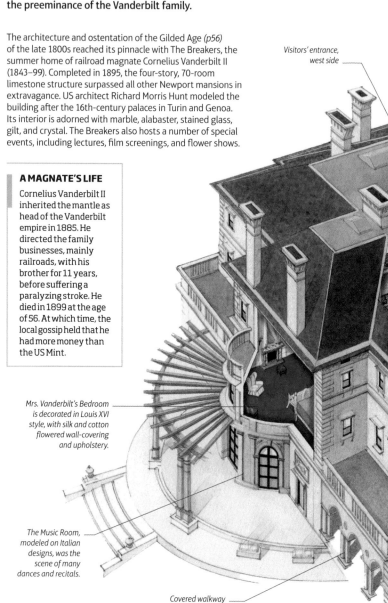

Visitors' entrance, west side

Mrs. Vanderbilt's Bedroom is decorated in Louis XVI style, with silk and cotton flowered wall-covering and upholstery.

The Music Room, modeled on Italian designs, was the scene of many dances and recitals.

Covered walkway

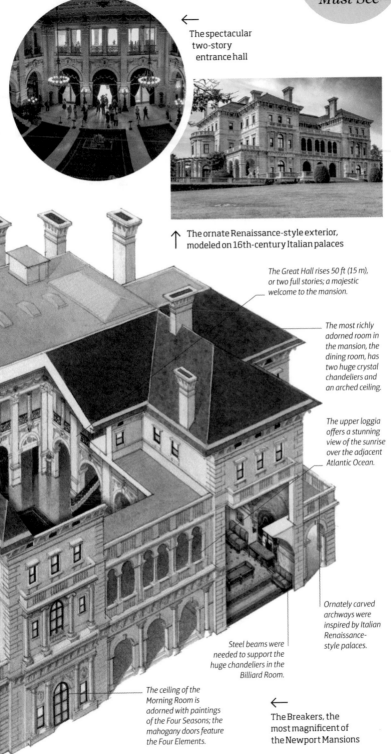

The spectacular two-story entrance hall

←

↑ The ornate Renaissance-style exterior, modeled on 16th-century Italian palaces

The Great Hall rises 50 ft (15 m), or two full stories; a majestic welcome to the mansion.

The most richly adorned room in the mansion, the dining room, has two huge crystal chandeliers and an arched ceiling.

The upper loggia offers a stunning view of the sunrise over the adjacent Atlantic Ocean.

Ornately carved archways were inspired by Italian Renaissance-style palaces.

Steel beams were needed to support the huge chandeliers in the Billiard Room.

The ceiling of the Morning Room is adorned with paintings of the Four Seasons; the mahogany doors feature the Four Elements.

← The Breakers, the most magnificent of the Newport Mansions

EXPERIENCE MORE

 3

Bristol

A A2 **i** 400 Hope St, Warren; www.bristolri.us

Bristol blossomed in the late 18th century when its status as a major commercial, fishing, whaling, and shipbuilding center made it the nation's fourth-busiest port. The many elegant Federal and Victorian mansions lining Hope, High, and Thames streets attest to those prosperous days. One such fine home is the 1810 **Linden Place**, where scenes from *The Great Gatsby* (1974) were filmed. The Federal-style mansion was built by General George DeWolf (1772–1844) with money he had made from his Cuban sugar plantations and the trade of enslaved people.

The trappings of wealth are also evident at **Blithewold Mansion and Gardens**. Built in 1894 for Pennsylvania coal baron Augustus Van Wickle (1856–98), the grounds offer spectacular views of Narragansett Bay.

Bristol's history as the producer of America's greatest yachts is traced at the **Herreshoff Marine Museum and America's Cup Hall of Fame**. The museum is set on Narragansett Bay, at the site of the Herreshoff Manufacturing Company, which built yachts for eight America's Cup races. The museum also operates a sailing school, and hosts classic yacht regattas.

Colt State Park, a 0.7-sq-mile (1.9-sq-km) shoreline park, features a 3-mile (5-km) drive along Narragansett Bay, a bicycle trail, many picnic areas, and playing fields. Also on the park grounds is the **Coggeshall Farm Museum**, a restored 1790s' coastal farm with a barn, blacksmith's shop, and heirloom breeds of domesticated animals.

Linden Place

⊘⊗⊚ **↟** 500 Hope St ◷ Jan-Apr & Nov: 10am-4pm Tue-Fri; May, Oct, & Dec: 10am-4pm Tue-Sat, noon-4pm Sun **w** lindenplace.org

Blithewold Mansion and Gardens

⊘ **↟** 101 Ferry Rd ◷ Times vary, check website ◷ Public hols **w** blithewold.org

Herreshoff Marine Museum and America's Cup Hall of Fame

⊘⊗ **↟** 1 Burnside St ◷ Jun-Sep: 10am-5pm daily; Oct-Dec: 10am-5pm Wed-Sun **w** herreshoff.org

↑ The scenic trail by Narragansett Bay, Bristol, a perfect spot for rollerblading and cycling

↑ Period interiors at the Old Slater Mill National Historic Landmark

Colt State Park
🏠 Rte 114 🕐 Daily
🌐 riparks.com

Coggeshall Farm Museum
♿ 🏠 Poppasquash Rd off Rte 114 🕐 Late-May-early-Sep: 10am-4pm Tue-Sun; check website for off-season hours 🌐 coggeshallfarm.org

---

4

Pawtucket

🅰 C6 ℹ 175 Main St; www.pawtucketri.com

This bustling city, built on hills sliced by the Blackstone, Ten Mile, and Moshassuck rivers is generally acknowledged to be the birthplace of America's Industrial Revolution. In 1793 mechanical engineer Samuel Slater (1768–1835) built the country's first water-powered cotton-spinning mill here.

The Old Slater Mill National Historic Landmark

A major historic site, the **Old Slater Mill National Historic Landmark** includes the restored Slater Mill and the 1810 Wilkinson Mill, complete with the only 8-ton (7-tonne) water wheel in the US.

At the **Slater Memorial Park** on the Ten Mile River, there are trails, paddleboats, tennis courts, and a seasonal 1895 Looff carousel. The stationary-style carousel is the oldest in the country still in its original building. The park also features the city's oldest dwelling, the 1685 Daggett House, which has been a museum since 1905. You can enjoy summer music as well as Halloween and winter wonderland events at the park.

Old Slater Mill National Historic Landmark
♿ ⓦ 🏠 Roosevelt & Slater aves 📞 (401) 725-8638 🕐 Mar, Apr, & Nov: 11am-3pm Sat & Sun; May-Oct: 10am-4pm Tue-Sun (Jul & Aug: also Mon)

Slater Memorial Park
♿ 🏠 Newport Ave 📞 (401) 728-0500 ext 252 🕐 8:30am-dusk daily

Woonsocket

🅰 C6 ℹ 175 Main St, Pawtucket; www.woonsocketri.org

Located on the busy Blackstone River, Woonsocket was transformed from a relatively small village to a booming mill town by the development of the local textile industry in the 19th and early 20th centuries. Although the textile industry declined after World War II, the city remains one of its major manufacturing hubs.

The **Museum of Work and Culture** focuses on the impact of the Industrial Revolution on the region. The daily lives of the factory owners and workers are examined with the help of multimedia exhibits.

Museum of Work and Culture
♿ 🏠 42 S Main St 📞 (401) 769-9675 🕐 9:30am-4pm Tue-Fri, 10am-4pm Sat, 1-4pm Sun

---

Tiverton

🅰 D6 🌐 tiverton.ri.gov

Sandwiched between the Sakonnet River and the Massachusetts border, the village of Tiverton is blessed with some of the richest farmland in New England. Handsome stone walls line the few roadways, and the rolling fields yield everything from pumpkins to succulent strawberries. The crossroads at Tiverton Four Corners is the *de facto* market village; Gray's Ice Cream parlor and Groundswell Cafe + Bakery two of the corners, while antiques dealers and art galleries fill many of the other beautifully preserved 18th- and 19th-century buildings.

→ Exhibit at the Museum of Work and Culture in Woonsocket

❼ Little Compton

🅰 D7 ℹ 23 America's Cup Ave, Newport; www.little-compton.com

Residents of Little Compton justifiably relish their isolated nook at the end of a peninsula that borders Massachusetts: it is one of the most charming villages in the entire state, sheltered by the surrounding farmlands and woods.

The white-steepled United Congregational Church stands over Little Compton Commons. Beside the church lies the Old Commons Burial Ground, with the gravesite of Elizabeth Padobie (c. 1623–1717), who was the first white woman born in New England. The 1680 **Wilbor House** is also a draw. It was home to eight generations of the Wilbor family, and is furnished with period pieces and antique household items.

Nearby **Carolyn's Sakonnet Vineyard** is the largest winery in the region. There are daily wine tastings and guided tours. Beyond the vineyard on Route 77 is Sakonnet Wharf, where curious onlookers can watch as fishermen arrive at shore with their catches.

Wilbor House

⊗ 🏠 548 W Main Rd 📞 (401) 635-4035 🕐 Call for hours

Carolyn's Sakonnet Vineyard

 ☺ 🏠 162 W Main Rd 🕐 11am–5pm daily 🅦 sakonnetwine.com

❽ Portsmouth

🅰 D6 ℹ 23 America's Cup Ave, Newport; www. portsmouthri.com

Portsmouth figures greatly in Rhode Island history. It was the second settlement in the old colony, founded in 1638 just two years after Providence.

> **Portsmouth figures greatly in Rhode Island history. It was the second settlement in the old colony, founded in 1638 just two years after Providence.**

The town was also the site of the 1778 Battle of Rhode Island, the state's only major land battle during the American Revolution. Bad weather and fierce British resistance forced the US troops to retreat. With the British in hot pursuit, only the courage of the American rear guard enabled most of the soldiers to escape to the sanctuary of Butts Hill Fort. Today some of the fort's redoubts are still visible from Sprague Street, where plaques recount the battle.

The **Green Animals Topiary Garden** is a much more whimsical attraction. Located on a Victorian estate, the garden is inhabited by a wild and wonderful array of topiary creations. In all, some 80 animal shapes – including elephants, giraffes, and even a dinosaur – have been trimmed and sculpted from a selection of yew, English box-wood, and California privet. Elsewhere on the grounds, formal flower gardens and a Victorian home with an extensive collection of period toys will delight younger visitors.

Green Animals Topiary Garden

⊗ 🏠 Cory's Lane 📞 (401) 847-1000 🕐 May–Oct: 10am–5pm daily

❾ Middletown

🅰 D7 ℹ 23 America's Cup Ave, Newport; www. middletownri.com

Nestled between Newport (p212) and the bustling town of Portsmouth, Middletown is known for its proximity to a number of popular beaches.

→

Gentle waves rolling in to the scenic coastal town of Middletown

Magnificent hedge-sculpted animal in Little Compton's Green Animals Topiary Garden

Third Beach is located on the Sakonnet River, where a steady wind and relatively calm water make it a favorite with windsurfers and young families. Third Beach runs into the largest and most beautiful beach in the area. Sachuest, or **Second Beach**, is widely considered one of the best places to surf in southern New England. This spacious strand is rippled with sand dunes and equipped with campgrounds. Purgatory Chasm, a narrow cleft in the rock ledges on the east side of Easton Point, provides a scenic outlook over both the beach and 50-ft-(15-m) high Hanging Rock.

Second Beach is adjacent to the **Norman Bird Sanctuary**, a wildlife area with 7 miles (11 km) of walking trails that are ideal for birding. Some 250 species have been sighted at this sanctuary, including herons, woodcocks, and swans. The refuge is home to numerous four-legged animals, such as rabbits and red foxes. You can also learn organic gardening on site, and during the winter months the sanctuary trails are used by cross-country skiers.

Third Beach

⊘ ⌂ Third Beach Rd ☎ (401) 849-2822 ⊙ Memorial Day–Labor Day: lifeguards on duty 9am–5pm daily

Second Beach

⊘ ⌂ Third Beach Rd ☎ (401) 849-2822 ⊙ Memorial Day–Labor Day: lifeguards on duty 8am–6pm daily

Norman Bird Sanctuary

⊘ ⊛ ⌂ 583 Third Beach Rd ☎ (401) 846-2577 ⊙ 9am–5pm daily ⊗ Thanksgiving, Dec 25

---

⑩

South Kingstown

⌜A⌟ C7 ⌜i⌟ 4808 Tower Hill Rd, Wakefield; www.south kingstownri.com

South Kingstown is a 55-sq-mile (142-sq-km) town that encompasses 15 villages, including Kingstown, Green Hill, Wakefield, and Snug Harbor. The town is home to the **Peace Dale Museum of Art and Culture**. Located in an 1856 post office, the museum displays weapons and tools of indigenous cultures around the world, including from prehistoric New England.

After visiting the museum, travelers can enjoy the region's outdoor charms. Enthusiastic sightseers, particularly those with cameras, should trek to the top of the observation post at Hannah Robinson Rock and Tower, where they'll

find expansive views of the Atlantic Ocean and the Rhode Island seashore.

The paved South County Bike Path starts at the Kingstown train station, and takes cyclists through Great Swamp, the scene of the 1675 slaughter of 2,000 Narragansett people at the hands of soldiers and settlers – one of New England's bloodiest ever battles. The swamp is now a wildlife refuge called the **Great Swamp Management Area**, crisscrossed with nature trails and home to creatures such as coyotes, mink, and wild turkeys.

Peace Dale Museum of Art and Culture

⊘ ⌂ 1058 Kingstown Rd ☎ (401) 783-5711 ⊙ Sep–Jun: 10am–2pm Wed

Great Swamp Management Area

⌂ Liberty Lane off Great Neck Rd ☎ (401) 789-0281 ⊙ Dawn–dusk daily

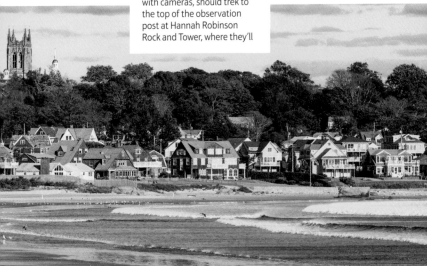

Jamestown

A C7 **i** 23 America's Cup Ave, Newport; (401) 849-8048 or (800) 326-6030

Named for England's King James II (1633–1701), Jamestown is located on Conanicut Island and linked to Newport *(p212)* and the mainland by a pair of bridges. During the Revolutionary War, British troops torched much of the town, sparing very few houses from that era.

The town is best known for the **Beavertail Lighthouse and State Park**, perched at the southernmost tip of the island. The first lighthouse here was built in 1749 and was replaced by the present structure in 1856. As with many New England lighthouses, the coastal vistas from Beavertail are beautiful. The winds, surf, and currents can be heavy at times, but on calm days hiking, climbing, and sunbathing are favorite pastimes here.

Situated on the site of an early fort and artillery battery, **Fort Wetherill State Park** offers great scenic outlooks. The park is a popular place for saltwater fishing, boating, and scuba diving. Legend has it that notorious privateer Captain Kidd (1645–1701) stashed some of his plundered loot in the park's Pirate Cave.

Beavertail Lighthouse and State Park

⊗ **A** Beavertail Pt **C** (401) 423-3270 Park: ⏱ Dawn-dusk daily (call for lighthouse hours)

Fort Wetherill State Park

⊗ **A** Fort Wetherill Rd **C** (401) 884-2010 ⏱ Dawn-dusk daily

---

Wickford

A C6 **i** 4160 Old Post Rd, Charlestown; (401) 789-4422 or (800) 548-4662

Considered a part of North Kingstown, the village of Wickford lies in the northern-most point of Washington County, also known as South County. Wickford's many 18th- and 19th- century houses are a magnet for artists and craftsmen. John Updike, author of *Rabbit Run* (1960), had family roots here. The 1745 Updike House on Pleasant Street is one of some 60 buildings constructed before 1804.

Day-trippers hailing from Providence and Connecticut are known to jam Wickford's picturesque harbor and shopping streets. At the corner of Brown and Phillips streets, the Kayak Centre of Rhode Island offers paddling tours on Narragansett Bay.

Old Narragansett Church (more commonly called Old St. Paul's) is one of the oldest Episcopal churches in the US, dating back to 1707, with an organ from 1660 and an upstairs gallery to which enslaved people were relegated. Artist Gilbert Stuart (1755–1828) was baptized here in a silver font given to the church as a gift by England's Queen Anne (1665–1714).

One mile north of town is **Smith's Castle**, one of the oldest plantation houses in America. In 1678 settler Richard Smith built a dwelling on the site. Hardly a castle, the structure served as a garrison for the soldiers who had

Did You Know?

John Updike's *The Witches of Eastwick* is set in a waterside village modeled on Wickford, RI.

↑ Gilbert Stuart Birthplace, set along the Mattatuxet River in Saunderstown

participated in the 1675 Great Swamp Fight. The battle was the first in a chain of tragic events, culminating in the retaliatory destruction of the garrison and the death of 40 soldiers. Later the structure was rebuilt and acquired by the Updike family in 1692. Subsequent renovations transformed it into one of the most handsome plantation houses on the Rhode Island shore. The house contains fine paneling, 17th- and 18th-century furnishings, china, and a chair once owned by Roger Williams (p211).

Smith's Castle

◈◉ ⌂55 Richard Smith Dr
☏(401) 294-3521 ⊙Times vary, call for hours

 13

Saunderstown

⌂C7 ℹ8045 Post Rd, North Kingstown; (401) 295-5566

Located between Wickford and Narragansett, this town has two main attractions. The gambrel-roofed **Gilbert Stuart Birthplace** was built in 1751. Stuart (1755–1828), whose portraits of US presidents were to bring him lasting fame, was born here. His best-known portrait, of George Washington, graces the US one-dollar bill.

On the lower level of the house, Stuart's father built a large kitchen and snuff mill. The upstairs living quarters are authentically furnished.

Also in town is the **Silas Casey Farm**, dating back to 1702, which offers guided tours and a farmers' market (May–Oct). The property is ringed by almost 30 miles (48 km) of stone walls.

Gilbert Stuart Birthplace

◈◉ ⌂815 Gilbert Stuart Rd
⊙May–mid-Oct; times vary, check website 🖥gilbert stuartmuseum.org

Silas Casey Farm

◈◉ ⌂2325 Boston Neck Rd ☏(401) 295-1030
⊙Jun–mid-Oct: 1–5pm Tue & Thu, 9am–2pm Sat

EAT

George's of Galilee
Fishermen from this small port town land a delicious array of fish and seafood. For an excellent selection, head to the open deck of George's, just a short drive down the coast from Jamestown.

⌂C7 ⌂250 Sand Hill Cove Rd, Galilee 🖥georgesofgalilee.com

⑤⑤⑤

Matunuck Oyster Bar
The salt ponds of Matunuck are acclaimed for briny farmed oysters. Here, pioneering aquaculturalist Perry Raso serves them alongside veggies from his farm.

⌂D6 ⌂69 Succotash Rd, Matunuck 🖥rhody oysters.com

⑤⑤⑤

←
The sun rising over the bridge linking Jamestown and Newport

14

Narragansett

🗺️ C7 ✈️ TF Green Airport
ℹ️ 36 Ocean Rd; www.
narraganettri.gov

In the late 19th century this town's waterfront area gained national fame as a fashionable resort, complete with a large casino. In 1900 a devastating fire razed the 1884 casino and many of the lavish hotels. All that remains of the former casino are **The Towers**, two stone towers linked by a Romanesque-Revival-style arch.

Today society digs have given way to rolling waves, as the town beach offers some of the best surfing on the East Coast. Nearby the **South County Museum** depicts early Rhode Island life with farm animals (including RI red chickens), a one-room schoolhouse, and a working print shop.

The Towers
🕐 🗺️ 35 Ocean Rd ⏰ Check website 🌐 thetowersri.com

South County Museum
♿ 🗺️ Strathmore St off Rte 1 📞 (401) 783-5400 ⏰ Times vary; check website 🌐 southcounty
museum.org

15

Charlestown

🗺️ C7 ✈️🚆 ℹ️ 4945 Old Post Rd; www.charles
townri.org

This small town stretches along 4 miles (6 km) of lovely beaches, encompassing the largest saltwater marsh in the state and several parks. The large **Burlingame State Park** on Watchaug Pond is equipped with campgrounds (note that these are ticketed), trails, swimming and picnic areas, as well as fishing and boating. Birders will enjoy the south side of the park, site of a former Audubon Society Wildlife Sanctuary. It remains a habitat for many kinds of waterfowl and migrating birds.

More outdoor enjoyment can be found at the smaller 0.3-sq-mile (0.7-sq-km) Ninigret Park, the grounds of which include an 18-hole disc-golf course. Every clear Friday night, the park leaves the gates open, so visitors can stargaze at the **Frosty Drew Observatory**, which is open year-round. (The facility is unheated, so be sure to dress accordingly). The Fantastic Umbrella Factory – a collection of quirky shops – is also worth a visit.

STAY

Weekapaug Inn
All the rooms at this shingle-style inn come equipped with a birding guide and binoculars, so guests can take full advantage of the naturalist-guided walks in the region.

🗺️ C7 🗺️ 25 Spray Rock, Westerly
🌐 weekapauginn.com

💲💲💲

Burlingame State Park
🗺️ Rte 1A 📞 (401) 322-8910 ⏰ Apr–early Sep: dawn–dusk daily

Frosty Drew Observatory
🗺️ 61 Park Lane, Ninigret Park
⏰ Fri (weather permitting)
🌐 frostydrew.org

16

Watch Hill

🗺️ C7 ℹ️ 1 Chamber Way, Westerly; (401) 596-7761

A village within the town of Westerly, Watch Hill has been an upscale beach haven for the rich and famous since the 19th century. Strolls along Bay Street yield beautiful views of Victorian houses on rocky hills above the beach. Visitors can enjoy the relaxed atmosphere, with a little window-shopping or sunbathing. The beach's 1867 Flying Horse Carousel is a favorite of children. The vantage point of the Watch Hill Lighthouse offers views of neighboring New York's Fishers Island.

←

Castle Hill Lighthouse, located at the water's edge in Narrangansett

↑ The rising sun burns away mist on Sachuest Beach, Newport

FIVE GREAT BEACHES IN THE OCEAN STATE

Rhode Island is so small that every resident lives within a half-hour drive of more than 400 miles (645 km) of coastline. Complex currents create a steady flow of sand along the shores, resulting in some of New England's finest recreational beaches.

EASTON'S BEACH

🅐D7 🅐Memorial Blvd, Newport

This white sand beach, beloved by surfers, also has a gentler end for safe swimming. Just 2 miles (3 km) to the east, Sachuest Beach, is a local favorite.

NARRAGANSETT BEACH

🅐C7 🅐Boston Neck Rd, Narragansett

Beachgoers flock to the downtown shore of Narragansett for swimming, sunbathing, and surfing.

CHARLESTOWN BREACHWAY

🅐C7 🅐Charlestown Beach Rd, Charlestown

Some 3 miles (5 km) of white sand sprawls to the west of Charlestown Breachway, which maintains a tidal flow between the salt pond and marshes of Ninigret National Wildlife Refuge and the Atlantic Ocean.

MISQUAMICUT BEACH

🅐C7 🅐Atlantic Ave, Westerly

This golden sand barrier beach shelters Winnapaug Pond, a favorite with sailors and swimmers. Adjacent is a retro amusement park.

NAPATREE POINT

🅐C7 🅐Watch Hill, Westerly

This 1.5-mile (2.5 km) sandy spit separates Little Narragansett Bay from the more turbulent waters of the Atlantic Ocean. Swimming and sunbathing are popular here.

↑ A seasoned surfer hits the waves at Narragansett Beach

↑ Beachgoers enjoying the sun on Misquamicut Beach

A DRIVING TOUR
BLOCK ISLAND

RHODE ISLAND

⚓ Block Island

Length 18 miles (29 km) **Starting point** Old Harbor, the island's only village, has several small inns and quaint restaurants that overlook the Atlantic ocean.

Locator Map
For more detail see p206

Lying 13 miles (21 km) off the coast, the haven of Block Island has long been a favorite getaway spot for New Englanders. With 25 per cent of its wild landscape under protection, Block Island is a wonderful destination for outdoor enthusiasts who enjoy such activities as swimming, fishing, sailing, bird-watching, kayaking, canoeing, and horseback riding. Some 30 miles (48 km) of natural trails entice hikers and cyclists alike to experience the island's natural beauty firsthand.

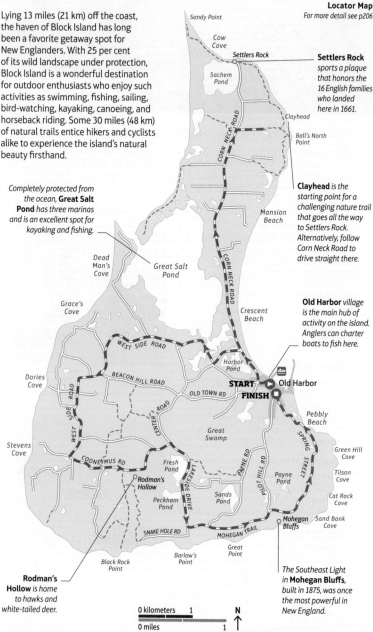

Settlers Rock *sports a plaque that honors the 16 English families who landed here in 1661.*

Completely protected from the ocean, **Great Salt Pond** *has three marinas and is an excellent spot for kayaking and fishing.*

Clayhead *is the starting point for a challenging nature trail that goes all the way to Settlers Rock. Alternatively, follow Corn Neck Road to drive straight there.*

Old Harbor *village is the main hub of activity on the island. Anglers can charter boats to fish here.*

START FINISH Old Harbor

Rodman's Hollow *is home to hawks and white-tailed deer.*

The Southeast Light in **Mohegan Bluffs**, *built in 1875, was once the most powerful in New England.*

0 kilometers 1
0 miles 1

N ↑

The historic and impressive
Southeast Light in
Mohegan Bluffs

CONNECTICUT

Coastal Connecticut was one of the first inhabited areas of New England, as it lay at the southern edge of the retreating glacial ice sheet. The most prominent coastal indigenous peoples at the time of European contact were the Pequot and the offshoot Mohegan. The powerful Pequots pushed back when the Plymouth colony tried to establish settlements on their land. However, the Pequot War (1634–38) resulted in the their dissolution, and English colonists claimed the entire area. But many Pequots remained there and, drawing on continuous records dating to tribal dissolution, they re-formed in 1975 and achieved federal recognition in 1983.

Connecticut has always been a trendsetter, beginning with its adoption in 1639 of the Fundamental Orders of Connecticut – the English Americas' first constitution. It was on Connecticut soil that the nation's first law school and amusement park were built. Scholars and soldiers can thank the fertile minds of state residents for giving them the first dictionary and pistol; gourmands, for the hamburger and corkscrew; and children, for the three-ring circus, lollipop, and frisbee.

Fueled by waterpower, mill towns sprang up along the rivers, eventually giving way to larger commercial centers. But Connecticut is as beautiful as it is industrious, as American artists demonstrated a century ago, when they painted the upland woods and the green and gold marshes of Long Island Sound.

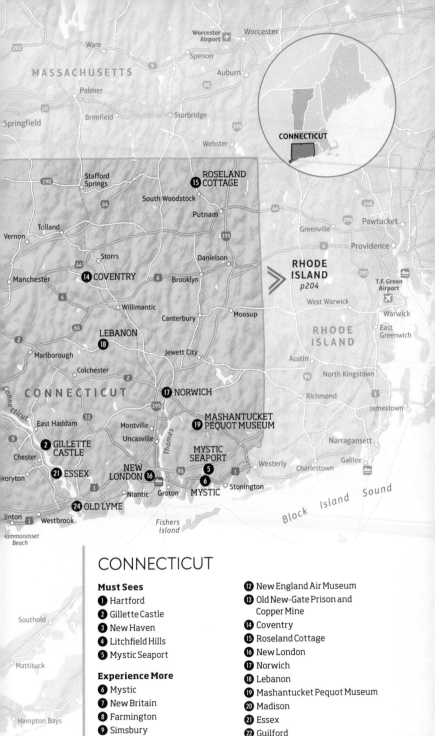

CONNECTICUT

↑ Hartford's glistening high-rise buildings seen from Founders Bridge

①

HARTFORD

🅐 B6 ✈ Bradley Intl Airport 🚆🚌 Union Station
ℹ 800 Main St; ctvisit.com/hartford

An ancient Saukiog settlement and later a Dutch trading post, Connecticut's capital was founded in 1636 by Reverend Thomas Hooker (1586–1647) and a group of 100 Englishmen from the Massachusetts Bay Colony. By the late 19th century, Hartford was flourishing, thanks to an economic boom in the insurance industry and a cultural flowering typified by resident authors Mark Twain and Harriet Beecher Stowe. A revitalization program has helped breathe new life into the downtown core.

① 〈icons〉

Wadsworth Atheneum

🅐 600 Main St 🕐 11am–5pm Wed–Sun (free 4–5pm); 10am–5pm Sat & Sun
🌐 thewadsworth.org

Established in 1842, Wadsworth Atheneum is the oldest continuously operating public art museum in the country. Its extensive collection has 50,000 pieces and spans five centuries. It is particularly strong in Renaissance, Baroque, and Impressionist works, as well as in European decorative arts. The museum is noted for its extensive collection of American paintings, including works by Thomas Cole (1801–48) and Frederic Church (1826–1900). Outside in the Burr Mall is the monumental sculpture, *Stegosaurus* (1973), by Connecticut resident Alexander Calder (1898–1976).

② 〈icons〉

Old State House

🅐 800 Main St 🕐 Jul–Sep: 10am–5pm Tue–Sat; Oct–Jun: 10am–5pm Mon–Fri
🌐 cga.ct.gov/osh

The 1796 State House, thought to have been designed by Charles Bulfinch (1763–1844) and slightly modified since, is the country's oldest Capitol building. It also claims to be the birthplace of democracy in the state of Connecticut, and was named a National Historic Landmark in 1960. Its graceful center hall, grand staircase, and ornate cupola make the Old State House one of the nation's finest examples of Federal architecture. An interactive audio tour highlights the Great Senate Room and the courtroom where enslaved Africans, who revolted aboard the Cuban schooner *Amistad*, won their freedom. Outdoors there is a seasonal farmers' market.

> Established in 1842, Wadsworth Atheneum is the oldest continuously operating public art museum in the country. Its extensive collection has 50,000 pieces and spans five centuries.

③ Center Church and Ancient Burying Ground

🏛 60 Gold St
🕐 10am–4pm daily

Five stained-glass windows designed by US artist Louis Comfort Tiffany (1848–1933) grace the 1807 Center Church (First Church of Christ in Hartford). Its Ancient Burying Ground was once Hartford's only graveyard and contains some 415 headstones dating back to 1648, including that of Hartford's founding father, the Reverend Thomas Hooker. Across Main Street is the 527-ft- (160-m-) high Travelers Tower office building, the tallest man-made observation post in the state.

④ Bushnell Park

🏛 Trinity and Elm sts
🕐 Dawn–dusk daily
🌐 bushnellpark.org

Shaded by 100 tree varieties, Bushnell Park, measuring some 40 acres (16 ha), is the lush creation of noted

↑ The Spanish American War Memorial in Bushnell Park

landscape architect and Hartford native Frederick Law Olmsted (1822–1903). Children adore the park's 1914 Bushnell Carousel, with its 48 hand-carved horses, ornate "lovers' chariots," and refurbished Wurlitzer band organ. The 115-ft- (35-m-) tall Soldiers and Sailors Memorial Arch – tours of which run every Thursday in May–Oct from 12-1:30pm – honors those who saw duty in the American Civil War.

⑤ The Bushnell

🏛 166 Capitol Ave
🌐 bushnell.org

This leading performing arts venue hosts Broadway-style extravaganzas as well as more modest productions. Highlights of the free tours include the historic theater, a state-of-the-art modern stage, and a 14-ft (4-m) glass chandelier.

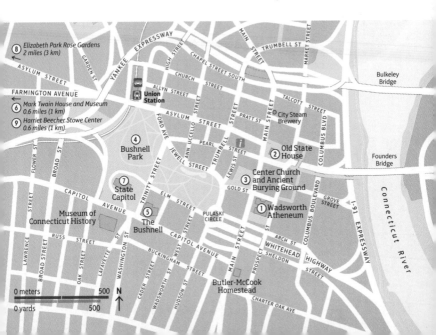

EAT

City Steam Brewery

Handcrafted ales, fish and chips, and similar hearty pub grub are served in the elegant interior of this wood-paneled late-19th-century department store building. There is additional seating outside on the terrace. As a bonus, there's a late-night comedy club in the basement.

942 Main St
w citysteam brewery.com

$ $ $

---

⑥

Mark Twain House and Museum

351 Farmington Ave
9:30am–5:30pm daily
Jan–Feb: Tue, public hols
w marktwainhouse.org

Samuel Clemens (1835–1910) who used the pen name Mark Twain, was a former Mississippi steamboat pilot, humorist, and author who lived here from 1874 to 1891 and penned seven books. Designed by architect Edward Tuckerman Potter, the 19-room home is a masterpiece of the Picturesque-Gothic style. Its expansive upper balconies, peaked gables, towering turrets, and painted brick combine the sense of high style and playfulness personified by its owners. The adjoining museum has extensive exhibits on Twain and his times, including a film produced by award-winning New England documentary filmmaker Ken Burns. Guided tours of the house are obligatory (last tour at 4:30pm).

Did You Know?

The pseudonym Mark Twain signifies a water depth of two fathoms, deep enough for a riverboat.

---

⑦

State Capitol

210 Capitol Ave **(860) 240-0222** **8am–5pm Mon–Fri**

Housing the Connecticut General Assembly, the State Senate, the House of Representatives, and the office of the Governor of the State of Connecticut, the State Capitol was designed by Richard Upjohn (1828–1903) in the High Victorian-Gothic style. It is built of marble and granite and has a golden dome. Highlights of the interior are the oak woodwork and the ornate charter chair. Tours run during the week.

The State Capitol with its resplendent gold dome, and *(inset)* the Victorian-Gothic-style House Chamber

Roses in full bloom at the splendid Elizabeth Park Rose Gardens ↑

Elizabeth Park Rose Gardens

🏠 Prospect Ave 📞 (860) 231-9443 🕐 Dawn-dusk daily

Each year in this delightful park, covering an expansive area, more than 900 varieties of roses bloom on around 15,000 bushes. The park also has herb, perennial, and rock gardens.

Harriet Beecher Stowe Center

🏠 77 Forest St 🕐 9:30am-5pm Mon-Sat, noon-5pm Sun 🕐 Public hols, Jan-Mar: Tue 🖥 harrietbeecher stowe.org

Harriet Beecher Stowe was already rich and famous when she built her Victorian Gothic home at Nook Farm on the west side of Hartford in 1871. Stowe's beautifully preserved home (where she lived until her death in 1896) was renovated in 2017; the house and adjacent buildings form the Stowe Center. Exhibits focus on the sweeping fame and influence of her famous novel *Uncle Tom's Cabin* and its role in abolishing slavery in the US, while giving some small coverage to her other novels. Highly engaging conversational interactive tours of the house range from discussions of Stowe's skill as a decorator to debates over her unapologetic use of melodrama and senti-mentality as political tools. You can also find out more about 19th-century social issues such as the role of women and slavery.

HARRIET BEECHER STOWE

An ardent abolitionist, Harriet Beecher Stowe (1811–96) believed her purpose was to write, and she penned over 30 books. She wrote her 1852 novel *Uncle Tom's Cabin* to publicize the suffering of enslaved African Americans. Although later appropriations of the character of Uncle Tom twisted him into a servile and self-hating stereotype, the original book galvanized anti-slavery movements around the world and hastened the onset of America's Civil War.

2

GILLETTE CASTLE

B7 **67 River Rd off Rte 82, Hadlyme** **(860) 526-2336** **Castle: late May-Labor Day: 11am-5pm Thu-Sun; Park: 8am-dusk daily**

Ostentatious and bizarre, Gillette Castle is the antithesis of New England's renowned architectural grace. However, visitors to this curious 24-room granite mansion and its impressive grounds, always leave with a smile.

Actor William Gillette based the design of his 1919 dream home on medieval castles, complete with battlements and turrets. The castle is rife with such oddities as homemade trick locks, furniture set on wheels and tracks, a cavernous living room, and a series of mirrors starting in his bedroom that permitted him to see who was arriving downstairs in case he wished to be "indisposed" or make a grand entrance.

Constructed on a steel framework, the castle is built of local fieldstone that was lifted up the hill on an aerial tram designed by Gillette himself. He had a generator installed to provide power, but the castle is still dark and baronial. Following Gillette's death, the castle and its 0.2 sq miles (0.5 sq km) of land became a state park. His railroad with its two locomotives used to carry guests on a 3-mile (5-km) tour through the property. Now visitors walk the many trails that surround the castle.

WILLIAM GILLETTE

An eccentric playwright and actor, William Gillette caught the acting bug early, leaving college at age 20 to tread the boards. His most famous role, repeated many times in repertory, was Sherlock Holmes. He is reputed to have made $3 million playing the fictional sleuth. Gillette spent $1 million on building his folly. His will stipulated that it should never fall into the hands of "any blithering saphead."

The castle's roof has a view of the Connecticut River and the many boats that travel along it.

Servants' quarters

The study is where Gillette spent much of his time.

At the main entrance, the huge oak door through which visitors must pass is equipped with an elaborate home-made lock.

→

Gillette's zainy castle, with its quirky interiors

1. The atmospheric interior of Gillette Castle, complete with a photograph of the castle's eccentric ocupant.

2. A covered bridge in the typical New England style allows visitors to traverse a stream in the castle grounds.

3. The impressive exterior of Gillette Castle.

1

2

Mezzanine

The Library holds self-educated Gillette's far-ranging book collection.

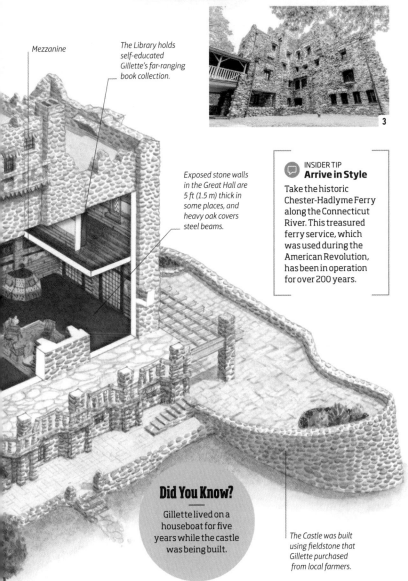

3

Exposed stone walls in the Great Hall are 5 ft (1.5 m) thick in some places, and heavy oak covers steel beams.

> **INSIDER TIP**
> ## Arrive in Style
>
> Take the historic Chester-Hadlyme Ferry along the Connecticut River. This treasured ferry service, which was used during the American Revolution, has been in operation for over 200 years.

Did You Know?

Gillette lived on a houseboat for five years while the castle was being built.

The Castle was built using fieldstone that Gillette purchased from local farmers.

→

Colorful terraced houses
on New Haven's beautiful
tree-lined Court Street

③

NEW HAVEN

🔺A7 **ℹ️Long Wharf Dr, exit 46 from I-95; www. visitnewhaven.com**

The land on which New Haven stands was purchased from the Quinnipiac people in 1638 for just a few knives, coats, and hatchets. Its coastal location meant that it was ideally placed to become a major manufacturing center. Over the centuries, items ranging from clocks to musical instruments and cannonballs have been made here. In 1716 Yale University moved from Saybrook to New Haven, establishing the city as a vibrant center for education, technology, and research.

①

New Haven Green

This park is the central section of the original nine symmetrical town squares laid out by the Puritans in 1638. The Green has been the focal point of local life ever since, serving as the setting for many of New Haven's activities and festivals. On the corner of Court and Church Streets is the monumental Greek Revival post office, now the Federal District Court. City Hall faces the Green on Church Street and epitomizes

High-Victorian style, with its limestone-and-sandstone facade. In front of City Hall, the Amistad Memorial honors Sengbe Pieh (also known as Joseph Cinqué), the leader of the *Amistad* revolt.

In late April the Green becomes the stage for Powder House Day, a reenactment of one of Benedict Arnold's few celebrated moments. At the beginning of the American Revolution, Arnold seized control of a municipal arsenal and led his troops to Boston to help bolster the sagging colonial forces.

②

New Haven Museum

🏠114 Whitney Ave
🕐10am–5pm Tue–Fri, noon–5pm Sat **🌐new havenmuseum.org**

This Colonial Revival building traces the city's history from 1638 to the present. Exhibits include Eli Whitney's cotton gin, the sign that hung over Benedict Arnold's George Street shop, a fine collection

EAT

Louis' Lunch

The self-proclaimed "Birthplace of the Hamburger Sandwich" has been serving their special mix of ground meat on white toast since 1895.

🏠261 Crown St
🌐louislunch.com

⑤⑤⑤

of colonial pewter and china, and permanent galleries on the *Amistad* and the city's maritime history.

___

③

Grove Street Cemetery

🏠 227 Grove St ⏰ 8am-4pm daily 🌐 grovestreet cemetery.org

Walking through the burial ground's 1848 Egyptian Revival gate, visitors will find a veritable who's who of New Haven. Eli Whitney, Noah Webster, and Lyman Beecher are just some of the highly distinguished citizens buried in this cemetery.

___

④

Eli Whitney Museum

🏠 915 Whitney Ave, Hamden ⏰ 10am-3pm Sat, noon-5pm Sun (Jun-Aug: 11am-4pm Sat & Sun) 🌐 eliwhitney.org

One of the nation's earliest inventors, Whitney (1765–1825) was best known for developing the cotton gin, thereby automating the labor-intensive task of separating cotton from its seeds. Another of his inventions, a musket with interchangeable parts, revolutionized manufacturing. The museum contains examples of Whitney's achievements as well as hands-on learning activities for children.

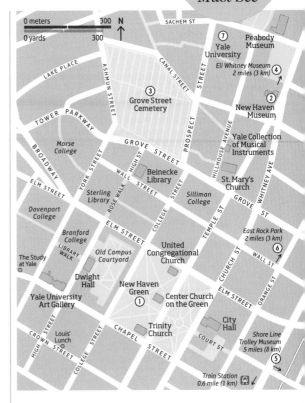

0 meters 300 N
0 yards 300

SACHEM ST
⑦ Peabody Museum
Yale University
Eli Whitney Museum 2 miles (3 km) ④
③ Grove Street Cemetery
② New Haven Museum
Yale Collection of Musical Instruments
Morse College
GROVE STREET
Beinecke Library
St. Mary's Church
Sterling Library
Silliman College
East Rock Park 2 miles (3 km) ⑥
Davenport College
ELM STREET
Branford College
Old Campus Courtyard
United Congregational Church
The Study at Yale
Dwight Hall
New Haven Green ①
Center Church on the Green
Yale University Art Gallery
Trinity Church
City Hall
Shore Line Trolley Museum 5 miles (8 km) ⑤
Louis' Lunch
CHAPEL STREET
COURT ST
Train Station 0.6 mile (1 km)

___

⑤

Shore Line Trolley Museum

🏠 17 River St, East Haven ⏰ Times vary, check website 🌐 shoreline trolley.org

Five miles (8 km) to the east of New Haven, in East Haven, is the Shore Line Trolley Museum. The oldest rapid-transit car and first electric freight locomotive are among 100 vintage trolleys on display. The museum also offers a 3-mile (5-km) trolley ride through salt marshes and woods on the country's oldest suburban trolley line.

___

⑥

East Rock Park

🏠 41 Cold Spring St
☎ (203) 946-6086
⏰ 8am-dusk daily

One of the finest of New Haven's many parks, East Rock Park is crisscrossed by 10 miles (16 km) of nature trails, offering spectacular views of Long Island Sound.

___

←

Visitors enjoying the ride at New Haven's Shore Line Trolley Museum

⑦

YALE UNIVERSITY

🕐 Times vary for each individual site, check website ℹ️ 149 Elm Street; www.yale.edu

Founded in 1701, Yale University is one of the most prestigious institutions of higher learning in the world. Since the Collegiate School moved to New Haven in 1716, town and gown have been inextricably linked. Collections at the Yale University Art Museums put larger cities to shame.

The list of Yale's distinguished alumni includes Noah Webster, who compiled the nation's first dictionary, Samuel Morse, inventor of Morse code, and five US presidents. President Bill Clinton and former First Lady and 2016 presidential candidate Hillary Clinton met while students at Yale Law School. Visitors can follow in their footsteps as they stroll through the grounds at their leisure, or join a free guided tour of the campus, departing from the visitor center.

Did You Know?

A Yale study found that one of the most familiar scents among adults is that of Crayola crayons.

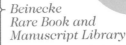

THE WOMEN'S TABLE

Located outside the Sterling Memorial Library, this sculpture commemorates women at Yale. It was designed by alumna Maya Lin, who is best known as the creator of the Vietnam War Memorial in Washington, D.C. Lin chose spiraling numbers to mark the presence – and absence – of registered female students since the inception of Yale in 1701.

Yale Museum Highlights

Beinecke Rare Book and Manuscript Library

▶ American architect Gordon Bunshaft built the library windows with translucent marble to filter the sunlight and prevent it from harming the library's priceless collection of illuminated medieval manuscripts and 7,000 rare books. Its prized possession is one of the world's few remaining Gutenberg Bibles.

Peabody Museum of Natural History

▼ Visitors entering the museum are dwarfed by the imposing skeleton of a 67-ft- (20-m-) high Brontosaurus - an apt introduction to this outstanding museum, famous for its collection of prehistoric beasts. The Peabody's third floor has a more contemporary feel, with displays ranging near and far, from daily life in ancient Egypt to modern biodiversity in Connecticut.

Yale University Art Gallery

This major collection of Asian, African, European, American, and pre-Columbian art comprises more than 100,000 objects. Among its prized American pieces is John Trumbull's 1786 painting depicting the battle of Bunker Hill. It also includes works by Picasso, Van Gogh, Monet, and Pollock.

Yale Collection of Musical Instruments

▶ A must-stop for the musically inclined, this stunning collection of instruments, considered among the top ten of its kind, has 800 objects, including historic woodwind and stringed instruments.

← Dwight Hall, formerly the college library at Yale University Old Campus

Fall foliage rises above a mist-
shrouded lake at Black Rock
State Park, Watertown ↑

④

LITCHFIELD HILLS

⚠ A6 ℹ Rte 202, On-the-Green, Litchfield; www.ctvisit.com/litchfield

Stretching west from the Connecticut River to the New York border, the
Litchfield Hills are arguably the most scenic section of Connecticut. Verdant
pastures drawing an array of wildlife are intersected by picturesque mountain
streams, steep valleys, and tranquil lakes, while a collection of model
18th- and 19th-century communities of white houses and clapboard churches
cluster around town greens. Stunning views from the summit of Mount Tom
entice hikers to the area, while Mount Tom State Park's lake is a favorite with
families and scuba divers alike.

Nestled in the folds and foothills of the
Berkshire Hills and Taconic Mountains in the
northwesternmost section of Connecticut, the
Litchfield Hills region covers some 1,000 sq miles
(2,590 sq km), or one-quarter of the state.
Anchored by the thundering Housatonic River,
this bucolic landscape of woods, valleys, lakes,
and wildlife offers unparalleled opportunities
for outdoor pursuits, such as canoeing,
kayaking, white-water rafting, tubing, fly-
fishing, and hiking to name just a few. In
autumn, traffic along the winding roads can
slow, as the brilliant fall foliage entrances
sightseers. A steady influx of wealth into
the area has resulted in the gentrification
of Litchfield's 26 towns and villages, with
boutiques and bistros popping up beside
traditional craft shops and historic homes.

↑ Admiring the clocks on display at
the Bristol Clock Museum

> **This bucolic landscape of woods, valleys, lakes, and wildlife offers unparalleled opportunities for outdoor pursuits.**

collection includes 5,000 clocks and watches. Bristol is also home to the Lake Compounce Theme Park, the nation's oldest amusement park, which has been entertaining families since 1846. More family fun can be found on Riverside Avenue in the form of the New England Carousel Museum. Its collection of antique carousel pieces is considered one of the finest in the world.

Just 15-minutes' drive east is the scenic Black Rock State Park, in the Mattatuck State Forest. The park offers excellent swimming and hiking opportunites, with scenic views over Thomaston, Watertown, and portions of Waterbury.

New Preston

The pretty town of New Preston offers access to the 0.2-sq-mile (0.5-sq-km) Lake Waramaug State Park. The lake is especially beautiful in the fall, when the glorious colors of the leaves are reflected on its mirrorlike surface. Visitors can rent canoes and enjoy peaceful paddles around the shoreline, and some 80 campsites cater to enthusiasts who want to linger and enjoy the great outdoors.

HIDDEN GEM
Glass Half Full

Farmland around New Preston's Lake Waramaug is temperate enough to grow wine grapes. Swing by Hopkins Vineyard (www.hopkins vineyard.com) to sample delicious wines served alongside local cheeses, country pâtés, and fresh bread.

Bristol

Bristol's past as a premier clock manufacturing center is celebrated at the American Clock and Watch Museum on Maple Street. Housed in an 1801 mansion, this vast

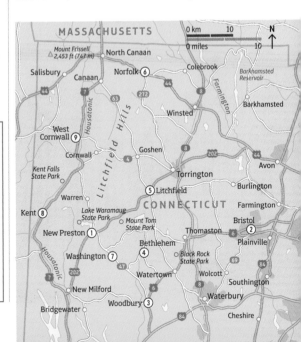

Woodbury

With many shops and dealers, this is a popular haunt for antiques lovers. The 18th-century Glebe House museum on Hollow Road shows period furniture *in situ*. The grounds of this minister's farmhouse feature the Gertrude Jekyll Garden, the noted English landscaper's only garden on US soil. The town is also blessed with five wonderfully preserved churches from various eras.

Bethlehem

One of the town's highlights is the Bellamy-Ferriday House and Garden, the 18th-century home of Reverend Joseph Bellamy (1719–90), founder of the first theological seminary

Did You Know?

The area attracts high-profile residents, including chef Jacques Pépin and actress Meryl Streep.

in America. Located on Main Street, this 13-room house (open May–Oct) displays Ferriday family Delftware, furniture, and Oriental art.

Litchfield

Picturesque Litchfield has many noteworthy historic buildings, such as South Street's 1784 Tapping Reeve House and Litchfield Law School, the country's first law school. On the outskirts of town, on Route 202, Mount Tom State Park has trails leading to the 1,325-ft (404-m) summit. The lake is a great spot for swimming, boating, and fishing.

Norfolk

Founded in 1758, this small village is located in the northwest corner of the state. Its village green is known for a fountain with spigots for both horses and people, designed by architect Stanford White. Just outside the town center is the Music Shed, an auditorium on the Ellen Batell Stoeckel Estate

GREAT VIEW
Take to the skies

For the ultimate birds-eye view over these beautiful hills, opt for a hot-air balloon flight. Spirit Ballooning (*www.spiritballooning.com*) is one of a number of experienced providers that operate in the area. All offer rides that last around one hour, taking off at dawn and dusk.

that hosts the highly acclaimed annual Norfolk Chamber Music Festival.

Washington

With five charming villages and abundant outdoor recreation, Washington is a peaceful town surrounded by idyllic countryside. Tucked high into the wooded hills surrounding the town, the **Institute for American Indian Studies** is well worth a visit. The museum and research center superbly re-creates

↑ Red-brick and clapboard houses line the streets of Norfolk

a pre-European-contact Algonkian village. With a collection of artifacts dating back 10,000 years, nature trails, and a healing garden, it's the perfect spot to learn about the woodlands culture of northwestern Connecticut.

Institute for American Indian Studies

⊕ 📷 🏠 38 Curtis Rd ⏰ Wed–Sat: 10am–5pm (from noon Sun) 🚫 Public hols 🌐 iais museum.org

---

SHOP

White Flower Farms
This isn't your average garden center. Greenfingered travelers will find endless inspiration in White Flower Farm's seasonal trial and display gardens, where staff will happily share gardening tips.

🏠 167 Litchfield Rd, Morris ⏰ Apr–Nov: 10am–4pm daily 🌐 whiteflowerfarm.com

---

⑧

Kent

Art lovers should go out of their way to visit this small community with the highest concentration of galleries in the region, including the interesting Heron American Craft Gallery and the Kent Art Association Gallery.

North of town travelers indulge in outdoor fun at Kent Falls State Park. A short hike into the park will reward visitors with stunning views of one of the state's most impressive waterfalls, known as Kent Falls. Follow the trail to the top of this

---

↑ Independent art and craft galleries in the small town of Kent

250-ft (76-m) cascade to see the most vigorous chute of all. Picnic facilities overlook the falls, giving fine views.

---

⑨

West Cornwall

Tiny West Cornwall is best known for its covered bridge. The 1841 bridge, which spans the Housatonic River, is only one of two such spans in the state open to car traffic.

↑ Covered West Cornwall Bridge spanning the Housatonic River

5 ⬡ ⬡ ⬡ ⬡ ⬡

MYSTIC SEAPORT

🅐C7 🏠75 Greenmanville Ave (Rte 27) 🕐Apr–Oct: 9am–5pm daily (call for off season hours) 🚫Dec 24 & 25 🌐mysticseaport.org

Walk the decks of a tall ship, or see carpenters replank a vessel at this "museum of America and the sea." Mystic Seaport replicates a 19th-century coastal village with craftspeople plying their trades, historic vessels, and a working shipyard.

What began as a modest collection of nautical odds and ends housed in an old mill in 1929 has grown into the world's largest maritime museum. This working replica of a 19th-century port comprises more than 40 buildings open to the public, including a bank, chapel, tavern, ship-carver's studio, and schoolhouse. The main attraction is the preservation shipyard and fleet of antique ships, including the *Charles W. Morgan*, the last remaining vessel of the nation's fleet of 19th-century whalers. Permanent and changing exhibitions display ship carvings and figureheads, nautical art, and vintage photography. Visitors can even master the art of celestial navigation, or at least learn how early sailors used the stars and planets to navigate stormy seas, at the Treworgy Planetarium.

↑ Historic sailing ship, *Joseph Conrad*, moored at Mystic Seaport

The Village Green Bandstand is used as a concert venue during holidays.

Here, shipcarvers created figureheads and decorations for shipbuilders.

A whaleboat exhibit on Chubb's Wharf displays all the gear carried in such vessels.

Burrows House is an early 19th-century home of a shopkeeper and his milliner wife.

Middle Wharf

The Charles W. Morgan, the last wooden whaling ship in the world.

The Joseph Conrad, one of the museum's largest ships, serves as a training vessel.

Mystic River Scale Model

Did You Know?

The original 19th-century buildings of Mystic Seaport were sourced from all over New England.

↑ The quaint seaport, with its historic ships moored alongside

EXPERIENCE MORE

💬 **INSIDER TIP**
All Aboard!

Visitors can board many rare and historic boats moored at Mystic Seaport Museum. Some make daily outings, and others you can even captain yourself. Short, full-day, and overnight charters are available, offering fantastic views from the top deck.

The LA Dunton, a 1921 schooner, is one of the last existing examples of New England round-bow fishing vessels.

The Sabino steamship takes passengers on cruises on the Mystic River.

This copy of the 1901 Brant Point Lighthouse on Nantucket Island is home to a multimedia exhibit.

❻
Mystic

🅐 C7 🛈 27 Coogan Blvd; www.mysticinfocenter.com

Once a prosperous port and shipbuilding village, Mystic turned to tourism when those industries waned. Today Mystic Seaport recounts the seafaring days and is the town's main attraction, though the tidy shops and splendid eateries are also worth exploring. Have your camera at the ready when the counter-weights of the bascule bridge over the Mystic River swing skywards to let boats pass; t's fascinating to watch.

Two miles north of the village, **Mystic Aquarium** aims to promote conservation of the environment and of the animals that inhabit it. Seals and sea lions cavort in the outdoor Seal Island; indoors is a colony of African black-footed penguins and 3,500 sea creatures. The Aquarium and its partners also help protect the wild beluga whale population through research and education.

Mystic Aquarium
♿ ⓟ 🅐 55 Coogan Blvd
🕐 Jan–Mar: 10am–5pm daily; Apr–Aug: 9am–6pm daily; Sep–Dec: 9am–5pm daily 🔒 Jan 1, Thanksgiving, Dec 25 🌐 mysticaquarium.org

↑ Mystic River Bascule Bridge, opening to allow boats to pass

↑ Tubers floating down the popular Farmington River on a bright summer's day

➐ New Britain

⛰B6 ℹ1 Constitution Plaza, 2nd Floor, Hartford; www.newbritainct.gov

New Britain, which was first recognised as a new parish in 1754, is located midway between Boston and New York, in the county of Hartford. Travelers to either city should stop to visit the **New Britain Museum of American Art**, whose distinguished collection spans art from the Colonial era to the present. Almost every major US artist of note is represented here, including Georgia O'Keeffe (1887–1986), Andrew Wyeth (1917–2009), Alexander Calder (1898–1976), and Isamu Noguchi (1904–88). The American Impressionist collection is also important. One gallery is dedicated to the seminal "Arts of Life in America" mural series by Thomas Hart Benton.

New Britain Museum of American Art

⊛⊛⊛ ⛰56 Lexington St ⊙11am–5pm Tue, Wed, Fri & Sun; 11am–8pm Thu; 10am–5pm Sat ⓦnbmaa.org

➑ Farmington

⛰B6 ℹ33 E Main St, Avon; www.farmington-ct.org

Perched on the banks of the surging Farmington River, this quiet enclave has long been the starting point for canoeists, fishermen, and birdwatchers. The skies above the Farmington River Valley are a busy place, popular with hang-gliders and hot-air balloonists taking in the spectacular vistas from on high. Several companies offer champagne flights over the scenic valley, while others offer candlelit tours of the town's historic homes.

The interior of the **Hill-Stead Museum** has remained unchanged since the death of its original owner, Theodate Pope Riddle (1867–1946). Pope, one of the country's first female architects, designed the Colonial-Revival mansion, which was finished in 1901. Her will stipulated that upon her death nothing in the house could be changed, altered, or moved. The result is a fascinating home frozen in the Edwardian period. On display is the Pope family's fine collection of French and American Impressionist paintings, including works by Edgar Degas, Edouard Manet, Mary Cassatt, and James Whistler. The museum also contains splendid examples of American and European furniture and decorative arts.

The **Stanley-Whitman House**, furnished with Colonial pieces, is a well-preserved example of early 18th-century architecture of New England. It is often used as a venue for craft demonstrations and exhibits.

Elsewhere in Farmington, admirers of old cemeteries will find many markers of interest in the Ancient Burying Ground, with gravestones dating back to 1661. In the Riverside Cemetery, one tombstone marks the grave of Foone, a former enslaved African who drowned in the town's canal after being freed in the *Amistad* trial.

Twenty miles (32 km) south of Farmington lies the blue-collar town of Waterbury, where the clock tower is modeled on that of the city hall in Siena, Italy. The **Mattatuck Museum** displays American art and relates Waterbury's industrial role as the "Brass City" during the 19th and early 20th century.

Hill-Stead Museum

⊛⊛ ⛰35 Mountain Rd ⊙10am–4pm Tue-Sun ⓧPublic hols ⓦhillstead.org

Stanley-Whitman House

⊛⊛ ⛰37 High St ☎(860) 677-9222 ⊙May-Oct: 10am–4pm Wed-Sun; Nov-Apr: call for hours

During the lower Jurassic period some 200 million years ago, the dinosaurs that roamed this region literally left their mark on the land.

Mattatuck Museum
 63 Prospect St, Waterbury ⏰ Noon-5pm Mon-Fri & 1st weekend of month 🚫 Public hols 🌐 mattmuseum.org

EAT

Roughly a fifth of New Britain's residents are of Polish ancestry. These restaurants and shops offer great, authentic Polish options.

Staropolska
 B6 📍 252 Broad St 🌐 starpolska.net

$ ⑤ ⑤

Belvedere
 B6 📍 82 Broad St 🌐 belvederenew britain.com

$ ⑤ ⑤

Polmart
 B6 📍 123 Broad St 🌐 polmartusa.com

$ ⑤ ⑤

---

⑨
Simsbury

🔼 B6 ℹ️ Hartford; www. simsbury-ct.gov

Originally a quiet colonial farming community, Simsbury grew into something of a boomtown in the early 18th century with the discovery of copper in the region. The wheels of US industry started turning here with the opening of the nation's first steel mill in 1728.

Three centuries of local history are squeezed into the **Phelps Tavern Museum**. The museum is located in the home of Sea Captain Elisha Phelps. Period rooms and galleries have been used to re-create an authentic inn that operated here from 1786 to 1849, an era when such wayside inns were central to New England's social life. The tavern museum is part of a 87,100-sq-ft (8,100-sq-m) complex that includes a 1790 schoolhouse and six period gardens.

Phelps Tavern Museum
 📍 800 Hopmeadow St 📞 (860) 658-2500 ⏰ Thu-Sat 🚫 Public hols

---

⑩
Dinosaur State Park

🔼 B6 📍 400 West St, Rocky Hill ⏰ Park: 9am-4:30pm daily; Exhibit center: 9am-4:30pm Tue-Sun 🚫 Public hols 🌐 dinosaur statepark.org

During the early Jurassic period some 200 million years ago, the dinosaurs that roamed this region literally left their mark on the land. The park opened officially in 1968, two years after a wealth of tracks were discovered by accident during construction excavations. Today some 500 prehistoric tracks are preserved beneath this park's huge geodesic dome. Also on display is a life-size model of an 8-ft (2.4-m) *Dilophosaurus*, the creature that most likely left the prints. Two large dioramas tell the story of the Connecticut Valley during the Triassic and Jurassic periods. Highlights of this exhibit are a model *Coelophysis* and a cast of a skeleton unearthed in New Mexico. A thrill for children and amateur paleon-tologists is the chance to make a plaster cast of one track from May through October (call ahead to find out what to bring). The park also has 2.5 miles (4 km) of hiking trails through a variety of habitats.

← Prehistoric tracks on display in Connecticut's Dinosaur State Park

11

Windsor

🅰B6 ℹ️Hartford; www.
townofwindsorct.com

Windsor was settled in the
early 1630s by Pilgrims from
Plymouth (p170), making it
the oldest permanent English
settlement in the state – a
claim that is fiercely disputed
by the residents of nearby
Wethersfield (p254).

The 1758 **Strong-Howard
House** is a surviving frame
structure named after the
newlyweds who built it. It has
an excellent collection of furnishings reflecting the history
of Windsor. Next door is the

Dr Hezekiah Chaffee House,
a brick Georgian-Colonial
built in the mid-18th century.
Tickets include entry to both
houses. Down the road stands
the 1780 home of the state's
first senator, Oliver Ellsworth
(1745–1807). The **Oliver
Ellsworth Homestead** contains interiors from the era.

Strong-Howard House

🅰96 Palisado Ave
(860) 688-3813 11am-
4pm Wed-Sat Public hols

**Dr Hezekiah
Chaffee House**

🅰108 Palisado Ave
(860) 688-3813 11am-
4pm Wed-Sat Public hols

↑ Visitors aboard an original trolley
at the Windsor Trolley Museum

**Oliver Ellsworth
Homestead**

🅰778 Palisado Ave
(860) 688-8717 By
appointment

12

New England
Air Museum

🅰B6 🏠Bradley Inter-
national Airport, Windsor
Locks 10am-5pm daily
Early Sep-late May: Mon;
Jan 1, Thanksgiving, Dec 25
🇼neam.org

Aviation fans can indulge their
flights of fancy at the largest
aviation museum in the Northeast. The impressive collection
of 80 aircraft spans the
complete history of aviation,
beginning with pre-Wright
Brothers flying machines
right up to present-day jets
and rescue helicopters. Located
near Bradley International
Airport since 1981, the museum
is housed in and around two
cavernous hangars. Highlights
include a replica Bunce-
Curtiss Pusher, a 1909 Blériot
and a Sikorsky VS-44 Flying
Boat, the last of the four-
engined flying boats.

To experience the thrill of
flying, visitors can strap themselves into a simulator of the
Grumman Tracer.

An imposing Sikorsky VS-44 flying-boat at New England Air Museum

13

Old New-Gate Prison and Copper Mine

🅰B6 ℹ️115 Newgate Rd, East Granby ☎(860) 655-1591 🕐Mid-Jul-Oct: 10am-1pm Mon, 1-5pm Fri, 10am-5pm Sat & Sun

When financial woes forced the sale of this 18th-century copper mine, its new proprietors found a novel but grim use for the dark hole. In 1773 the local government transformed the mine into the state's first colonial prison. The jail has held everyone from horse thieves to captured British soldiers, and represented a particularly brutal form of punishment, with prisoners living in damp, sunless tunnels. Mercifully, the prison was abandoned in 1827, though tours of its chamber still inspire shivers.

14

Coventry

🅰B6 ℹ️Hartford; www.coventryct.org

Coventry is the birthplace of Nathan Hale (1755–76), one of the heroes of the American Revolution. Before he was to be hanged by the British as a spy, the 21-year-old uttered his now famous last words, "I only regret that I have but one life to lose for my country."

The **Nathan Hale Homestead** is an anomaly in that its namesake never actually lived in the building. The house, located on the site where Hale was born, was built by Hale's father and brothers in the year he was executed. Hale's belongings are on display, including his army trunk.

Between June and October, the homestead is the site of the popular Coventry Regional Farmers' Market every Sunday, with organic and heirloom produce for sale.

Nathan Hale Homestead
 🏠2299 South St ☎(860) 742-6917 🕐Times vary, call for hours

15

Roseland Cottage

🅰C6 🏠556 Rte 169, Woodstock ☎(860) 928-4074 🕐Jun-mid-Oct: 11am-4pm Wed-Sun

This Gothic Revival style "cottage" is unmissable; it is painted bright pink, with

SHOP

Antiques Marketplace

The old mill town of Putnam has reinvented itself as an antiques capital. Hit this marketplace to sample the wares of more than 175 dealers, then stroll the town streets for smaller, quirkier shops.

🅰C6 🏠109 Main St, Putnam ☎(860) 928-0442 🕐Mon & Tue

21 flowerbeds and peaked gables that bloom in a profusion of color from summer through fall. The house was built in 1846 as a summer retreat for Henry and Lucy Bowen and their growing family. Bowen, a Woodstock native who made his fortune in the silk wholesale business in New York, was also an ardent abolitionist and advocate for women's suffrage. The cottage interior features stained-glass windows, Gothic arches, and many of the original furnishings. Bowen entertained three US presidents here, and the house remained in his family until 1968.

↑ The eye-catching exterior of Roseland Cottage in Woodstock

16

New London

🅰B7 🚌 ℹ️ Mystic; (860) 536-8822 or (800) 863-6569

British forces led by traitor Benedict Arnold razed New London during the American Revolution. Rebounding from the attack, the town enjoyed newfound prosperity with the whaling industry during the 19th century.

Downtown, the **Custom House Maritime Museum** tells the stories of New London's waterfront and other aspects of the city's nautical history. It also remains the oldest operating custom house in the country, dating from 1833. Tours of the site are available, though they must be booked in advance.

Connecticut College houses the Lyman Allyn Art Museum, particularly known for its 19th-century American paintings. Also on campus, is the college Arboretum. At the edge of town is **Monte Cristo Cottage**, boyhood home of Nobel Prize-winning playwright Eugene O'Neill (1888–1953). The cottage, which served as the setting for his Pulitzer Prize-winning play *Long Day's Journey into Night* (1957), is now a research library, with some of O'Neill's belongings on display.

Directly across the river Thames from New London is the town of Groton, where the USS *Nautilus* – the world's first nuclear-powered submarine – is berthed at the Submarine Force Museum on the Naval Submarine Base. Nearby, Fort Griswold Battlefield State Park is where British troops under Benedict Arnold killed surrendering American soldiers in 1781. A 134-ft (41-m) obelisk memorial and a battle diorama mark the terrible event.

Custom House Maritime Museum

♿🕐 🏠150 Bank St
🕐 Times vary, check website
🌐 nlmaritimesociety.org

Monte Cristo Cottage

♿ 🏠325 Pequot Ave ☎(860) 443-5378 ext 227 🕐 Jun-Aug: noon–4pm Thu–Sun

---

🔍 HIDDEN GEM
New London Street Art

A series of larger-than-life murals and vibrant street art by local artists color the streets of New London. See them for yourself on a self-guided walking tour of the city center, starting at Hygienic Art *(79 Bank St)*.

17

Norwich

🅰C7 ℹ️ Mystic (860) 536-8822 or (800) 863-6569

Norwich has the somewhat dubious distinction of being the birthplace of Benedict Arnold (1741–1801), known for his betrayal of colonial forces during the American Revolution. In contrast, the Colonial Cemetery contains graves of French and American soldiers who died fighting for the American cause.

The city is also home to a number of notable museums. A two-story Colonial structure, the **Christopher Leffingwell House**, is named after a financier of the colonial side in the American Revolution. During the war, Leffingwell's house and tavern were used for secret meetings. The interior has never been remodeled, and is full of late 17th- and 18th-century furniture.

The **Slater Memorial Museum** is also worth a visit; its displays of fine and decorative art represent a broad range of world cultures, including the Americas, Asia, Europe and Africa.

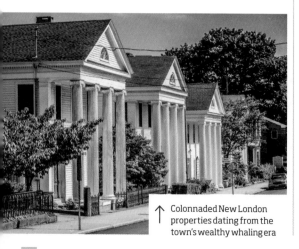

↑ Colonnaded New London properties dating from the town's wealthy whaling era

↑ Statues on display in the Slater Memorial Museum in Norwich

Christopher Leffingwell House

 348 Washington St (860) 889-9440 Apr-Oct: 11am-4pm Sat Public hols

Slater Memorial Museum

108 Crescent St 9am-4pm Tue-Fri; 1-4pm Sat & Sun Jan 1, Dec 25 slatermuseum.org

18
Lebanon

B6 Hartford New London Mystic; (860) 536 8822 or (800) 863-6569

This Eastern Connecticut community is steeped in American Revolution history. It was on the 0.25-sq-mile (0.7-sq-km) common here that French hussars trained before joining their American allies in Yorktown for the climactic battle of the conflict. Lebanon native and artist John Trumbull (1756–1843), whose paintings can be seen in Hartford's Wadsworth Atheneum (p230) and New Haven's Yale University Art Gallery, designed the town's 1807 Congregational Church.

Nearby is the **Governor Jonathan Trumbull House**. Father to John and governor of the colony and the state of Connecticut from 1769 to 1784, Trumbull was the only governor of the 13 colonies to remain in office before, during and indeed after the Revolutionary War.

Twelve miles (19 km) east of Lebanon, Canterbury is home to the **Prudence Crandall Museum**. Crandall (1803–90) raised the ire of citizens when, in 1832, she admitted a young Black student to her private school for girls. Undaunted by threats of boycotts, Crandall kept the school open and attracted students, many of whom were Black, from other states. Public outcry was such that the local government pushed through a law forbidding private schools to admit Black children from out of state. Crandall was subsequently jailed and brought to trial. However, it was only after an angry mob attacked the school in 1834 that she reluctantly closed her doors forever. Today the museum commemorates Crandall's struggle and traces Black history in the area.

Governor Jonathan Trumbull House

 169 W Town St (860) 429-7194 Mid-May-mid-Oct: 1-5pm Sat & Sun

Prudence Crandall Museum

 Canterbury Green (860) 546-7800 For renovations until spring 2022

19
Mashantucket Pequot Museum

 C7 110 Pequot Trail Late-Mar-early-Dec: 9am-5pm Wed-Sat (Nov: also Tue) pequotmuseum.org

When European colonists landed in what would become New England, the prosperous Pequot nation controlled much of the land on which the state of Connecticut now sits. The Mashantucket Pequot Tribal Nation opened this modern museum in 1998 to celebrate Native American culture and relate the history of European contact from a Pequot perspective. Full-scale dioramas and exhibits sketch a way of life in harmony with nature, and show the resilience of a people almost wiped out in the 17th century. In a video commentary, a number of tribal members relate how cultural traditions influence and enrich modern life. The on-site restaurant offers Native American dishes, and the gift shop specializes in arts and crafts by Indigenous peoples. A challenging trail leads up nearby Lantern Hill for a five-state view.

Did You Know?

Lebanon was the first town in the Connecticut colony to be given a Biblical name.

↑ Sun setting over the sands of Hammonasset Beach State Park in Madison

20

Madison

🅐B7 🔳1 Constitution Plaza, 2nd Floor, Hartford (860) 787-9640

Madison is a resort town full of antiques stores and boutiques. Several historic homes are open for viewing, including the 1685 **Deacon John Grave House**. It has served as tavern, armory, courthouse, and infirmary, but has always belonged to the Graves. One of the oldest artifacts on display is the family's bookkeeping ledger, with entries from 1678 to 1895.

Madison is also home to **Hammonasset Beach State Park**, the largest shoreline park in the state. Poking into Long Island Sound, the peninsula has a 2-mile (3-km) beach that attracts swimmers and sunbathers. The park has a nature center, a campground, walking trails, and picnic areas.

Deacon John Grave House
 🚪581 Boston Post Rd ☎(203) 245-4567 ⏰Mid-Jun–early Sep: call for hours

Hammonasset Beach State Park
⏰🚶 🚪I-95, exit 62 ☎(203) 245-2785 (campground: 877 668-2267) ⏰8am–dusk daily

> Local lore maintains that the Thimbles are named after the thimbleberry - a shrub that looks rather like a black raspberry - although it is not widely found in this region.

21

Essex

🅐B7 🔳1 Constitution Plaza, 2nd Floor, Hartford (860) 787-9640

In surveys naming America's top small towns, Essex is often found at the head of the list. Sited on the Connecticut River, the village is surrounded by a series of sheltered coves and has a bustling marina and tree-lined, largely crime-free streets.

The **Connecticut River Museum**, a restored 1878 warehouse, overlooks the water. Its collection and exhibits of maritime art and artifacts tell the story of this once-prominent shipbuilding town, where the *Oliver Cromwell* – the first warship built for the American Revolution – was constructed. The museum's star exhibit is a replica of the world's first submersible craft, the *Turtle*, a squat, single-seat vehicle built in 1775.

Transportation is also the focus at the **Essex Steam Train and Riverboat**, where guests take an authentic, coal-belching steam engine for a 12-mile (19-km) tour. At the midpoint, passengers can cruise down the river for 90 minutes aboard a riverboat.

Connecticut River Museum
 🚪67 Main St ☎(860) 767-8269 ⏰10am–5pm Tue–Sun (late May–mid Oct: also Mon) 🚫Jan 1, Labor Day, Thanksgiving, Dec 24 & 25

Essex Steam Train and Riverboat
 🚪Exit 3 off Rte 9 ⏰May–Oct: check website for schedule 🌐essexsteamtrain.com

---

22

Guilford

🅐B7 🔳1 Constitution Plaza, 2nd Floor, Hartford; www.visitguilfordct.com

In 1639 Reverend Henry Whitfield (1597–1657) led a group of Puritans from Surrey,

England, to a wild parcel of land near the West River, where they established the town of Guilford. A year later, fearing an attack by local Menuncatuck people, the colonists built a defensible home out of local granite. It is the oldest stone dwelling of its type in New England, and now serves as the **Henry Whitfield State Museum**. The austere interior has a 33-ft (10-m) great hall and 17th-century furnishings.

Guilford is graced by dozens of historic 18th-century homes. Both the **Hyland House**, a classic early saltbox, and the 1774 **Thomas Griswold House** are open to view. **Dudley Farm**, a 19th-century working farm and living-history museum, demonstrates agricultural techniques of the era. In July craftsmen gather on the scenic Guilford Green to celebrate the arts at the annual Guilford Craft Expo.

Henry Whitfield State Museum

 🏠 248 Old Whitfield St
📞 (203) 453-2457 🕒 May–Oct: 10am–4:30pm Wed–Sun; Nov–Jan: by appt only

Hyland House

♿ ✍ 🏠 84 Boston St 📞 (203) 453-9477 🕒 Jun–Sep: 11am–4pm Fri & Sat, noon–4pm Sun 🚫 Public hols

Thomas Griswold House

♿ ✍ 🏠 171 Boston St 📞 (203) 453-2263 🕒 Call for hours

Dudley Farm

🏠 2351 Durham Rd 📞 (203) 457-0770 🕒 Jul–Oct: 10am–2pm Thu–Fri, 9am–2pm Sat, 1–4pm Sun

---

㉓
Thimble Islands

🅰 B7 🚢 From Stony Creek Dock; (203) 488-8905 ℹ️ (203) 777-8550

From Stony Creek, travelers can cruise to the Thimble Islands aboard one of several tour boats that operate in the area. Local lore maintains that the Thimbles are named for the thimbleberry – a shrub that looks rather like a black raspberry – although it is not widely found in this region. Many of the 365 islands are little more than large boulders visible only at low tide, but some of the bigger, privately owned islands sport small communities. One colorful legend about this clutch of islands centers on circus performer General Tom Thumb (1838–83) courting a woman on Cut-In-Two Island (so named because a bridge connecting two tiny islands was destroyed). Another has the privateer Captain Kidd (1645–1701) hiding plundered treasure on Money Island while being pursued by the British fleet. Today cruisers can watch seals or take in glorious fall colors.

㉔
Old Lyme

🅰 B7 ℹ️ 52 Lyme St; oldlyme-ct.gov

Once a major shipbuilding center, Old Lyme is still home to a number of grand 18th- and 19th-century houses, originally built for wealthy merchants and sea captains. The picturesque village and surrounding natural areas attracted a summer colony of *plein-air* painters.

The **Florence Griswold Museum** is intimately linked to the arts. The mansion was once the home of Captain Robert Griswold and his daughter Florence. An art patron, Florence began letting rooms in the 1890s to artists from New York looking to escape the city and spend the summer by the sea. Among others, she hosted Henry Ward Ranger (1858–1916), Childe Hassam (1859–1935), and Clark Voorhees (1871–1933), spawning the Old Lyme Art Colony.

This stop on the Connecticut Art Trail features some of the works by more than 200 artists, who at one time lived in the house or nearby. Many of Griswold's guests painted on the wall panels of the dining room as thanks for her generosity. There is also a modern gallery that houses changing exhibitions. It is a work of art in itself, with a rippling aluminum canopy entrance, curvilinear walls, and skylights to provide soft illumination.

Florence Griswold Museum

♿ ✍ 🎧 🏠 96 Lyme St, Old Lyme 📞 (860) 434-5542 🕒 10am–5pm Tue–Sat, 1–5pm Sun

Small boats sailing between the remote Thimble Islands ↑

A SHORT WALK
WETHERSFIELD

Distance 0.5 miles (1 km) **Time** 15 minutes
Nearest train station Hartford

Now an affluent Hartford suburb, Wethersfield began as the state's first settlement in 1634. In 1640 its citizens held an illegal public election – America's first act of defiance against British rule. The town also hosted the 1781 Revolutionary War conference between George Washington (1732–99) and his French allies, during which they finalized strategies for the decisive American victory in Yorktown. Preserved within a 12-block area, Old Wethersfield stands as a primer of American architecture, with numerous houses from the 18th to 20th centuries. The centerpiece is the Webb-Deane-Stevens Museum, a trio of dwellings depicting the differing lifestyles of three 18th-century Americans: a wealthy merchant, a diplomat, and a leather tanner.

↑ Visitors exploring the charming and historic Webb-Deane-Stevens Museum

> **Preserved within a 12-block area, Old Wethersfield stands as a primer of American architecture.**

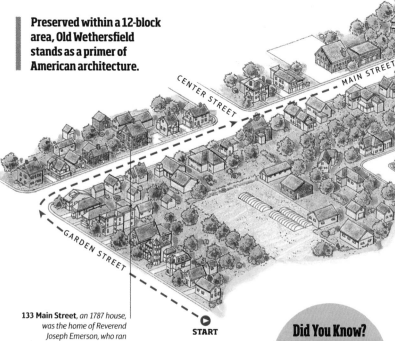

133 Main Street, *an 1787 house, was the home of Reverend Joseph Emerson, who ran the Female Seminary at the Old Academy at 150 Main Street.*

START

Did You Know?

Four trials and three executions for witchcraft took place in Wethersfield in the 17th century.

0 meters 75
0 yards 75

N ↑

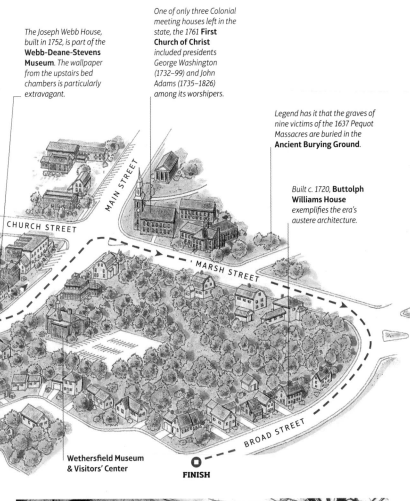

The Joseph Webb House, built in 1752, is part of the **Webb-Deane-Stevens Museum**. The wallpaper from the upstairs bed chambers is particularly extravagant.

One of only three Colonial meeting houses left in the state, the 1761 **First Church of Christ** included presidents George Washington (1732–99) and John Adams (1735–1826) among its worshipers.

Legend has it that the graves of nine victims of the 1637 Pequot Massacres are buried in the **Ancient Burying Ground**.

Built c. 1720, **Buttolph Williams House** exemplifies the era's austere architecture.

CHURCH STREET

MAIN STREET

MARSH STREET

BROAD STREET

Wethersfield Museum & Visitors' Center

FINISH

↑ A pretty street in Wethersfield during winter

A DRIVING TOUR
COASTAL FAIRFIELD COUNTRY

Length 44 miles (71 km), including a detour to New Canaan
Stopping-off points There are a number of waterfront restaurants in Greenwich and Norwalk

Travelers following Interstate 95 are bound to strike it rich along the "Gold Coast," so nicknamed because of the luxurious estates, marinas, and mansions concentrated between Greenwich and Southport. This, the southernmost corner of Connecticut, has attractions sure to meet everyone's taste. The shoreline is dusted with many beaches offering a variety of summer recreation opportunities. Nature preserves, arboretums, and planetariums, will appeal to naturalists of all ages. People of a more artistic bent can visit the area's numerous small galleries or its well-established museums.

↑ Grand homes on Greenwich's pretty coastline

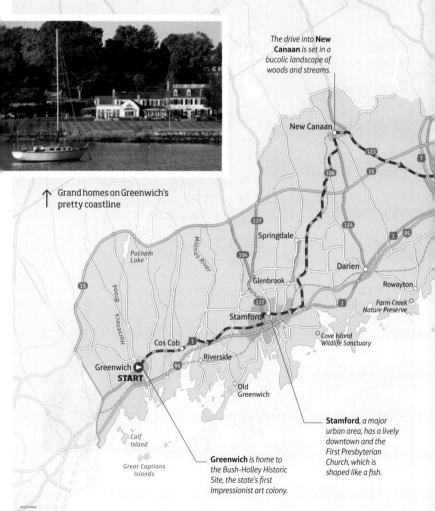

The drive into **New Canaan** is set in a bucolic landscape of woods and streams.

Greenwich is home to the Bush-Holley Historic Site, the state's first Impressionist art colony.

Stamford, a major urban area, has a lively downtown and the First Presbyterian Church, which is shaped like a fish.

↑ Philip Johnson's Glass House in a strikingly bucolic landscape in New Canaan

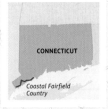

CONNECTICUT

Coastal Fairfield Country

Locator Map
For more detail see p228

Westport, *a charming town on the banks of the Saugatuck River, is home to the Sherwood Island State Park.*

Circus owner P. T. Barnum was once mayor of **Bridgeport**.

□ Bridgeport
FINISH

Seaside Park

Mill River

Lillian Wadsworth Arboretum

Westport

Southport

Fairfield

Jennings Beach

Black Rock

Norwalk

East Norwalk

Sherwood Island State Park

0 kilometers   5
0 miles   5

N ↑

Cockenoe Island

Grassy Island

Shea Island

Chimon Island

Sheffield Island

Norwalk *has a trendy waterfront district of South Norwalk, with its busy restaurants, shops, and cafes.*

→
Signboard for the 19th-century Sheffield Island Lighthouse in South Norwalk

VERMONT

Vermont was thinly settled in the millennia prior to the arrival of Europeans, since the land was ill-suited to agriculture and the hilly terrain made travel difficult. When the French arrived, the shores of Lake Champlain were populated by the Iroquois, the southern edge of the region was the domain of Mahicans, while the woodlands were the province of Wabanaki hunters.

The state was given its current name by French explorer Samuel de Champlain in 1609. Translating as "Green Mountain" in French, it must have seemed most suitable when he gazed upon the verdant landscape. Settled by both the French and British in the early 18th century under conflicting land grants from New York and New Hampshire, this expanse of thick forest and rolling pasture was eventually ceded to the British in 1763 on their defeat of French forces during the French and Indian War (1754–1763). The Wabanaki areas that would become Vermont, New Hampshire, and Maine had allied with the French. When the British prevailed, most of the Indigenous people's lands were seized.

Vermont operated as an independent republic from 1777, becoming the 14th US state in 1791. A rugged independence persists in Vermonters, who despite severe winter weather seem to be outdoors year-round, hiking, skiing, skating, sledding, cycling, kayaking, hunting, and fishing, sometimes against a brilliant background of fall leaves. Vermonters may be small in number, but they are also fiercely patriotic, and often lead the country's conscience on social and political issues.

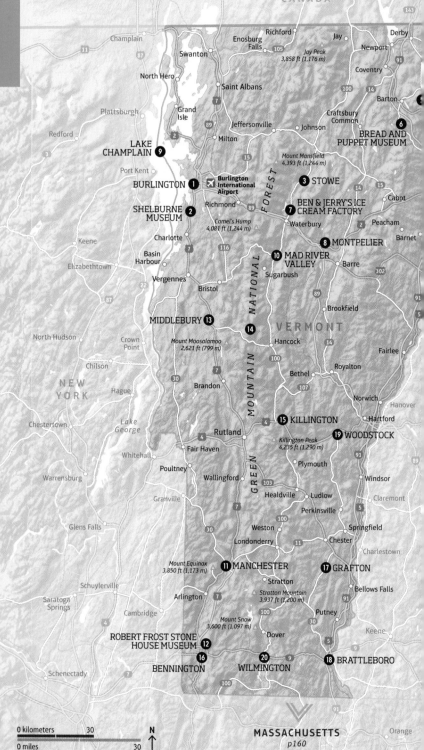

VERMONT

Must Sees
1 Burlington
2 Shelburne Museum

Experience More
3 Stowe
4 St. Johnsbury
5 Lake Willoughby
6 Bread and Puppet Museum
7 Ben & Jerry's Ice Cream Factory
8 Montpelier
9 Lake Champlain
10 Mad River Valley
11 Manchester
12 Robert Frost Stone House Museum
13 Middlebury
14 Green Mountain National Forest
15 Killington
16 Bennington
17 Grafton
18 Brattleboro
19 Woodstock
20 Wilmington

NEW
HAMPSHIRE
p280

VERMONT

❶

BURLINGTON

🅰 A2 ✈ Burlington International Airport 🚌🚢 King St Dock
ℹ Suite 100, 60 Main St; www.vermont.org

The lively university town of Burlington is one of Vermont's most popular tourist destinations. The town is rich in grand old mansions, historic landmarks, enticing shops, and restaurants, and it has an attractive waterfront. The famed American Revolution patriot Ethan Allen (1738–89) has his final resting place here in Greenmount Cemetery.

Did You Know?

The only battle fought within city limits was in 1813; it lasted 20 minutes and had zero casualties.

①

Battery Street

The center of Burlington is compact and easy to explore on foot. Battery Street, near the waterfront, is the oldest, most historic part of the city and a jumping-off point for ferries to New York State and sightseeing trips around Lake Champlain. More than 200 handsome buildings in the downtown core have been renovated, and visitors will find many architectural landmarks, including the First Unitarian Church.

Battery Park, at the north end of Battery Street where it meets Pearl Street, was the site of a battle between US soldiers and the British Royal Navy. Burlington saw several skirmishes during the War of 1812, and scuba divers have found military artifacts at the bottom of the lake. Ten shipwrecks, three lying close to Burlington, can be explored by divers who register with the Waterfront Diving Center on Battery Street.

These days Battery Park is a much more peaceful place. Lake Champlain is at its widest point here, and visitors who stroll through the park are rewarded with lovely views of Burlington.

💬 INSIDER TIP
Jazz Festival

Burlington's cultural life comes to the fore during its annual jazz festival in June. Venues for this popular concert series include City Hall Stage, Waterfront Park, and the Flynn Center for the Performing Arts.

②

Spirit of Ethan Allen

🏠 Burlington Boat House, College Street 🕙 May–Oct: 10am–6:30pm 🌐 soea.com

Tall-stack steamers used to ply the waters of Lake Champlain. Today visitors can board a three-decker cruise ship, *Spirit of Ethan Allen*, for a 90-minute narrated cruise or for brunch, lunch, dinner, and sunset cruises. Reservations are essential.

←

Christmas lights in Church Street Marketplace in downtown Burlington

③

Fleming Museum of Art

🏛 **University of Vermont, 61 Colchester Ave** 🕐 **Sep-May: 10am–4pm Tue–Fri (to 7pm Wed), noon–4pm Sat & Sun; call for summer hours** 🗓 **Mid-Dec–mid-Jan, public hols** 🌐 **uvm.edu/fleming**

The Fleming Museum of Art is located on the campus of the University of Vermont (UVM), perched on a wooded hillside that overlooks the city. Built in 1931, this elegant Colonial Revival building houses an impressive collection of anthropological artifacts totalling more than 25,000 items and ranging from ancient Mesopotamia to modern times. Items on display include European and American paintings and sculptures, Japanese prints, Qing Dynasty textiles from China, Native American art and crafts, jewelry and glassware, and West and Central African sculpture.

④

Shelburne Farms

🏛 **1611 Harbor Rd** 🕐 **10am–5pm daily** 🌐 **shelburnefarms.org**

Seven miles (11 km) south of town are the Shelburne Museum (*p266*) and Shelburne Farms, a historic 2.2-sq-mile (5.7-sq-km) estate. The grounds of the latter include rolling pastures, woodlands, and a working farm. From March to October visitors can enjoy informative tours of the dairy. There is also a children's farmyard on site.

Shelburne Museum (*p266*)

EAT

Hen of the Wood
Locally grown and foraged food in an intimate setting.

🏛 **55 Cherry St**
🌐 **henofthewood.com**

$$$

Farmhouse Tap & Grill
Gastropub with locally sourced food and 30 taps of local craft beer.

🏛 **160 Bank St**
🌐 **farmousetg.com**

$$$

→

Visitors walking by large carved wooden figures at Shelburne Farms

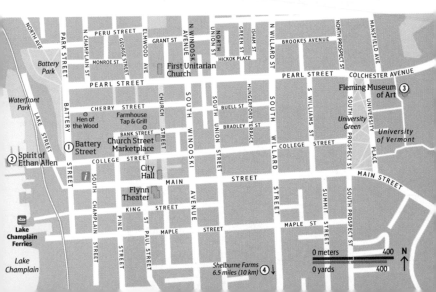

A SHORT WALK
HISTORIC DISTRICT

Distance 0.5 miles (1 km) **Time** 15 minutes

The four-block section known as the Church Street Marketplace is located at the center of Burlington's historic district. The neighborhood has been converted into a pedestrian mall complete with trendy boutiques, patio restaurants, specialty stores, factory outlets, craft shops, and, naturally, a Ben & Jerry's (p270).

The marketplace, thronged with shoppers and sightseers throughout the year, is at its most vibrant in the summer months, with numerous street performers and musicians adding color and action. The district also has its share of historical attractions, including the 1816 First Unitarian Church.

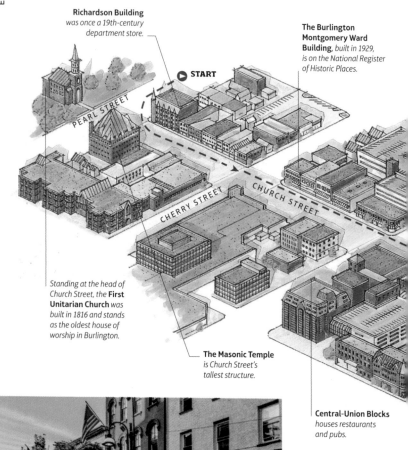

Richardson Building *was once a 19th-century department store.*

▶ **START**

The Burlington Montgomery Ward Building, *built in 1929, is on the National Register of Historic Places.*

PEARL STREET

CHERRY STREET

CHURCH STREET

Standing at the head of Church Street, the **First Unitarian Church** *was built in 1816 and stands as the oldest house of worship in Burlington.*

The Masonic Temple *is Church Street's tallest structure.*

Central-Union Blocks *houses restaurants and pubs.*

← Bustling Church Street, with its many restaurants

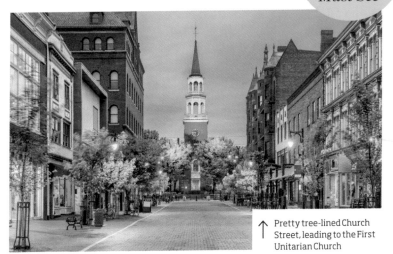

↑ Pretty tree-lined Church
Street, leading to the First
Unitarian Church

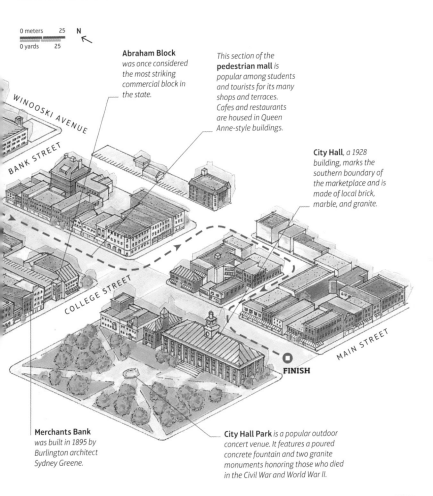

0 meters 25
0 yards 25

N ↖

Abraham Block
*was once considered
the most striking
commercial block in
the state.*

*This section of the
pedestrian mall is
popular among students
and tourists for its many
shops and terraces.
Cafes and restaurants
are housed in Queen
Anne-style buildings.*

WINOOSKI AVENUE

BANK STREET

COLLEGE STREET

MAIN STREET

City Hall, *a 1928
building, marks the
southern boundary of
the marketplace and is
made of local brick,
marble, and granite.*

FINISH

Merchants Bank
*was built in 1895 by
Burlington architect
Sydney Greene.*

City Hall Park *is a popular outdoor
concert venue. It features a poured
concrete fountain and two granite
monuments honoring those who died
in the Civil War and World War II.*

SHELBURNE MUSEUM

🅐 A2 🅠 Rte 7, 7 miles (11 km) S of Burlington
🅞 Mid-May-late Oct: 10am-5pm Mon-Sat, noon-5pm Sun
🅦 shelburnemuseum.org

The Shelburne Museum offers a unique insight into American history, art, and design. Within its many collections, all manner of trinkets and treasures are waiting to be discovered.

100,000

The number of items in the Shelburne Museum's growing collection.

Established in 1947 by collector Electra Webb (1888–1960), the Shelburne Museum celebrates four centuries of American ingenuity, creativity, and diversity. Here folk art, antique tools, duck decoys, and circus memorabilia share display space with pieced quilts and paintings by US artists such as Winslow Homer. The 39 buildings include a school-house, a stagecoach inn, and a covered bridge. Opened in 2013, the Pizzagalli Center for Art and Education offers year-round programs and exhibitions.

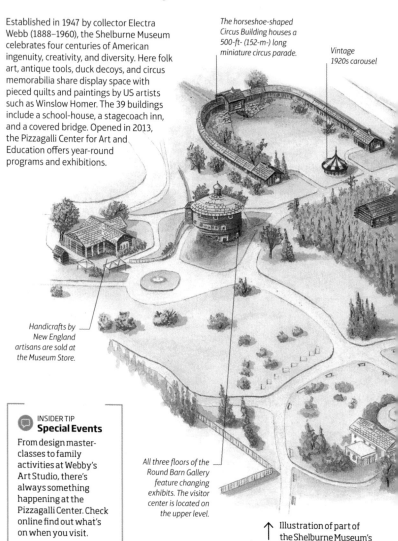

The horseshoe-shaped Circus Building houses a 500-ft- (152-m-) long miniature circus parade.

Vintage 1920s carousel

Handicrafts by New England artisans are sold at the Museum Store.

All three floors of the Round Barn Gallery feature changing exhibits. The visitor center is located on the upper level.

↑ Illustration of part of the Shelburne Museum's expansive grounds

💬 INSIDER TIP
Special Events

From design masterclasses to family activities at Webby's Art Studio, there's always something happening at the Pizzagalli Center. Check online find out what's on when you visit.

← The striking Round Barn Gallery dates back to 1901

→ Visitors boarding the former Lake Champlain steamship, *Ticonderoga*

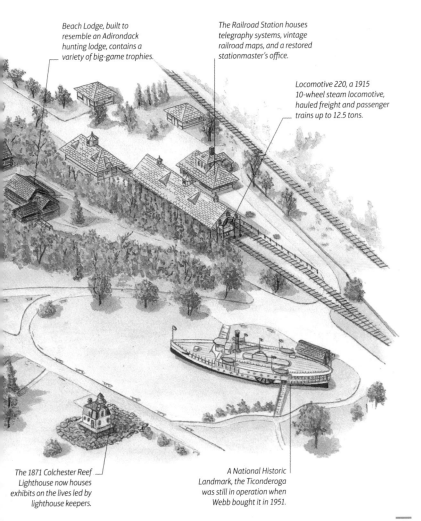

Beach Lodge, built to resemble an Adirondack hunting lodge, contains a variety of big-game trophies.

The Railroad Station houses telegraphy systems, vintage railroad maps, and a restored stationmaster's office.

Locomotive 220, a 1915 10-wheel steam locomotive, hauled freight and passenger trains up to 12.5 tons.

The 1871 Colchester Reef Lighthouse now houses exhibits on the lives led by lighthouse keepers.

A National Historic Landmark, the Ticonderoga was still in operation when Webb bought it in 1951.

EXPERIENCE MORE

③ Stowe

B2 ⛰40 miles (64 km) W in Burlington ℹ51 Main St; www.gostowe.com

It is hardly surprising that the von Trapp family, whose daring escape from Austria during World War II inspired the 1965 movie *The Sound of Music*, chose Stowe as their new home. The pretty village is ringed by mountains, reminiscent of their beloved Austrian Alps. The estate's giant wooden chalet, the Trapp Family Lodge, and cross country ski trails are among the most popular in the area.

Thanks to 4,393-ft (1,339-m) Mount Mansfield, this idyllic town has been a major ski and outdoor activity center since the 1930s. In winter it draws hordes of skiers to Stowe Mountain Resort. Lined with chalets, motels, restaurants, and pubs, Mountain Road runs from the village to the peak of the mountain. Many local spas and resorts offer gourmet meals, as well as massages and other health treatments. In the village the Vermont Ski and Snowboard Museum traces the development of downhill sports.

In summer there are still opportunities to enjoy the outdoors. Visitors can hike, rock-climb, fish, and canoe; or they can walk, cycle, or inline skate along the paved, meandering 5.5-mile (8.5-km) Stowe Recreational Path. It winds leisurely from Stowe's village church across the West Branch River, then through woodlands.

> **INSIDER TIP**
> **Sled Hire**
> You don't have to clip on skis to experience a downhill rush. Umiak Outdoor Outfitters (*www.umiak.com*) in Stowe rents out performance sleds for maximum speed and maneuverability.

> **Visitors can walk, cycle, or inline skate along the paved, meandering 5.5-mile (8.5-km) Stowe Recreational Path.**

④ St. Johnsbury

C2 ⛰Burlington 🚌 ℹ2000 Memorial Dr; www.stjvt.com

This small industrial town, the unofficial capital of Vermont's northeast region, sits on a promontory at the convergence of the Moose, Sleeper, and Passumpsic rivers. The town is named after St. Jean de Crèvecoeur, a friend of the Revolutionary War hero Ethan Allen. It was suggested that "bury" be added to the name because there were simply too many towns called St. John. It was here in 1830 that mechanic Thaddeus Fairbanks (1796–1886) invented the platform scale, a much more

Stowe's charming community church, amid magnificent fall colors ↑

Interior of the Fairbanks Museum and Planetarium in St. Johnsbury

accurate method of weighing than the balances of the time. The Fairbanks scale, as it came to be known, put St. Johnsbury on the map and boosted the growth of other pioneer industries, notably the manufacturing of maple products.

The Fairbanks family collected art and antiques, which are now housed in the fine **Fairbanks Museum and Planetarium**. This brick Victorian building, which is

on the National Historic Register, contains over 175,000 artifacts. Also on Main Street is the **St. Johnsbury Athenaeum Art Gallery**, a Victorian gem with gleaming woodwork, paneled walls, and circular staircase. It highlights the landscapes of the Hudson River School of painting. This 19th-century movement was the first school of American art, and focuses on the beauty of the natural world. Albert Bierstadt (1830–1902), whose canvas *Domes of Yosemite* hangs here, was one of its leaders.

Fairbanks Museum and Planetarium

🔘🔘 📍1302 Main St
🕐Museum: 9am–5pm daily; planetarium: call for show times 🌐fairbanks museum.org

St. Johnsbury Athenaeum Art Gallery

🔘🔘 📍1171 Main St
🕐10am–5:30pm Mon, Wed & Fri, noon–7pm Tue & Thu, 10am–3pm Sat
🌐stjathenaeum.org

5

Lake Willoughby

🅰B2 📍Rte 5A near Barton
📞(802) 239-4147

Travelers heading east from Barton climb a crest on the road only to be met with the breathtaking view of this beautiful body of water. The narrow glacial lake, which plunges 300 ft (90 m) in certain areas, is flanked by two soaring cliffs: Mount Pisgah at 2,750 ft (840 m) and Mount Hor at 2,650 ft (810 m). Jutting straight out of the water, the mountains give the lake a distinctly Nordic or even Alpine cast, earning

Willoughby the nickname the "Lucerne of America."

With trails leading around both promontories, this is a haven for hikers and swimmers seeking a secluded spot. There are wonderful picnic and camping areas along the beaches at either end of the 5-mile (8-km) lake, while several resorts ring the shores.

6

Bread and Puppet Museum

🅰B2 📍Exit 25 Rte 122 near Glover 🕐Jun–Oct: times vary, check website
🌐breadandpuppet.org

An extraordinary place down a quiet rural road, this museum is a century-old building that once served as a barn to shelter dairy cattle. The cows have gone, but every inch of space is taken up by paintings, masks, and other theatrical knickknacks, most notably costumed puppets of all shapes and sizes. The props belong to the Bread and Puppet Theater company, founded in 1962. Guided tours of the museum are the best way to glimpse the history behind the brilliant artistry. The troupe members live communally on the surrounding farm. Their popular productions are most notable for the masterful use of giant puppets.

→

Outlandishly costumed puppets at the Bread and Puppet Museum

→ Golden sunlight reflecting off the calm surface of Lake Champlain

⑦ Ben & Jerry's Ice Cream Factory

🅰B2 📍Rte 100, Waterbury
🕐Jul-mid-Aug: 9am-9pm daily; mid-Aug-Oct: 9am-7pm daily; Nov-Jun: 10am-6pm daily 🌐benjerry.com/waterbury

Although Ben Cohen and Jerry Greenfield hail from Long Island, New York, they have done more than any other "flatlanders" to put Vermont's dairy industry on the map. In 1977 these childhood friends paid $5 for a correspondence course on making ice cream and parlayed their knowledge into a flourishing empire.

Ben and Jerry use the richest cream and milk from local farms to produce their ice cream and frozen yogurt. The Ben & Jerry trademark is the black-and-white Holstein cow, embellishing everything in the gift shop.

Factory tours start every 15 to 30 minutes and run for half an hour, during which visitors learn all there is to know about making ice cream. They are given a bird's-eye view of the factory floor, with the chance to sample the products and sometimes test new flavors at the tour's end.

⑧ Montpelier

🅰B2 ❌Burlington 🚉🚌
ℹ️39 Main St; www.montpelier-vt.org

Montpelier is the smallest state capital in the US, but its diminutive stature is advantageous. The city is impeccably clean, friendly, and easily seen on foot. Despite Montpelier's size, its state politicians and legislators are housed in an imposing building. **Vermont State House**, which dates back to 1859, replaced an earlier building that was destroyed by fire. It is now a formidable Greek Revival structure, complete with a gilt cupola and fluted pillars of granite.

The **Vermont History Museum** is housed in a replica of a 19th-century hotel. The museum has an additional center in neighboring Barre.

Vermont State House
🕐🕐 📍115 State St
🕐7:45am-4:15pm Mon-Fri (mid-Jul-late Oct: also 11am-3pm Sat) 🚫Public hols
🌐statehouse.vermont.gov

Vermont History Museum
🕐🕐 📍109 State St
🕐10am-4pm Tue-Sat
🌐vermonthistory.org

⑨ Lake Champlain

🅰A2 ❌Burlington 🚌
ℹ️60 Main St, Burlington; (802) 863-3489 or (877) 686-5253

Lake Champlain was named for French explorer Samuel de Champlain (1574–1635), the first European to explore much of the surrounding

 ↑ Visitors sampling the wares of Ben & Jerry's Ice Cream Factory

Did You Know?

Lake Champlain is said to be the home of "Champ," a water serpent similar to the Loch Ness Monster.

region. Some 120 miles (190 km) long and 12 miles (19 km) wide, this vast expanse of water has its western shore in New York State, while the eastern sector is in Vermont. Seasonal hour-long ferry rides run regularly between Burlington and Port Kent, New York.

Sometimes called the sixth Great Lake because of its size, Champlain has miles of shore-line and about 70 islands. At its northern end, the Alburg Peninsula and a group of thin islands (North Hero, Isle La Motte, and Grand Isle) give glimpses of the region's color-ful past. At Ste. Anne's Shrine on Isle La Motte is a statue of Champlain. Grand Isle is home to America's oldest log cabin (1783). The villages of North and South Hero were named in honor of brothers Ethan and Ira Allen. Their volunteers, the Green Mountain Boys, helped secure Vermont's status as a state.

Some of Lake Champlain's treasures are underwater, preserved in a marine park where scuba divers can explore the shipwrecks resting on sandbars and at the bottom

of the lake. Displays at the **Lake Champlain Maritime Museum** at Basin Harbor focus on some of the historic ship-wrecks, as well as the many steamboats that once plied these waters. Visitors can board a full-scale replica of a 1776 gunboat and visit the Hazelett Watercraft Center.

Lake Champlain Maritime Museum

 ⓝ 4472 Basin Harbor Rd, Vergennes ⓞ Late May-early Oct: 10am–5pm daily ⓦ lcmm.org

---

⑩
Mad River Valley

ⒶB2 ⓝCentral VT along Rte 100 ⓘRte 100, Waitsfield; www.madriver valley.com

Located in central Vermont, Mad River Valley is most famous for outdoor activities that include hiking, cycling, hunting, and especially skiing.

One popular stop is the Mad River Glen ski area, which attracts die-hard tradition-alists who enjoy their sport the old-fashioned way: without high-speed gondolas (though there are four chairlifts) or snowmaking equipment. With about four dozen trails, Mad River Glen

caters to the country's most skilled skiers – in fact, its motto is "Ski it if you can."

Another ski area, Sugarbush has over 100 trails. It is the polar opposite of Mad River Glen, catering to all levels of skiers with the most modern snowmaking facilities and lifts. A state-of-the-art "people mover" connects what used to be two separate ski areas: Lincoln Peak and Mount Ellen.

Activities in and around fashionable Waitsfield include hiking, hunting, and polo. The local landmark is a round barn, one of only a dozen remaining in the state. It is now a venue for functions.

EAT

Capitol Grounds

Now a two-generation roastery, Capitol Grounds crafts Montpelier's famous 802 Coffee. Try their delightful chocolate chip cookies.

ⒶB2 ⓝ27 State St, Montpelier ⓢSun ⓦcapitolgrounds.com

⑪ Manchester

Ⓐ A4 **↻Rutland** **⬜ ℹ18 Depot St, Manchester Center; www.manchester vt.com**

Manchester is actually made up of three separate communities: Manchester Depot and Manchester Center, the outlet centers of New England, and Manchester Village. The sum of these parts is a picturesque destination surrounded by mountains, typical of scenic southern Vermont. There are two major ski areas: Stratton,

---

STAY

Equinox Resort

This luxury golf resort and spa has been welcoming guest for over 200 years. Fly-fishing, falconry, and shooting schools are offered on-site.

Ⓐ A4 **⌂3567 Main St, Manchester** **ⓦ equinox resort.com**

💲💲💲

↑ Skiers gathering at the foot of the slopes in Stratton Mountain Resort, Manchester

---

The compact campus of Middlebury College is a delightful place to explore, with graceful architecture, an art gallery, and green spaces.

a large complex with more than 90 trails and a hillside ski village with shops and restaurants; and Bromley, a busy, family-oriented ski area.

Manchester has been a popular vacation resort since the 19th century, when wealthy urbanites used to head to the mountains to escape the summer heat. The town's marble sidewalks fringed by old shade trees, the restored Equinox Resort, and several stately homes evoke that era.

One of Manchester's most elegant houses is **Hildene**, a 24-room Georgian Revival manor house built by Robert Lincoln (1843–1926), the son of President Abraham Lincoln (1809–65). Among the mansion's most notable features are its 1,000-pipe Aeolian organ and Lincoln family memorabilia. In winter, 8 miles (13 km) of trails are open to cross-country skiers. The **Southern Vermont Arts Center** presents performances and exhibitions in a stately Georgian mansion as well as a modern museum building. The vast estate features the state's

largest sculpture garden. Elsewhere, the **American Museum of Fly Fishing** claims to house the world's largest collection of fly-fishing paraphernalia. It includes hundreds of rods, reels, and flies used by famous people such as Bing Crosby and Ernest Hemingway.

Manchester is also where Charles Orvis established his fly rod shop in 1856; the finest of the company's rods are still built there. The extensive Orvis Flagship Store carries the full line of equipment and supplies, as well as offering fly-fishing classes on select dates throughout the summer.

Hildene

⊘ ⊘ **⌂ Rte 7A** **🕐 9:30am-4:30pm daily** **🚫 Easter, Thanksgiving, Dec 24-26** **ⓦ hildene.org**

Southern Vermont Arts Center

⊘ ⊘ **⌂930 SVAC Dr** **🕐10am-5pm Tue-Sat, noon-5pm Sun** **ⓦsvac.org**

American Museum of Fly Fishing

⊘ **⌂4070 Main St** **🕐 Jun-Oct: 10am-4pm Tue-Sun; Nov-May: 10am-4pm Tue-Sat** **ⓦamff.org**

---

⑫ Robert Frost Stone House Museum

Ⓐ A4 **⌂121 Historic Rte 7A, Shaftsbury** **📞(802) 447-6200** **🕐May-Oct: 11am-5pm Wed-Sun**

In this 1769 house surrounded by stone walls and apple trees Robert Frost wrote what is perhaps his best known poem, "Stopping by Woods on a Snowy Evening." Frost and his family lived in the Dutch Colonial home from 1920 to

→ The picturesque Robert Frost Stone House Museum, encircled by apple trees

1929. Just as in Derry, New Hampshire (p281), the rural landscape inspired Frost to write his distinctive verse pitched with a laconic New England cadence. While he was living here, the poet wrote several key volumes and was awarded the first of four Pulitzer Prizes for literature. Frost was instrumental in developing the educational philosophy of Bennington College in the 1930s, and the institution now owns this property and opens the house and grounds to the public.

 13

Middlebury

🅐 A3 ✈ 36 miles (58 km) N in Burlington 🚌 🛈 93 Court St; www.townof middlebury.org

Middlebury, founded in 1761, is the archetypal New England town. It has not one, but two village greens, or "commons," tall-spired churches, a prestigious college, and a collection of Colonial-era homes. Chief among the town's earliest buildings are the Battell and Beckwith commercial blocks, the Congregational Church, and the Middlebury Inn, a brick Georgian-style hostelry that dates back to 1827.

The town gets its name from the days of stage coaches when it served as the transit point on Vermont's main north-south and east-west routes. Morgan horses, one of the first US native breeds, were often seen on this route. Today visitors can tour the **University of Vermont Morgan Horse Farm**, which is dedicated to the preservation and improvement of this versatile and historic breed. Between 60 and 80 stallions, mares, and foals are cared for by agricultural science students.

History buffs will enjoy the **Henry Sheldon Museum of Vermont History**, an 1829 house that documents the early 19th century through its collection of furniture, textiles and clothing, and art.

At the town's **Vermont Folklife Center,** multimedia exhibits help bring rural culture to life. The center's Heritage Shop features quilts, decoys, baskets, and other objects made by contemporary folk

artists. The compact campus of Middlebury College is a delightful place to explore, with graceful architecture, an art gallery, and green spaces.

University of Vermont Morgan Horse Farm

♿ 🚫 🏠 Rte 23 NW of Middlebury in Weybridge 📞 (802) 388-2011 🕐 May-Oct: 9am-4pm daily

Henry Sheldon Museum of Vermont History

♿ 🏠 1 Park St 📞 (802) 388-2117 🕐 10am-5pm Tue-Sat, 1-5pm Sun 🚫 Nov-Apr: Sun, Jan 1, Jul 4, Thanksgiving, Dec 24 & 25

Vermont Folklife Center

🅟 🏠 88 Main St 📞 (802) 388-4964 🕐 10am-5pm Mon-Fri

→ A ceramic horse, on display in Middlebury College's art gallery

14

Green Mountain National Forest

🄰C5 ℹ️ Forest Supervisor, Green Mountain National Forest, 231 N Main St, Rutland; (802) 747-6700

This huge spine of greenery and mountains runs for 550 sq miles (1,425 sq km) – almost the entire length of the state – along two-thirds of the Green Mountain range. The mountains have some of the best ski centers in the eastern US, including Sugarbush (p271) and Mount Snow (p279).

The National Forest encompasses six wilderness areas – sections of the forest that have remained entirely undeveloped. While hard-core backcountry hikers may enjoy this challenge, the majority of travelers will prefer to roam the less primitive areas of the forest. There are more than 500 miles (800 km) of hiking paths, including the challenging Long and Appalachian trails (p10), and picnic sites and camp-grounds are found throughout.

Lakes, rivers, and reservoirs offer excellent boating and fishing opportunities. On land, bike paths are numerous and specially designated trails are open to horseback riders. Visitors are encouraged to stay on the paths in order to pre-serve the delicate ecosystem. Markers indicate designated lookout points and covered bridges. The town of Stratton

in the southern portion of the mountain range offers a variety of recreational activities, and nearby Bromley Mountain Ski Center has been a popular family resort since the 1930s.

15

Killington

🄰B3 ➡️Rutland ℹ️Rte 4, West Killington; www.killington.com

Outdoor adventurers seeking a lively social life head for this year-round resort. Killington has dozens of hotels, B&Bs, and condo clusters, as well as golf courses, hiking and bike trails, and an adventure center. It operates the largest ski center in the eastern United States, with 200 runs spread across seven peaks. Killington itself is the second-highest peak in Vermont, at 4,240 ft (1,292 m). Mountain Mountain Meadows

Did You Know?

Annual snowfall at Killington Peak averages 250 inches (6.4 m).

Cross Country Ski & Snowshoe Center and Mountain Top Inn – both excellent cross country ski centers – are also situated in the Killington area.

The ski season here usually lasts eight months, longer than anywhere else in Vermont, with one of the gondolas running during the summer and fall as well. It is worth taking a ride to the top for the spectacular views; on a clear day, visitors can glimpse parts of five states and distant Canada.

16

Bennington

🄰A4 ➡️🚌 ℹ️Bennington Area Visitor's Center, Rte 7; www.bennington.com

Though tucked away in the southwest corner of Vermont's iconic Green Mountain National Forest, Bennington is no backwoods community. The third-largest city in the state, it is an important manufacturing center and home to Bennington College.

Three bridges herald the approach to town. These 19th-century wooden structures, built with roofs to protect them against the harsh Vermont winter, were nicknamed "kissing bridges," because in the days of horses and buggies

A snowboarder spraying powder at Sugarbush, in the Green Mountain range

The Revolutionary era comes alive during a walking tour of the Old Bennington Historic District, where a typical New England village green is ringed by pillared Greek Revival structures. The 1806 First Congregational Church is a striking and much-photographed local landmark. Next to it is the Old Burying Ground, resting place of five Vermont governors and the beloved poet Robert Frost.

Looming over the Historic District is the **Bennington Battle Monument**, a massive stone obelisk that, when it was built in 1891, was the tallest war monument in the world. It commemorates a 1777 battle in nearby Willoomsac Heights. An elevator takes visitors to an observation area that offers panoramic views of Vermont and its neighboring states.

The turbulent times of the Revolutionary War are also recalled in the Sloane Gallery at the **Bennington Museum**. But better

they provided shelter for courting couples to embrace.

Bennington was established in 1749, and a few decades later Ethan Allen arrived to lead the Green Mountain Boys, a citizen's militia created to protect Vermont from the expansionist advances of neighboring New York. Allen would later make his name as a patriot during the Revolutionary War by leading his men to several decisive victories against British forces.

known is the museum's Grandma Moses Gallery, named for famed local folk artist Anna Mary "Grandma" Moses (1860–1961). A farmer's wife with no formal training in art, Moses began painting landscapes as a hobby when she was in her mid-70s. She was "discovered" in 1940 and hailed as an important new talent.

Bennington Battle Monument
⊗ 🕐 🚹 15 Monument Circle
📞 (802) 447-0550 🕐 Mid-Apr–Oct: 9am–5pm daily

Bennington Museum
⊗ 🕐 🚹 75 Main St 🕐 10am–5pm Thu-Tue (Jun-Oct: daily)
📅 Jan, Thanksgiving, Dec 25
🌐 benningtonmuseum.org

> 🔍 HIDDEN GEM
> **Bennington Farmers' Market**
> Visitors can sample local food year-round here, on the first and third Saturdays of each month. Fresh produce dominates in season; opt for baked goods when the market moves indoors in winter.

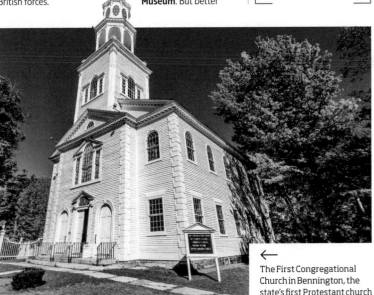

The First Congregational Church in Bennington, the state's first Protestant church

Morning in Beaver Meadow, Green Mountain National Forest

GREAT VIEW
Quechee Gorge

Head 6 miles (10 km) east of Woodstock to take in this stunning chasm. Best views can be found from Route 4, which crosses the gorge via a steel bridge; there is a parking lot, where you can stop and stare.

 17

Grafton

A B4 **↦** Rutland
W graftonvermont.org

A thriving industrial center in the early 19th century, Grafton suffered a steady decline until by the 1960s it was almost a ghost town. But in 1963 Dean Mathey, a wealthy investment banker, established a foundation with the mandate to restore historic structures and revitalize commercial life. Today the village is an architectural treasure trove of 19th-century buildings.

Two attractions are also thriving commercial enterprises. The 1801 Grafton Inn is one of the country's oldest hostelries. The **Grafton Forge Blacksmith Shop** produces ironware on-site and displays an array of historic tools and artifacts of the trade. Visitors can watch the blacksmith work.

Eighteen miles (29 km) to the north lies the hamlet of Plymouth Notch, the birth-place of Calvin Coolidge (1872–1933), 30th president of the US. The **Calvin Coolidge State Historic Site** encompasses an 1850s' general store and post office once run by Coolidge's father, as well as the Coolidge family home.

Grafton Forge Blacksmith Shop
🅿 **A** School St **C** (603) 998-0720 **O** Times vary, call for hours

Calvin Coolidge State Historic Site
♿🅿 **A** Rte 100A **C** (802) 672-3773 **O** Late May–mid-Oct: 9:30am–5pm daily

---

18

Brattleboro

A B4 **↦** 20 miles (32 km) NE in Keene, NH 🚌🚆 **i** 180 Main St; www.brattleboro chamber.org

Perched on the banks of the Connecticut River on the New Hampshire border, Brattleboro is the first major town that northbound travelers encounter as they enter the state. Fort Dummer was established here in 1724 as the first colonial settlement in what would become Vermont.

Brattleboro has consequently adopted the slogan "Where Vermont Begins."

A center of commerce and industry, the town is also a hub of tourism. As with so many other Vermont towns, there is a historic district with many Federal-era buildings of architectural interest. In the 1840s, after the Vermont Valley Railroad was laid to provide a vital link to the outside world, natural springs were discovered in the area, and Brattleboro took on a new personality as a spa town.

The former railroad station now houses the **Brattleboro Museum and Art Center**, which offers rotating exhibitions by artists of regional and international stature. The Brattleboro Music Center, on Walnut Street, stages a broad range of programs, including a chamber music series. The town's **Estey Organ Museum** is housed in the former factory building where the famous reed, pipe, and electronic organs were manufactured, prior to being shipped around the world.

Brattleboro Museum and Art Center
♿ **A** 10 Vernon St **O** 11am–5pm Wed–Mon **W** brattle boromuseum.org

→ Brick facades within Brattleboro's historic downtown district

↑ Children watching grazing Jersey cows at the Billings Farm & Museum in Woodstock

Estey Organ Museum

 📍108 Birge St 🕐Mid-May-early Oct: 2-4pm Sat & Sun 🌐esteyorgan museum.org

---

19

Woodstock

🅰B3 🚆Rutland 🚌 ℹ️59 Central St; www. woodstockvt.com

Even in Vermont, a state where historic, picturesque villages are a common sight, the pretty town of Woodstock stands out. Founded in 1761, it is an enclave of renovated brick and clapboard Georgian houses. The restoration of the town was the result of the generosity of philanthropists such as the Rockefeller family and railroad magnate Frederick Billings (1823–90). An early proponent of reforestation, Billings personally financed the planting of 10,000 trees in the Woodstock area.

Billings Farm & Museum is still a working entity. The 1890 farmhouse has been restored, and there are seasonal events such as plowing competitions in the spring and apple-cider pressing in the fall. The museum also traces Vermont's agricultural past with old photographs and exhibits of harvesting implements. Half an hour's drive northeast of Woodstock is the **King Arthur Flour Bakery + Café**. Its a mecca for bakers who are inspired by the popular range of baking ingredients and utensils, and delicious treats are sold in the café. A robust schedule of cooking classes is also on offer here.

Billings Farm & Museum

🍽 📍River Rd 🕐Apr-Oct: 10am-5pm daily; check website for winter hours 🌐billingsfarm.org

King Arthur Flour Bakery + Café

🍽🛍 📍135 US Route 5, Norwich 🕐7:30am-6pm daily 🌐kingarthurbaking.com

---

20

Wilmington

🅰B4 🚆West Dover ℹ️21 W Main St; (802) 464-8092

Wilmington is the largest village in Vermont's Mount Snow Valley, with several buzzing restaurants and stores catering to the numerous tourists who come to enjoy outdoor sports at the nearby mountain. Like so many of Vermont's small towns, its Main Street is lined with restored 18th- and 19th-century buildings, many listed on the National Register of Historic Places.

Standing 3,600 ft (1,100m) tall, **Mount Snow** is in fact named after the original owner of the land, farmer Reuben Snow – although most visitors believe the name refers to the abundance of white powder that arrives during winter. In the late 1990s, more than $35 million was spent on upgrading the ski center, which now has 102 trails, many of them wooded. Mount Snow was one of the first ski resorts in the US to provide facilities for snowboarders, with dedicated learning areas for beginners and facilities for advanced surfers. The center also opened the first mountain-bike school in the country. Outdoor summer attractions include challenging bike trails (some are also ski runs), hiking routes, an inline skate and skateboard park, and a climbing wall. The 18-hole Mount Snow Golf Club provides a more sedate diversion.

Mount Snow

🍽 📍Rte 100 🕐Daily 🌐mountsnow.com

NEW HAMPSHIRE

The Wabanaki peoples of New Hampshire lost their lands after the Treaty of Paris in 1763 as a consequence of their alliance with France in the French and Indian War (1688–1763). Native American villages of the coastal region had already been destroyed by the 1616–19 plague, which gave English settlers cultivated land for the taking. Initial settlements in the 1620s remained coastal, but within a generation explorers had ventured deep into the region's woods for furs and timbers.

Today there can be no better expression of New Hampshire's individualistic spirit than the state motto, "Live Free or Die," which is stamped on the state license plate. Six months before the signing of the Declaration of Independence on July 4, 1776, New Hampshire became the first state to formally reject British rule.

The landscape that helped forge the determined mindset of early settlers has changed little in the ensuing centuries. It is estimated that more than 90 percent of the state is undeveloped, with dense forest covering around three-quarters of its land.

0 kilometers 30

0 miles 30

CANADA

Connecticut
Lakes

Pittsburg

Richford

Canaan

Saint Albans

Colebrook

Dixville
Notch

Errol

Richard

Browningon

Island Pond

Blue Mountain
3,274 ft (998 m)

Stark

Berlin

Jeffersonville

Craftsbury
Common

Groveton

Mount Cabot
4,160 ft (1,268 m)

Gorham

Milton

Lyndonville

Lancaster

Burlington

Burlington
International Airport

Stowe

St. Johnsbury

Whitefield

WHITE MOUNTAIN
NATIONAL FOREST

Richmond

Cabot

Littleton

22 PINKHAM
NOTCH **17**

Waterbury

VERMONT
p258

Franconia

BRETTON
WOODS **18**

16

Montpelier

Barre

Bath

FRANCONIA
NOTCH STATE PARK **3**

CRAWFORD
NOTCH
STATE PARK **19**

Glen

Bristol

VERMONT

Brookfield

LINCOLN-WOODSTOCK **20**

21

Middlebury

Royalton

Woodstock

KANCAMAGUS
HIGHWAY

Warren

Tamworth

Brandon

NEW HAMPSHIRE

Squam
Lake

Plymouth

Lake
Winnipesaukee

Mendon

HANOVER **12**

Mount Cardigan
3,120 ft (951 m)

Meredith

Killington

Enfield

Bridgewater

Weirs Beach

Wolfeboro

Woodstock

Lebanon

14 ENFIELD
SHAKER
MUSEUM

Bristol

Rutland

Danbury

Laconia

Plainfield

28

SAINT-GAUDENS
NATIONAL
HISTORIC SITE **15**

Franklin

CANTEREBURY
SHAKER
VILLAGE **2**

Wallingford

NEW LONDON **13**

Newport

10 LAKE SUNAPEE
REGION

Canterbury

Pittsfield

Claremont

Newbury

Loudon

Weston

Springfield

Charlestown

Henniker

8 CONCORD

Suncook

Manchester

Londonderry

Bellows Falls

Hillsborough

Hooksett

Arlington

Walpole

Marlow

MANCHESTER **11**

Manchester
Boston
Regional
Airport

Hancock

KEENE **9**

Dublin

Merrimack

Derry

MONADNOCK
STATE PARK **6**

Peterborough

Milford

Salem

Wilmington

Brattleboro

RHODODENDRON
STATE PARK **7**

Jaffrey

Nashua

Hudson

NEW HAMPSHIRE

Must Sees

1 Portsmouth
2 Canterbury Shaker Village
3 Franconia Notch State Park

Experience More

4 Hampton
5 Exeter
6 Monadnock State Park
7 Rhododendron State Park
8 Concord
9 Keene
10 Lake Sunapee Region
11 Manchester
12 Hanover
13 New London
14 Enfield Shaker Museum
15 Saint-Gaudens National Historic Site
16 Jackson
17 Pinkham Notch
18 Bretton Woods
19 Crawford Notch State Park
20 Lincoln-Woodstock
21 Kancamagus Highway
22 White Mountain National Forest
23 North Conway

NEW HAMPSHIRE

❶ PORTSMOUTH

🅰D4 ✈36 Airline Ave 🚌10 Ladd St 🛈500 Market S; www.goportsmouthnh.com

When settlers established a colony here in 1623, they called it Strawbery Banke in honor of the berries blanketing the banks of the Piscataqua River. In 1653 its name was changed to Portsmouth, a reflection of the town's reputation as a hub of maritime commerce. First a fishing port, the town enjoyed prosperity in the 18th century as a link in the trade route between Great Britain and the West Indies. In the lead up to the American Revolution, Portsmouth was a hotbed of revolutionary fervor.

①
Governor John Langdon House

🅰143 Pleasant St ☎(603)-436-3205 🕐Jun–mid-Oct: 11am–5pm Fri–Sun

The son of a farmer of modest means, John Langdon (1741–1819) was a captain, merchant, and shipbuilder before becoming the governor of New Hampshire and a US senator. In 1784 he built this imposing Georgian mansion. The house is known for its ornate Rococo embellishments. The grounds boast a grape arbor and rose garden.

②
Moffatt-Ladd House

🅰154 Market St ☎(603) 436-8221 🕐Mid-Jun–mid-Oct: 11am–5pm Mon–Sat, 1–5pm Sun

One of Portsmouth's first three-story homes, this elegant 1763 mansion was built for wealthy maritime trader and sea captain John Moffatt. The house's boxy design was a precursor to the Federal style of architecture that would later become popular throughout the country. The house, located on the Portsmouth Harbor Trail (a walking tour of the Historic District), is graced by a grand entrance hall, a series of family portraits, and many period furnishings.

③
Wentworth-Gardner House

🅰50 Mechanic St ☎(603) 436-4406 🕐Jun–Oct: 11am–4pm Thu–Mon

Also on the Portsmouth Harbor Trail, this 1760

↑ Portsmouth's waterfront, lined with grand houses

house, built by wealthy merchant and landowner Mark Hunking Wentworth (1709–85), is considered to be one of the best examples of Georgian architecture in the entire country. The house's beautiful exterior has rows of multi-paned windows, symmetrical chimneys, and a grand, pillared entrance. The interior contains 11 fireplaces, and is decorated with hand-painted wallpaper, and graceful carvings that took artisans a year to complete.

④

USS Albacore

🏠 Albacore Park 🕐 Mid-May–mid-Oct: 9:30am–5pm daily; mid-Oct–mid-Jan & mid-Feb–mid-May: 9:30am–4pm Thu–Mon 🌐 ussalbacore.org

This submarine was the fastest underwater vessel of its type when it was launched from the Portsmouth Naval Shipyard in 1953. Visitors can access its cramped quarters and get an idea of what life was like for the crew. Exhibits in the visitor center trace the vessel's history.

---

⑤

Water Country

🏠 Rte 1 S of Portsmouth 🕐 Jun–Labor Day: check website for hours 🌐 watercountry.com

Thrilling water rides, a pirate ship, and a man-made lagoon await visitors to New England's largest water park. Smaller children can enjoy the slides and fountains, while the more adventurous can careen down looping water slides.

↑ The USS *Albacore*, offering a glimpse of life on board a submarine

GREAT VIEW
Water Views

Onboard Portsmouth Harbor Cruises, choose from narrated history cruises around the harbour, gorgeous sunset and city-light night trips, or offshore visits to spot seabirds on the Isles of Shoals, nine islands located off the coast. "Foliage cruises" head inland up the Piscataqua River.

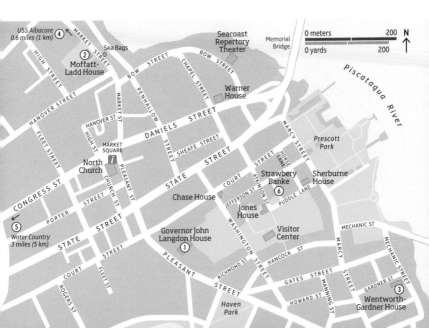

⑥ 🗝 Ⓜ 🍴 🖥 🛍

STRAWBERY BANKE

📍14 Hancock St ⏰May–Oct: 10am–5pm; Nov & Dec: special events only
🚫Jan–Apr 🌐strawberybanke.org

Visitors can fully immerse themselves in Portsmouth's colonial past at this indoor-outdoor museum, where costumed guides bring more than 300 years of history to life with tours, demonstrations, and workshops.

Situated near Portsmouth's vibrant waterfront district, the 10-acre (4-ha) site of Strawbery Banke contains 38 historic buildings where costumed guides show local life from 1695 to 1955. Houses open to the public are furnished in period style and hold collections of decorative arts, ceramics, and assorted artifacts. Many buildings are set amid gardens cultivated according to their eras, from early pioneer herb gardens to formal Victorian flower beds. Highlights include Pitt Tavern, where Patriots plotted against the Crown, and Jones House, now a popular spot for families thanks to its child-friendly Discovery Center.

> **Houses open to the public are furnished in period style and hold collections of decorative arts, ceramics, and assorted artifacts.**

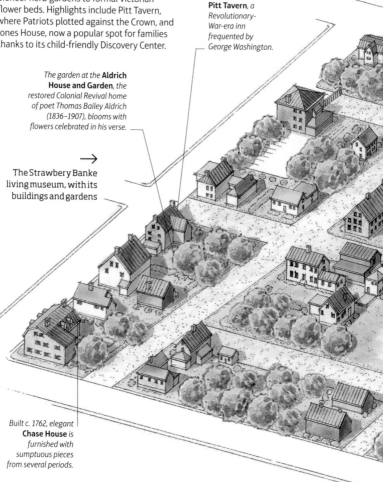

Pitt Tavern, a Revolutionary-War-era inn frequented by George Washington.

*The garden at the **Aldrich House and Garden**, the restored Colonial Revival home of poet Thomas Bailey Aldrich (1836–1907), blooms with flowers celebrated in his verse.*

→
The Strawbery Banke living museum, with its buildings and gardens

*Built c. 1762, elegant **Chase House** is furnished with sumptuous pieces from several periods.*

1 This is one of many colonial houses at Strawbery Banke, some of which are open to the public to explore.

2 There are various demonstrations at the museum; here a craftsman shows the technique of making pottery.

3 The Victorian hothouse at the Goodwin Mansion contains many species of exotic plants that may have been grown here in 1870.

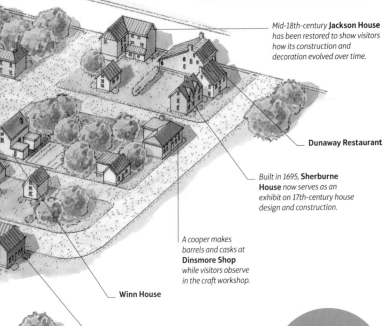

Mid-18th-century **Jackson House** has been restored to show visitors how its construction and decoration evolved over time.

Dunaway Restaurant

Built in 1695, **Sherburne House** now serves as an exhibit on 17th-century house design and construction.

A cooper makes barrels and casks at **Dinsmore Shop** while visitors observe in the craft workshop.

Winn House

The Discovery Center for Children's Activities at **Jones House** entertains and educates youngsters in this c. 1790 structure.

Did You Know?

Strawbery Banke is located on the site of Portsmouth's original seaport, known as "Puddle Dock."

② ⬦ ⬥ ▭ ⬗

CANTERBURY SHAKER VILLAGE

⬛C4 🏠288 Shaker Rd, Cantebury ⏰May–Aug: 10am–4pm Tue–Sun; Sep–Oct: 10am–5pm daily; Nov: 10am–4pm Sat & Sun 🅦shakers.org

Canterbury Shaker village, surrounded by lush green fields and tranquil hardwood forest, embodies the sect's belief in orderly design and craftsmanship as prayer.

Founded in 1792, this Shaker community remained active until the last sister died in 1992, making it one of the longest-lasting communities of the religious group in the US. This museum presents the Shaker legacy of entrepreneurship, innovative design, and simple living through 25 restored and four reconstructed Shaker buildings, plus extensive forests, fields, gardens, and trails. Guided tours and self-guided exhibits are available. Visitors have basement-to-attic access to the 1793 Dwelling House.

↑ Exterior of the 1793 Dwelling House, the heart of this Shaker community

↑ Spinning wheels exhibited in a sewing room

Did You Know?

The common flat broom was invented in 1798 by Shaker Brother Theodore Bates.

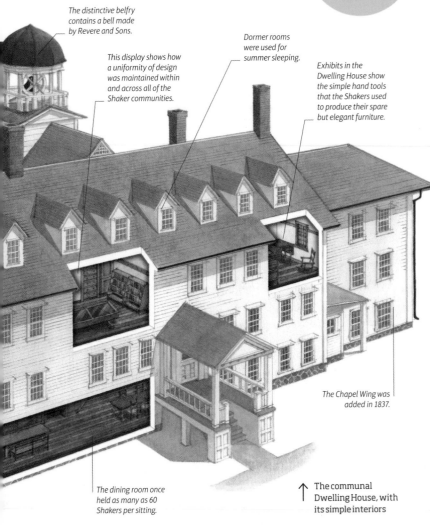

The distinctive belfry contains a bell made by Revere and Sons.

This display shows how a uniformity of design was maintained within and across all of the Shaker communities.

Dormer rooms were used for summer sleeping.

Exhibits in the Dwelling House show the simple hand tools that the Shakers used to produce their spare but elegant furniture.

The Chapel Wing was added in 1837.

The dining room once held as many as 60 Shakers per sitting.

↑ The communal Dwelling House, with its simple interiors

WHO WERE THE SHAKERS?

Mother Ann Lee founded this offshoot sect of the Quakers and brought her acolytes from England to America in 1774. Officially known as The United Society of Believers in Christ's Second Appearing, the Shakers acquired their name "Shaking Quakers" through their ecstatic behavior during worship. Essentially monastic, the Shakers believed in equality of the sexes and practiced celibacy – which turned out to be their ultimate undoing, as new converts failed to materialize.

FRANCONIA NOTCH STATE PARK

🄰C2 🄰I-93, Franconia Notch Parkway 🄲Dawn-dusk daily
🄸Visitor Center: 260 Tramway Drive; www.nhparks.state.nh.us

In the heart of the White Mountain National Forest, the sweeping valley of Franconia Notch State Park, with its abundance of lofty peaks, tranquil lakes, winding trails forested trails, and secluded camping grounds, is an outdoor enthusiast's haven, just waiting to be explored.

This spectacular mountain pass carved between the Kinsman and Franconia ranges is graced with some of the state's most spectacular natural wonders. Attractions include Flume Gorge, a narrow, granite chasm carved by rushing Flume Brook, and an aerial tramway car that carries passengers to the summit of Cannon Mountain. Boise Rock is an ideal picnic spot with views of the Cannon Cliffs and Echo Lake.

The Appalachian Trail spans part of Franconia Notch before it continues north. Known as the Franconia Ridge Trail, this 9-mile (15-km) hike skirts the second highest range of peaks in the White Mountains. Its excellent views and relative accessibility make it one of the most popular routes in New England, with up to 700 hikers a day.

Did You Know?

The northern part of the park is in the town of Franconia, while the southern part is in Lincoln.

Vibrant fall foliage coloring the banks of Echo Lake, Franconia Notch State Park ↑

← Winter hikers on the snowy summit of Mount Lafayette on the Franconia Ridge Trail

→ Visitors walking alongside the fast-flowing waters of the Flume Brook as it carves its way through Flume Gorge

OLD MAN OF THE MOUNTAIN

The old Man of the Mountain, a mysterious and much-loved rock formation that resembled the profile of a wise old man once protuded proudly from the side of a cliff above Profiler Lake. Also known as The Great Stone Face or The Profile, the Old Man has been the state emblem since 1945.

Sadly the Old Man met a bitter end in 2011 when the rocky profile crumbled and fell down the mountain-side. A monument now stands in Profiler Plaza as testament to the Old Man's enduring legacy. An interactive sculpture by artist Shelly Bradbury and Ron Magers helps visitors visualise the Old Man in all his former glory.

EXPERIENCE MORE

4

Hampton

D4 Portsmouth
📍1 Lafayette Rd; www.
hamptonchamber.com

One of New Hampshire's oldest towns, Hampton is situated at the geographic center of the many state parks and public beaches that line Highway 1A, the coast road. Public recreation areas stretch from Seabrook Beach, a sandy shore dotted with dunes, to the rugged shoreline of **Odiorne Point State Park** in Rye to the north. The park has biking trails, tidal pools, and a boardwalk spanning a saltwater marsh. The park's Science Center also runs interpretive nature programs that are especially appealing to young visitors.

Ten miles (16 km) to the south of the factory outlet shopping center in North Hampton, travelers will come upon the popular **Hampton Beach**. This miniature version of Atlantic City (without the gambling) comes complete with a venue that hosts big-name entertainers and an old-fashioned boardwalk lined with video arcades, ice-cream shops, and stalls selling T-shirts and tacky souvenirs.

Open year-round, Hampton Beach is busiest during hot summer months, when vacationers come to enjoy the miles of clean, golden beaches, including a separate area designated for surfers. Swimmers and jet skiers test the waters, parasailors soar overhead, and deep-sea fishing and whale-watching charter boats are available from Hampton Harbor. The bustling strand is not the place for people seeking a quiet beach vacation, but instead it is geared toward family fun, with numerous game arcades, water slides, magic shows, and an impressive series of free concerts and fireworks.

Odiorne Point State Park
⊗ 🅐Rte 1A, Rye Beach
📞 Park: (603) 436-7406
🕐 Park: 8am-dusk daily;
Science Center: 10am-5pm daily (Nov-Mar: Sat-Mon only), seacoastscience center.org 🚫Jan 1, Thanksgiving, Dec 25

Hampton Beach
🌐hamptonbeach.org

5

Exeter

D4 Portsmouth
📍120 Water St; www.
exeterarea.org

The quiet little town of Exeter, southwest of Portsmouth, was much less tranquil during the century and a half leading up to the American Revolution (1775–83). The community sprang up around the falls, linking the tidal Squamscott River and the freshwater Exeter River. It was founded in 1638 by the Reverend John Wheelwright (1592–1679), an outspoken cleric whose radical views resulted in

---

🔍 HIDDEN GEM
Skywatchers

The origins of America's Stonehenge (www. stonehengeusa.com), south of Exeter, in the remote Salem woods are obscure, but the formation is an evocative site during solstices and equinoxes.

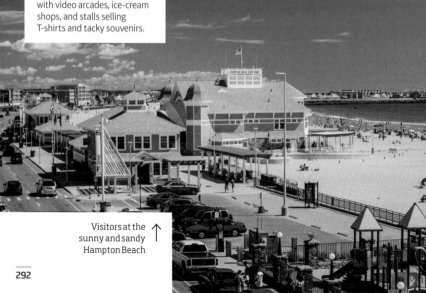

Visitors at the
sunny and sandy ↑
Hampton Beach

↑ Hikers tackling the popular peak of Mount Monadnock

him being thrown out of the Massachusetts colony.

During the turbulent years leading up to American Independence, outraged townspeople here openly defied the British government. They drove off officials dispatched to cut down trees for the British Navy, burned their leaders in effigy, and finally declared independence from Britain, setting a precedent for the rest of the colonies.

Dominating the center of town, Phillips Exeter Academy stands as one of the country's most prestigious preparatory schools. Founded in 1781, the grand complex comprises more than 100 ivy-clad brick buildings fronted by manicured lawns.

Other points of interest include the Gilman Garrison House, a late 17th-century fortified log building, and the **American Independence Museum**, which displays an original copy of the Declaration of Independence in mid-July, and also owns two drafts of the US Constitution.

American Independence Museum

 ⬛1 Governors Lane
☎(603) 772-2622 ◯May–Nov: 10am–4pm Tue–Sat

6

Monadnock State Park

🅰B4 ◯Off Rte 124, W of Jaffrey ◯Dawn-dusk daily ⬤nhstateparks.org

Standing some 3,165 ft (965 m) high, Mount Monadnock has two claims to fame. It is said to be one of the world's most climbed mountains (it is not unusual to find several dozen hikers milling around its peak), and it has spawned a geological term. A "monadnock" is an isolated hill or mountain of resistant rock rising above a plain that has been created by glacial activity.

The mountain's popularity has a lot to do with its seasonal campgrounds, scenic picnic areas, and hiking trails. Within the park, there are 40 miles (64 km) of trails, many of which lead to the summit. The climb to the peak of the metamorphic schist pinnacle takes more than 3 hours, but on clear days intrepid hikers are rewarded with views of all six New England states. Along the trails, markers have been erected in memory of such men of letters as Ralph Waldo Emerson (1803–82) and Henry David Thoreau (1817–62),

both of whom climbed to the peak. The visitor center gives an overview of the hiking trails (which are popular with cross-country skiers in winter) and information about the local flora and fauna.

7

Rhododendron State Park

🅰B5 ◯Off Rte 119, W of Fitzwilliam ◯Dawn-dusk daily ⬤nhstateparks.org

New England's largest grove of wild rhododendrons bursts into a celebration of pink and white in June through mid-July. Walking through the shrubs, some of which grow to more than 20 ft (6 m) high, is a feast for the senses in summer, but there are floral highlights in other seasons as well. In the spring the woodland park is carpeted with trilliums; by May the apple trees are heavy with blossoms. During summer, visitors will find flowering mountain laurel and wild flowers such as jack-in-the-pulpit. The park features picnic areas and hiking trails that offer spectacular views of Mount Monadnock and the surrounding peaks.

ROBERT FROST AND NEW HAMPSHIRE

New Hampshire's natural beauty was an inspiration to one of America's best-loved poets: Robert Frost (1874–1963). Born in San Francisco, the four-time winner of the Pulitzer Prize moved to Massachusetts with his family when he was 11. After working as a teacher, a reporter, and a mill hand, Frost moved briefly to England in 1912, and upon his return to the US in 1915 he settled in the Franconia Notch area (p290). The majestic setting inspired him to pen many of his greatest works.

8

Concord

⚠C4 🚗🚌 ℹ49 S Main St; (603) 224-2508

New Hampshire's capital is a quiet little town, but because it is the seat of government of a county, it has been associated with a number of important historical figures. Mary Baker Eddy, founder of the Christian Science Church, spent much of her life here. The Pierce Manse was the one-time home of Franklin Pierce, the 14th president of the US, and the 1819 State House is one of the oldest state capitol buildings in America. Inside are several hundred paintings of the state's better-known residents and political figures. In its heyday, the Eagle Hotel on Main Street hosted the likes of presidents Andrew Jackson and Benjamin Harrison, as well as aviator Charles Lindbergh, and former First Lady Eleanor Roosevelt. Concord schoolteacher Christa McAuliffe (1948–86) unfortunately gained her fame through tragedy. On January 28, 1986, McAuliffe boarded the *Challenger* space shuttle as

↑ The colonnaded exterior of Concord's 19th-century State House

the first civilian to be launched into space by NASA. Just 71 seconds after liftoff, with her husband and children watching from the ground, the shuttle exploded into a fireball and crashed, killing McAuliffe and her six fellow astronauts. Her memory lives on at **The McAuliffe-Shepard Discovery Center**, which also honors New Hampshire native and astronaut Alan Shepard, who was the first American to be launched into space. The futuristic center is capped by a giant glass pyramid, and features exhibits and scale models of spacecraft.

The McAuliffe-Shepard Discovery Center

♿♻ 🅿 📍2 Institute Dr
🕐10:30am–4pm Fri–Sun
(late Jun–Aug: daily)
🌐starhop.com

9

Keene

⚠B4 🚌 ℹ48 Central Sq; (603) 352-1303

Keene is the largest town in southern New Hampshire's Monadnock region. The nation's first glass-blowing factory was founded in nearby Temple in 1780, and soon after Keene became one of the region's hotbeds of arts and crafts. By the 19th century the

town was famous for the production of high-quality glass and pottery and for its thriving wool mill. The **Horatio Colony Museum** is the former home of a descendant of the mill-owning family. Its period furnishings give a good idea of upper-class life in the mid-19th century. Today the focus of Keene's thriving cultural life is Keene State College, which has several theaters and art studios where events are staged throughout the year.

Horatio Colony Museum

♿ 📍199 Main St 📞(603) 352-0460 🕐May-mid-Oct: 11am–4pm Wed-Sun

→ Visitors admiring the works on display at Manchester's Currier Museum of Arts

DRINK

Stark Brewing Co

This craft brewing company occupies one of Manchester's massive historic mill buildings along the Merrimack River. Milly's Tavern, the site's brewpub, offers hearty meals and a minimum of 18 beers on tap. In the same facility, the Stark Distillery crafts a rye-based vodka

⚠A4 📍500 Commercial St, Manchester 🌐stark brewingcompany.com

⑩ Lake Sunapee Region

Ⓐ C4 **ⓘ 328 Main St, New London; (603) 526-6575 or (877) 526-6575**

This scenic region, dominated by 2,743-ft- (835-m-) high Mount Sunapee and the 10-mile (16-km) lake at its feet, is a major draw for outdoor enthusiasts, particularly skiers and boaters. Many locals have vacation homes here, and an increasing number of retirees are also moving to the region, attracted by both the scenery and the active lifestyle.

Lake Sunapee (its name is said to be derived from the Pennacook words for "wild goose water") has been attracting visitors for well over a century. In the mid-1800s, trains and steamships used to transport tourists to hotels that rimmed the lake. The steamships have long since gone, but vacationers can still rent canoes or take a sightseeing boat. Mount Sunapee State Park's namesake peak attracts hikers and climbers during the summer months and skiers in winter. The Mount Sunapee resort in the park is the largest ski area between Boston and the White Mountains.

CONCORD COACHES

In 1827 Concord-based wheelwright Lewis Downing and coach builder J. Stephens Abbot built the first Concord Coach, designed to withstand the unforgiving trails of the undeveloped West. In their own way, the stagecoaches were as revolutionary as the Internet is today, because they helped facilitate communications across the vast emerging hinterland of the US.

⑪ Manchester

Ⓐ A4 **🚍 1 Airport Rd** **ⓘ 54 Hanover St; (603) 666-6600**

In 1805 the modest Amoskeag Mill was built on the east bank of the Merrimack River. It continued to expand, until, by the beginning of the 20th century, it was the largest textile mill in the world, employing some 17,000 people at its peak.

Today this former industrial city is known for the **Currier Museum of Art**, which is home to an excellent collection of European and Contemporary art .The entire second floor is dedicated to 18th- and 19th-century American artists, including the Impressionists and members of the Hudson River School. Another gallery features regional artists.

The museum's largest piece is the nearby Zimmerman House, designed in 1950 by pioneering American architect Frank Lloyd Wright (1867–1959) as an exemplar of his Usonian homes. Shuttles take visitors from the museum to the house, and guided tours (by advance reservation mid-April through January) of its interior highlight textiles and furniture designed by Wright.

Currier Museum of Art

🅐🅒🅔🅑 ⓕ 🏠 150 Ash St 🕐 11am–5pm Wed–Mon (from 10am Sat) ⓦ currier.org

12

Hanover

 B3 🔁 Lebanon 🚌
ℹ️ 53 S Main St; www.
hanoverchamber.org

Hanover, with a traditional village green ringed by historic brick buildings, is the archetypal New England college town. It is a pretty stop for visitors following the Appalachian Trail, which goes right through the center of town. Hanover is also the home of **Dartmouth College**, the northernmost of the country's Ivy League schools. Originally known as Moor's Indian Charity School, the college was founded in 1769 to educate and convert Native Americans. Today some 4,500 students participate in programs that include one of the oldest medical schools in America, the Thayer School of Engineering (1867), and the Amos Tuck School of Business (1900). Famous graduates include former vice president Nelson Rockefeller.

The college's **Baker-Berry Library** is decorated by a series of intriguing murals tracing the history of the Americas painted by Mexican artist José Clemente Orozco (1883–1949) in the early 1930s. The newly expanded **Hood Museum of Art** has a diverse collection that includes Native American and African art, plus early American and European paintings, and works by such noted modern artists as Pablo Picasso.

Dartmouth College
⊗ 🆆 dartmouth.edu

Baker-Berry Library
🅐 Dartmouth College
📞 (603) 646-2567 🕐 Daily; times vary, call for hours

Hood Museum of Art
⊗ 🏛 🅐 Dartmouth College 🕐 Times vary, check website 🆆 hood museum.dartmouth.edu

---

 13

New London

🅐 C4 🔁 Lebanon 🚌 ℹ️ 328 Main St; www.nl-nh.com

New London's perch atop a crest gives it an enviable view of the surrounding forests during the fall foliage season. The bucolic setting also serves as a wonderful backdrop for the town's rich collection of colonial and early 19th-century buildings. Of these, the architectural centerpiece is **Colby-Sawyer College**, a private undergraduate liberal arts school founded in 1837. The college organizes numerous cultural programs, including plays, lectures, films, concerts, and art exhibitions. More cultural fun can be had farther down the street at the **New London Barn Playhouse**. Housed in a refurbished 1820s' barn, the theater stages popular plays and musicals during the summer.

←

The charming brick bell tower of Dartmouth's Baker-Berry Library

The sparsely decorated interior of the Enfield Shaker Museum

Colby-Sawyer College

  Main St ⏱9am-5pm Mon-Fri 🌐colby-sawyer.edu

New London Barn Playhouse

🅿 84 Main St ⏱Mid-Jun-Sep: times vary, check website 🌐nlbarn.org

14

Enfield Shaker Museum

B3 Rte 4A, Enfield ⏱May-Dec: 10am-5pm Mon-Sat, noon-5pm Sun 🌐shakermuseum.org

Facing religious persecution in Britain in the mid-18th century, several groups of Shakers, a sect that broke away from the Quakers, fled to North America under the spiritual guidance of Mother Ann Lee (1736–84). The Shaker village at Enfield was founded in 1793, one of 18 such communities in the US.

Between the founding of Enfield and the 1920s, the Shakers constructed more than 200 buildings, of which 13 remain. And while they farmed more than 4.6 sq miles (12 sq km) of land, property was under the ownership of the community, not individuals. Members were celibate and they were strict pacifists, devoting their "hands to work and hearts to God." At one time the Enfield Shakers numbered over 300, but, as in similar communities, their numbers gradually dwindled. In 1923 the last 10 members moved

to the Canterbury Shaker Village (p288), north of Concord. The last Canterbury Shaker died in 1992 at the age of 96.

The exhibits at the museum illustrate how the Shakers lived and worked. Visitors will come across fine examples of Shaker ingenuity, including one of their many inventions: sulfur matches. The buildings are filled with the simple but practical wooden furniture for which the Shakers, who were consummate craftspeople, were famous. The 160-year-old Great Stone Dwelling, the largest such structure ever built by these industrious people, is available for overnight stays.

15

Saint-Gaudens National Historic Site

B3 Rte 12A N of Cornish-Windsor Bridge ⏱Buildings: late May-Oct: 9am-4:30pm daily; Grounds: dawn-dusk daily 🌐nps.gov/saga

This national historic site celebrates the life of Augustus Saint-Gaudens (1848–1907), the country's preeminent sculptor of his time. When he began to summer here in 1885, it marked the beginning of the town's evolution into an art colony. Artists, writers, and musicians alike were attracted to the town by the talent of Saint-Gaudens, whose family had emigrated to the US from Ireland when he was a baby. Something of a world traveler, Saint-Gaudens became an apprentice cameo cutter in New York and later studied at the Ecole des Beaux-Arts

in Paris. He also won several commissions in Rome. By the time that he returned to New York, his reputation as a brilliant sculptor had been well established. His work, usually of heroic subject matter, can be found throughout the country. New England is home to many Saint-Gaudens masterpieces, including Boston's Shaw Memorial (1897).

Saint-Gaudens grew tired of the big-city pace, buying an old inn near the Connecticut River and turning it into a home and studio. Many of his greatest works were created here, including the famous statue of Abraham Lincoln (1809–65) that stands in Lincoln Park, Chicago. Today this historic 1805 home is filled with the sculptor's furniture and samples of his small, detailed sketches for large bronzes. A number of his sculptures are displayed around the 0.2-sq-mile (0.5-sq-km) property, which is laid out with formal gardens and pleasing walking trails flanked by tall pines and hemlocks.

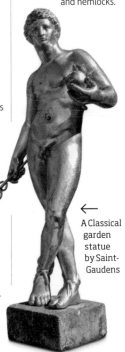

← A Classical garden statue by Saint-Gaudens

16

Jackson

C2 📍18 Main St; (603) 383-9356

This mountain village is tucked away on a back road off Route 16B, but drivers will not miss it, because the entrance is marked by its distinctive red-and-white covered bridge. The picturesque 200-year-old community is, along with the nearby villages of Intervale, Bartlett, and Glen, the main center for accommodation in the Mount Washington area.

Jackson was at one time a favorite getaway spot for big-city Easterners, but the hard times of the Great Depression of the 1930s saw the town slip into disrepair. Developers rediscovered this quiet corner of New Hampshire in the 1980s and began restoring several of the town's best hotels.

Jackson is a popular base camp for skiers, as the region is blessed with more than 110 downhill runs and a network of over 200 miles (320 km) of cross-country trails. The main ski centers are Black Mountain, the Wildcat Ski Area, and the Attitash Mountain Resort, the state's biggest ski center.

Summer sports abound here as well. The region's numerous peaks and valleys make this prime hiking and mountain-biking country, and a restored 18-hole course is set against one of the most scenic backdrops in New England. After having worked up a sweat, bikers and hikers can cool off under the water-falls of the Wildcat River in Jackson Village.

Did You Know?

On average, hurricane-force winds occur at the summit of Mount Washington 110 days of the year.

↑ A waterfall cascading through scenic Pinkham Notch

17

Pinkham Notch

C2 📍Rte 16 N of North Conway; (603) 466-2721; 6:30am–10pm daily

Named after Joseph Pinkham, who according to local lore explored the area in 1790 with a sled drawn by pigs, this rocky ravine runs between Gorham and Jackson. The Presidential Range girds the western flank of Pinkham Notch, while the 4,415-ft (1,346-m) Wildcat Mountain looms to the east.

Backcountry adventurers can enjoy a great variety of activities. Skiing at the Wildcat Ski Area is excellent, while in the summer visitors can ride to the summit aboard the aerial gondola to take in great views of Mount Washington and the Presidential Range.

Hiking trails to suit all skill levels lace Pinkham Notch, including a section of the Appalachian Trail (p10). Along the way, visitors are led past some of the region's most captivating sights, including waterfalls, scenic overlooks, and pristine ponds tucked away in thick woodland. Lucky travelers may spot raccoons, beaver, deer, and even the occasional moose.

18

Bretton Woods

C2 📍(603) 278 - 3320 🌐brettonwoods.com

This tiny enclave situated on a glacial plain at the base of the Presidential Range has an unusual claim to fame: it hosted the United Nations Monetary and Financial Conference in 1944. The meetings laid the groundwork for the World Bank, a response to the need for currency stability after the economic upheavals of World War II. The delegates also set the gold standard at $35 an ounce and chose the American dollar as an international standard for monetary exchange.

The setting for this vital meeting was the **Omni Mount Washington Resort**. It is easy to imagine the reaction of delegates when they first caught sight of this Spanish

Renaissance-style hotel from a sweeping curve in the road. Opened in 1902, the hotel has a sparkling white exterior and crimson roof that stand in stark contrast to Mount Washington, which looms 6,288 ft (1,917 m) skyward behind the edifice. The hotel has entertained a host of distinguished guests, including three presidents, Winston Churchill (1874–1965), inventor Thomas Edison (1847–1931), and baseball star Babe Ruth (1895–1948). Designated a National Historic Landmark, the 200-room structure was built by 250 Italian craftsmen. Today the hotel is surrounded by parkland, with facilities including an 18-hole golf course laid out by Donald Ross (1872–1948). Nearby Bretton Woods ski area offers alpine skiing along with 62 miles (100 km) of cross-country trails.

The Mount Washington Valley, in which Bretton Woods is located, is dominated by the peak of Mount Washington, which is the highest in the northeastern United States. It also has the distinction of having the worst weather of any mountain in the world. Unpredictable snowstorms are not unusual, even during summer months, and the now second-highest wind speed recorded on earth was clocked here in April 1934: 231 mph (372 kph). During the last century, the mountain has claimed the lives of almost 100 people caught unaware by its climate. On clear days, however, nothing compares to the panoramic view from the top. Brave souls hike to the summit by one of the many trails, drive their own cars, or puff slowly to the top aboard the deservedly famous **Mount Washington Cog Railroad**. Billed as "America's oldest tourist attraction," the railroad started operating in 1869 along one of the steepest tracks in the world, climbing at a heart-stopping 37 percent gradient at some points. At the top, passengers can visit the Sherman Adams Summit Building, with the Summit Museum, and Mount Washington Observatory.

Omni Mount Washington Resort

Rte 302, Bretton Woods omnihotels.com

Mount Washington Cog Railroad

Off Rte 302, Marshfield Base Station Apr–Nov: check website for timetable thecog.com

The eye-catching terrace of Mount Washington Resort, and *(inset)* nearby Cog Railroad ↓

19

Crawford Notch State Park

🅰C2 📍Rte 302 between Twin Mountains & Bartlett ⏱Daily; campground: late May–mid-Oct 🌐nhstate parks.org

This narrow pass, which squeezes through the sheer rock walls of Webster and Willey mountains, gained notoriety in 1826. One night severe rain sent tons of mud and stone careening into the valley below, heading straight for the home of innkeeper Samuel Willey and his family. Alerted by the sounds of the avalanche, the family fled outdoors, where all seven were killed beneath falling debris. Ironically, the lethal avalanche bypassed the house, leaving it unscathed. Several writers, including New Englander Nathaniel Hawthorne, have immortalized the tragedy in literature. The historic house still stands and is now in service as a visitor center.

At one point the notch was threatened by overlogging. However, the establishment of the state park in 1911 has ensured protection of this rugged wilderness. Today white-water boaters come here to test their mettle on the powerful Saco River, which carves its way through the valley. Fishermen ply the park's more tranquil ponds and streams in search of sport and a tasty dinner of trout or salmon.

People who prefer to keep their feet dry can still enjoy the water on a short hiking trail leading to the Arethusa Falls. Towering more than 200 ft (61 m) in the air, this magnificent cascade is New Hampshire's tallest waterfall. Elsewhere in the park, drivers are afforded wonderful views of the Silver Cascades and Flume Cascades waterfalls without leaving the comfort of their car.

→

A spectacular sunset illuminating the Kancamagus Highway

 GREAT VIEW
Majestic Mountains

Painted bright yellow, the 1865 Mountain View Grand Resort is as familiar a feature of the landscape as the mountains themselves. Nab a rocker on the front porch for the best views of the Presidential Range.

20

Lincoln-Woodstock

🅰C3 🚗66 miles (106 km) SW in Lebanon 🛈126 Main St, N Woodstock; (603) 745-6621

Located near the White Mountains, North Woodstock offers ski-bum winter ambience and hiker-chic sensibility for the rest of the year. While the **Woodstock Inn Brewery**, set in an old train station, is a favorite with the hikers, visitors can also head to the village general store, Fadden's, which dates back to 1896. Learn how maple syrup has been produced over the years in its maple sugar house out back.

Tiny Lincoln is located just 3 miles (5 km) northeast of North Woodstock. The town's location at the western end of the Kancamagus Highway and at the southern entrance to Franconia Notch State Park (p290) have turned it into a base camp for both backwoods adventurers and

←

The enduring Willey House, within Crawford Notch State Park

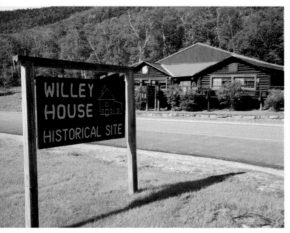

> **Located near the White Mountains, North Woodstock offers ski-bum winter ambience and hiker-chic sensibility for the rest of the year.**

stick-to-the-road sightseers. Nearby **Loon Mountain** is one of the state's premier ski resorts. In the summer it offers a number of activities, from a climbing wall and ziplines to disc golf, mountain biking, and gondola rides to the summit.

Woodstock Inn Brewery
 135 Main St, N Woodstock
w woodstockinn
brewery.com

Loon Mountain
E of I-93, near Lincoln w loonmtn.com

21

Kancamagus Highway

C3 Rte 112 between Lincoln & Conway Saco District Ranger Station, 33 Kancamagus Hwy; (603) 447-5448

Touted by many as the most scenic fall-foliage road in New England, this stretch of highway runs through the White Mountain National Forest *(p302)* between Lincoln and Conway. The road covers about 34 miles (55 km) of Route 112 and offers exceptional vistas from the Pemigewasset Overlook as it climbs approximately 3,000 ft (914 m) through the Kancamagus Pass. Descending into the Saco Valley, the well-traveled road joins up with the Swift River, following the aptly named waterway into Conway. The highway provides fishermen with easy access to the river, which is home to brook and rainbow trout.

Campgrounds and picnic areas along the entire length of highway give travelers ample opportunity to relax and eat lunch on the banks of cool mountain streams. Maintained by the US Forest Service, the campgrounds are equipped with toilets, and one has shower facilities; most are operated on a first-come, first-served basis.

Well-marked trails also allow drivers to stretch their legs in the midst of some of the most beautiful scenery in the state. One of the most popular trails is a short loop that leads travelers to the oft-photographed Sabbaday Falls. Closer to Conway, road signs guide drivers to several scenic areas that offer views of cascades, rapids, and rivers.

The area is home to a wide variety of wildlife, including resident birds such as woodpeckers and chickadees, as well as migratory songbirds who breed here in the summer. Larger inhabitants include deer, moose, and the occasional black bear.

EAT

Half Baked and Fully Brewed
This bakery-café is a good place to stop for a healthy lunch, or to pick up tasty sandwiches and cookies for a picnic along the scenic Kancamagus Highway.

C3 187 Main St, Lincoln (603) 745-8811

White Mountain National Forest

🏛️C2 ℹ️71 White Mountain Dr, Campton; www.fs. fed.us

New Hampshire's heavily forested northland is an outdoor paradise, encompassing a national forest, several state parks, more than 1,200 miles (1,930 km) of hiking trails, several dozen lakes, ponds and rivers, and 23 campgrounds. The White Mountain National Forest, a small portion of which lies in neighboring Maine, sprawls over an impressive 1,203 sq miles (3,116 sq km).

The most beautiful wilderness area in the state, the White Mountain National Forest is home to an abundance of wildlife, including a large population of moose. These giant members of the deer family are very shy, but they can be seen from the road at dawn or dusk, lumbering back and forth from their feeding grounds or standing in a swampy pond.

This spectacular region offers all manner of outdoor activities – from bird-watching and skiing to rock climbing and kayaking – but even less sporty travelers will revel in the spectacular scenery visible from the comfort of their car. The park is home to more than 20 summits that soar to over 4,000 ft (1,220 m). Driving through the White Mountains, visitors encounter one scenic vista after another: valleys flanked by forests of pine, a collection of stunning waterfalls tumbling over rocky outcrops, and trout streams burbling beside the meandering roads.

In 1998 a stretch of road, the 100-mile- (160-km-) long White Mountains Trail, was designated as a National Scenic and Cultural Byway. The trail loops across the Mount Washington Valley, through Crawford Notch (p300), North Conway, and Franconia Notch (p290). Brilliant fall foliage colors, interspersed with evergreens, transform the rugged countryside into a living palette. The leaves of different trees manifest a rich variety of shades: flaming red maples, golden birch, and maroon northern red oaks.

> **The White Mountain National Forest, a small portion of which lies in neighboring Maine, sprawls over an impressive 1,203 sq miles (3,116 sq km).**

Winter hikers brave the snow near Lion Head, White Mountains

Driving during the fall can be a beautiful but slow-moving experience, since thousands of "leaf peepers" (visitors who have traveled solely to see the autumn colors) are on the roads. Accommodations can also be difficult to find during this busy period, unless booked well in advance.

23 North Conway

C3 **2617 Main St; (603) 356-5701 or (800) 337-3563**

The gateway to the sublime beauty of the White Mountains, North Conway is, surprisingly, also a bustling shopping center. This mountain village now has more than 70 factory outlets and specialty shops lining the main road. Prices are low in the first place, even for designer names such as Michael Kors, Ralph Lauren, and Tommy Hilfiger, but,

HIKING HIGH IN NEW HAMPSHIRE

It's almost mandatory that visitors take a hike in New Hampshire, where the White Mountains alone stretch across a quarter of the state. There are plenty of sky-scraping trails to take your fancy; in Franconia Notch State Park, the moderate, 1.5-mile (2.5-km) Artist Bluff loop rewards with a striking view of Echo Lake. Or head to Crawford Notch State Park, where it's a similar distance each way to reach Arethusa Falls. With a 140-ft (43-m) drop, the waterfall is among the most dramatic in the state. To try this more advanced hike, follow Bemis Brook Trail until it connects to Arethusa Falls Trail. The *White Mountain Guide*, published by the Appalachian Mountain Club, is a comprehensive guide to help serious and casual hikers alike safely discover the beauty of the region.

because there is no sales tax in New Hampshire, all purchases become even better bargains.

Locals are quick to point out that there are many other attractions in and around North Conway, including canoe trips on the Saco River and a ride along the **Conway Scenic Railroad**, which takes visitors into the mountains aboard an old-fashioned train. Also nearby, the **Story Land** theme park was founded in 1954, a year before Disneyland opened in California. Children

can ride on an antique German carousel, a pirate ship, or Cinderella's coach.

Conway Scenic Railroad

Rte 16 in North Conway Check website for schedule conwayscenic.com

Story Land

Rte 16 in Glen Late May–Jun & Labor Day–Columbus Day: 9:30am–5pm Sat & Sun; Jul & Aug: 9am–6pm daily storylandnh.com

↑ The historic train station in North Conway, painted in cheerful colors

A DRIVING TOUR
LAKE WINNIPESAUKEE

Length 70 miles (113 km) **Stopping off points** Wolfboro, Center Sandwich, and Weirs Beach.

This stunning lake has a shoreline that meanders for 240 miles (386 km), making it the biggest stretch of waterfront in New Hampshire. Ringed by mountains, Winnipesaukee is scattered with 264 islands. Around its shores are sheltered bays and harbors, with half a dozen resort towns where visitors can enjoy activities ranging from canoeing to shopping for crafts and antiques.

Locator Map
For more detail see p282

The surrounding woodland makes **Center Sandwich** a top destination during fall.

The pristine **Squam Lake** was where the movie On Golden Pond *(1981)* was filmed.

A mansion called **Castle in the Clouds** looms on the crest of a hill some 750 ft (229 m) above the lake.

Upscale **Meredith** has many beautiful lakeside homes and is a center for shopping and dining.

A bustling holiday town, **Weirs Beach** has a sandy beach, a boardwalk, fairground rides, souvenir shops, and water parks.

One of the country's oldest vacation spots, **Wolfeboro** is the largest community on the lake and one of the prettiest.

Center Sandwich · Squam Lake · Moultonborough · Holderness · East Holderness · Center Harbor · Ashland · Lake Waukewan · Meredith · Weirs Beach · Glendale · Lakeport · Laconia · Belknap Mountain 2,382 ft (726 m) · Melvin Village · Moultonborough Bay · Long Island · Bear Island · Governors Island · Lake Winnipesaukee · Rattlesnake Island · West Alton · Mirror Lake · Lake Wentworth · Wolfeboro · Merrymeeting Lake · Alton Bay · Alton · **START/FINISH** · Castle in the Clouds

0 kilometers 8
0 miles 8

N

↑ Colorful houses reflected in the water of Lake Winnipesaukee

MAINE

Archaeological evidence on Maine's offshore islands points to a seasonal Basque presence dating back to 1480, and some historians speculate that Norse sailors probed the rocky coast as early as the 11th century. The Penobscot and Passamaquoddy people were the first in New England to have extensive contact with Europeans, and they began trading furs with the French in the early 17th century. European settlement began in earnest with the Popham Beach colony of 1607. Although short-lived, it spawned a succession of similar settlements at Monhegan (1622), Saco (1623), and Georgeana (1624). The last – renamed York in 1652 – became the English America's first chartered city in 1642.

While Maine has always been one of the more sparsely populated states in the Union, it has been at the center of numerous territorial disputes, beginning with its abrupt seizure by Massachusetts in 1652 (an unhappy union, which ended in 1820). At the outset of the Revolutionary War (1775–83), Portland was bombarded and burned by the British as an example to other colonies harboring similar anti-Loyalist sentiments.

Traveling through Maine, it is easy to see what all the fuss was about. The state's trove of unspoiled wilderness is interspersed with wonderfully preserved relics of its past. The importance of seafaring in the region's history is evident in maritime museums, sea captains' mansions, and the many lighthouses found along the coast.

MAINE

Must Sees

1 Portland
2 Penobscot Bay
3 Acadia National Park
4 Campobello Island

Experience More

5 Kittery
6 Calais
7 Ogunquit
8 Bangor
9 The Kennebunks
10 Freeport
11 Brunswick
12 Old Orchard Beach
13 Northeast Harbor
14 Boothbay Harbor
15 Bar Harbor
16 Augusta
17 Machias
18 Bethel
19 Sugarloaf
20 Baxter State Park
21 Moosehead Lake
22 Rangeley Lakes Region
23 Aroostook Country

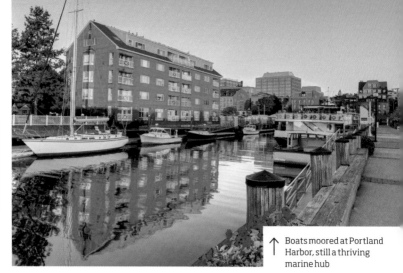

↑ Boats moored at Portland Harbor, still a thriving marine hub

PORTLAND

 E3 ✈ 7000 NE Airport Way 🚌 950 Congress St & 100 Thompson's Pt Rd 🚆 Commercial & Franklin sts ℹ 14 Ocean Gateway Pier; www.visitportland.com

Located on the crest of a peninsula, Portland was described by poet and Portland native Henry Wadsworth Longfellow as "the beautiful town that is seated by the sea." Portland has been devastated by no less than four major fires, resulting in its preponderance of sturdy stone Victorian buildings.

Victoria Mansion

🏛 109 Danforth St ⏰ Times vary, check website 🌐 victoriamansion.org

This sumptuous brownstone villa was completed in 1860 to serve as the summer home of hotelier Ruggles Sylvester Morse (c. 1816–93). The interior has striking decorative details, such as painted trompe l'oeil walls and ceilings, wood paneling, marble mantels, and a flying staircase.

> **INSIDER TIP**
> **Seasonal Bounty**
>
> At the Portland Farmers' Market almost 40 vendors present a smorgasbord of everything that can be grown or foraged in southern Maine (www.portland farmermarket.org).

Portland Museum of Art

🏛 7 Congress Sq ⏰ 10am–6pm Sat-Wed; 10am-8pm Thu-Fri 🔒 Nov-late May: Mon & Tue 🌐 portland museum.org

Portland's fine art museum occupies three buildings in Federal, Beaux-Arts, and postmodern styles. It has a collection of paintings and graphic art by Winslow Homer (1836–1910) and arranges seasonal tours to his studio on Prouts Neck. Other highlights include works by artists Fitz Henry Lane, Alex Katz and Andrew Wyeth.

Children's Museum & Theatre of Maine

🏛 Thompson's Pt ⏰ Times vary, check website 🌐 kitetails.org

This waterfront facility opened in 2021, and is home to a 100-seat theater, vast science center, an arts and culture floor, and an outdoor play area.

Wadsworth-Longfellow House

🏛 489 Congress St ⏰ Times vary, check website 🌐 mainehistory.org

Poet Henry Wadsworth Longfellow (1807–82) grew up in this 1785 house, which contains family mementos, portraits, and furnishings.

⑤ Tate House Museum

🏠 1270 Westbrook St
🕐 Jun-Oct: 10am-4pm
Wed-Sat, 1-4pm Sun
🚫 Jul 4, Labor Day
🌐 tatehouse.org

In 1755 George Tate, an agent of the British Royal Navy, constructed an elegant gambrel-roofed home. Now a National Historic Landmark, the house has fine period furnishings. Garden and architectural tours can be arranged by appointment.

⑥ Maine Narrow Gauge Railroad Co. & Museum

🏠 49 Thames St 📞 (207) 828-0814 🕐 May-Oct: 9:30am-4pm daily (Apr: weekends only); Train ride: departures on the hour

Scenic trips along a stretch of the waterfront are the highlight of this museum

dedicated to the railroad that served much of Maine from the 1870s to the 1940s.

⑦ Portland Observatory

🏠 138 Congress St 📞 (207) 774-5561 🕐 Late May-mid-Oct: 10am-4:30pm daily

This landmark is the last surviving 19th-century signal tower on the Atlantic. The climb to the top is worth it.

⑧ Portland Head Light

🏠 1000 Shore Rd, Cape Elizabeth 📞 (207) 799-2661 🕐 Call for hours

First illuminated in 1791 by order of President George

Washington (1732–99), the lighthouse has been the subject of poetry, postage stamps, and photographs. The keeper's house is now a museum with exhibits on the history of the world's beacons. The surrounding park, just 4 miles (6.5 km) from downtown, has a beach and picnic areas.

→

The historic Portland lighthouse on Cape Elizabeth at sunrise

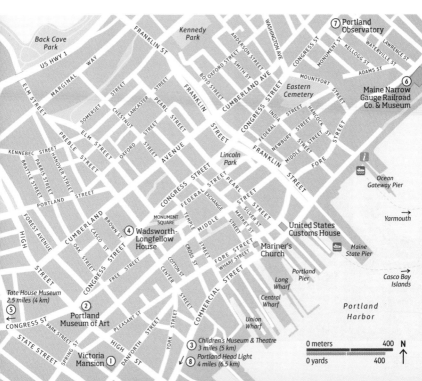

A SHORT WALK
OLD PORT

Distance 0.5 miles (1 km) **Time** 15 minutes

This once-decaying neighborhood near the harbor has been restored and is now one of the city's liveliest neighborhoods, filled with shops, art galleries, restaurants, and bars. The Old Port's narrow streets are lined with classic examples of Victorian-era commercial architecture, including venerable structures that once served as warehouses and ships' chandleries. From the docks, ships take passengers out for deep-sea fishing excursions and harbor tours. Cruises include mail-boat rides and excursions to the Calendar Islands, where visitors can enjoy everything from cycling to sea kayaking.

START

The distinctive **Charles Q. Clapp Block** was designed by self-taught architect Charles Quincy Clapp in 1866.

The **Centennial Block** has a facade made of Maine granite.

The **First National Bank** was Portland's grandest building when erected in 1884. Its sandstone and brick exterior features a corner tower and tall chimneys.

MARKET STREET

MIDDLE STREET

EXCHANGE STREET

MARKE

A statue of dolphins is situated in the small cobblestone area in the middle of the Old Port district.

Designed for the prominent Deering family, the **Mary L. Deering Block** is a mix of Italian and Colonial Revival styles.

FOR STRE

Constructed after the fire of 1866, the **Seaman's Club** is known for its striking Gothic windows.

← One of the brightly lit shops that line the streets of Old Port at dusk

The United States Custom House standing in front of the docks ↑

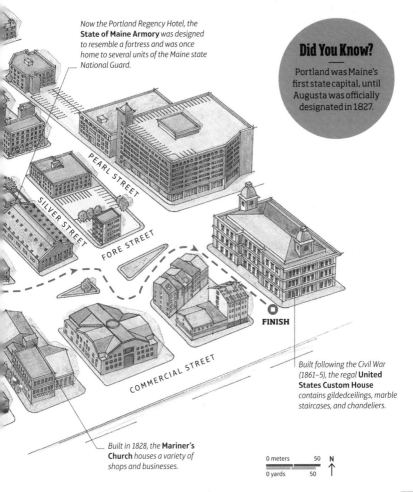

Now the Portland Regency Hotel, the **State of Maine Armory** was designed to resemble a fortress and was once home to several units of the Maine state National Guard.

Did You Know?

Portland was Maine's first state capital, until Augusta was officially designated in 1827.

PEARL STREET

SILVER STREET

FORE STREET

COMMERCIAL STREET

FINISH

Built following the Civil War (1861–5), the regal **United States Custom House** contains gilded ceilings, marble staircases, and chandeliers.

Built in 1828, the **Mariner's Church** houses a variety of shops and businesses.

0 meters	50	N
0 yards	50	↑

↑ A fleet of boats bobble on the ocean in Penobscot Bay

2

PENOBSCOT BAY

⚑F2

Penobscot Bay is picture-book Maine, with verdant hills that roll straight into the ocean, wave-pounded cliffs, sheltered harbors bobbing with fishing boats, and lobster traps piled high on the docks. Windjammer sailboats and ferries carry passengers to offshore islands, setting sail from Rockland, Camden, and Lincolnville, popular stops on the bay's western shore, while the more remote eastern shore is dotted with perfectly preserved villages.

The year-round mix of fishermen, artists, and musicians makes Penobscot Bay an intriguing destination. The triangular sails of sightseeing schooners billow in the breeze as they cruise through the bay's archipelago, while craft galleries stretch the imagination of what can be fashioned from wood and rock.

The western shore is home to the bustling communities of Rockland, Camden and hipster Belfast with its dynamic working waterfront. Between them are the scenic harbor villages of Rockport, Lincolnville, and Northport. Farther north, the streets of Searsport and Bucksport are lined with gracious homes of 19th-century sea captains. The rockier eastern shore has fewer harbor towns, but Castine rules as a yachting center, while salty Stonington, where every dooryard has a heap of wire traps and striped buoys, is a reminder that this is where Maine's thriving lobster industry began.

↑ Painting by Marguerite Thompson Zorach at the Farnsworth Art Museum, Rockland

Rockland

 1 Park Dr; www.camden rockland.com

An old fishing town and commercial hub, Rockland is now a top tourist destination. The Lobster Festival, on the first weekend of August, is the town's main event. The **Farnsworth Art Museum** showcases artists inspired by Maine's landscape, while the **Center for Maine Contemporary Art** spotlights a new generation. **The Maine Lighthouse Museum** is worth a visit for its superb collection of lenses and other artifacts.

Farnsworth Art Museum

◈ 16 Museum St 10am-4pm Wed-Sun farnsworth museum.org

Center for Maine Contemporary Art

◈ 21 Winter St 10am-5pm Wed-Sat; noon-5pm Sun cmcanow.org

Maine Lighthouse Museum

◈ 1 Park Dr Late Mar-Dec mainelighthouse museum.org

② Monhegan Island

monheganwelcome.com

Ten miles (16 km) offshore, this unspoiled enclave is a favored retreat for birders and hikers. Excursions depart from Port Clyde, Boothbay Harbor, and New Harbor.

Did You Know?

The Penobscot Nation has called Penobscot Bay home for over 10,000 years.

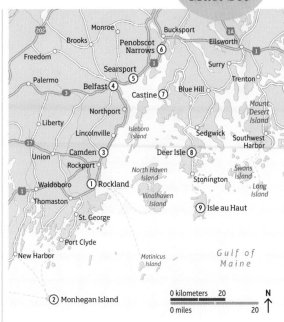

② Monhegan Island

0 kilometers 20
0 miles 20
N

③ Camden

Commercial St, 2 Public Landing visitcamden.com

Elegant homes and spired churches line Camden's shady streets, and a host of shops border the waterfront. Among the fine inns on High Street is the Whitehall, with a room dedicated to Pulitzer Prize-winning poet Edna St. Vincent Millay, who was schooled in Camden. From May through October, a short road at Camden Hills State Park on Route 1 leads to the top of Mount Battie, where Millay found inspiration.

④ Belfast

14 Main St belfast maine.org

Boasting America's oldest shoe store and a busy water-front with a brewery and restaurants, Belfast has emerged as center for the arts thanks to a major performing arts venue and a restored Art Deco theater. It is the market town for organic farmers from nearby Waldo County villages and features competing farmers' markets on Fridays and Saturdays. The bar and dining scene ranks among the best north of Portland.

PENOBSCOT BAY AND ITS ISLANDS

Penobscot Bay is famous for its numerous islands. Although some are no more than a pile of bald granite boulders, others are lush paradises that cover thousands of acres and are prime territory for birders, hikers, and sea kayakers. While some of these retreats are inhabited, most are completely wild, home only to harbor seals and seabirds such as puffins and great cormorants.

↑ A lobster boat on display in Penobscot Marine Museum, Searsport

The water churns with glow-in-the-dark plankton when you paddle beneath night skies in Castine Harbor. Stars above and stars below make Bioluminescence Night Paddles with Castine Kayak Adventures a truly memorable experience (castinekayak.com).

⑤
Searsport

🏳 14 Main St, Belfast
Ⓦ searsport.maine.gov

Searsport was a major shipbuilding port during the 19th century. **The Penobscot Marine Museum**, which is housed in a complex of restored sea captains' homes, recalls the glory days of the last half of the 19th century, when one American deepwater captain in ten hailed from Searsport. The extensive collections of maritime art are augmented by a vast collection of historic photographs – many made from glass-plate negatives – that chronicle the building of Searsport vessels and some of their around-the-world voyages as well as details of the fishing trade.

Searsport is considered the antiques capital of Maine, and its edges are chockablock with second-hand and vintage stores practically bursting at the seams with trinkets and treasures. Roadside flea markets are held on summer and fall weekends.

Just off Route 1 as you approach the Belfast town line, Moose Point State Park – once a dairy farm – offers those who visit panoramic views, hiking trails, tidal pools, and picnicking facilities.

Penobscot Marine Museum

◈ 2 Church St Ⓞ May–Oct daily Ⓦ penobscotmarine museum.org

⑥
Penobscot Narrows

This deep canyon of the Penobscot River between Prospect and Verona Island, just downriver from the town of Bucksport, provides a tremendous scenic view of the headwaters of Penobscot Bay. The Penobscot Narrows Bridge and Observatory span the gorge, carrying Routes 1 and 3 from Fort Knox in Prospect downeast toward Acadia. Tiny Fort Knox State

→ The Isle au Haut Light House standing tall in Duck Harbor

→

The *State of Maine* at the Maine Maritime Academy in Castine

Park surrounds a pentagonal Civil War-era fortress. Visitors can explore old barracks, storehouses, and underground passages that were used to smuggle goods. The park is also the gateway to the Penobscot Narrows Bridge Observatory, which provides 360-degree views from 420 ft (128 m) above the river.

⑦ Castine

ℹ Emerson Hall, 67 Court St; www.castine.me.us

Founded in the early 17th century and coveted for its strategic location overlooking the bay, Castine has flown the flags of France, Britain, the Netherlands, and the US.

Relics of Castine's turbulent past can still be seen at Fort George on Wadsworth Cove Road, the highest point in town. Fort George was built by the British in 1779 and witnessed the American Navy's worst defeat during the Revolutionary War, a battle in which more than 40 colonial ships were either captured or destroyed.

The fort is always open. Located across from Fort George, on Battle Avenue, is the Maine Maritime Academy.

⑧ Deer Isle

🚍 ℹ 114 Little Deer Isle Rd; (207) 348-6124

Deer Isle, reached from the mainland via a suspension bridge, is actually a series of small islands. Island highlights include the village of Deer Isle itself, the famous Haystack Mountain School of Crafts, and the town of Stonington.

⑨ Isle au Haut

🚍 ℹ 114 Little Deer Isle Rd (207) 348-6124

Lobster fishermen and wealthy summer rusticators occupy this mountainous island that marks the east end of Penobscot Bay. A mail boat from Stonington covers the 8 miles (13 km) to Isle au Haut twice a day. Almost half the island, some 4 sq miles (11 sq km), actually belongs to Acadia National Park *(p318)* and offers visitors a plethora of scenic hiking routes and stunning viewpoints.

STAY

Sleep in a slice of Maine's maritime history at a Penobscot Bay sea captain's home-turned-bed and breakfast inn.

The Captain A.V. Nickels Inn
🏠 127 E Main St, Searsport 🌐 captain nickelsinn.com

$$$⑤

Captain Swift Inn
🏠 72 Elm St, Camden 🌐 captainswiftinn.com

$$$⑤

The Homeport Inn
🏠 121 E Main St, Searsport 🌐 homeport historicinn.com

$$$⑤

Did You Know?

The 1,527-ft- (465-m-) tall Cadillac Mountain is the highest point on the Atlantic Coast.

ACADIA NATIONAL PARK

🅰 G2 🚌 Bangor–Bar Harbor 🕐 Dawn–dusk daily
ℹ️ Hulls Cove Visitor Center, off Rte 3 in Hulls Cove; www.nps.gov/acad

Located primarily on Mount Desert Island, Acadia National Park is a wild, unspoiled paradise where wave-beaten shores and inland forests await.

The park's main attraction is the seasonal Loop Road, a 27-mile (43-km) drive that climbs and dips with the pink granite mountains of the east coast of the island before swinging inland past Jordan Pond, Bubble Pond, and Eagle Lake.

Acadia is home to numerous animals including woodchucks, whitetailed deer, red foxes, and the occasional black bear. Visitors who want a closer, more intimate look at the flora and fauna can do so on foot, bike, or horseback on more than 45 miles (72 km) of old crushed-rock carriage roads ideal for hiking and cycling. On the coast, numerous isolated bays and rocky coves line the island's perimeter. Sand Beach is one of only two lifeguarded beaches in the park, but only the truly brave take the plunge into the chilly ocean water, which rarely exceeds a bracing temperature of around 55°F (13°C).

↑ Lush vegetation blanketing the rocky coastline of Acadia National Park

← Visitors watching the water being sucked into Thunder Hole, caused when the tide rises and there are heavy winds

→ Beautiful red foxes, one of many animal species that thrive in the diverse habitats of Acadia National Park

CAMPOBELLO ISLAND

G7 **Rte 774** **Cottage: late May–mid-Oct: 9am–5pm daily** **visitcampobello.com**

At the northeast tip of the United States, Campobello Island is a place of tranquil seclusion and natural beauty. It shaped the character of Franklin Delano Roosevelt, and gave him a special sympathy for America's Canadian neighbors.

In 1964, some 4.5 sq miles (11.5 sq km) of Campobello Island's rugged terrain were designated as a memorial to President Franklin Delano Roosevelt (1882–1945). The main settlement of Welshpool was where the future president spent most of his summers, until 1921, when he contracted polio. Undaunted, Roosevelt went on to lead the US through the Great Depression and World War II. The highlight of the park – which actually lies just across the border in Canada – is Roosevelt Cottage, a 34-room summer home that displays Roosevelt's personal mementos. A passport is required for border crossing.

GREAT VIEW
Liberty Point

Observation decks on the cliffs afford far-ranging views. Gaze across the Lubec Channel to West Quoddy Head Lighthouse from the west deck, or admire Liberty Cove and the bluffs of Grand Manan Island from the east.

→ A visitor taking in the eastern view from Liberty Point

1 Franklin D. Roosevelt's stunning 34-room summer residence is the centerpiece of Roosevelt Campobello International Park.

2 Campobello Island is home to many pretty buildings and a quaint country church.

3 Kayaking from the Bay of Fundy is a great way to explore the rugged coastline of Campobello Island.

↑ A dramatic sky over East Quoddy Head Lighthouse at sunset

EXPERIENCE MORE

⑤ Kittery

🅐D4 🚇Portland 🚆I-95 and US Rte 1; www.mainetourism.com

Founded in 1647, Kittery boasts the oldest church in Maine, the 1730 First Congregational Church. Many fine old mansions line the streets, including the John Bray House, one of the oldest dwellings in Maine. **Fort McClary**, now a state historic site, dates back to the early 1800s. The **Kittery Historical and Naval Museum** is filled with ship models and exhibits. However, Kittery is best known for a more contemporary lure – over 100 factory outlet stores along Route 1, where shoppers can buy name brands at a discount.

Fort McClary State Historic Site

⌖ 🅟 Pepperell Rd, Kittery Point 📞(207) 439-2845 🕐Late May-early-Oct: 10am-dusk daily

Kittery Historical and Naval Museum

⌖ 🅟 Rogers Rd 📞(207) 439-3080 🕐Jun-mid-Oct: 10am-4pm Wed-Sun; winter: times vary, call for hours

⑥ Calais

🅐G7 🚇Bangor 🚆39 Union St; (207) 454-2211

Perched on the west bank of the St. Croix River, Calais is Maine's busiest border crossing with Canada. The two countries share jurisdiction over nearby St. Croix Island, where in 1604 explorers Samuel de Champlain and the Sieur de Monts established the first European settlement in North America north of Florida. The island is accessible by boat, a difficult trip due to strong currents and tides.

Calais was devastated by a huge fire in 1870. One of the few buildings that survived is Hamilton's Folly mansion at No. 78 South Street. This Victorian house was so dubbed by locals because of its ostentatious design – a tribute to the excess that bankrupted its owner. Outdoor activities abound here. The St. Croix River is a challenging waterway for canoeists and a prime spot for salmon fishing.

Three miles (5 km) southwest of Calais is the Baring Unit of the **Moosehorn National Wildlife Refuge**, a wilderness that beckon hikers, bird-watchers, and naturalists. An observation deck offers the best views, and there are also a number of commercial farms that allow visitors to pick their own blueberries.

Moosehorn National Wildlife Refuge

🅟103 Headquarters Rd, Baring 🕐Park: Dawn-dusk daily 🌐fws.gov

⑦ Ogunquit

🅐D4 🚇Portland 🚆36 Main St; www.ogunquit.org

It is easy to see why the Abenaki people called this enclave Ogunquit, meaning "Beautiful Place by the Sea." Maine beaches don't come any better. From late June to Columbus Day, trolleys shuttle along this powdery stretch of sand and dunes that curves around a backdrop of rugged cliffs. Atop the cliffs is the 1.25-mile (2-km) Marginal Way, a footpath that offers walkers dramatic vistas of the ocean. Perkins Cove, home of the only pedestrian drawbridge in the US, is a quaint jumble of fisher-men's shacks now transformed into galleries, shops and restaurants.

Did You Know?

Maine covers nearly as many square miles as the other five New England states combined.

←

The white-washed walls of Fort McClary State Historic Site in Kittery

The peaceful harbor setting of Perkins Cove in Ogunquit

This picturesque outpost attracted an artist's colony as early as 1890, establishing it as a haven for the arts. The **Ogunquit Museum of American Art** was built in 1952 by the eccentric but wealthy Henry Strater, who served as its director for more than 30 years. Built of wood and local stone, the museum has wide windows to allow views of the rocky cove and meadows.

Ogunquit Museum of American Art

⊕ 🏠 543 Shore Rd ⏰ May-Oct: 10am-5pm daily 🚫 Labor Day 🌐 ogunquitmuseum.org

---

8

Bangor

🏠 F1 🚗 287 Godfrey Blvd
🚌 ℹ️ 2 Hammond St; (207) 947-0307

The world's leading lumber port in the 1850s, Bangor remains the commercial center of northern Maine. The town's Penobscot River harbor was once loaded with ships carrying pine logs from nearby sawmills. Industrial might aside, Maine's second-largest city also draws visitors because of its ideal location as a base camp for treks to Acadia National Park *(p318)* and the forestlands that stretch to the north.

The city has a number of noteworthy residences. Stately homes line the West Market Square Historic District and the Broadway area. Maine-born horror author Stephen King lives in a mansion at No. 47 West Broadway, complete with a wrought-iron fence festooned with iron bats and cobwebs. The Greek Revival 1836 Thomas Hill House is headquarters for the Bangor Historical Society and offers historic walking tours. One of Bangor's most pleasant green spaces is the **Mount Hope Cemetery**. Established in 1834, the cemetery is beautifully landscaped with ponds, bridges, and paved paths that attract strollers and inline skaters. The **Cole Land Transportation Museum** is also a big draw. The museum's collection contains more than 200 vehicles dating from the 19th century, ranging from fire engines and horse-drawn logging sleds to antique baby carriages.

Mount Hope Cemetery

⊛ 🏠 State St
⏰ 7:30am-dusk Mon-Fri
🌐 mthopebgr.com

Cole Land Transportation Museum

⊕ 🏠 405 Perry Rd
⏰ May-early Nov: 9am-5pm daily 🌐 colemuseum.org

← A statue of lumberjack Paul Bunyan, representing Bangor's lumber trade

9

The Kennebunks

🅰D4 ✈30 miles (48 km) NE in Portland ℹ16 Water St, Kennebunk; www.visitthe kennebunks.com

First a thriving port and busy shipbuilding center, then a summer retreat for the wealthy, the Kennebunks are made up of two villages: Kennebunk and Kennebunkport. Many fine Federal and Greek Revival structures in Kennebunkport's historic village indicate the fortunes made in ship-building and trading from 1810 to the 1870s. History of another sort can be found at the **Seashore Trolley Museum**, where some 200 antique streetcars are housed. Visitors can tour the countryside aboard one of the restored trolleys.

The scenic drive along Route 9 offers views of surf along rocky Cape Arundel. Kennebunk is famous for its beaches, most notably Kennebunk Beach, which is actually three connected strands. One of the town's most romantic historic homes is the 1826 Wedding Cake House. According to the local lore, shipbuilder George Bourne was married hastily with no time to bake the traditional wedding cake. He vowed to his bride that he would

↑ A charming street in Kennebunkport, presided over by the belfry of South Congregational Church

remodel their home to look like a wedding cake when he returned from sea. Today the Gothic spires and ornate latticework offer proof that Bourne was a man of his word. Housed in four restored 19th-century buildings, The Brick Store Museum offers displays of decorative arts and local history. Pick up a bilingual map for a downtown walking tour.

Seashore Trolley Museum

◈ 🅰195 Log Cabin Rd, Kennebunkport ⏰Late May-mid-Oct: 10am-5pm daily; early May & late Oct: 10am-5pm Sat & Sun 🌐trolleymuseum.org

---

10

Freeport

🅰E3 ✈17 miles (27 km) SW in Portland ℹ23 Depot St; www.visitfreeport.com

Although Freeport dates back to 1789, shoppers would argue that it did not arrive on the scene until 1917, when the first L. L. Bean clothing store

opened its doors. Today this retail giant is open 24 hours a day, 365 days a year, and is easily Maine's biggest man-made attraction.

Travelers who make it past the shops will discover a working harbor in South Freeport, where seal-watching tours and sailing cruises depart. The shoreline includes Wolfe's Neck Woods State Park, 0.4 sq miles (1 sq km) of tranquility wrapped along Casco Bay.

Freeport's most unusual sight is the **Desert of Maine**. Originally a late 1700s' farm, its over-tilled, over-logged topsoil eventually disappeared

EAT

The Clam Shack

This teeny fish shack serves the best lobster rolls around. Grab one to eat *al fresco*, along the shores of the Kennebunk River.

🅰D4 🅰2 Western Ave, Kennebunk ⏰Early-May-mid-Oct 🌐theclamshack.net

$⑤$ $⑤$

→ Pastel-colored stores and attractions lining the pier at Old Orchard Beach

altogether, creating a vast desert of sand dunes. Visitors can walk the nature trails with a guide, or ride on an open cart. The farm museum is housed in a 1783 barn.

Desert of Maine

♿ 🕐 🏠 95 Desert Rd 🕐 Mid-May–mid-Oct: tours 9:30am–4:30pm daily 🌐 desertof maine.com

⓫
Brunswick

🅰 E3 🚗 33 miles (53 km) SW in Portland ▭ 🛈 8 Venture Ave, Brunswick; (207) 725-8797

Brunswick is best known as the home of Bowdoin College and as the land entry for the scenic panoramas of the town of Harpswell – a peninsula and three islands in Casco Bay.

Founded in 1794, the college claims a number of eminent alumni, including explorers Robert Peary (1856–1920) and Donald MacMillan (1874–1970). The **Peary-MacMillan Arctic Museum** honors the two, who in 1909 became the first people to reach the North Pole, though this is disputed.

The **Pejepscot History Center** offers displays of Brunswick history in its three

LIGHTING THE WAY SINCE 1791

For centuries, mariners have been guided to safety by Maine's picturesque lighthouses. The coast is dotted with 65 such beacons, some accessible from the mainland, and others perched on offshore islands. Portland Head Light was commissioned by George Washington and built in 1791, making it the oldest lighthouse in the state. It is open to the public and houses a small museum focusing on local marine and military history.

museums, as well as tours of both Skolfield-Whittier House, a 17-room Italianate mansion built in 1858, and the Joshua L. Chamberlain House, a Civil War museum.

Peary-MacMillan Arctic Museum

🏠 Hubbard Hall, Bowdoin College 📞 (207) 725-3416 🕐 10am–5pm Tue–Sat, 2–5pm Sun 🚫 Public hols

Pejepscot History Center

♿ 🕐 🏠 159 Park Row 📞 (207) 729-6606 🕐 Jun–Oct: call for opening hours and tour times

⓬
Old Orchard Beach

🅰 E3 🚗 13 miles (21 km) NE in Portland ▭ 🛈 11 First St; oldorchardbeach maine.com

One of the oldest seashore resorts in Maine, Old Orchard Beach's 7 miles (11 km) of beautiful sandy shoreline and low surf make it a favorite, family-friendly spot for swimming and boogie boarding. Kids love the pier – which is lined with fantastic shops and tempting food stands – the games arcade, and the Palace Playland amusement park. The latter features a carousel, a Ferris wheel, a steel roller coaster, and other thrill rides.

↑ Visitors clambering across the bluff to reach Pemaquid Point Light, near Boothbay Harbor

 13

Northeast Harbor

G2 ✈Trenton ℹ18 Harbor Dr; www.mount desertchamber.org

Northeast Harbor is the center of Mount Desert Island's social scene. The village has a handful of upscale shops, restaurants, handsome summer mansions, and a scenic harbor.

High above the harbor, the **Asticou Terraces and Thuya Lodge and Garden** house collections of excellent paintings, books, and a reflecting pool that descends to the harbor's edge.

Somes Sound, a finger-shaped natural fjord that juts 5 miles (8 km) into Mount Desert Island, separates Northeast Harbor from quiet

↑ Colorful landscaping at the Thuya Gardens, Northeast Harbor

Southwest Harbor, famed for its yacht-builders Hinckley and Morris. The village is home to the **Wendell Gilley Museum of Bird Carving**. A village artisan was a pioneer in the art of decorative bird carving, and the museum preserves about 100 of more than 10,000 birds he carved.

A short drive or bike ride beyond Southwest Harbor are unspoiled villages, including Bass Harbor, where visitors can view the 1858 Bass Harbor Head Light.

Asticou Terraces and Thuya Lodge and Garden

✦ 🚗Rte 3 S of Rte 198 Jct 📞(207) 276-3727 🕐Lodge: Jun–Sep; Garden: May–Oct: call for hours

Wendell Gilley Museum of Bird Carving

✦ 🚗4 Herrick Rd, Southwest Harbor 📞(207) 244-7555 🕐Times vary, check website 🌐wendell gilleymuseum.org

 14

Boothbay Harbor

E3 ℹ192 Townsend Ave; www.boothbayharbor.com

The boating capital of the mid-coast, Boothbay Harbor bustles with the influx of summer tourists. Dozens of

 PICTURE PERFECT
Harbor Views

Northeast Harbor is best viewed from the stunning Asticou Terraces, where a granite path snakes along the hillside, yielding ever-wider vistas as it ascends; pure panorama perfection.

boating excursions cast off from the dock. Visitors might choose to take an hour's sail along the coast aboard a majestic windjammer, or the popular trip to the artists' retreat on Monhegan Island (p315). The harbor is at its best in late June, when majestic tall ships parade in for the annual Windjammer Days festival.

The town itself is packed with shops and galleries. **Maine State Aquarium**, a haven for parents of restless children on rainy days, focuses on the creatures of Maine's important fisheries industry.

A scenic 30-mile (48-km) drive up the coast brings travelers to Pemaquid Point, where the 1827 **Pemaquid Point Light** houses the Fisherman's Museum in the old lightkeeper's home. The Pemaquid Art Gallery is on the grounds and shows the work of local artists. Nearby is the Colonial Pemaquid State

Historic Site, which includes a 1695 graveyard and a replica of **Fort William Henry**. English colonists fought French invaders at this spot in several forts that date from the early 17th century onward. A small museum contains a diorama of the original 1620s' settlement and displays a collection of tools and household items that reflect the rustic lives of the early settlers.

Maine State Aquarium
 194 McKown Point Rd ☎(207) 633-9559 ◯Late May-Sep: 10am-5pm daily ◯Sep: Mon & Tue

Pemaquid Point Light
Rte 130 ☎(207) 677-2492 ◯Mid-May-mid-Oct: 10:30am-5pm daily (museum & gallery: call for hours)

---

⑮
Bar Harbor

G2 ⊕Trenton Island Explorer 1201 Bar Harbor Rd, Trenton; www. barharbormaine.com

With a commanding location on Frenchman Bay, Bar Harbor is Mount Desert Island's lively tourist center. Artists Thomas Cole (1801–48) and Frederic Church (1826–1900) discovered the area's beauty in the 1840s' and their brilliant work attracted the wealthy. In the

19th century, the town was a haven for the Astors and the Rockefellers, among other rich American families. In 1947 a fire destroyed 26.5 sq miles (69 sq km) of wilderness and a third of Bar Harbor's lavish summer homes, all but ending the village's reign as a high-society enclave. A display of early photographs at the **Bar Harbor Historical Society Museum** shows the grand old days and the devastating effects of the fire. Several of the remaining summer showplaces have been turned into gracious inns.

Today Bar Harbor is a thriving waterside resort that attracts 5 million visitors a year. From here people can explore Acadia National Park (*p318*) or the Maine coastline. Downtown, the Art Deco **Criterion Theater** is a perennial favorite that is listed on the National Register of Historic Places. It offers films, live music, and theater performances.

The **Abbe Museum** is also of special note as one of New England's top museums of Native American heritage. It is devoted to the principal tribal groups of the Wabenaki people – the Abenaki, Maliseet, Mi'kmaq, Passamaquoddy, and Penobscot Nations of Maine and the Canadian Maritimes. Exhibits trace archeology as well as modern and recent history of the tribal communities with abundant photos and artifacts. The Abbe also hosts a spring Indian Market featuring contemporary Native American artists, as well as the summer Native American Festival and Basketmakers Market. A branch, next to the Wild Gardens of Acadia, has almost 300 species of local plants.

The **Kisma Preserve** is located in Trenton. The pastures, streams, and woods are home to numerous species of animals, but it is difficult to predict which will be visible. Guided tours that provide background on the animals.

Bar Harbor Historical Society Museum
33 Ledgelawn Ave ☎(207) 288-0000 ◯Mid-Jun-Oct: 1-4pm Mon-Fri

Criterion Theater
⊛ 35 Cottage St ☎(207) 288-0829

Abbe Museum
⊛ 26 Mount Desert St ◯May-Oct: 10am-5pm daily; Nov-Apr: 10am-4pm Thu-Sat ◯Jan ⊛ abbemuseum.org

Kisma Preserve
⊛ Rte 3 in Trenton ☎(207) 667-3244 ◯By appointment

↑ An exhibit on the Wabanaki people at the Abbe Museum in Bar Harbor

16
Augusta

🅰 E2 🔼 75 Airport Rd
🚌 🛈 269 Western Ave;
(207) 623-4559

Maine's state capital is a relatively quiet city of 19,000. The 1832 **Maine State House** was built of granite quarried from neighboring Hallowell. Major expansions have left only the center block from the original design by Boston architect Charles Bulfinch (1763–1844). Across the street, the **Blaine House** has been serving as the governor's mansion since 1919. The 28-room Colonial-style home was built in 1832 for a local sea captain.

The **Maine State Museum** has exhibits spanning "12,000 years of Maine history." One highlight is the "Made in Maine" exhibit, which re-creates a water-powered woodworking mill. The **Old Fort Western** is a restoration of one of New England's oldest wooden forts, dating from 1754. It was built on the site where the Plymouth Pilgrims had established their trading post the previous century.

Heading southwest from Augusta, travelers will get a rare look at the last active Shaker community in the US.

Established in 1783, the **Sabbathday Lake Shaker Village** is home to a few residents who still adhere to their traditional beliefs of simplicity, celibacy, and communal harmony.

Maine State House
🖔 🅰 State & Capitol sts
☎ (207) 287-1400 🕘 8am–5pm Mon-Fri

Blaine House
🖔 🅰 192 State St ☎ (207) 287-2301 🕘 Call for appt

Maine State Museum
🖔🖔 🅰 2301 State St
🕘 Until 2023; check website for details 🌐 mainestate museum.org

Old Fort Western
🖔 🅰 16 Cony St 🕘 Jun-Oct; times vary, check website 🌐 oldfortwestern.org

Sabbathday Lake Shaker Village
🖔🖔 🅰 707 Shaker Rd, New Gloucester 🕘 Late May-mid-Oct: 10am-4:30pm Mon-Sat 🌐 maineshakers.com

> Situated at the mouth of a river of the same name, Machias retains many of the handsome homes that sprang up during its days as a prosperous 19th-century lumber center.

17
Machias

🅰 G7 🔼 Bangor 🛈 2 Kilton Lane; (207) 255-4402

Situated at the mouth of a river of the same name, Machias retains many of the handsome homes that sprang up during its days as a prosperous 19th-century lumber center. The town's name comes from the Micmac language and means "bad little falls," a reference to the waterfall that cascades in the center of town.

Machias lays claim to the region's oldest building, the 1770 **Burnham Tavern**, now a museum with period furnishings. It was here that plans were made for the first naval battle of the Revolutionary War in 1775. Following that meeting, local men sailed out into Machias Bay on the small sloop *Unity* and captured the British man-of-war HMS *Margaretta*. Models of the two ships can be seen at the Gates House, a restored 1807 home in nearby Machiasport.
Roque Bluffs State Park,

to the southwest of town, offers swimming in a large freshwater pond and a 1-mile (1.6-km) sweep of beach. Birders reserve months in advance for boat trips from Cutler to Machias Seal Island, home to puffins, Arctic terns, and razorbill auks.

Burnham Tavern
🖐 🚻 🏠 Main St 🅲 (207) 255-6930 🕐 Jul & Aug: times vary, call for hours

Roque Bluffs State Park
🖐 🏠 145 Schoppee Point Rd, Roque Bluffs 🅲 (207) 255-3475 🕐 Mid-May–Oct: 9am–dusk daily

---

 18

Bethel
🅰 D2 ✈ Portland
🛈 8 Station Place; www.bethelmaine.com

A picturesque historic district, a major New England ski resort, and proximity to the White Mountains give Bethel year-round appeal. Settled in 1796, the town grew into a farming and lumbering center, and with the 1851 arrival of the railroad it quickly became a popular resort. The lineup of classic clapboard mansions on the town green includes the

↑ Downtown Augusta skyline, on the banks of the Kennebec River

↑ A snowboarder speeding down a tree-lined run at Sugarloaf

Federal-style Moses Mason House (c 1813), which has Rufus Porter murals on two floors.

Scenic drives are found in all directions, taking in tiny, unspoiled colonial hamlets to the south and beautiful mountain terrain to the north. Sunday River Ski Resort, just north of town in Newry, has 8 mountains and more than 100 ski trails. Evans Notch, a natural pass through the White Mountain peaks, offers many memorable views, including from abutments to a vanished bridge high above the Wild River. Grafton Notch State Park has even more spectacular scenery along its drives, hiking trails and picnic areas.

19

Sugarloaf
🅰 D1

Maine's highest ski mountain, and the state's second-highest peak after Mount Katahdin, Sugarloaf is the centerpiece of this touristic village packed with hotels, restaurants, and hundreds of condominiums. Downhill skiers have been flocking to the **Sugarloaf ski center** for years, attracted by more than 160 trails and a vertical drop of 2,800-ft (870-m). The center also offers cross-country skiing, and other winter activities, such as snowboarding, snow-shoeing, and ice skating.

In summer months, the emphasis shifts to the resort's impressive 18-hole golf course, boating on the many lakes and rivers, and hiking in the surrounding Carrabassett Valley. The resort is also famous for a network of more than 50 miles (80 km) of mountain-biking trails from flat routes to challenging circuits full of steep climbs and scenic descents.

Sugarloaf ski center
🖐 🚻 🏠 Carrabassett Valley 🕐 8:30am–3:50pm daily 🌐 sugarloaf.com

20

Baxter State Park

🅰 F6 ℹ️ 64 Balsam Dr, Millinocket; www.baxter statepark.org

This park was named for Governor Percival Proctor Baxter (1876–1969), who was instrumental in the effort to preserve this magnificent land, purchasing more than 300 sq miles (800 sq km) and donating it to the state with the stipulation that it was never to be developed. The park encompasses 46 mountain peaks, 18 of them over 3,000 ft (900 m), including Katahdin, Maine's tallest.

The park's hiking trails are unsurpassed, and offer a range of difficulty. Hundreds of hikers successfully summit Katahdin each year, and the trails can be crowded in summer and fall. Some hardy souls can be seen completing the last steps of the famous Appalachian Trail (p10), which runs from Springer Mountain, Georgia, to Katahdin.

21

Moosehead Lake

🅰 F6 ℹ️ 480 Moosehead Lake Rd, Greenville; www.destinationmoose headlake.com

Forty miles (64 km) long and blessed with 320 miles (515 km) of mountain-rimmed shoreline, Moosehead Lake is one the largest bodies of fresh water within any state in the Northeast. Popular with hunters, hikers, and fishermen since the 1880s, the region is attracting a whole new breed of outdoor enthusiasts: mountain bikers, skiers, and snowmobilers.

Greenville, the region's largest town, is the starting point for excursions into the Great North Woods, including seaplane services that fly visitors to remote fishing camps. It is also the chief base for moose-watching expeditions, which can take the form of aerial reconnaissance, exploration of boggy sites via timber roads, or boat or canoe trips to observe moose as they feed in hallow waters. The **Moosehead Marine Museum** tells of the history of the steamboat in Greenville, beginning in 1836, when the town was a logging center. One of the museum's prized possessions is the *Katahdin*, a restored 1914 steamboat that plied the lake during the peak lumbering years. It offers lake cruises and excursions to Mount Kineo, the most prominent landmark on the lake.

Moosehead Marine Museum

 🏠 12 Lily Bay Rd, Greenville 🕐 Late Jun–mid-Oct: 10am–4pm Mon–Sat 🌐 katahdincruises.com

22

Rangeley Lakes Region

🅰 D1 ℹ️ 6 Park Rd; www. rangeleymaine.com

Set against a backdrop of mountains, this rustic area encloses a series of pristine lakes that have long been a draw for outdoor enthusiasts. In summer fishermen ply the

Did You Know?

Moose are strong swimmers, and can dive up to 16 ft (5 m) underwater to search for food.

↑ Traversing the white runs at Saddleback Mountain, Rangeley Lakes Region

waterways for trout and salmon, while canoeists frequently spot a moose or two lumbering along the shoreline. The area is now popular with mountain bikers, but the beauty of the place has never been a secret. Hikers have been enjoying the vistas from the summit of Bald Mountain and tramping the section of the Appalachian Trail running along Saddleback Mountain for decades.

Elsewhere, the popular **Rangeley Lake State Park** provides vacationers with facilities for swimming, fishing, birding, boating, and camping, plus 1.2 miles (2 km) of lakefront. Toward the southeast, **Mount Blue State Park** is home to Webb Lake, a favorite haunt of fishermen due to its plentiful population of smallmouth bass, brown trout, and pickerel. The park is dominated by the towering 3,187-ft (971-m) Mount Blue.

Rangeley Lake State Park

⊛ 🅐 South Shore Dr, Rangeley 🄲 (207) 864-3858 🄾 Facilities: May–Oct: 9am–dusk daily

Mount Blue State Park

⊛ ⊛ 🅐 West Rd, Weld 🄲 (207) 585-2347 🄾 9am–dusk daily

←

A lake in Baxter State Park, a favored watering hole for *(inset)* moose

 ㉓

Aroostook County

🅐 G6 🄻 11 W Presque Isle Rd, Caribou; www.visit aroostook.com

Maine's largest and most northern county, Aroostook covers an area greater than the combined size of Connecticut and Rhode Island. The region is best known for agriculture, producing nearly 2 billion lb (907 million kg) of potatoes each year, plus lush crops of clover, oats, barley, and rapeseed. In summer acres of potato fields are covered with blossoms, a vision in pink and white. Another 6,250 sq miles (16,200 sq km) of land is forested, mostly owned by

paper companies that process the trees in nine local pulp and paper mills.

In summer, fly-fishermen, hikers, and canoeists flock to **Aroostook State Park**. When the heavy winter snows come, snowmobilers arrive in large numbers to explore the entire 3,500 miles (5,600 km) of the Interstate Trail System.

Aroostook County begins in Houlton, a quiet town with a Market Square Historic District of 28 buildings from the 19th century. A French dialect can be heard in the northern St. John Valley, the legacy of Acadians who settled here in 1785. The **Acadian Village** consists of 16 original and reconstructed buildings from the early days. In New Sweden, a cluster of historic buildings recalls a Swedish colony that settled not far from Caribou in the late 19th century.

Aroostook State Park

⊛ ⊛ 🅐 87 State Park Rd, S of Presque Isle 🄲 (207) 768-8341 🄾 Mid-May–mid-Oct: dawn–dusk daily; accessible for snowsports in winter

Acadian Village

⊛ 🅐 Rte 1, Van Buren 🄲 (207) 868-5042 🄾 Mid-Jun–mid-Sep: noon–5pm daily

---

MAINE'S GREAT RAFTING RIVERS

Maine is famous for three whitewater rivers: the Kennebec, the Dead, and the west branch of the Penobscot. The first two meet near a town called The Forks, southwest of Moosehead Lake, where several rafting companies offer equipment and guided trips. The Millinocket area services paddlers bound for the Penobscot, famed among rafters for its challenging drop through a vertical walled canyon downriver from the Ripogenus Dam.

NEED TO KNOW

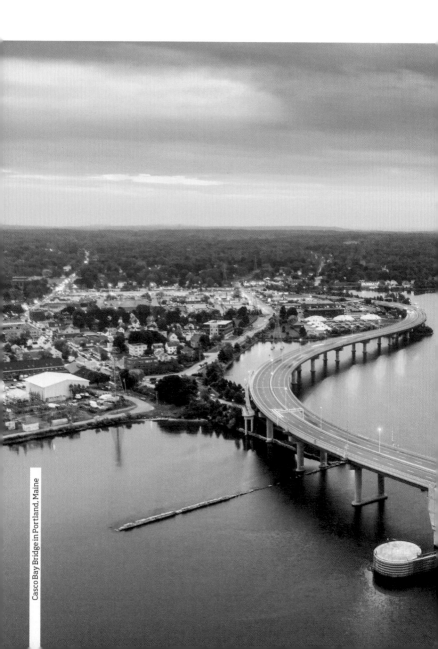

Casco Bay Bridge in Portland, Maine

BEFORE
YOU GO

Things change, so plan ahead to make the most of your trip. Be prepared for all eventualities by considering the following points before you travel.

AT A GLANCE

CURRENCY
US Dollar (USD)

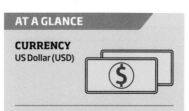

AVERAGE DAILY SPEND

SAVE	SPEND	SPLURGE
$100	$175	$275+

BOTTLED WATER	COFFEE	BEER	DINNER FOR TWO
$1.50	$2-$3	$6	$100

CLIMATE

 The longest days occur May–Sep while Nov–Feb sees the shortest daylight hours.

 Temperatures average 73°F (23°C) in summer, and regularly drop below 25°F (-4°C) in winter.

 Mar–Apr and Oct–Dec see the heaviest rainfall. Expect snowfall Dec–Feb.

ELECTRICITY SUPPLY

The standard US electric current is 110 volts and 60 Hz. Power sockets are type A and B fitting plugs with two flat pins.

Passports and Visas

For entry requirements, including visas, consult your nearest US embassy or check with the **US Department of State**. All travelers to the US should have a machine-readable biometric passport that is valid for six months longer than their intended period of stay. Citizens of the UK, Australia, New Zealand, and the EU do not need a visa, but must apply to enter in advance via the Electronic System for Travel Authorization (**ESTA**). Applications must be made at least 72 hours before travel, and applicants must have a valid passport and a return airline ticket. Visitors from all other regions will require a visa and passport to enter. Be sure to allow plenty of time for the US border agency's thorough passport and visa checks.

ESTA
🆆 esta.cbp.dhs.gov/esta
US Department of State
🆆 travel.state.gov

Government Advice

Now more than ever, it is important to consult both your and the US government's advice before traveling. The US Department of State, the **UK Foreign and Commonwealth Office**, and the **Australian Department of Foreign Affairs and Trade** offer the latest information on security, health and local regulations.

Australian Department of Foreign Affairs and Trade
🆆 smartraveller.gov.au
UK Foreign and Commonwealth Office
🆆 gov.uk/foreign-travel-advice

Customs Information

You can find information on the laws relating to goods and currency taken in or out of the US on the **Customs and Border Protection Agency** website. All travelers need to complete a Customs and Border Protection Agency form when crossing the US border.

Customs and Border Protection Agency
🆆 cbp.gov/travel

Insurance

We recommend that you take out a comprehensive insurance policy covering theft, loss of belongings, medical care, cancellations and delays, and read the small print carefully. All medical treatment is private and US health insurers do not have reciprocal arrangements with other countries. Car rental agencies offer vehicle and liability insurance; check your policy before traveling.

Vaccinations

No inoculations are needed for the US.

Reserving Accommodations

New England offers a huge variety of accommodations, from luxury five-star hotels and resorts to B&Bs, roadside motels, and homestays. Lodgings can fill up and prices shoot up during key seasons. An extensive list of accommodations can be found on the **Visit New England** website. Camping is allowed only in sanctioned campgrounds in New England.
Visit New England
ⓦ visitnewengland.com

Money

Most establishments accept major credit, debit, and prepaid currency cards. Contactless payments are becoming widely accepted, however, it is always worth carrying some cash for smaller items and tips. Cash machines can be found at banks, airline terminals, train and bus stations, and on main streets in major towns. Waiters will expect to be tipped 15 to 20 per cent of the total bill, hotel porters and housekeeping should be given $1 per bag or day, and you should round up taxi fares to the nearest dollar.

Travelers with Specific Requirements

The Society for Accessible Travel and Hospitality and **Mobility International** offer information for people with disabilities. Most hotels and restaurants are equipped for wheelchair users, and many outdoor recreation areas have wheelchair-friendly trails and tour buses.

Mobility International
ⓦ miusa.org
Society for Accessible Travel and Hospitality
ⓦ sath.org

Language

English is the principal language spoken in New England, although parts of the region near the border with Quebec also speak French.

Opening Hours

COVID-19 The pandemic continues to affect New England. Some museums, tourist attractions, and hospitality venues are operating on reduced or temporary opening hours, and require visitors to make advance bookings for a specific date and time. Always check ahead before visiting.

Mondays Some museums are closed for the day.
Sundays Many shops open late and close early.
Public holidays Shops, museums, and attractions generally close early or for the day.
Winter Some places close weekdays from mid-October to the end of December and close entirely from January to early May.

PUBLIC HOLIDAYS

Jan 1	New Year's Day
Mid-Jan	Martin Luther King Day
Late Feb	President's Day
Mar/Apr	Easter
Mid-Apr	Patriots' Day (ME and MA only)
Late May	Memorial Day
Jul 4	Independence Day
Early Sep	Labor Day
Mid-Oct	Columbus/Indigenous Peoples' Day
Nov 11	Veterans Day
Late Nov	Thanksgiving
Dec 25	Christmas

GETTING AROUND

Whether you're exploring by car or making use of the region's public transportation, here is all you need to know to navigate New England.

AT A GLANCE

PUBLIC TRANSPORTATION

BOSTON

$2.40
One-way subway fare

PORTLAND

$2.00
Single local bus journey

PROVIDENCE

$2.00
Single local bus journey

SPEED LIMIT

INTERSTATE HIGHWAYS	MAJOR HIGHWAYS
65 mph (105 km/h)	**55** mph (95 km/h)

TOWN CENTERS	URBAN ZONES
30 mph (45 km/h)	**25** mph (40 km/h)

Arriving by Air

Boston's Logan International Airport (BOS) is the region's busiest airport, although some domestic and international carriers use Manchester Boston Regional Airport (MHT) in New Hampshire, which serves Vermont and Maine; Portland International Jetport in Maine; T. F. Green Airport (PVD) in Warwick, Rhode Island; and Bradley International Airport (BDL) in Windsor Locks, Connecticut, which serves Hartford, Connecticut, and Springfield, Massachusetts.

Rail Travel

Amtrak trains from New York follow two main routes in New England. The Northeast Regional route covers Long Island Sound, Connecticut, and Providence, and continues to Boston's South Station. The Vermonter follows the same route to New Haven, Connecticut, then turns north along the Connecticut River. Amtrack's Downeaster service leaves Boston's North Station with stops in New Hampshire and Maine, ending in Brunswick, Maine.
Amtrak
W Amtrak.com

Bus Travel

Concord Coach Lines serves Maine and New Hampshire. **Peter Pan** has stops in Connecticut, Rhode Island, New Hampshire, and western Massachusetts. Other parts of Massachusetts, such as Cape Cod and the South Shore are served by **Plymouth & Brockton**. **Bolt Bus** runs from Boston to New Haven and New York. **Megabus** serves Portland, Boston, and New York.
Bolt Bus
W boltbus.com
Concord Coach Lines
W concordcoachlines.com
Megabus
W megabus.com
Peter Pan
W peterpanbus.com
Plymouth & Brockton
W p-b.com

GETTING TO AND FROM THE AIRPORT

Airport	Distance to City	Taxi Fare	Public Transport	Journey Time	Price
Logan International, Boston	4 miles (7 km)	$30	MBTA Silver Line	15 mins	$2.75
Bradley International	14 miles (23 km)	$40	Bradley Flyer	30 mins	$1.75
Manchester Boston Regional	5 miles (8 km)	$30	MTA bus	20 mins	$2.00
T. F. Green	10 miles (16 km)	$40	MBTA Commuter Rail RIPTA bus	17 mins 20 mins	$3.25 $2.00

JOURNEY PLANNER

Plotting the main routes by journey time, this map is a rough guide to driving between New England's main towns and cities. The times given reflect the fastest and most direct routes. Allow extra time for driving in bad weather, morning or evening rush hours, and high season, when roads will be buser.

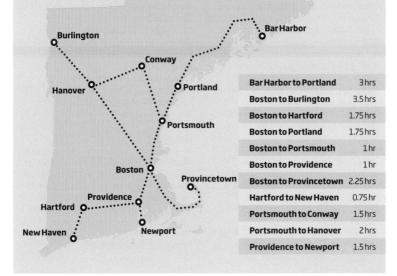

• • • Major Driving Routes

Bar Harbor to Portland	3 hrs
Boston to Burlington	3.5 hrs
Boston to Hartford	1.75 hrs
Boston to Portland	1.75 hrs
Boston to Portsmouth	1 hr
Boston to Providence	1 hr
Boston to Provincetown	2.25 hrs
Hartford to New Haven	0.75 hr
Portsmouth to Conway	1.5 hrs
Portsmouth to Hanover	2 hrs
Providence to Newport	1.5 hrs

Boats and Ferries

The CAT high speed car ferry connects Bar Harbor, Maine, and Yarmouth, Nova Scotia in about 3.5 hours from spring to fall. The **Steamship Authority** and **Hy-Line Cruises** depart Hyannis and Woods Hole, Massachusetts, for Nantucket and Martha's Vineyard islands.

The CAT
🆆 ferries.ca/thecat
Hy-Line Cruises
🆆 hylinecruises.com
Steamship Authority
🆆 steamshipauthority.com

Public Transportation

Very little public transportation in New England is integrated between regions. **RIPTA** (Rhode Island Public Transit Authority) operates an extensive bus service throughout Rhode Island with special beach buses from urban centers in the summer. The **MBTA** (Massachusetts Bay Transportation Authority) operates the subway (known more commonly as the "T") and bus lines in the Metropolitan Boston area as well as commuter rail options stretching north to Newburyport, west to Worcester, and south to Providence, Rhode Island. Safety and hygiene measures, timetables, ticket information, transport maps, and more can be obtained from individual operators' websites.

MBTA
🆆 mbta.com
RIPTA
🆆 ripta.com

Bus

City bus networks are generally frequent and reliable. In most cities, a single fare applies for all bus travel within city limits. Multiple trip tickets and one-day travel passes are available in major cities. Single-trip tickets can also be bought from the driver when boarding your bus but change is not given so you must pay the exact fare.

In Boston, the MBTA bus system expands the transit network to cover more than 1,000 miles (1,600 km). Buses are often crowded and schedules vary. Two useful sightseeing routes are Haymarket–Charlestown (from near Quincy Market to Bunker Hill) and Harvard–Nubian (from Harvard Square via Massachusetts Avenue to Back Bay and South End to Nubian Square in Roxbury). Public transportation in rural areas is less extensive.

Subway

Boston's combined subway and trolley network, known as the "T", is run by the MBTA. It operates 5am–12:45am daily (from 6am on Sundays). Weekday service is every 3–15 minutes; less frequent at weekends. There are five lines: Red, from south of the city to Cambridge; Green, from the Museum of Science westward into the suburbs; Blue, from near Government Center to Logan International Airport and on to Revere; Orange, linking the northern suburbs to southwest Boston; and Silver, a surface bus that runs from Roxbury to Logan International Airport via South Station.

Maps of Boston's subway system are available at Downtown Crossing MBTA station, or online. Admission to subway stations is via turnstiles into which you insert a paper "Charlie" ticket or tap a plastic "Charlie" card. The plastic cards offer a small discount and are intended largely for residents; details on obtaining one can be found on the MBTA website. The paper "Charlie" ticket can be purchased at any MBTA vending machine. It can be loaded with a single trip ($2.40 subway/$1.70 bus), or a 24-hour pass ($12.75) or 7-day pass ($22.50) and is valid on all subway and bus routes.

Taxis

Due to the popularity of Lyft and Uber ride-hailing services, taxicabs are becoming increasingly scarce, though cabs can be still be picked up at taxi ranks and hotels in larger city centers as well as at airports. Cab companies that operate in the Boston Metropolitan area are limited to picking up in the cities where they are chartered. A Boston cab cannot pick up in Cambridge or vice versa.

Arrow Cab Company (Hartford, CT)
🆆 arrowcabct.com
ASAP Taxi (Portland, ME)
🆆 asaptaxi.net
Boston Cab (Boston, MA)
🆆 bostoncab.us
Cambridge Cabs (Cambridge, MA)
🆆 cambridgecabs.info
MetroCab (Boston, MA)
🆆 boston-cab.com
Providence Taxi (Providence RI)
🆆 providence-taxi.business.site
Vermont Ride Network (Burlington, VT)
🆆 greencabvt.com

Driving

Much of New England's charm is found in the region's scenic open roads and on driving tours during fall-foliage season. Major cities' public transportation systems makes it easy to be without a car, but driving is by far the easiest way to explore beyond urban centers.

Driving to New England

The I-95 superhighway is the main entry to New England from New York and points south. This major highway runs close to the coast through Connecticut and Providence, and Rhode Island to the outskirts of Boston. Circumventing the city, the highway continues up through New Hampshire and Maine. From the north, the two major gateways into New England are I-89 and I-91. The latter crosses from Canada into Vermont, then follows a relatively straight line south along the Vermont/New Hampshire border, through Massachusetts and Connecticut to New Haven. I-89 starts in northwestern Vermont, then cuts diagonally from Burlington to Concord, New Hampshire, where it links up with I-93 into Boston. The major western points of entry are I-84 and I-90 (toll road) from New York state.

Driving in New England

Driving in Boston, where traffic can be heavy and erratic and parking costly, is not advised. Most New England roads are good, with divided highways connecting most major cities. Winter and early spring driving have their challenges. Snow and ice call for special driving skills, and frost heaves create sidewalk cracks and potholes. Heavy traffic can slow progress on popular roads during peak summer season.

Car Rental

To rent a car in New England you must be at least 21 years old and have a valid credit card. Some rental companies charge an extra fee to drivers under age 25. Major international car rental agencies have outlets at all main airports and in all major towns and cities.

Rules of the Road

Third party insurance is required. Drive on the right. Seat belts must be worn at all times by the driver and passengers. Young children should be restrained in child seats buckled into the back seat. Laws vary on using a mobile phone while driving; err on the side of caution and pull over to call or text.

Pass only on the outside or left-hand lane, and when approaching a traffic circle, give priority to traffic already on the circle. All vehicles must give way to emergency services vehicles.

The legal blood alcohol limit for drivers is 0.08%. Avoid drinking alcohol if you plan to drive.

Cycling

New England offers many options for cyclists of all ages and abilities. Trails in state parks and national parks forests are perfect off-road riding territory, and most ski resorts permit mountain biking (for a fee) in the summer. The commercial website **Bike New England** has compiled guides and links to cycling in the six states.

Bike New England
w bikenewengland.com

Bicycle Hire

Most major cities in New England have urban bike sharing programs, some of which include electrically assisted e-bikes. Cyclists are expected to stay off pedestrian sidewalks. In non-urban areas, outfitters who rent canoes and kayaks usually also rent touring and mountain bicycles, and can advise on local touring routes to suit all abilities.

Blue Bikes (Boston)
w bluebikes.com
Lime
w li.me/en-us/home
Zagster (Portland)
w zagster.com

Bike Touring

Several companies operate guided and self-guided bike tours around New England. **VBT** covers much of the region, while **Backroads** and **DuVine** focus on Vermont. **Summerfeet Cycling** specializes in Maine tours. The **Rails-to-Trails Conservancy** provides information and maps on 1,359 trails along abandoned railroad tracks that have been converted into convenient and accessible paths for cyclists and pedestrians.

Backroads
w backroads.com
DuVine
w duvine.com
Rails-to-Trails Conservancy
w railstotrails.org
Summerfeet Cycling
w summerfeet.net
VBT
w vbt.com

Cycle Safety

Helmets and high-visibility clothing are not obligatory but wearing them is strongly advised, especially when cycling on rural roads.

Walking and Hiking

Most New England city centers can be explored on foot. Even Boston is a great walking city: it is compact and most streets are flanked by adequate sidewalks.

Hiking trails crisscross almost all of New England, with the two most popular being the **Appalachian Trail** and Vermont's 265-mile (426-km) **Long Trail**. If going off the beaten path, be sure you have good hiking boots, waterproof outerwear, warm inner clothing, a map, and a compass. Make sure your phone is fully charged but don't count on having cell service in remote areas.

Appalachian Trail
w appalachiantrail.org
Long Trail
w greenmountainclub.org/the-long-trail

PRACTICAL
INFORMATION

A little local know-how goes a long way in New England. Here you can find all the essential advice and information you will need during your stay.

AT A GLANCE

EMERGENCY NUMBER

GENERAL
EMERGENCY

911

TIME ZONE
EST/EDT
Eastern Daylight Time
(EDT) is observed
Mar 14–Nov 7, 2021;
Mar 13–Nov 6, 2022;
Mar 12–Nov 5, 2023.

TAP WATER
Unless otherwise
stated, tap water is
safe to drink.

WEBSITES
NECN.com
  The regional cable news company's
  website offers real-time traffic updates.
nws.com
  The National Weather Service offers
  detailed weather information at every
  weather station in the region.
visitnewengland.com
  New England's official tourist board
  website for overseas visitors

Personal Security

New England is generally safe, but petty crime does take place. Pickpockets work known tourist areas and busy streets. Use your common sense, keep valuables in a safe place, and be alert to your surroundings. Lock your car and always store valuables in the trunk.

If you have anything stolen, report the crime as soon as possible at the nearest police station. Get a copy of the crime report to claim on your insurance. Contact your embassy or consulate immediately if your passport is stolen or in the event of a serious crime or accident.

As a rule, New Englanders are very accepting of all people, regardless of their race, gender or sexuality. The country's abolitionist and women's suffrage movements both started here, and the region was early to support same-sex marriage. In fact, Vermont was the first US state to introduce civil unions in 2000, and Massachusetts became the first state to legalize same-sex marriage in 2004. Today, Boston has the largest LGBT+ population in the region, but even small towns are accepting. If you do feel unsafe, the **Safe Space Alliance** pinpoints your nearest place of refuge.
Safe Space Alliance
🌐 safespacealliance.com

Health

New England has a number of acclaimed hospitals should you need medical treatment. The US does not have a government health program, so emergency medical and dental care, though excellent, can be very expensive. Medical travel insurance is highly recommended in order to cover some of the costs related to an accident or sudden illness. The price of basic care at a hospital emergency room can rise incredibly quickly. Should you be in a serious accident, an ambulance will pick you up and charge later.

If you need a prescription dispensed, there are pharmacies (drugstores) in every city in the region, some staying open 24 hours. Ask your hotel for the nearest one.

Smoking, Alcohol, and Drugs

Smoking and "vaping" are banned in all public spaces such as bus and train stations, airports, and enclosed areas of bars, cafes, restaurants, and hotels. However, many bars and restaurants have outdoor areas where smoking is permitted.

Alcohol may not be sold to or bought for anyone under the age of 21. The drink-drive limit is strictly enforced. Recreational cannabis use is decriminalized in all New England states, and fully legal in Massachusetts, Vermont, and Maine.

ID

Passports are required as ID at airports. (American citizens may use a state driver's license to board domestic flights.) Anyone who looks under 25 may be asked for photo ID to prove their age when buying alcohol or tobacco.

Visiting Places of Worship

Show respect by dressing modestly. Do not talk loudly or use cameras, phones, or other mobile devices without first asking permission.

Cell Phones and Wi-Fi

Do not rely on mobile phones or other devices for navigation or emergency communications in remote areas such as northern Maine and New Hampshire, where reception can be intermittent.

Free wi-fi hotspots are widely available in towns and cities. Almost all hotels, motels, and inns offer free wi-fi, as do many cafes, bars, and restaurants.

Visitors from outside the US can buy pay-as-you-go SIM cards at airports and most phone stores, which can be used in compatible phones. Some networks also sell basic flip phones (with minutes) for as little as $25 (no paperwork or ID required). Canadian residents can usually upgrade their domestic cell phone plan to extend to the US. Pre-paid phone cards usually offer the best rates for long-distance calls, and are sold in most drugstores.

Post

Main post offices are found in the centers of major towns and cities. Post offices are open 9am–5pm weekdays, with some branches open on Saturdays. All are closed on Sundays and public holidays. Letters and small parcels – less than 13 oz (370 g) – with correct postage can be placed in any blue mailbox.

Taxes and Refunds

It is important to remember that listed prices rarely include applicable taxes. All New England states, with the exception of New Hampshire, levy their own sales tax (usually somewhere between 5 and 8 per cent) All states charge taxes on hotel rooms and restaurant meals, and some cities also have tax surcharges. Since none of these taxes are levied at a national level, international visitors cannot claim refunds.

Discount Cards

Many New England museums, galleries, and attractions offer discounts to students and senior citizens. A valid form of ID is required. Students from abroad should carry an International Student Identity Card (**ISIC**) to claim discounts on hostel accommodation, museums, and theaters. Over-50s should look into buying an **AARP** membership (open to non-Americans), which can provide discounts at hotels and on car rentals.

AARP
w aarp.org
ISIC
w isic.org

Responsible Tourism

Long considered one of the US's most environmentally conscious regions, New England continues to gain national acclaim for its forward-thinking initiatives and policies. Forty per cent of the region's energy is from renewable sources; Boston is recognized by the Natural Resources Defense Council as the greenest city on the East Coast; and both Maine and Vermont are national leaders in environmental initiatives. Visitors find it easier than ever to be environmentally aware when touring the area. Recycling facilities are common, and community farmers' markets selling local produce and artisan foodstuffs can be found in every corner of every state.

INDEX

ACKNOWLEDGEMENTS

DK would like to thank the following for their contribution to the previous edition:
Patricia Harris and David Lyon, Eleanor Berman, Tom Bross, Patricia Brooks, Helga Loveseed, Pierre Home-Douglas, Clare Peel, Zoe Ross

The publisher would like to thank the following for their kind permission to reproduce their photographs:

Key: a-above; b-below/bottom; c-centre; f-far; l-left; r-right; t-top

123RF.com: Jon Bilous 164-5t; James Kirikis 81tl; Sara Winter 311cr.

Alamy Stock Photo: 506 collection 70tr; AF archive 105cra; age fotostock / Steve Dunwell 92bl, 123tl, / Georges Lis 112bl; Cheri Alguire 316-7b; All Canada Photos / Robert Chiasson 134t; Alpha and Omega Collection 53br; Alpha Stock 257tl; ES Tech Archive 57tr; Andy Arthur 156-7b; Artokoloro Quint Lox Limited 54br; Brian Atkinson 320br; Avalon / Photoshot License 102-3t; Marcus Baker 81c; Rob Barr 319br; Norman Barrett 202bl; Vicki Beaver 190t; Jon Bilous 84-5t, 136-7b, 141tr, 143br, 156t, Russ Bishop 101br; Pat & Chuck Blackley 298tr, 316t, 320cr; Paul Brown 137crb; David Brownell 158-9; Ron S Buskirk 313t; Cal Sport Media / Eric Canha 196-7t; Chris Cameron 272bl; Susan Candelario 120-1b; Carpe Diem - UK 38-9b; Cavan Images 26cr, / Josh Campbell 274-5t; Clarence Holmes Photography 195tr; Classic Image 53cla; Peter Conner 263cr; gary corbett 323bc; CPC Collection 52t; Tom Croke 46bl, 139b, 302-3b; Ian G Dagnall 22tl, 117t, 170t, 244cra; Daniel Dempster Photography 293br; DanitaDelimont.com 201br, / Walter Bibikow 248t, / Cindy Miller Hopkins 33cra, / Jerry And Marcy Monkman 302t, / Susan Pease 47b, 176-7b; Christian Delbert 35br; Erin Paul Donovan 300bl; Douglas Peebles Photography 212t; Randy Duchaine 45br, 133cra, 189tl, 201t, 217cl, 231tr, 239tr, 239c, 239br, 240br, 247b, 250-1t, 269tl, 269br; Michael Dwyer 64cb, 68-9t, 105b, 126-7; EcoPhotography 293tl; Education & Exploration 1 124-5b; Education & Exploration 4 124clb; Norman Eggert 287br; Chad Ehlers 93tl; Encore 180cr; Envision Stock Photography, Inc. 20cr; Everett Collection Inc 56tl; eye35 stock 314t; Franck Fotos 11br; Kevin Galvin 26crb; georgesanker.com 19br, 306-7; Bob Gibbons 10-11b; GL Archive 233cr; Granger Historical Picture Archive 55t, 56cla, 295cra; H. Mark Weidman Photography 288bl; Hemis / Walter Bibikow 323t; Christian Hinkle 278b; Historical image collection by Bildagentur-online 53cb; Cindy Hopkins 216br; IanDagnall Computing 54tr; Ivy Close Images 54tl; Jannis Werner (Harvard Images) 155tr; Brian Jannsen 268-9; EcoPhotography.com / Jerry and Marcy Monkman 32-3t, 43cr; JLImages 117cla; Jon Arnold Images Ltd 321; Stuart Kelly 35cl; Scott Kemper 318-9t, 325cra; Albert Knapp 36cla; Erik Lattwein 89tr; Marianne Lee 211br; Paul Light 71br; Lighthouses by Allan Wood 8cl; Felix Lipov 326bl; Melvyn Longhurst 82bl, 116bc; LOOK Die Bildagentur der Fotografen GmbH / Elan Fleisher 86t; Luscious Frames 40-1t; David Lyons 36tr; Major Pix 39cl; Picade LLC / James Marshall 49cl; Martin Thomas Photography 66crb; mauritius images GmbH 216-7t, / Walter Bibikow 47cl, 187br, 297tl, 297br, 317tr; Buddy Mays 320clb; MCT / Columbus Dispatch / Barbara J. Perenic 71cl; Megapress 81cl; Mira 33cl, 197bl, 218-9b, 273t, 322bl; Dawna Moore 222bl; Cavan Images / Aurora Photos / Karsten Moran 312bl; Jenna Nace 267tl; National Geographic Image Collection 70cla, / Brian Drouin 255b, / Richard Seeley 330clb; Nature Picture Library / Onne van der Wal 35tl; Steve Nichols 149cb; Niday Picture Library 53tr, 98clb; Nikreates 87br, 154tr; George Ostertag 331br; Stockimo / Dianna Owen 223br; George Oze 290-1b; Painting 133cla; Gabe Palmer 49tr; Sean Pavone 112cl, 200b, 328-9b; The Picture Art Collection 273br; Art Phaneuf 188b; Pictorial Press Ltd 54cb; Pierre Rochon photography 291tl; Enrico Della Pietra 324-5b; PJF Military Collection 75tr; Robert Proctor 84br; Edwin Remsberg 44tl; Peter Righteous 289br; robertharding 184b, / Alan Copson 30-1t; Earl Robicheaux 194-5b; pierre rochon 324tr; Stillman Rogers 287tl, 287tr, 299cr; Henryk Sadura 83tr; Jorge Salcedo 80-1b, 131cra, 135bl; Philip Scalia 262t; Doug Schneider 267cra; James Schwabel 140-1b, 326t; Kevin Shields 331tl; Lee Snider 44-5b, 218tr; Cavan Social 223cr; Visions of America, LLC / Joseph Sohm 101tl; Antony Souter 41cl; Kumar Sriskandan 33tr, 42-3t, 99tr, 100bl, 182br, 291cra, 299b; Stephen Saks Photography 173tl; Charles Stirling 200clb; StockShot 32bl, / Gary Pearl 329tr; SuperStock 81br; Stan Tess 10clb, 22cl, 56-7t, 98-9b, 100cl, 110, 110br, 111t, 112clb, 114b, 115bl, 123b, 165cr, 191bc, 198tl, 233t, 235tc, 237bl, 239, 239tl, 242b, 243t, 246tl, 248bl, 249b, 250bl, 252t, 253br, 254tr, 257br, 264bl, 275b, / *Harbor Fog (2009)* by Ross Miller 68bl; The Granger Collection 52br; TNS / Miami Herald / Charles Trainor Jr. 70b; Mauro Toccaceli 20bl, 81cra,173cra; Rodney Todt 285tr; Tricia Toms 148-9; Steve Tulley 215cra; Vespasian 54cla; Visions of America, LLC 90b; Mark Waugh 122tl; Jim West 279tl; Yakoniva 198-9b; ZUMAPRESS.com / Sun-Sentinel 71t.

AWL Images: Adam Jones 17tl, 160-1.

Billings Farm and Museum: 28crb.

Boston Book Fair: Mike Ritter 40bl.

Photo Courtesy Museum of Fine Arts, Boston: 132-3b, 133tl, Tony Rinaldo 36br, 66cr.

Bridgeman Images: 57bl; Private Collection / American School 53tl, Prismatic Pictures / American School, (20th century) 55bl; Yale University Art Gallery, New Haven, CT, USA / American School, (19th century) 52cb.

Courtesy of The Mary Baker Eddy Library, Boston, MA: 136t.

Depositphotos Inc: alex9500 235tr; christianhinkle 236t, ugljevarevic 130bl, zrfphoto 294tr.

Dreamstime.com: 1miro 50bl; Anderm 118-9; John Anderson 300-1t; Mihai Andritoiu 34tr, 332-3; Jerry Coli 211tr, 225; Demerzel21 210b; Wangkun Jia 23tr, 55br, 115tr, 168br; Jndphoto 28t; Kenneth Keifer 26bl; James Kirkikis 125tr, 256cl; Chee-onn Leong 50cl; Lequint 215tl; Marazem 43br; Sean Pavone 26t, 64tl, 74cl, 106-7; Peanutroaster 24cr; Susan Peterson 172bl; Enrico Della Pietra 25cl; Jorge Salcedo 66bl; Marcio Silva 63, 94-5; Joe Sohm 39br; Sphraner 39tr; Debra Tosca 245br; Tneorg 131tc; Whbouton 192-3; Oscar C. Williams 51cr; Sara Winter 34br; Mark Zhu 142cl.

Farnsworth Art Museum: *Land and Development of New England (1935)* by Marguerite Thompson Zorach, Oil on canvas, 96 x 76 in, Museum purchase, 1991.17 314br.

Getty Images: 2thirdsphoto 56bc; Jose Azel 19tl, 30bl, 280-1; Bettmann 56br, 189br; bhofack2 13cr; Boston Globe 51tl, 91t, 91cra, 138t, 294-5b, / John Tlumacki 41br, Joanne Rathe / Lincoln (2012) DeWitt Godfrey 37crb, / David L. Ryan 38tl; Corbis Documentary / David H. Wells 217br; DenisTangneyJr 11t, 240-1t; DigitalVision / Walter Bibikow 292b; franckreporter 51br; Daniel Grill 42br; Corey Hendrickson 28bl; ivanastar 65,144 -5; Icon Sportswire / Leslie Plaza Johnson 57br; jonathansloane 270bl; KenWiedemann 20crb; Corbis / Brooks Kraft LLC 49crb; Paul Marotta 72-3t; mtcurado 99ca; Michael Piazza 8clb; Photodisc / Justin Cash 18bl, 258-9; Portland Press Herald 50cra, 327bl; Joseph Prezioso 50br; Nicholas Rhodes 73b; shakzu 12clb; George Steinmetz 276-7; travelview 12-3b; Universal Images Group / Education Images 296b; Jeremy Woodhouse 330b.

Hancock Shaker Village: 23c.

Harvard Art Museums: Katya Kallsen 152bl.

Harvard Museum of Natural History: Jeffrey Blackwell 153t.

The House of Seven Gables: 166tc, 166-7t**Idletyme Brewing Company:** 45tr.

International Festival of Arts & Ideas: Judy Sirota Rosenthal 50cr.

iStockphoto.com: aimintang 210clb, 220-1b; AlbertPego 62, 76-7, 270-1t; AlexPro9500 235cra; Allard1 221tl; APCortizasJr 120tr; Roman Babakin 149br; Arpad Benedek 66t; benedek 18tr, 20t, 226 -7; buzbuzzer 99tl; cmart7327 48-9t; connerscott1 4; DenisTangneyJr 6-7, 13br, 22-3c, 31cr, 46-7t, 88-9b, 104tl, 154b, 174t, 178b, 182t, 203tr, 243br, 305, 310t; E+ / DenisTangneyJr 2-3; Elijah-Lovkoff 82cl; f11photo 238-9b; Liran Sokolovski Finzi 180t; Franckreporter 69cr; gnagel 232cl; janniswerner 150br, 150-1t; jimfeng 82bc; jorgeantonio 102bc; josanmu 179t; KenWiedemann 171cr, 176tr, 178tl; kickstand 51cl; Kirkikis 135tr; Sean Pavone 11cr, 208t, 265t, 284-5t; rickberk 24t; Andrew Roque 223t; sbossert 51tr; SeanPavonePhoto 230t; shananies 121cra; Studio-Annika 51bl; Ron Thomas 12t; Torresigner 10ca; traveler1116 232-3b; travelview 16, 58-9; Ultima_Gaina 25tr; Zoran_Photo 8cla.

Maine Mead Works: 45cl.

Courtesy of Mass MoCA - Massachusetts Museum of Contemporary Art: Emma Franco / Zoran Orlić Campus Building 7 / *Wall Drawing 614 and Wall Drawing 630* Sol LeWitt © ARS, NY and DACS, London 2019 22-3t, / *Wall Drawing 340* by Sol LeWitt © ARS, NY and DACS, London 2019 37t.

Courtesy of the Nantucket Historical Association: 48bl.

New England Aquarium: 110cl.

New England Conservatory: Andrew Hurlbut 69bl.

Photo courtesy of Norman Rockwell Museum, Stockbridge, Massachusetts: Walt Engels 185t.

Old Sturbridge Village: Kan Photography 186tr.

Peabody Museum of Archaeology & Ethnology Harvard University: President and Fellows of Harvard College / Mark Craig 153bl.

Picfair.com: Andrew Dow 168-9t; Education Exploration 1 212br; John Greim 28cr, 31b, 319clb, 320bl.

Portland Museum Of Art: 24-5t.

The Providence Athenæum: Cat Laine 208br; Nat Rea 17cb, 204-5.

Regattabar: Lenny White 72br.

This edition updated by

Contributors Patricia Harris and David Lyon
Senior Editor Alison McGill
Senior Designer Stuti Tiwari Bhatia
Project Editors Dipika Dasgupta, Rebecca Flynn
Project Art Editor Ben Hinks
Editor Nayan Keshan
Picture Research Coordinator Sumita Khatwani
Assistant Picture Research Administrator Vagisha Pushp
Jacket Coordinator Bella Talbot
Jacket Designers Bess Daly, Ben Hinks
Senior Cartographic Editor Subhashree Bharati
Cartography Manager Suresh Kumar
DTP Designer Tanveer Zaidi
Senior Production Editor Jason Little
Production Controller Kariss Ainsworth
Deputy Managing Editor Beverly Smart
Managing Editors Shikha Kulkarni, Hollie Teague
Managing Art Editors Bess Daly, Priyanka Thakur
Art Director Maxine Pedliham
Publishing Director Georgina Dee

First edition 2001

Published in Great Britain by Dorling Kindersley Limited, One Embassy Gardens, 8 Viaduct Gardens, London SW11 7BW

Published in the United States by DK Publishing, 1450 Broadway, Suite 801, New York, NY 10018

Copyright © 2001, 2021 Dorling Kindersley Limited
A Penguin Random House Company
21 22 23 24 10 9 8 7 6 5 4 3 2 1

A CIP catalog record for this book is available from the British Library.

A catalog record for this book is available from the Library of Congress.

ISSN: 1542 1554
ISBN: 978 0 2414 7402 0

Printed and bound in China.

www.dk.com

A NOTE FROM DK EYEWITNESS

The rapid rate at which the world is changing is constantly keeping the DK Eyewitness team on our toes. While we've worked hard to ensure that this edition of New England is accurate and up-to-date, we know that opening hours alter, standards shift, prices fluctuate, places close and new ones pop up in their stead. So, if you notice we've got something wrong or left something out, we want to hear about it. Please get in touch at travelguides@dk.com